Sociology of Education in India

Sociology of Education in India

SECOND EDITION (Revised and Enlarged)

N. Jayaram

RAWAT PUBLICATIONS
Jaipur • New Delhi • Bangalore • Guwahati • Kolkata

ISBN 978-81-316-0695-7

First edition published 1990
Second revised edition 2015

Reprinted, 2022

Published by
Prem Rawat for **Rawat Publications**
Satyam Apts, Sector 3, Jawahar Nagar, Jaipur 302 004 (India)
Phone: 0141 265 1748 / 7006 Fax: 0141 265 1748
E-mail: info@rawatbooks.com
Website: www.rawatbooks.com

New Delhi Office
4858/24, Ansari Road, Daryaganj, New Delhi 110 002
Phone: 011 2326 3290

Also at *Bangalore, Guwahati* and *Kolkata*

Printed and bound in India.

Dedicated to

my parents and **my father-in-law**

in memory

No educational activity or research is adequate in the present stage of consciousness unless it is conceived in terms of a sociology of education.

Mannheim and Stewart (1962: 159)

Contents

Preface to the First Edition

During one of his visits to Bangalore in 1987, Professor T.K. Oommen enkindled in me the idea of bringing out in the form of an anthology my articles in the area of sociology of education. What is published in journals and periodicals has obviously only a limited readership, and in a way even gets dated. Also, individual articles constitute only disjointed bits of our thinking, which over a period of time happen to fall into a somewhat consistent pattern. These are certainly valid reasons for publicising in book form what has already been published here and there.

In this anthology I have tried to arrange thirteen of my papers in the area of sociology of education written over the last decade. All but the first two of them have been either published earlier in journals or edited volumes, or were presented at conferences or symposia, and remained as yet unpublished. The texts of these papers have now been revised and the statistical information therein has been updated to the extent possible.

The first essay provides an historical introduction to the scope of the sociology of education. The second essay introduces the basic concepts and substantive themes in the sociological analysis of the relationship between education and society. The third essay analyses the development of 'western' education in India from the perspectives of the dependency theory and the colonial-neo-colonial framework. The fourth and the fifth essays deal with the relationship between education, economy, and society by focussing respectively on urbanisation and educational growth, and the education-employment mismatch. The next three essays (6, 7, and 8) examine education in relation to social stratification, focussing respectively on inequality and social change, protective discrimination, and the oppressed and the value-oriented education. The ninth essay, co-authored with Dr G. Sivaramakrishnan, deals with teachers and unionism, and the tenth essay discusses student political activism. The last three essays (11, 12, and 13) dwell on education in relation to politics with emphasis on democracy, peace, and the 'new' educational policy.

In the case of any such volume, notwithstanding considerable effort at careful editing and revision, some amount of repetition of themes, ideas, and even sentences and paragraphs is inevitable. Overlooking such repetitions and overlaps, a reader could read through the essays as a sociological analysis of education in India, or s/he can read any particular essay as a self-contained thematic unit. To avoid repetitions of citations, I have put all the references at the end, with a notation in brackets indicating the number of the essay in which a particular reference is cited.

I have incurred an immense debt of help and gratitude from many senior fellow professionals in various ways in the course of the last decade and a half. While they are far too many to be listed completely, I cannot but single out the names of Professors Philip G. Altbach, Chris Bagley, Suma Chitnis, Y.B. Damle, M.S. Gore, C. Rajagopalan, the late M.S.A. Rao, Satish Saberwal, Suresh Shukla, and Asher Tropp. I thank them all.

On the family front, I have received unstinted help and guidance from my father-in-law, Shri V. Vasudevan. Despite his old age he has had the kindness and patience to go through these essays in their several drafts. His scrutiny of their language and his meticulous proofreading has contributed in no small measure to making these essays more readable than they would have otherwise been. My wife Viji cheerfully took upon herself most of my domestic responsibilities, and my son Vinay, who considers my time as his own, ungrudgingly spared me enough of it to bring out this compilation. They deserve my sincere thanks.

I have acknowledged separately my gratitude to the publishers and copyright holders for permitting me to reprint my papers. I thank Sri K. Rawat for his keen interest in publishing this anthology.

N. Jayaram

Preface to the Second Edition

Nothing gives an author more pleasure than to know that a book that he authored a quarter century back is still being consulted and sought after. The first edition of this book was published in 1990. Though not intended as a textbook, it came to be adopted as one by many departments offering sociology of education as a specialisation, mainly because there was a dearth of India-oriented reading material for students pursuing the subject as a course. Although it has been out of print for more than a decade now, it remains on the reading list and is used in classroom transactions on the subject.

The idea of revising the book and enlarging its contents occurred to me many times earlier. It has often been suggested to me by teachers and students, too. But given my other academic commitments, it was never put on my list of priorities. Thanks to Shri Pranit Rawat, who refused to be dissuaded by my excuses for further deferment, I had to embark on the project forthwith and complete it within a definite deadline. Now that the work is done, I feel both relieved and happy.

Of the thirteen chapters in the first edition, I have retained all but one, namely, 'Urbanisation and Educational Growth', which I found totally out of date in its argument as well as data. Though the chapter on '"New" Educational Policy, 1985: A Critique' is also out of date, given its archival significance, I have retained it. The texts of the chapters have been revised and the statistical information and citations therein have been updated (often using endnotes) to the extent possible. In some portions of some chapters, the data are old, but the descriptions and arguments remain as relevant now as they were made a quarter century ago.

Besides retaining the twelve chapters, I have now included seven new chapters. These new chapters focus on school-community relations, demographic dividend, the educational saga and ideology of Dr Ambedkar, the educational backwardness of Indian Muslims, the decline of the university as a public institution, the changing status of the academic profession in China and India, and multiculturalism and education, respectively. The nineteen chapters in the book are now organised under five parts as follows: (i) Introductory (four chapters), (ii) Education and Economy (two chapters), (iii) Education, Emancipation, and Social Change (five chapters), (iv) University, Teachers, Students (four chapters), and (v) Political Aspects of Education (four chapters). A comprehensive list of references follows.

I am overwhelmed by the debt of gratitude that I have accumulated from many fellow professionals since the publication of the first edition of the book. The good wishes of my octogenarian teacher Professor C. Rajagopalan and the unstinted encouragement and support of my septuagenarian long-distance guru Professor Philip G. Altbach have stood me in good stead. Among those who have shown interest in my work and supported it in many different ways, I would like to mention Professors D.N. Dhanagare, R. Govinda, Shyam Menon, S. Parasuraman, K. Ramachandran, and Avinash Kumar Singh. I, however, miss the affection and counsel of Professor Satish Saberwal, who passed away on 20 October 2010.

I am thankful to all students and teachers who have given me feedback on the first edition of the book. To the library staff at Bangalore University, Goa University, The University of the West Indies (St Augustine, Trinidad), Tata Institute of Social Sciences (Mumbai), Institute for Social and Economic Change (Bengaluru), and Indian Institute of Advanced Study (Shimla) I owe a special word of thanks for making available to me books, articles, and reports at various stages of writing/revising the book.

As always, my wife Viji has been supportive of my academic work; my son Vinay keeps me wondering whether it was worthwhile devoting my time to sociology. I thank them both.

I have acknowledged separately my gratitude to the publishers and copyright holders for permitting me to reproduce my papers. I thank Shri Kailash Rawat and Shri Pranit Rawat not only for assiduously persuading me to work on this edition of the book, but also for the special care they have taken in bringing it out so well and in record time.

N. Jayaram

Acknowledgements

The author acknowledges with grateful thanks the following copyright holders and publishers for permitting him to revise and reprint the articles mentioned against their names:

1. The Editor and Publisher, *Mainstream,* Perspective Publications Private Limited, New Delhi:
   (a) 'Protective Discrimination and Education: A Critique of a Strategy for Change', *Mainstream,* Republic Day Special Issue, 1983, pp. 28–34 (appearing as Chapter 8).
   (b) 'Education: Colonial Legacy and Neo-Colonial Dependency', *Mainstream,* 23 (35), 27 April 1985, pp. 19–23 (appearing as Chapter 4).
   (c) 'Education: "New" Policy: A Critique', *Mainstream,* Republic Day Special Number, 1986, pp. 44–48 (appearing as Chapter 19).
2. The Managing Editor, *Seminar,* New Delhi:
   (a) 'Towards a "Culture of Silence"', *Seminar,* 297, May 1984, pp. 31–34 (appearing as Chapter 9).
3. The Publisher, *Religion and Society,* The CISRS Publications Trust, Bangalore:
   (a) 'Peace and Conflict vis-à-vis Education: Some Sporadic Thoughts', *Religion and Society,* 33 (4), December 1986, pp. 27–36 (appearing as Chapter 18).

4. Professor Krishna Kumar, Department of Education, University of Delhi and Professor Ravinder Kumar, Director, Nehru Memorial Museum and Library, New Delhi:
   (a) 'Educational Muddle and Degeneration of Democracy: Reflections on the Indian Scenario', Paper presented (in absentia) at the Symposium on 'Education and Democracy', held at Nehru Memorial Museum and Library, New Delhi, on 10–12 December 1988 (appearing as Chapter 17).
5. Professor Suma Chitnis, Tata Institute of Social Sciences, Bombay and Professor Philip G. Altbach, State University of New York, Buffalo:
   (a) 'Teachers and Unionism: The Organization of the Academic Profession' (co-authored with G. Sivaramakrishnan), in Suma Chitnis and Philip G. Altbach (eds.): *The Indian Academic Profession* (105–33). Delhi: Macmillan, 1979 (appearing as Chapter 14).
6. Professor Philip G. Altbach, State University of New York, Buffalo:
   (a) 'India', in Philip G. Altbach (ed.): *Student Political Activism: An International Reference Handbook* (91–102). New York: Greenwood Press, 1989 (appearing as Chapter 15).
7. Professor Orlando Albornoz, President, and Professor Jaap Dronkers, Secretary, International Sociological Association's Research Committee (RC 04) on Sociology of Education:
   (a) 'The Education-Employment Mismatch: A Sociological Appraisal of the Indian Experience', Paper presented at the Committee's Mid-Term Conference held at Salamanca (Spain), on 23–26 August 1988 (appearing as Chapter 5).
8. The Executive Editor, *Rajagiri Journal of Social Development,* Rajagiri College of Social Sciences, Kalamassery, Kochi:
   (a) 'Multiculturalism and Education: The Indian Experience', *Rajagiri Journal of Social Development,* 2 (2), December 2006, pp. 131–57 (appearing as Chapter 16).
   (b) 'Beyond Demographic Dividend: Some Aspects of the Sociology of Youth in India', *Rajagiri Journal of Social Development (Registered Series),* 1 (1), December 2009, 1–16 (appearing as Chapter 6).

9. The Editor, *Journal of Educational Planning and Administration,* National University of Educational Planning and Administration, New Delhi:
   (a) 'The School and the Community', *Journal of Educational Planning and Administration,* 23 (4), October 2009, pp. 387–400 (appearing as Chapter 3)
   (b) 'Confucius and the Guru: The Changing Status of the Academic Profession in China and India' (with Philip G. Altbach), *Journal of Educational Planning and Administration,* 20 (4), 2006: 395–410 (appearing as Chapter 13).
10. Managing Editor, *Sociological Bulletin,* Indian Sociological Society, New Delhi:
   (a) 'Ethnicity and Education: A Socio-Historical Perspective on the Educational Backwardness of Indian Muslims', *Sociological Bulletin,* 39 (1 and 2), March–September 1990, pp. 115–29 (appearing as Chapter 11).
11. Professor Avinash K. Singh, National University of Educational Planning and Administration, New Delhi:
   (a) 'Education and Emancipation: The Saga and Ideology of Dr B.R. Ambedkar', Paper presented (in absentia) at the Anil Bordia Memorial Policy Seminar on 'Education and Social Empowerment: Policies and Practices', National University of Educational Planning and Administration, New Delhi, 16–17 December 2013 (appearing as Chapter 10).

References

Chapter 7 appeared as Chapter 7: 'Inequality and Education' (pp. 121–37) in the author's book titled *Higher Education and Status Retention: Students in a Metropolis,* New Delhi: Mittal Publications, 1987, of which he is the copyright holder.

Chapter 12 appeared as Chapter 2: 'The Decline of the University as a Public Institution in India' (pp. 23–40), in Ishwar Modi (ed.): *Modernization, Globalization and Social Transformation (Volume 3: Education, Religion and Creativity – Essays in Honour of Professor Yogendra Singh).* Jaipur: Rawat Publications, 2013, of which he is the copyright holder.

Part I

Introductory

1

Sociology of Education

An Historical Introduction

Sociology of education is one of the most rapidly developing areas of special study within the larger frontiers of sociology. It consists in the application of the sociological perspective to the concept of education. Broadly, it is defined as a study of the institutions and processes of education, on the one hand, and the relation between education and the other facets of society, on the other. The exact scope of this field of study has not, however, remained the same in the course of its chequered history of nearly a century and a quarter now. To understand the scope of this subject and the contemporary trends in it, one should bear in mind its long history and complex tradition. This chapter provides an historical introduction to the scope of the sociology of education.

Durkheim and the Origin of the Sociology of Education

The historical roots of the sociology of education can be traced to the earliest Greek thinkers on education like Plato (428/427–348/347 BCE) and Isocrates (436–338 BCE) who recognised the social significance of education and its possible role in supporting the state. However, the emergence of a distinct study of education from a sociological point of view is of comparatively recent origin.

It is generally agreed among sociologists that it was Émile Durkheim (1858–1917), the classical French sociologist, who first clearly indicated the need for a sociological approach to the study of education. During his career as a teacher at the Universities of Bordeaux and Paris, Durkheim taught educational theory and practice as well as sociology. In fact, by a special ministerial decree the name of Durkheim's chair at Paris was re-designated as 'Science of Education and Sociology'. Three of his posthumous works, namely, *Education and Sociology* (1956/1922), *Moral Education* (1925), and *The Evolution of Educational Thought* (1938) are admirable products of Durkheim's lifelong interest in the educational process and the relation of formal education to social structure and to the channels of socialisation in society.[1]

Durkheim viewed education as a sociologist. He considered education as 'an eminently social thing in its origins as in its functions' and, as a result, the theory of education relates more clearly to sociology than to any other science (1956: 114). He conceived of education as intimately related to a society's structure. It reflects and maintains the society, and can only partially change it. In its role as an agency of social change, it can, at best, instil 'the inclination for collective life' and transmit emergent social ideals and cultural values.

In the true spirit of his sociology, Durkheim emphasised the socio-cultural relativity of educational ideals. That is, according to him, there is no single ideal or perfect type of education for all individuals. The differences in socio-cultural milieu and needs play an important role in the type of educational programmes which are established in different societies. Moreover, education is not a static phenomenon; rather it is an ever changing social process. And, the transformations in education are always the result and the symptom of the social transformations in terms of which they are to be explained. Many of the current innovations in education like open schools, community education, adult education, etc. underscore the validity of Durkheim's observations and insights.

In order to better explain the social phenomenon of education, Durkheim identified four areas of research appropriate for sociologists. They are:

1. identification of the current social facts of education and their sociological function,
2. identification of the relationships between education and social and cultural change,

3. cross-cultural and comparative research in various types of educational systems, and
4. investigation of the classroom and school as an on-going social system.

In spite of the great insights of Durkheim and his strong plea for a sociological approach to the study of education, it was many years before sociologists appreciated his research guidelines. This unfortunate apathy and negligence on the part of sociologists are explained by the nature of human concerns among intellectuals during and for many years after Durkheim's time and also, to some extent, by a relative lack of scientific sophistication in sociology itself.

The Rise and Fall of Educational Sociology

Around the turn of the last century, educators in the United States of America and Canada were faced with numerous social problems. The large influx of immigrants, the shift to a younger and more urban population, the increased complexity and demands imposed by growing industrialisation, etc. presented a succession of dilemmas. What are the most effective means by which immigrants can be integrated into the school and community? What types of educational programmes are best for the majority of children who are from the rural background and are embarking on their first formal educational experience? In what ways are differences in European languages, ethnic identities, and religious affiliations influencing patterns of learning behaviour? These were the types of questions that social analysts of education asked and sought to answer.

This implied a growing need to comprehend the social tasks and problems of education. Not surprisingly, the social problems of education were among the first concerns of educators like William James (1842–1910) and John Dewey (1859–1952) as well as sociologists like Lester Frank Ward (1841–1913) and Albion Woodbury Small (1854–1926). These educators and sociologists in America worked together closely. The result of this 'mixed marriage' of educationalists and sociologists, as Ronald G. Corwin (1965) has described it, was the development of the so-called 'educational sociology'.[2]

Ward, the pioneering sociologist in America, is usually regarded as the most influential figure in this quest. In his *Dynamic*

Sociology, Or Applied Social Science published in 1883, Ward viewed education as 'the proximate means of progress' and recognised its power to stimulate 'social telesis'. According to him, ignorance is the stumbling block in the way of righteousness and happiness. He argued, therefore, that education should chiefly be 'a system for extending to *all* the members of society such of the extant knowledge of the world as may be deemed most important' (quoted in Fletcher 1972: 498). Ward's views illustrate the emphasis on the moral and practical aspects in the discipline, which took it away from theory and research.

Dewey was another influential figure. His collection of three lectures, *The School and Society,* published in 1899, created widespread interest in the role of the school as a social institution and its relation to the community. His ideas exercised a profound influence on the development of educational sociology as a distinct discipline.

According to Francis J. Brown (1961: 47), the first course in educational sociology was offered by Henry Suzzallo at Teachers College, Columbia University, as early as 1910. Apparently, this was a revolt against the largely metaphysical educational philosophy current then. A separate department for educational sociology was established in the same University in 1916 under the chairmanship of David Sneedden.

In this context, the contribution of E. George Payne, whom Francis J. Brown calls the 'father of educational sociology' (ibid.: 38), deserves special mention. Payne's *Principles of Educational Sociology: An Outline,* published in 1928, contained a clear conception of the meaning of educational sociology as well as an inspiring conviction as to its role. He established a separate department of educational sociology in the School of Education of the New York University. He was also largely instrumental in organising the National Society for the Study of Educational Sociology in 1923. This Society issued three year-books between 1923 and 1931. In 1927, Payne started the *Journal of Educational Sociology,* which became the official organ of the Society.

In the first half of this century, there was considerable enthusiasm in the United States of America for the development of educational sociology. Between 1910 and 1926, the number of colleges offering courses in this field grew from 40 to 194. Walter Robinson Simth's *Introduction to Educational Sociology,* which was the first textbook to incorporate the phrase 'educational sociology' in its title, was published in 1917. In the span of the next two decades (1916–36), twenty-five textbooks were published in this area.

The phenomenal growth and popularity of the subject is understandable in the light of the late nineteenth century and early twentieth century optimism of the 'Progressive Era' in America. The hallmark of this was the rejection of the prevailing belief that human affairs are governed by destiny and the insistence that intellect could guide social evolution. The educational sociologists believed that humanity and society could be perfected, and that schools could contribute toward such perfection by developing the human intellect and by inspiring the students to devote themselves to the noble task of reforming society.

The immense popularity of the subject does not imply that it had developed in a homogeneous fashion. On the contrary, a survey of literature in educational sociology makes it clear that the development of the concept of educational sociology has been divergent and varied (see P.M. Smith 1959). According to Wilbur B. Brookover and David A. Gottlieb (1964: 5–10), at least seven distinct points of view could be delineated in educational sociology. They are:

1. Educational sociology as the means of social progress.
2. Educational sociology as a basis for deciding the objectives of education.
3. Educational sociology as applied sociology.
4. Educational sociology as an analysis of the socialisation process.
5. Educational sociology as training for educational workers.
6. Educational sociology as an analysis of the place of education in society.
7. Educational sociology as an analysis of social interaction within the school, and between the school and the community.

The nexus between educationalists and sociologists did not, however, last long.[3] In America, the development of sociology came under the influence of the German tradition of scholarship, which laid emphasis upon theory and research. Educational sociology was sadly wanting in the requirements of theory and research. It was viewed by sociologists as an applied field with narrow pragmatism, which was theoretically fragmented and devoid of adequate research methods. Also, the American sociologists were not too impressed with the emphasis on moral philosophy which generally characterised educational sociology.

On the other hand, educationalists also became disillusioned with educational sociology. They felt that educational sociology promised too much with regard to the importance of education and that the grand claims of perfecting society were not being realised. Sociology, they complained, was obsessed with highly technical research methods and grandiose and unrealistic theories. Sociologists, they discovered, could hardly offer even a few definite solutions to educational problems.

Consequently, educationalists and sociologists shifted their attention to other problems and other areas. Turning inward toward their own disciplines, they confined themselves to their own points of view. In course of time, educational sociology fell into disrepute and slowly became a historical relic. By the 1950s, the number of colleges offering educational sociology as a course of study had dwindled considerably. The exit of educational sociology was officially marked in 1963 when the *Journal of Educational Sociology* became *Sociology of Education,* and when the Educational Sociology section of the American Sociological Association became its section on the Sociology of Education.[4] Today, sociology of education is regarded as a legitimate part of the broader field of sociology rather than that of pedagogy or education.

Orville G. Brim (1958) and Corwin (1965) have analysed the weaknesses of the early attempts to develop the subject. According to them, in essence, all the faults arose from the same source, namely, its separation from the mainstream of sociology. Firstly, many of the courses in the subject were developed in colleges or schools of education and had little to do with the main body of sociology. Moreover, these courses were taught by educationalists, rather than by sociologists. Secondly, most of the educationalists who taught the subject had very little knowledge of or interest in the developments in sociology itself. Thirdly, most of the students of the subject were teachers-in-training. And finally, as regards research, the techniques remained at a primitive level and the focus was on a limited area of problems of interest to the practising teacher.

Writing in 1965, Neil Gross described sociology of education as 'a relatively underdeveloped and unfashionable subfield of sociology' (1965: 128). According to him, certain factors are related to the low prestige of the subject. A large body of literature published under the rubric has little or no sociological relevance. The existent literature in the field lays undue emphasis on description in contrast to analysis, lacks theoretical orientation, and is deficient in methodological standards. Moreover, the environment in which sociologists of education work is not conducive to their development. Their association with the faculty of education, which is 'at or near the bottom of the academic prestige hierarchy' with its emphasis on applied science, has not enhanced their prestige. In the following section we shall see how this underdeveloped and unfashionable field became a fashionable one.

The Scope of Sociology of Education

The rejuvenation of the subject since the 1950s with a symbolic change in its nomenclature – 'sociology of education' instead of 'educational sociology' – has been mainly the result of the efforts of sociologists taking an interest in education as a field of study. The number of sociologists studying education from a consistently sociological rather than 'applied education' frame of reference has steadily increased since the publication of Brookover's *A Sociology of Education* in 1955. A number of distinguished American sociologists like Talcott Parsons, Samuel Stouffer, Robert Merton, Everett Hughes, etc. have made outstanding contributions in general theoretical sociology which have taken the form of studies in educational institutions. In view of all this, there arose an optimism that educational institutions constitute 'a fertile field for sociological research and provide unique laboratories in which to deal with strategic sociological problems' (Gross 1965: 129).

Today, most sociologists recognise that education, in both its formal and non-formal aspects, plays a very important role in regard to individuals and society. It follows then that the understanding of individual behaviour and social processes requires an understanding of the nature of education. This perhaps explains the present preoccupation with the sociology of education as a subfield of sociology.

What is the scope of sociology of education as different from educational sociology? According to Brookover and Gottlieb

(1964), there are both negative and positive criteria for delineating the field of sociology of education. Sociology of education will *not* include all sociology simply because sociology is good training for teachers, and it is *not* a technology of education either. On the positive side, the sociology of education *is* 'the scientific analysis of the social processes and social patterns involved in the educational system' (ibid.: 11). It includes both formal education and 'the multitude of informal communicative processes which serve educational functions' (ibid.). Such an analysis is assumed to lead to 'the development of scientific generalisations about human relations in the educational system' (ibid.: 12).

Based on the research and analysis of the educational system, Brookover and Gottlieb (ibid.: 12–14) present a tentative outline of the sociology of education as follows:

Relationship of the educational system to other aspects of society. This category includes several subdivisions, namely, (a) the function of education in the preservation and development of culture, (b) the relationship of the educational system to the process of social control and the power system, (c) the function of the educational system in the process of social and cultural change or in the maintenance of the *status quo,* (d) the relationship of education to the social class or status system, and (e) the functioning of the formal educational system in the relationships among racial, cultural, and other groups.

The school as a social system. This envisages an analysis of the social structure within the school and the nature of the school culture. The two general types of sociological analyses to be included in this area are (i) the nature of the school culture, particularly as it differs from the culture outside the school, and (ii) the patterns of social interaction or the structure of the school society. The latter includes (a) definitions of the various social positions in the school, (b) the relationship between actors in these positions, (c) leadership and power relations, (d) social stratification, and (e) informal patterns of interaction as seen in school cliques and congeniality groups. Other subjects for analysis in this area are the social roles of the teacher, the nature of the teacher's personality, and the impact of the teacher on the student.

The school and the community matrix. This envisages an analysis of the patterns of interaction between the school and other social groups in the immediate community. Among the key subject areas in this category are (a) the delineation of the community as it affects school organisation, (b) analysis of the educational process as it occurs in non-school social systems of the community, (c) the relationship between the school and the community in the educational function, and (d) demographic and ecological factors of the community in relation to the school organisation.

Sociology of Education in the United Kingdom

The foregoing outline of the early history of the sociology of education in the United States of America does not apply to the United Kingdom. In the United Kingdom, the American brand of educational sociology failed to capture the interest of the educationalists. Even after the World War II, sociology of education was rarely taught in teacher-training colleges or university education departments. Only in the 1960s did it gain recognition as a valuable part of a teacher's education. Thus, in the United Kingdom, the sociological study of education, in so far as it has existed at all, has developed in departments of sociology rather than in colleges of education.

According to Asher Tropp, the origins of the sociology of education in the United Kingdom could be traced to 'the first half of the nineteenth century with empirical investigations of educational facilities by Royal Commissions, Select Committees, Her Majesty's Inspectors of Schools, and private social investigators' (1967: 287). However, the real development of the subject could be said to have begun only with the appointment of Sir Fred Clarke as the Director of the Institute of Education, University of London, in 1936. Clarke recognised the importance of the contribution which sociology could make to the development of educational thought as well as to planning in education. In his *Education and Social Change,* Clarke proposed 'to accept unreservedly what may be called the sociological standpoint and to exhibit as well as we can its concrete application to the field of English education' (1940: 1). Unfortunately, Clarke's emphasis on 'the sociological standpoint' did not gain much acceptance among the educationalists.

Behind Clarke's appreciation of the sociological approach to the study of education was Karl Mannheim (1893–1947), a refugee from Nazi Germany. Settled in London and lecturing on sociology at the London School of Economics, Mannheim exercised considerable influence on the intellectual deliberations at the Institute of Education, University of London, where he was subsequently appointed to the Chair of Education in 1946. Mannheim viewed education as a dynamic element in society. It was a social technique in itself and a means of social control.

In his *Man and Society in an Age of Reconstruction*, Mannheim wrote:

> Sociologists do not regard education solely as a means of realizing abstract ideals of culture, such as humanism or technical specialisation, but as part of the process of influencing men and women. Education can only be understood when we know for what society and for what social position the pupils are being educated (1940: 271).

According to him,

> The principal contribution of the sociological approach to the history and theory of education is to draw attention to the fact that neither educational aims nor educational techniques can be conceived without a context, but rather, that they are to a very large extent socially directed. Who teaches whom for what society, when and how, as the sociological questions were once framed (Mannheim and Stewart 1962: 159).

He very firmly believed that, by analysing the society, and diagnosing its ills, we might be able to plan an educational programme for a new and better society.

As a regular academic discipline, sociology of education developed in the United Kingdom only after the World War II, when both it and the parent discipline of sociology came into their own. In the emancipation of sociology of education from a low status field and its establishment as a full-fledged subject, the London School of Economics, whose brand of sociology held sway till the late 1960s, played an important role.

In the immediate post-War period, David Glass and his associates at the London School of Economics carried out the now classic study on *Social Mobility in Britain* (see Glass 1954). More than a third of this book is about education. The interest among these sociologists at that time was largely with problems of social structure and economy. As Jean E. Floud, one of the sociologists associated with the mobility research at the School, has said, they were fascinated 'by the spectacle of educational institutions struggling to respond to the new purposes of an advanced industrial economy' (quoted in Banks 1976: 3).

It must be specially mentioned here that two products of the London School of Economics, namely, Floud and A.H. Halsey, exercised considerable influence on the development of the sociology of education in the United Kingdom. Their book *Social Class and Educational Opportunity*, written along with F.M. Martin in 1957, was extremely influential both among sociologists and policy makers. Equally significant was their review of the sociology of education in Europe and America for *Current Sociology* (see Floud and Halsey 1958). On the basis of this review and their previous work, they compiled, with Arnold Anderson, *Education, Economy, and Society* (Halsey et al. 1961), which has remained an invaluable pioneering reader in the sociology of education even to this day.[5]

These scholars, along with others interested in the field, like J.W.B. Douglas (1964), were basically concerned with the twin problems of social justice and efficiency in education. As Olive Banks (1976) has shown, their work is legitimately located as part of a much longer tradition of 'political arithmetic' in the United Kingdom. Broadly, the substantive focus of their research was the relationship between social class and educational opportunity. It embraced a variety of discrete questions leading to studies of streaming practices in schools, of secondary school reorganisation policies, of the effects of different kinds of schooling on the occupational aspirations of children, of the special problems of so-called deprived areas, social determinants of educability, etc.

One point needs special mention here. For nearly two decades, the subject developed with a rather uncritical framework of structural functional theory. According to Basil Bernstein, this theoretical framework laid emphasis upon macro-structural relationships as 'these controlled the relationships between levels of the educational system, the organisational features of schools and their selective principles, and the interrelationships with the division of labour, social stratification and social mobility' (1974b: 151). Its basic unit was an element of a social structure, for example, a role, or a structure examined in its relation to another. The major technique of enquiry of this approach was the social survey. Furthermore, this approach, 'tended to assume a normative system, and the problems of its acquisition' (ibid.: 152).

In the absence of any alternative theoretical model there was very little discussion about the theoretical basis of the subject. The only readily available alternative, namely, the Marxist perspective, was not organised as far as education was concerned and it produced no textbook in this period.[6]

Another influence which has shaped the general direction of the subject has been its pragmatic interest in educational policy. Scholars like Halsey and Douglas demanded that educational policies should be based on the knowledge of the social facts of inequality of educational opportunities. Their basic orientation was governed by a desire for a peaceful and piecemeal democratic change to a more egalitarian society – a concern for social policy which was rooted by and large in Christian pragmatism and Fabian socialism. Not surprisingly, they received public recognition as well as the continued attention of successive education ministers in United Kingdom. B. Williamson (1974: 7) has shown the close links between the sociology of education and political decision-making and the extent to which the research itself has been sponsored by official and semi-official agencies.

As regards the teaching of the sociology of education,[7] the most significant factors were the changes in teacher education in United Kingdom. The most prominent of these was the lengthening of the teacher-training course from a two-year certificate to a four-year degree in 1962, and an increase in the number of students admitted to colleges of education – which rose from 16,785 in 1961 to 39,574 in 1968, and reached an all-time high of 42,133 in 1972. 'At the same time there was a move to make education, as a discipline, more academically respectable, by attempting to identify it with the separate disciplines of which it is composed' (Reid 1978: 20).

The 'New' Sociology of Education

In the early 1970s, the sociology of education entered upon a state of transition. The theoretical frameworks within which the subject operated began to be redesigned. Sociologists of education became greatly excited about the potential gains to be made in applying to questions of education such diverse theoretical perspectives as Marxism, symbolic interactionism, phenomenology, and ethno-methodology. Although there are major differences between these approaches, they share certain common features:

1. A view of man as a creator of meanings.
2. An opposition to macro-functional sociology.

3. A focus upon the assumptions underlying social order, together with the treatment of social categories as themselves problematic.
4. A distrust of forms of quantifications and the use of objective categories.
5. A focus upon the *transmission and acquisition* of interpretative procedures (Bernstein 1974b: 150).

The upshot of this theoretical ferment is the hope that new questions can be posed about old problems and new ones identified. This trend is fashionably called the 'new' sociology of education, after D. Gorbutt (1972), as different from the 'conventional' or the 'old' sociology of education.

As early as 1968, Martin D. Shipman's *Sociology of the School* presented alongside a structural-function analysis of the school a conflict theory one. But the watershed for most was in April 1970 when the British Sociological Association organised a conference on the sociology of education at Durham. To the surprise of many of those who were teaching the sociology of education, a number of papers presented at the conference (see Richard Brown 1973) revealed new, or at least different theoretical perspectives.

Another significant development in this context is the reader *School and Society* prepared by the Open University in 1971 (see Cosin et al. 1971) for the revamped education course. This reader, which was based on an entirely new approach, came to be used as a textbook not only by the Open University students, but also those in teacher-training colleges and university departments.

To those in the field who had all along been cloistered in structural-functionalism and whose sociology of education contained few theoretical concerns, these developments portended a rather uncomfortable and disquieting future. Thus, one can view the emergence of the 'new' sociology of education as a challenge to the structural-functional approach to the study of education.

After the Durham conference, three figures of eminence in the sociology of education, namely, Pierre Bourdieu, Basil Bernstein, and Michael F.D. Young, met and debated on its theoretical foundations and empirical concerns. The outcome of their discussion was the seminal volume *Knowledge and Control: New Directions for the Sociology of Education* edited by Young

(1971b). The theoretical perspectives presented in this book, as also the ideas of its editor, established the phase of the 'new' sociology of education.

Basically, this book marks an attempt to redefine the kinds of questions that sociologists should ask of education by taking into serious consideration some of the theoretical insights of Karl Marx, Max Weber, and Durkheim together with those of George Herbert Mead and Mannheim. The starting point of this redefinition is the view very strongly expressed by both Young and Bernstein. This view may be briefly summarised as follows.

In the study of education, sociologists have far too long 'taken' the educators' and administrators' definition of what the problems are. And, 'by not making their assumptions explicit', they 'have necessarily taken them for granted' (Young 1971a: 1). In fact, 'early research in the determination of educational opportunity treated as unproblematic the concept of "what is to be educated" or the nature of education at which pupils fail' (Eggleston 1978: 64). Thus, sociologists have refrained from asking questions about the way in which knowledge is selected and transmitted in schools. They have trivialised the study of school socialisation.

The proponents of the 'new' sociology of education argue that schools should no longer be viewed merely as people-processing organisations which are engaged in selecting and grading the input to make sure of a satisfactorily unequal output. Rather they should be viewed as knowledge-processing organisations and as agents of cultural transmission and social control. This directs attention towards the selection and transmission of knowledge in the school. Young advocates that the sociology of education should enquire into 'the social organisation of knowledge in educational institutions' (1971a: 3). This shift in the major focus of the sociology of education has important implications for the organisation of sociological knowledge. 'Sociology of education is no longer conceived as the area of enquiry distinct from the sociology of knowledge' (ibid.).

The 'new' sociology of education seems to be preoccupied with two kinds of problems, or it could be said to be operating at two levels of analysis. In the first place, there is a concern with what is regarded as appropriate knowledge to be passed on in schools. It is believed that if we know more about the selection of knowledge, we would know more about the structure of power in society. And, in the second place, there is the concern with the structure of classroom interaction between teacher and pupil. This is indicative of the attraction of interactionist social psychology.

According to Williamson, much of the 'new' sociology of education 'is neither new nor illuminating, and the relevance of some of the perspectives employed even to the supposedly new questions being posed is questionable indeed' (1974: 4). No doubt, at first sight, the 'new' sociology of education appears to be markedly different from the old. But there is very little in it which cannot be found in Marx and Durkheim, and which is not presupposed in the old sociology of education.

It should be recognised, however, that the 'new' sociology of education is excitingly critical in its perspective and orientation. It makes problematic the assumptions about school and education which have been taken for granted by most educationalists and not a few sociologists. The more conventional emphasis is considered to be 'disastrous for the development of a sociology of education', as it is not primarily about education at all (Davies 1971: 267–68). The 'new' sociology of education turns away from a preoccupation with the social structure. It sees itself as a part of the sociology of knowledge. The perspectives incorporated in it raise difficult questions about teaching, learning, evaluating learning, curriculum, school organisation and control, and the *raison d'être* of educational institutions.

It should be noted that this kind of fundamental questioning is sustained with sociological theory, something which is generally weak in the conventional sociology of education. In this way, the new sociology of education represents a considerable departure from the 'empirical plodding' and 'political pragmatism' of earlier approaches. It is not in the least concerned with questions of educational policy. But it does not preclude studies of the social construction of educational policy.

Before concluding this brief note on the 'new' sociology of education, one observation has to be made. That is, as Bernstein (1974b) has argued, the new developments in the sociology of education cannot be separated from the general development that have been taking place in sociological theory. In fact, they can be viewed as reflections of the latter. This means that the changes prescribed by the 'new' sociology of education have to be understood in the wider context of intellectual movements in sociology itself.

According to J. Karabel and Halsey, the formidable problem that the advocates of the 'new' sociology of education are faced with is legitimating their approach. Not only are their formulations new, but also the institutional base from which they operate is fragile. With its 'institutional incubator' being the Institute of Education, University of London, and holding only a tiny base in the universities, the 'new' sociology of education has not gained much prestige or institutional support. However, 'the "new" sociology of education is too new to permit a confident assessment of its contribution.[8] Its influence so far derives less from research findings than from the distinctively different research priorities it proposes' (1977: 51–52).

Significant changes have taken place in the sphere of education in the West since the publication of Karabel and Halsey's foregoing review and interpretation of educational research. Student radicalism declined rapidly, the significance of education for economic development was reappraised, and expansion of education at all levels offered wider opportunities to women and minorities. But with educational budgets being in crisis virtually everywhere, old issues of selection, social class, and diversity reappeared. In the light of all the evidence, towards the close of the twentieth century, Halsey wrote, '... the prospects for a sociology of education as political arithmetic in the service of the great values of a truly modern democracy are, as always, difficult but also extraordinarily bright' (1997: vi). The 819-page reader – *Education: Culture, Economy, and Society* (1997) – that Halsey put together with Hugh Lauder, Phillip Brown, and Amy Stuart Wells pointed to the direction in which sociology of education was developing. Besides the introduction, which delineated the transformation of education and society over the decades, the fifty-one chapters of the anthology were organised under six parts whose headings are self-explanatory: 'Education, Culture, and Society'; 'Education, the Global Economy, and the Labour Market'; 'The State and the Restructuring of Teachers' Work'; 'Politics, Markets, and School Effectiveness'; 'Knowledge, Curriculum, and Cultural Politics'; and 'Meritocracy and Social Exclusion'.

Sociology of Education in India

In India, the serious engagement of sociologists in the area of education began only in the mid-1960s. Prior to 1965, our sociologists had not paid much attention to the social problems related to education. Except for a pioneering study by I.P. Desai (1953) and a few other studies by his students, systematic studies on the sociological aspects of Indian education were few and far between.

The credit for visualising the need for a sociology of education in the country goes to the late J.P. Naik. It was he who, as the Member-Secretary of the Education Commission (1964–66), sponsored a seminar on 'The Sociology of Education in a Modernising Society'. The main aim of this seminar was to call together a group of sociologists to discuss the scope of a sociology of education and the possible contributions of sociologists in the formulation of educational policy in the country.

This seminar, which was organised by the Tata Institute of Social Sciences, Bombay (now Mumbai), in December 1964, resulted in a fruitful exchange of ideas between a group of distinguished sociologists from all over the country, on the one hand, and experts on education associated with the Education Commission, on the other. At this seminar, two courses of future action for a systematic study of various problems concerning education in the context of 'modernising Indian society' were drawn up.

The first one was the preparation of a set of thematic papers on some of the issues involved. After a 'follow-up' seminar held in October 1965 at the Tata Institute of Social Sciences, Bombay, to discuss the drafts of these thematic papers, they were published as *Papers in the Sociology of Education in India* in 1967 (see Gore et al. 1967). And, in the second place, the group of sociologists embarked upon an all India field survey to obtain empirical data concerning the social and economic background of students, teachers and parents, their values, attitudes and aspirations, and the general conditions obtaining in educational institutions of different kinds in the country (ibid.: viii). The all India report of the findings of the field survey conducted in eight states was published in 1970 as *Field Studies in the Sociology of Education* (Gore et al. 1970).

With these initial efforts at theoretical discussion and empirical investigation a systematic tradition of the sociology of education could be said to have started in the country.[9] Since then there has been a steady increase in the number of studies undertaken in this area. Several organisations like the National Council of Educational Research and Training (NCERT), the National Institute of Educational Planning and Administration (NIEPA; subsequently designated as the National University of Educational Planning and Administration [NUEPA]), the Indian Council of Social Science Research (ICSSR), and the University Grants Commission (UGC) have taken a special interest in the subject. The Tata Institute of Social Sciences, Mumbai has set up a separate Unit for Research in the Sociology of Education (since renamed as the Centre for Studies in the Sociology of Education). The subject has also gained popularity as a course of study in several university departments of sociology.

Outlining the scope of a sociology of education, M.S. Gore and I.P. Desai write:

> The sociological analysis of any concrete system of education can be conveniently organised along two dimensions – one, a discussion of the relationship between the education system and the other segments of the social system, and, two, a discussion of the system of education itself (1967: 2).

The former involves an attempt at ascertaining 'the specific function or functions performed by the system of education and the nature of functional and dysfunctional consequences that it may have for one or other aspect of the larger system' and 'the conditions under which the system of education may be able to fulfil the specific function that a sociologist attributes to it' (ibid.: 3). The latter starts with the fact that 'the basic unit of the system is provided by the interaction between the teacher and the pupil' (ibid.). However, 'the two discussions cannot always be neatly separated, but the internal organisation of the system and its external relationships do offer two points of vantage for discussion' (ibid.: 2).

As far as the major areas of research in the subject in the country are concerned Gore and Suma Chitnis (1967: 336–49) emphasised the following:

1. Education and culture: (a) Education as an agency for socialisation, (b) Education as an agency for the development of knowledge, and (c) Education as an agency for value change.
2. Education and social system: The relationship between the family, the political structure, the system of stratification, and

the occupational system on the one hand, and the educational system on the other.

3. The internal organisation of the system of education.

It has been revealed by the trend reports on the research in the sociology of education (see Chitnis 1974a, 1985; Thirtha and Mukhopadhyay 1974; Shah and Joshi 1979) that, in the first two decades, researchers in the country mainly concentrated on the second area of research noted above. Unmistakably, the sociology of education in the country had developed predominantly on the lines of the conventional brand of sociology of education, as it was taught and researched upon in the United States of America and the United Kingdom. It was dominated by the structural-functional theoretical framework and the survey method of research. The 'new' directions in the sociology of education were conspicuous by their absence.

Concluding her assessment of the trends in the sociology of education in India during 1969–79, Chitnis (1985: 229–31) observes that the prospects for the future of the subject in the country are bright. The subject has hitherto, no doubt, been preoccupied with empirical survey type and descriptive studies. But with more than two decades of experience of research in a developing society, we now seem to be 'very advantageously placed for the development of theory regarding education in such societies' (ibid.: 231).

Surveys of research in the sociology of education conducted since then have vindicated Chitnis' optimism. Surveying the literature on the subject produced during the period from 1979 to 1989, Jacob Aikara compiled a sixteen-page bibliography (1994: 31–46).[10] He found that research was concentrated on three sub-areas: '(i) education and stratification/equality, (ii) education and social change/development, and (iii) alternatives in education or non-formal education' (ibid.: 28). Among the areas which have been neglected or inadequately researched, he lists the impact of education on social placement or social mobility; the relationship between education, on the one hand, and polity, religion, and family, on the other; and innovations and reforms in education; educational administration (ibid.: 29–30).

In her recently published review of literature, Geetha B. Nambissan (2014) focuses on sociological research on school education in India. 'Unlike many of the earlier reviews, which broadly included social science research on education', she 'specifically focuses on contributions by sociologists or by scholars who draw on sociological theories and concepts'. Considering her delimitations – school education and sociological focus – her list of references is short (ibid.: 95–101). Her review indicates the 'need for scholars to identify key issues and concerns in contemporary schooling and carry out systematic empirical research' (ibid.: 94).

It must be noted that in the last two decades or so, some significant studies have been published on the sociology of education. Sureshchandra Shukla and Rekha Kaul (1998) have put together a volumes of essays focussing on education vis-à-vis development and underdevelopment. The compilation by Geetha B. Nambissan and S. Srinivasa Rao (2013b) examines the changing contours of and the emerging concerns in the sociology of education in India.

Since the publication of Meenakshi Thapan's ethnography of life at the Rishi Valley School (2006/1991) and Padma Sarangapani's ethnography of learning in a north Indian village (2003), scholars have been interested in the ethnography of school culture and the schooling process (see Thapan 2014). Karuna Chanana (2001) has explored the trends and issues in women's education. Another useful compilation on women's education is by Jandhyala B. Tilak (2007). Avijit Pathak has examined the social implications of schooling (2013/2002) and reflected on education vis-à-vis the moral quest (2009). Another useful analysis of the sociological perspectives on education is provided by Aikara (2004).

Thus, during the last quarter century, the sociology of education in India has developed a substantial body of literature focussing on a variety of themes and issues. All the same, there is considerable scope for its substantive growth as well as for its theoretical and methodological refinement. Introducing their anthology, Nambissan and Rao observe,

> ... the *sociological imagination* has a critical contribution to make as we still lack an understanding of education as a social institution and its interlinkages with poverty, cultural diversity, and the world of work. How do structural inequalities, cultural diversity, and identities of different social groups mediate

institutional practices and influence learning? These are areas of research where sociologists of education in India have a critical role to play (2013a: 19; emphasis in original).

Notes

1. For a brief critical appraisal of Durkheim's contribution to sociology of education, see Lukes (1973: 128–36), and of Durkheim and the functionalist tradition, see Blackledge and Hunt (1985: 5–109).
2. According to Reid, the phrase 'educational sociology' has a curious ring to, it:

   It could suggest that this type of sociology is educational, implying either that the other types are not, or one might argue that it includes all sociology, since the subject itself is educational (that is, helps with 'the systematic training and development of the moral and intellectual faculties') (1978: 17).
3. For a more detailed discussion of the divergence between the disciplines of education and sociology, see Hansen (1967: 3–35).
4. Of course, it is not uncommon to find scholars maintaining a distinction between 'educational sociology' and 'sociology of education' (see, for example, Taylor 1966; Hansen 1967: 21–24; Jensen 1967; Znaniecki 1970). Stalcup (1968) in addition to these two also uses a third category, namely, 'social foundation of education'.
5. The two other comparable readers to have appeared since then are those put together by Karabel and Halsey (1977b) and Halsey et al. (1997).
6. The Marxist perspective in the sociology of education was articulated better in the 1970s and the early 1980s (see, for example, Levitas 1974; Sarup 1978; Matthews 1980; Demaine 1981).
7. The first taught masters' degree course in the sociology of education was introduced at the Institute of Education, University of London, in 1964, and the first degrees were awarded in 1966 (Bernstein 1974b: 148).
8. Nevertheless, Karabel and Halsey (1977: 52–61) provide an 'early assessment' of the 'new' sociology of education.
9. For a 'personal account' of the establishment of the sociology of education in India, see Chitnis (2013); see also Chanana (2013).
10. Another related survey focuses on the sociology of youth in India (see Jayaram 2000b).

2

Education and Society

Concepts and Themes

Human beings live in a more or less organised cluster called *society*. If we look at the societies around the world from the past to the present, we will be impressed by the fact that members of human societies have always shared distinctive ways of behaviour, beliefs and values, laws and customs, language and knowledge, etc. To the ensemble of these and other characteristic qualities and habits that human beings have acquired as members of a given society the name *culture* is given.

It is hard to exaggerate the importance of culture for an understanding of human beings and society. It is culture that distinguishes one human being from another and human beings as a species from other species. It is culture that makes human beings 'human'. At the societal level, culture provides solidarity and cohesion for the society by binding its members together. It broadly distinguishes one society from another. Most important, it is culture which is responsible for maintaining the continuity of a society despite periodic changes in membership due to birth, death, and migration.

How is such continuity possible? Each generation of a society passes on its social heritage and cultural traditions to the next generation. This is known as the *transmission of culture.* Culture is not transmitted through genes or heredity. This transmission takes place essentially through learning, and learning is a social process as it involves interaction. More than this, in every society, there exist more or less formalised processes to partially determine the learning of the young. The whole process of transmission of culture from one generation to another through learning – the process by which a naked infant is clad in the uniform of his culture – is called *socialisation.*

Socialisation enables a society to perpetuate itself beyond a single generation and it enables an individual to learn the values, beliefs, and behaviour patterns of her/his society or social group. This is necessary for the individual in order to adjust herself or himself and associate with others in a predictable and efficient way in a given society or social group. In brief, socialisation helps to transform the biological organisms into social personalities, and to make the individual fit to be a part of society. After all, human beings are not born social, but with the potentialities to learn the ways of society.

A word of caution is necessary here. First, human beings exhibit in varying degrees certain capabilities, limitations, and requirements as biological organisms. This should not be forgotten in our enthusiasm about the determining power of culture. And second, the fact that the culture of a society is transmitted from one generation to another through socialisation does not mean that it is rigid and unchanging. It is quite the contrary. In every generation of its existence the culture of a society undergoes a subtle process of change. This change in culture may take place either through accretions or through revision of the existing patterns by the members of that society.

Thus, the reciprocal relationship between society and culture renders possible not only the continuity of the former over generations, but also the refinement and enrichment of the latter. What is inherited by a generation is modified and added to, however little, during the course of that generation, before being transmitted to the succeeding generation. This process goes on and on and, over a period, the culture of a given society may undergo significant changes. But for events like revolution, war and conquest, and famine and pestilence, changes in culture are generally slow and gradual.

Coming back to socialisation, it is a process that continues throughout the life of an individual. There is no point in an individual's life when s/he has learnt everything about her/his society and thereafter s/he ceases to learn. Human beings belong to different groups, and even subgroups, at different stages of their life. As these groups change they must learn new things, rules, and patterns of behaviour. This involves what is called *re-socialisation.* Moreover, as a member of one social group an individual is not always confined to the same role; s/he may constantly change her/his roles within it: acquire new ones, drop or modify old ones. With each role there are new patterns of behaviour to be learnt. Furthermore, some individuals may also learn the culture of groups to which they do not belong, with the anticipation of becoming members of those groups. This is called *anticipatory socialisation.* Thus, the process of socialisation begins at birth and ends only with death. And, as a process of transmission of culture, it is very complex and has wide-ranging implications.

There are various agencies, both formal and informal, which directly or indirectly contribute to the process of socialisation. The specific agencies involved in the process of socialisation and the way they contribute to it are to a great extent relative to the type of society and the level of its development. Thus, in simpler societies, not only is the process of socialisation less complex, but also the agencies of socialisation are few, simple, and informal. But, as societies grow in complexity, the process of socialisation also tends to become so, with the arrangements for socialisation tending towards greater formality.

This is not meant to imply that in simpler preliterate societies the process of socialisation is entirely informal, whereas in complex urban-industrial societies it is totally formal. In any given society there are many agencies which in combination socialise its members. But, in simpler societies the agencies of socialisation are few and more informal, whereas in urban-industrial societies they are more in number and the process of socialisation tends to be more formal. In what follows we shall briefly discuss the relationship between the type of society and the process of socialisation at three broad levels of societal development (or the kind of culture that underlies the mode of production), namely, tribal, pre-industrial or agrarian, and urban-industrial societies.[1] Approximately, these three form a continuum of increasing social differentiation and cultural complexity.

In tribal society, life is based on simple technology. There is correspondingly simple division of labour with roles ascribed according to age and/or sex. Cultural life of this society may be considered as simple and as 'a repetitive cycle of generations'. As in every society, in tribal society too there is a need for handing down from generation to generation the language and ways of life as well as the skills which provide for the daily needs of the community. Broadly, three levels of socialisation can be outlined in tribal communities. At the outset, the young must learn the tribal language and the elementary rules of behaviour. Then boys and girls must be trained in the arts and crafts which are the basis of the community's livelihood. And finally, adolescents have to be initiated into the tribal lore, myths, and taboos so that they can be accepted as full members of the community. The transition to adult status is often socially emphasised by the ceremonies known as, what French ethnographer and folklorist Arnold van Gennep (1960) called, as *rites of passage*.

Generally, there are no special institutions and no professional teachers in tribal communities to perform the above tasks. The entire family or clan, in general, and the mother and elderly women, in particular, play a crucial role in transmitting the tribal language and elementary rules of behaviour, etiquette and customs, and restrictions and taboos to the child. A major part of the socialisation of boys and girls consists in becoming familiar with the economic functions and duties of adult life which centre on the community's sources of livelihood. The father and male relatives train the boy in hunting, fighting, making weapons, attaining proficiency in tribal arts and crafts, and knowing the local geography. On their part, the mother and female relatives perform a similar role in the case of girls, in addition to preparing them for marriage and household management. Finally, the *shaman* or witch doctor, the prototype of the scholar or professional man, initiates the adolescents into the tribal lore, myths, and taboos.

The child learns and absorbs the elements of the tribal culture through trial and error, play and observation, involving unconscious imitation as well as conscious inculcation. However, the extent to which the enforcement of taboos on and the assumption of responsibilities by the children are deliberately directed varies with the tribe, as shown in Margaret Mead's interesting contrast of the children of Manus (1936) and those of New Guinea (1930).

Among some groups, like the Incas of Peru, there prevailed a system of age-grades. 'The Incas classified all males into ten age-grades on the basis, principally, of their capacity to work' (Murdock 1934: 415). Such a system also apparently prevailed among the Tasmanians. Promotion from one grade to the next depended upon age and merits recognised by the tribe, and secret ceremonies accompanied initiation into each. There was an unusual degree of mystery about admission to the third and highest grade, the members of which possessed certain regulatory powers (ibid.: 9).

Among some African tribes socialisation beyond a particular age took place in places specially built for the purpose, away from the village (see Watkins 1965). The novices lived there until they were ready for initiation. During their stay, which varied from a few months to a few years, they were taught to fight, herd cattle, do a variety of crafts, and to perform dances and religious rituals. In some tribal societies in India, there is a special social arrangement called dormitory (see Majumdar and Madan 1956: 127–40). Dormitory is a kind of recreational club where boys and girls of particular age groups meet during evenings. It also functions as an agency of socialisation training adolescents in heterosexual social relationships and initiating them into sexual life.

Among some peoples of the Caucasus (Georgians, Abkhazians, Circassians, Abazins, Karachayevs, Balkars, Ossets, and others) children were compulsorily brought up outside their parents and family. This custom is called *atalychestvo* in Russian ethnographic literature, and in English it is denoted by the term 'fosterage' (see Gardanov 1976). 'The key to fosterage is not the content of the education, but its structural characteristic of being carried outside the family' (ibid.: 29).

As we move from tribal to the pre-industrial societies we find that the latter are numerically large, structurally differentiated, and culturally complex. Medieval Europe, pre-colonial India, pre-revolutionary China, and the Azetics of Mexico approximate the notion of pre-industrial agrarian society. In these societies, though the process of socialisation is still predominantly informal in nature, we find gradual differentiation in the agencies of socialisation.

In pre-industrial society, the family continues to play a general and dominant role in socialisation. More importantly, the family trains the new generation in agriculture and allied occupations. The guilds of various sorts impart training in different skills and trades like carpentry, smithy, etc. The formal element in socialisation is confined to the initiation by priests and instruction by the religious bodies. Pre-industrial state system had built into it some arrangement for training the royal heirs and the children of nobles in the art of statecraft and warfare. The class of priests was trained in a special exclusive centre.

An important feature of socialisation in both tribal and pre-industrial societies is that the process of learning and transmission of the verbal elements of culture is by oral means. It took place in a long chain of interlocking conversations between members of the group, involving face-to-face contact. Moreover, as distinct from the material content of the cultural tradition, the verbal content is stored only in human memory (Goody and Watt 1968: 29). In some pre-industrial societies, like traditional China and India, the Buddhist Northeast Thailand, and the pastoral Somalis of East Africa, where a tradition of script prevailed, its transmission was socially restricted to a select few, who were specially initiated into the rank of *literati* (Goody 1968: 11–20, 69, 85, 265).[2] Furthermore, the process of cultural transmission was largely utilitarian in character, with emphasis on the preservation of knowledge. It was basically concerned with ensuring cohesion and continuity of the society.

The rapid industrialisation and urbanisation during the last two centuries or so have given rise to the modem urban-industrial societies. These processes, which originated in Europe, have rapidly spread the world over, changing the socio-cultural milieu of the existing pre-industrial societies. A vital problem of modern urban-industrial societies is the transmission of a vast variety of accumulated knowledge and a complex culture which are constantly on the anvil of change. Not altogether unexpectedly, the whole process of socialisation and the institutional arrangements for this transmission have changed. A significant landmark of this phase is the emergence and institutionalisation of *education* as a crucial mechanism of socialisation and cultural transmission. How has this come about? And, what is the role of education in socialisation?

Urban-industrial societies are characterised by large-scale organisations, advanced techniques of production, and a complex division of labour. They require sophisticated and specialised knowledge in various fields. This has to be expanded, revised, and disseminated on a large scale. In order to maintain scientific and industrial techniques, to run massive bureaucracies at various levels, and also to manage the innumerable variety of occupations, there is need for a large number of knowledgeable and trained people. Such societies also presuppose the existence of a large number of productive workers skilled in a variety of trades. Industrial societies also imply innumerable adult roles which did not exist earlier and which have to be learnt so that individuals can function as full-fledged members of the society.

Obviously, the process of socialisation as it was in tribal and pre-industrial societies is not adequate or suitable for the efficient performance of the above functions in modern societies. It is true that the family still provides not only physical care, but also teaches the ways of society to its younger ones. Parents continue to be the 'first educators of the child', and it is within the family that the child's personality is developed in its early and formative years. But, as far as teaching of the skills that are necessary to earn a living in modern society is concerned, the family has been progressively relegated to the side line. Institutions like schools and colleges have taken over the responsibility of imparting knowledge and providing training in skills. They are supposed to fulfil these responsibilities more formally and also efficiently. The institutions of education are also presumed to provide the scope and avenue for acquiring the critical outlook and innovativeness which are very necessary for development.

Moreover, not all the roles which an adult in modern society needs to learn and perform can be taught within the family. The same is true of the rules of behaviour, norms and customs, and ways of life at the larger social levels beyond the family. The effectiveness of the family as an agency of socialisation becomes gradually weak and insignificant beyond the formative years of a child. The school can provide experience of a wider range of adults and in a less emotional frame of reference than the family. This is an important point which is often overlooked in the excessive stress on the role of schools in imparting knowledge and inculcating moral virtues.

A few points need clarification here. Firstly, other than family, educational institutions are not the only ones which are engaged in the process of socialisation in industrial societies. Among other agencies that contribute to socialisation mention may be made of peer groups, work groups, and the neighbourhood. With the passage of time, mass media have also been playing an important role in socialisation: the socialising role of the present day mass media like the press, radio, television, and films can hardly be exaggerated. Unlike education, the process of socialisation through these agencies is predominantly informal in nature. But in many modern societies it is also found that formal organisations like political parties, trade unions, religious bodies, etc. are offering formal instruction to socialise people, though that is not their main role.

Secondly, the reader must have observed that, in the foregoing discussion, the word education has been used sparingly. This is because, conventionally, the word education has been used very loosely and ambiguously. There are as many definitions of education as there are scholars defining it. Sometimes the word is used so broadly as to be synonymous with socialisation. In fact, etymologically, the English word education is derived from the Latin root *educare*, which means 'bringing up of children physically and mentally'. Even Émile Durkheim defined education as consisting of 'a methodical socialisation of the young generation' (1956: 71). According to him, education is the influence exercised by adult generations on those that are not yet ready for social life. Its object is to arouse and to develop in the child a certain number of physical, intellectual, and moral states which are demanded of her/him by both the political society as a whole and the special milieu for which s/he is specifically destined.

Eminent anthropologists and sociologists like Herbert Spencer, George Herbert Mead, Margaret Mead, and James Stroud, among others, share such a broad definition of education. The chief argument in defence of such a broad usage of the term seems to be that the total effect of education is not to be achieved only through formal agencies like schools and colleges.

However, for analytical rigour and practical considerations, it is necessary to distinguish between socialisation and education. The word socialisation may be used to refer to the whole process of cultural learning, from birth to death, including the instruction imparted in formal settings. The word education may be reserved to refer to the process of socialisation that takes place consciously and formally within the facilities specifically provided for the purpose like schools, colleges, institutes, polytechnics, universities, etc. It involves deliberate transmission of knowledge, skills, and values. Society institutionalises these facilities by organising the process, designating the personnel to carry it out, elaborating norms, providing equipment, and so on. It is in this more specific sense that the word education is used in the following pages.

In recent literature on the subject a distinction is sometimes made between formal education and non-formal education. These two phrases have not been defined precisely. Consequently, this, along with reference to such phrases as 'incidental education' and 'informal education', has led to some terminological confusion. The term 'education' here refers to the mode or content of teaching. *Formal education* may be defined as the teaching of certain knowledge or instruction in a particular branch of learning or trade, in a structured and programmed way, in institutions specifically designed and set up for the purpose such as schools, colleges, polytechnics, etc. *Non-formal education* refers to programmed (that is, consciously organised and patterned) and purposeful instruction in certain areas of knowledge and skill or some other element of culture which takes place outside of 'school' or similarly designated institutions. It is offered to a particular category of people – like adults, farmers, women, dropouts, etc. – who cannot be covered under the scheme of formal education, either because they have passed the age for it or because they are employed. It is relatively more flexible and free from the structural rigidities found in formal education. *Incidental education* refers to that process of learning which takes place in the course of life, as a result of which an individual absorbs enlightenment from the environment in which s/he lives and grows up. The phrase *informal education* is used almost synonymously with socialisation.

According to a recent view, however, the entire basis for the distinction between formal and informal education is unfounded, and the phrase non-formal education is a misnomer. It is argued that there is no definite line distinguishing one from the other. What is called non-formal education contains many characteristics of formal education. And, many a time, formal education is offered in a way devoid of some of its crucial characteristics. Alternatively, it is suggested that it would be meaningful to distinguish between structured and unstructured education.

As any other institution, education also has certain goals or objectives. As pointed out earlier, modern urban-industrial societies require a variety of humanpower to keep the society going. Educational institutions impart knowledge of a variety of types and train people in various skills so that they can fill the manifold adult roles in society. Moreover, educational institutions are endowed with the responsibility of creating and expanding knowledge. While this is the primary function of education, it is not the only one. Education also contributes towards socialisation by providing its clientele with a context and experience of adult roles in a wider social framework.

In order to achieve the foregoing objectives, the institution of education has to be structured in a particular way. Accordingly, the educational system of any country has a definite pattern. The whole process of education is divided into several types and stages. Movement from one stage to another is defined and predetermined. Within a setting where education takes place there will be organisation, that is, a set of roles, rules of behaviour, norms, and values. Depending on the level and type of education and the number of people involved, such organisation is relatively less or more complex. For example, a single-teacher school in a village is very simple in organisation compared to a big college in a city, which is more complex. The organisational structuring of educational settings is related to the functions which they are expected to perform in the pursuit of their objectives.

The foregoing discussion may give the impression that education is a full-fledged and self-contained institution, separable from the wider network of society. But we should hasten to add that this is far from being so. Education as an institution is firmly entrenched in society. Society consists of several other institutions like family, religion, economy, polity, etc. and education is inseparably related to these institutions. It is only for analytical purposes that we can isolate education from other social institutions.

The nature of the relationship between education and other social institutions is reciprocal. Education not only affects other social institutions but other social institutions also affect education. To the extent that all these social institutions are interwoven, changes in one will definitely have an impact on the others either directly or indirectly. In the light of the crucial position that education occupies in relation to other social institutions as a mechanism of transmission and innovation of knowledge and skills, it has great potentialities for social change and modernisation. Hence, in all the developed and the developing countries the role of education in national development is treated as axiomatic.

In the rest of this chapter, we shall briefly examine the reciprocal relationship between education and a few key social institutions such as family, economy, politics, religion, and stratification. This is intended to outline in general terms the scope of the subject embodied in the title of the chapter. And, therefore, the following discussion will be more conceptual than substantive in orientation.

Education and Family

The role of family as a social institution engaged in the transmission of culture has already been noted. It has been appropriately described as the 'incubator for culture' (Goldschmidt 1971: 195). Though with the advance of industrialisation and the growing complexity of the industrial societies many of the functions traditionally served by the family have been taken over by other agencies, the fundamental importance of the family can hardly be denied. In fact, attempts at liquidating the institution of family, as in the erstwhile Soviet Union after the Russian Revolution and in the institution of Kibbutz in Israel, were given up for obvious reasons. The current trend in all societies is to endow greater attention to the family and its welfare. Our interest in the family here is limited to the relationship it bears to education.

Both family and education have one purpose in common, that is, the socialisation of the younger generation. Whereas the family provides the earliest context for socialisation, socialisation by school starts later, when the child has reached five or six years of age. Thus, the socialisation of the child in its crucial formative years takes place in the family, and the child enters the school with some mould of socialisation. Even after entering the school the child normally continues to live with its parents and to be deeply influenced by the behaviour and attitude of its family members. There are two problems here. First, at what age should socialisation outside the family begin? And, the second, what alternatives should be available both at the start and later? The answers to these questions have implications both for the process of socialisation and for the personality of the child being socialised.

Socialisation in the school continues for a period of over ten years. This period is significant from the point of view of the child. During this period, the school works alongside the family, which also continues to be a very potent influence on the child. It is possible that there may develop a partnership between these two institutions engaged in the same activity. But it is also likely, and more so in large-scale societies with multiple groups and heterogeneous cultural traditions, that the two may come into conflict with each other. In the latter case, the consequences for the development of the personality of the child being socialised could be adverse.

Other than socialisation and personality development, which are the common grounds where family and school meet, there are some specific ways in which the two are related. For any school-going child, the academic environment of the family is really vital. It has been observed that, other things being normal, a favourable academic environment at home contributes towards academic achievement and better life chances compared to the unfavourable. Academic environment of the family is a broad concept comprising certain material and non-material factors. Among these, mention may be made of the financial position of the family members, the feedback provided to the child in terms of encouragement and kindling up of aspirations, etc. These factors reinforce what goes on in the school, thus affecting the academic placement and achievement of the students.

On the other hand, the structure of the family is itself affected to a considerable extent by education. The impact of education on urban-ward migration is well known. Rural people seeking education, especially higher and professional education, have to go out of their village. And such of those who thus get educated have to look for jobs outside the home and village. This has considerably affected the structure of the joint family in rural areas.

Social demographers have observed that, generally, educated people tend to have less number of children compared to the uneducated ones. In other words, education seems to be a key factor affecting the family size. In the area of marriage, the available evidence suggests the existence of a direct relationship between the educational level of individuals and the age at which they get married. Generally, educated people tend to marry relatively later compared to the uneducated ones. Therefore, education may be a key factor in raising the age at marriage and thereby bringing down the rate of growth of population. Incidentally, the incidence of inter-caste and inter-religious marriages is relatively more among the educated people compared to their uneducated counterparts.

Yet another area in which education has affected the family is in the sense of individual freedom and economic independence. While this is expected in the case of men, it is interesting to note that this has affected the status of women also. More and more women are now getting education and taking up salaried occupations and entering professions. This has brought in its wake some amount of role change and role conflict among the educated and working women. This may, in turn, act as a further source of change in the structure of the family.

Education and Economy

The significance of economy as a social institution has long been recognised. In fact, scholars like Karl Marx and his followers have argued that it is the pivotal institution of any society determining the nature and functioning of other social institutions. The institution of economy broadly includes all those organisations and structures, rules and regulations, and personnel which are engaged, directly or indirectly, in the production and distribution of goods and services. The level of economic development in any society determines to a great extent its development in other spheres. The developmental plan of all countries, therefore, lays the greatest emphasis on economic planning.

An integral feature of economic planning is the faith that is reposed in education as an important instrument in national development. This seems to be based on the fact that, with the growing complexity of urban-industrial society, economy and education have become intertwined, each affecting the other in significant ways. Economists have long been aware of the importance of this relationship and its implication for development in general.

Adam Smith in his concept of 'fixed capital' included the acquired and inherent abilities of 'all the inhabitants or members of a society'. David Ricardo and Thomas Malthus favoured education as the means of limiting the size of the family and, thereby, increasing the well-being of the masses. Alfred Marshall emphasised the importance of education as a national investment by underscoring the point that the most valuable of all capital was that 'invested in human beings'.

The relationship between education and economy is reflected in the close link that has developed between education and occupation in modern urban-industrial societies. The earlier types of society were, as a rule, small and relatively self-sufficient. The process of production was simple, based on hand and handmade tools. The mode of exchange and distribution was barter, which was replaced at a later stage by a crude form of money. Occupations were hereditary and required very little or no education. But, in modern societies, which are by their very nature large and dependent, the process of production is very complex. Mental work as different from manual work has gained importance. Modern occupations call for trained talent in the application of vision, knowledge, and concepts. In brief, the increasingly technical nature of industry has raised the level of education required in occupations of all types whether scientific, financial, or administrative.

Education influences economic development in two distinct but related ways. In the first place, the educational system provides the labour force that matches the needs of economy. This is called the humanpower allocation function of education, and is broadly discussed as the problem of human resource development. Conventionally, economists distinguish between two types of resources, namely, physical and human. Physical resources include all resources other than human labour and knowledge, that is, land, water, raw materials, machinery, and so on. However, it is the human beings who utilise the physical resources and bring about economic growth and development. In economics the phrase 'human resource development' is used narrowly to mean the development of people's productive ability or humanpower preparation for the production of goods and services. But, used in a wider sense, it means the development of all such capacities and abilities as can be of some use to the society and the individual. In modern society, education has assumed the greatest importance in human resource development. Among the other factors that are involved in human resource development, mention may be made of on-the-job training, self-development or self-education, improved health and nutrition, provision for basic amenities and suitable incentives, and organisation.

Education is a prerequisite of economic development in another way. Economic development assumes a particular set of attitudes and values, or broadly a new culture of its own. In the absence of rationality, impersonality, bureaucracy, and the qualities of thrift and planning, economic development can hardly become a reality. Education seems to be an important agency for fostering such values and attitudes among the people and preparing them for economic development. Briefly, education is capable of generating a 'climate for growth'.

It is a widespread belief now that in the context of economic development education can yield both financial and non-financial returns. This belief gains additional support in view of the fact that countries like the USA, Japan, and Denmark have become advanced mainly by gearing their educational system to the needs of their economy. It is true, however, that it is difficult to measure the returns from education in precise terms.

Till now we have emphasised the role of education in economic development. But, reciprocally, economy itself can influence education in a number of ways. A growing economy constitutes the base for educational development. Economic development increases employment opportunities and a country's real income, thereby making it easier for people to receive education. And, finally, economic growth itself is a major stimulus to the demand for more and higher education.

A word of caution is necessary here about the causative role of education. A highly developed system of education can be supported only by a sound and developed economy. In the absence of the latter, whatever education exists may lead to 'educated unemployment', social unrest, and destructive frustration. Thus, the relationship between education and economic development is not only reciprocal, but it should also be optimal. While economic development is almost impossible in the absence of educational development, undue development of education in the absence of matching economic development is detrimental to both.

Education and Politics

The relationship between education and political life has been a subject of discussion among philosophers and social scientists for centuries. Aristotle and Plato were among the first to highlight the crucial role of education in the polity. Jean-Jacques Rousseau, John Stuart Mill, John Locke, and later philosophers like John Dewey and Dean Rusk have all stressed the importance of education in a democratic political order. As early as 1808 John Gottleib Fichte was making a strong case for investing in national education rather than in a national army, because education would fulfil the same purpose that standing armies fulfil, namely, the support and maintenance of the state.

The relationship between education and politics is reciprocal. Education not only influences the political process and environment of a given society, but it also, in turn, gets influenced by political dynamics. As regards the functions that formal education performs in the political system we may emphasise the following: (a) political socialisation, (b) selection, recruitment, and training of leaders, (c) national integration, and (d) political input role.

Political socialisation is a recent phrase, but the concept that it connotes, namely, citizenship education, has been known to political philosophers for ages. Briefly, it refers to the process through which the individual internalises the norms and values of the political system. From the point of view of society, it is the process by which its socio-political values and political culture are transmitted from one generation to another. Of the many agencies influencing the process of political socialisation education seems to be singularly significant. Education can be used in a directed process of political socialisation, as was done in Nazi Germany and Soviet Russia and is being done in Communist China now. But education is also capable of contributing to the process of political socialisation indirectly.

The second function of education in relation to the political system is the selection, recruitment, and training of political leaders. As Gunnar Myrdal observes, 'in countries where the colonial powers were reluctant to relinquish their authority it was members of the educated elite who launched nationalist liberation movements' (1968: 1650). When India became independent after long years of colonial rule, the type of constitution that our leaders hammered out was in no small measure the product of the liberal education that most of them had received in the West. Moreover, their success and failure as the political elite of the country also had much to do with the ideals, skills, and wisdom they had derived from their education.

National integration, which is defined as the strengthening of nation-consciousness within a given group of people either through a natural process of development or through the deliberate application of stimulating techniques, is crucial to the creation of a strong and united country. It is also an essential precondition for all progress. National integration needs people's confidence in the nation's future, a continuous improvement in the standard of living of the masses, a deep sense of values and obligations of citizenship and an identification of people with the nation, assurance of good and impartial administration, and mutual understanding and respect for the culture of different sections of the population. The problem of national integration assumes greatest significance in a country like ours where diverse factors act as forces of disintegration. The evils of communalism, casteism, regionalism, and linguistic chauvinism in the country are too well known to need any discussion here.

In what specific ways can education help in national integration? Firstly, it can generate among pupils the right attitudes and values. Secondly, it can acquaint them with the common culture of the country, inculcate in them a feeling of belonging, and promote inter-cultural understanding. Finally, it can ensure, or at least create conditions conducive to, equality of opportunities. However, education cannot do all this automatically. There is need for deliberate and persistent efforts. The Education Commission (1964–66) had suggested four measures in this direction:

1. introducing a common school system of public education,
2. making social and national service an integral part of education at all stages,
3. developing all modern Indian languages, and taking necessary steps to enrich Hindi as quickly as possible so that it is able to function effectively as the official language of the Union, and
4. promoting national consciousness (see Ministry of Education 1971: 17).

The National Council of Educational Research and Training has set up a National Integration Cell to develop programme for promoting national integration.

Education also performs what could be called a political input role. The special educational bodies such as teachers' associations and students' unions act as interest groups and have a definite bearing on the political system. Moreover, education may enlarge the political consciousness of members of a society. From the perspective of political development this function of education appears to be as crucial as, if not more than, the first three functions.

In brief, for coming to grips with a formidable list of political problems in modernising pre-industrial societies – like extending governmental authority, establishing popular feeling of legitimacy, institutionalising political participation, improving administration, and creating a sense of national identity – education seems to be the only panacea. However, under certain circumstances, education may turn out to be politically dysfunctional. For example, in pluralistic societies, in societies with a high rate of 'educated unemployment', and in societies in which there is general dissatisfaction with the government, education may lead to disaffection, alienation, and even anomic behaviour.

We may now turn to the other side of the reciprocal relationship between education and politics, that is, the influence of the political system on education. Social scientists generally assume that the state is one of the most important institutions of any society. As an institution of decision-making and social control which can authoritatively allocate values, the state (and, hence, the political system) is very much in a position to influence the other institutions of society. Education is no exception. In fact, it is most vulnerable, as the state finds in education an instrument of great potential that can be manipulated to serve its own ends. In conformity with the law of self-preservation, every political system tends to evolve a system of education that it thinks can best serve to sustain and strengthen it.

More specifically, the influence of politics on education can be noticed in the constitutional provisions relating to education, and in the rules and laws framed from time to time to govern educational matters. When the educational objectives of a nation are too many and the problems involved are too complex, it is inevitable for the state to assume the role of a general director and coordinator of the entire system. One of the important measures of state control over the educational system is through financial allocations.

Thus, while education can contribute a lot to the political system through political socialisation, recruitment and training of leaders, national integration, and input roles, how best it can perform these functions itself seems to be determined by the political system and its objectives. A healthy rather than strained relationship between these two institutions seems to be a prerequisite for any efficient social organisation.

Education and Religion

Religion is a socio-cultural universal. Every society has some kind of religion manifesting itself in certain beliefs and rituals associated with the supernatural and the unknown. Traditionally, religion has been a dominating force influencing society in a variety of significant ways. In some societies, the influence of religion is so pervasive that they are called theocracies. Whether a society is theocratic or not, whether a society has only one religion (monotheistic) or many (polytheistic), religion and issues associated with it inevitably come into relationship with other social institutions.

Throughout human history religion has played a prominent role in the socialisation of the younger generation. In many societies, the significance of religion as an agency of socialisation has been next only to that of the family. Among some of the earliest things learnt by a child, elements of religion form an essential part. But religious behaviour itself is learnt behaviour. Therefore, not only is religion an agency of socialisation, but also the very process of learning religious behaviour is itself a part of socialisation.

Since the very existence of religion rests upon the transmission of the religious heritage from one generation to another, from the earliest times religion has understandably endorsed religious 'education'. In fact, religion has been largely responsible for the initial establishment of formal systems of education. As mentioned earlier, the medicine man or priest initiated the adolescents into the tribal lore and myths in preliterate societies. Among the ancient Hebrews, education was primarily a matter of transmitting the religious culture. The Bible and Jewish scriptures were compendiums of knowledge. Since the sixteenth century, the monasteries of the Christian church have taken a deep interest not only in religious education, which they are expected to, but also in secular education. Boys of ancient Egypt learned moral precepts from priestly literature of which the most important work was the

Book of the Dead. For a long time, among the Muslims, education (which was exclusively imparted by the clergy) was almost identified with the learning of the Qur'ran. In pre-Buddhist India, education was considered to be coterminous with the study of the Vedas. The ancient Indian universities like Nalanda, Takshasila, Nagarjuna, and Kanchipura imparted religious education. The educational institutions established and managed by monastic orders and other religious bodies are paramount in the private sector of education in the country.

In some societies, religious groups have influenced the content of education (see Cannon 1970). This is generally achieved through the mechanism of censorship, that is, by proscribing certain books or reading materials. While this may be expected in the case of theocratic societies, such occurrences are not altogether absent even in secular societies.

As regards the influence of education on religion, it is interesting to note that, in modern society, education has been called upon to perform a task which is quite antithetical to what it had done in earlier societies. Earlier, education functioned as the agency through which the religious heritage of the society was transmitted from one generation to another. But many modern societies proclaim themselves to be secular, and they expect their educational system to train people for secular occupations. Also, in multi-religious societies, education is expected to inculcate certain secular values and attitudes like equality, tolerance, adjustment, etc. It is argued that educational institutions could, or rather should, be the first secular environment in multi-religious societies.

Education and Social Stratification

Stratification is a ubiquitous phenomenon of human society. The essence of *social stratification* is social inequality which manifests in various forms. It may involve the differential allocation of income, status, and privileges; the differential distribution of opportunities for various social utilities; and even the differential evaluation of positions. Thus, any society could be conceived of as a ladder or hierarchy into which its population is distributed. The higher one's place in this ladder, the greater is the status and privileges enjoyed by her/him.

Based on the movement that is possible between the strata (called *social mobility*) broadly two systems of social stratification are distinguished. First, there is the fluid system of stratification or the open society, in which there is greater scope for movement up and down the hierarchy, and such movements actually take place. The contemporary American society with its class system of stratification is often cited as a typical illustration of this. And second, there is the rigid system of stratification or the closed society, in which the boundaries of various strata are rigid and movement between the strata is extremely difficult, if not impossible. The caste system, in which membership in a caste group was determined by birth, as it was prevalent in traditional India, is cited as the best illustration of this. However, these two do not exhaust the possible forms of stratification. And, even as two broad ideal types, they are not found in pure form in any society; societies lean towards one or the other type depending upon certain socio-economic and cultural conditions.

There are various correlates of social stratification. These correlates vary from society to society depending upon the level of their socio-economic and technological development. But, generally, in urban-industrial societies, education, occupation, income, and wealth stand out as the principal correlates of social stratification. In many technologically advanced countries, education has become the most important criterion of social stratification. This is so for the reason that, in such societies, occupation is the determinant of income, and recruitment to various occupations is determined by the educational level of the individuals. Furthermore, in such societies, status gradation is also defined by the occupational and educational levels of the individuals. Briefly, in view of the close relationship between education and occupation, and to the extent that occupation is an important if not the only avenue for income and social status, education acquires significance as a determinant of social placement and social stratification.

An important function of education in the context of social stratification in urban-industrial societies is to act as a generator of upward social mobility and as a solvent of inequalities. In such societies, occupation is the principal channel of social mobility. Since occupations carrying mobility potential require certain educational qualifications, education acquires significance as far as mobility is concerned. This seems to be true also of societies where the traditional systems of stratification did not permit large-scale social mobility. Here, the introduction of formal education (as was done by the British colonial rulers in India) gave an opportunity for people who were hitherto confined to lower or intermediary statuses in the traditional system of stratification to stake a claim to higher status in the new stratification system. Thus, education, under certain conditions, has the potentiality of dismantling the erstwhile system of stratification and has, therefore, been hailed as a solvent of inequalities.

However, the foregoing analysis of the role of education as a generator of upward social mobility and as a solvent of inequalities takes many things for granted and assumes certain factors are constant. But empirical evidence suggests it is not so. In fact, it has been observed, in the reciprocal relationship between education and social stratification, it is stratification that affects education primarily and to an extent far greater than the effect of education on stratification. We shall now turn our attention to this.

In many societies, the facilities for education leading to higher levels of occupations and professions like medicine, engineering, management, etc. are limited. But the number of aspirants who would like to make use of such facilities is invariably very high. With the cost of education being high and the constraints imposed on admission to such educational courses being both numerous and complex, only a select section of the society, which is invariably at the upper levels of the stratification system, manages to enter such courses of study and the occupations to which they lead. Such a system of education is often defended on meritocratic grounds. But the so-called merit itself is observed to be a function of some non-academic and socio-economic factors. Thus, education, instead of being a generator of upward social mobility, is forced by the existing system of stratification to function as an agency of 'status retention' (Jayaram 1987a).

Social stratification affects lower levels of education also, especially in the rural areas. In many of the developing countries, the rate of wastage and stagnation in school education is very high. This problem seems to exist, though not with the same intensity, even in some of the advanced countries. It has been found that it is generally students coming from the lower stratum background who drop out of the school. Even when education is provided free and additional incentives are given, the situation does not seem to improve much. The practical logic of the lower stratum people seems to run counter to the generally accepted beliefs of policy makers.

It must be clear that the relationship between education and social stratification is more complex than it appears on the surface. While education has enough the potentiality for changing the system of stratification, this potentiality itself seems to be governed by the existing system of stratification.

Summary

Every society has its own arrangements for passing on its cultural traditions to the succeeding generation. For centuries, the institution of family had played a predominant role in the socialisation of the younger generation. But, because of certain changes introduced by industrialisation and urbanisation during the last two centuries, the role of the family in this regard has gradually weakened. In order to meet the multifarious needs of modern society there emerged education, which has in the course of time developed as one of the most important social institutions.

However, education as a social institution does not function in isolation. It is firmly entrenched in the wider social network and is reciprocally related to other social institutions. Among the principal social institutions which are influenced by education and which, in turn, have influenced it, mention may be made of family, economy, politics, religion, and social stratification. In view of the crucial position that education occupies in relation to these institutions, it seems to have immense potentialities for social change and modernisation.

Notes

1. These are what Max Weber calls 'ideal types'. They are useful as guides in analysis, but they are nonetheless fictions. That is, they constitute benchmark for, *not* descriptions of, actual societies. In reality, no existing society may fit neatly into these types.
2. Certainly, in traditional societies, there is often a distinctive intellectual elite, but they are not so much teachers as guardians of knowledge, and knowledge is esoteric, sacred, aristocratic. It is frequently the knowledge of the gods, revealed to inspired seers; its guardians are priests or literati. The literati do not transmit new ideas, but rather keep pure old dogmas.

3

The School and the Community

Some Theoretical and Methodological Considerations

It is a sociological axiom that the school does not exist and function in a socio-cultural vacuum and that it is inextricably intertwined with the community in which it exists. However, the fact that the school in India, as we understand it today, is an implanted institution both in its structure and functions, challenges the conventional understanding of school-community relations. The subject is further complicated considering that (a) there are various types and levels of schools and in different locales, and (b) the connotation of the concept of community has changed from its original association with geographical space to its current association with socio-cultural identity/identification. Keeping these considerations in mind, this chapter explores the theoretical and methodological issues in the study of school-community relations in India.

Introduction

The school, as the formal social institution we know today, is of recent origin (see Chapter 2). It originated in response to the need for the transmission of a vast variety of accumulated knowledge and for socialisation in a complex culture associated with modern urban-industrial society. It is not that tribal and pre-industrial societies did not have arrangements for transmission of knowledge and socialisation, but the scope and scale of the institutions performing these functions were limited. In terms of their numbers, geographical spread, and the number of years that children spend in them, the modern school system is unprecedented.

The growth and spread of the modern school system does not, however, mean that traditional institutions, like family, which once performed the socialisation and knowledge-transmission functions, have lost their significance. The family still provides not only physical care but also teaches the ways of society to its younger ones. Parents continue to be the 'first educators of the child', and it is within the family that the child's personality is developed in its early and formative years. It is in the neighbourhood and wider community and culture that the child continues to interact intimately and is socialised further. Located as it is in a socio-cultural milieu, the school can hardly be an autonomous institution. It is inextricably intertwined with the community in which it exists. The reciprocal relationship between the school as a formal social institution and the wider community in which it exists is captured under the rubric 'school-community relations'.

Not surprisingly, from early on, in the classical tradition of 'educational sociology' (as different from the later tradition of the 'sociology of education' or the 'sociology of school'), the school was viewed as the focal point of the community. In fact, the village school best represented the social integration of school and community. The teachers not only knew the pupils but also their families. The immediate neighbourhood provided much of the subject matter for the school. However, with community life undergoing change, it became increasingly difficult to hold the school as the focal point of community interest. This also necessitated the attempts to establish and maintain school-community relationships. In the West, these attempts took many forms such as:

1. the encouragement of parent-teacher associations;
2. the development of school-community councils;
3. cooperation of the school with various organisations and interests in the community, including religious and political groups; and
4. increasing recognition of the importance of public relations in school administration at all levels.

Based on an appreciation of the focal significance of school vis-à-vis the community in which it is situated, educational sociologist Francis J. Brown (1961) even enunciated the following as the appropriate principles of school-community relations:

1. *Flexibility to meet the changing services of other organisations:* that is, 'the school should be sufficiently flexible to continually readapt its programme in the light of the changing services of other community agencies'.
2. *Adaptability to community background of the child:* that is, 'the role and function of the school should be determined in the light of the needs of the specific community backgrounds of the child'.
3. *Capability of extension to service the entire community:* that is, 'the school should develop a programme of activities and services to extend, refine, and integrate human experience for all age groups and at all levels'.
4. *Responsiveness to national and world needs:* that is, 'the school must relate itself to the larger community of the nation and the world'.
5. *Organisation for community-wide participation:* that is, 'effective service within the community for all its citizens can be achieved only through organisation in which the school should play a vital, but not necessarily the leading role'. In other words, the effective implementation of the first four principles requires definite organisation and community cooperation.

What such formulations ignored was the fact that the school-community relation is neither a one-way process nor is it static. In relation to the community, the school performs two functions: (i) the transmission of a formally authorised body of knowledge and (ii) secondary socialisation. The school serves and impacts the community by providing services which would not otherwise be available to the community. The functional outcome of the school vis-à-vis the community could often be conflictual: reproducing society and reinforcing its norms and values, on the one hand, and changing the societal patterns and norms and values, on the other.

The structure and functioning of the school is influenced significantly by the key human inputs that the community provides, namely, teachers and students; material inputs, including money; and cultural inputs in the form of values, including the value of education. Both teachers and students generally vary in their background characteristics, and communities differ in terms of the material/monetary support that they can extend to the school and in their value systems. These diversities in the community's input into school impact it both directly and indirectly, determining the functioning of the school and the outcome of its educational efforts.

It is important to note that, in specific instances, the nature of school-community relations and the outcome of the reciprocal relation between the two are a matter of empirical investigation rather than theoretical postulation. Since both school and community are variables, the matrix of relations between the two is complex.[1] Thus, generalisations about school-community relations can hardly be universal without provisos; they can only be context specific. This point has methodological significance for sociologists and educationists studying school-community relations, in terms of both the logic of procedure that it entails and the tools/techniques of data collection and analysis that it demands. This has also policy significance in that the policy prescriptions on school-community relations have to be flexible and the policy formulation must keep in view the context specificity of school-community nexus.

It was noted earlier that the school as an independent formal social institution originated in the West in response to specific historical and socio-economic conditions there. During the colonial era, this institution was transplanted into India and other colonies. This fact must be kept in mind in the discussion on the nature of school-community relations in India today. The nature of school-community relations with reference to the pre-colonial indigenous institutions of school-level learning, such as Buddhist *viharas*, Hindu *pathashalas* and *tols*, and Muslim *madrasahas* will obviously be different.

The School: One Concept, Many Referents

At the most general level, the term 'school' refers to 'an institution for educating children' (Pearsall 1999: 1281). Sociologically speaking, it is 'a social unit devoted specifically to the process of education. It ordinarily includes some physical setting, particularly a building or buildings, and personal participants divided into the two categories of teacher and pupil' (Fairchild 1976: 267). However, such general, dictionary definitions do not tell us much about the nature of school as a formal social institution that we encounter as students of social sciences. Even a cursory analysis would reveal that there is a great variety of schools and, at the empirical level, this variety makes for substantial differences in the way schools relate to the community (presuming for the time being that the community is homogeneous and invariant, which it is not) or vice versa.

To start with, schools vary in terms of the level at which schooling takes place and the age-group to which they cater. There are primary or elementary schools, secondary schools, and higher/senior secondary schools. The meanings that these labels carry in different countries vary, though at the entry and exit levels there are likely to be more agreements. For comparative purposes, in India, the accepted division is in terms of 'standards' – from I to XII. The age composition of each successive 'standard' is more or less comparable: with entry into Standard I at around the age of six and the progress through each standard per year and exiting out of Standard XII at around the age of eighteen. To this, if we also add the pre-school 'schools' – called variously as kindergarten (KG, to be short), pre-primary, nursery, play home, etc. – with their own internal gradation in terms of successive years (as in Upper KG and Lower KG), the range of institutions called 'school' would widen.

It is easy to understand that the nature and significance of school-community relations is vastly different at successive levels of schooling. Perhaps the community is in closest association with the school in the first couple of years that the child is in it. Accordingly, one has to give the greatest attention to school-community relations at the primary level. Irrespective of their previous pre-school experience, 'for most children the move into statutory schooling requires the most formidable readjustment' (Grugeon 1993: 11). The child entering a new cultural field in the school has to learn new patterns of behaviour and relationships, which are predominantly adult-directed. The cultural resources that the child brings from the community may, no doubt, help it negotiate the new social situation. However, the cultural orientations of the school and the community need not necessarily gel. Often, right in the first few years 'school' becomes an alien institution to the child, and schooling an alienating experience. This dimension is often missed out in our understanding of the problem of drop-out of children from schools. This dimension is also crucial for understanding the phenomenon of 'counter culture' and 'subversive culture' – that is predominantly initiated and mediated by the children – in later years of schooling.

The second important dimension of the variations in school is its location. Schools located in villages (some of which are remote or interior) or tribal hamlets (which are generally inaccessible) are undoubtedly different from schools in small towns or big cities. Some of the village schools are one-teacher schools, which are structurally different from the multi-teacher schools. Even in towns and cities, it matters where the school is located. In a spatially circumscribed village, the school best represents the focal point of the community and an ideal typical case for the study of *organic* school-community relations. As mentioned earlier, in such a school, the teachers not only know the students, but also their families. Members of the village community, whether they have school-going children or not, invariably know the school teacher(s). In fact, for a long time now, the village school master has been a key actor/agent in rural life.

The dynamics of school-community relations in city schools is markedly different. Here, the school functions more as an association in which the involvement of both students and teachers is segmentary and the role interplay is more formal. The community's interest in school is mediated more by governmental channels rather than by community members *per se*. Compared to the organic nature of school-community relations in rural areas, the school-community relations in urban areas (especially, the big cities) appear to be *synthetic*, if not forced. In fact, let alone the members of the community at large, even the parents may not know the teachers of their wards. This is particularly so once the status passage of the child from family to school is completed. Of course, the community baggage of the child is never shed; the reference to school as an alienating experience and the development of counter/subversive culture made earlier is apposite here, too.

Schools vary also in terms of their gender composition. There are single-sex schools meant exclusively for boys or girls, and co-educational schools, catering to both boys and girls. Some schools are co-educational in the first few years and become single-sex at a later stage. Given the strong imprint of patriarchy on our society and the prevalence of gender-based dual value system, the orientation to the education of boys and girls remains significantly different. The social construction of gender and gendered socialisation in our schools is reinforced by the socio-cultural orientations of the community at large. Obviously, the gender dimension in the variety of schools offers yet another direction to our understanding of school-community relations.

Who owns/manages the school for what/whose interests is yet another significant dimension in the typology of schools. To the extent that school education is a public good and a responsibility of the state, the government schools (or those run by its allied agencies like the board, corporation, or municipality) constitute an important segment of schools. These schools, by and large, cater to the educational needs of the socio-economically weaker sections in the rural areas. There is a large number of schools in the private (not-for-profit) sector, which receive grant-in-aid from the government. And, finally, there are private (for-profit) schools catering to the well-to-do sections of the society and those who are aspirants for upward social mobility.

It is well known that schools vary widely in terms of the quality of education they impart and the quality of products they turn out. In the popular imagination, good quality education is associated with private schools (ironically, some of them are called 'public schools') and poor quality education is coterminous with government schools. Exceptions to this, no doubt, are easy to find. What is particularly noteworthy about the government schools is their strain towards uniformity and rigidity, and pronounced indifference to the overall cause of education because of the bureaucratic way in which the school system is administered. However, considering the socio-economic background of the vast majority of the population, especially those living in the rural areas and inaccessible regions, government schools appear to be their only hope for educational deliverance.

Regrettably, however, the indifference of the teachers and administrators of the government schools is matched by the apathy of the community towards these schools. Reading reports about community orientation to government schools in urban as well as rural areas makes one wonder whether it makes any sense to speak of school-community relations with regard to such schools. It is in this context that the much touted idea of 'community participation' in schools becomes meaningful (see below). Contrastingly, considering their profit orientation, private schools are more sensitive to the community needs. Selfish as their motives may be, they devote some attention to school-community relations, even if the community members (especially in the urban areas) are not interested in it.

Finally, their orientation to primordial considerations such as religion/sect/denomination, caste, and region/language adds another dimension to the variety of schools. There are schools run by religious/sectarian/denominational and caste groups, tacitly or explicitly proclaiming their bias in favour of their respective groups. Interestingly, such groups are often called 'communities', and in that sense the meaning of 'school-community relations', or 'community-school relations', assumes a different connotation altogether, especially if the 'community' is not coterminous with a geographical boundary (as in the case of village community). Minority religious communities have the constitutional right to administer schools (and other educational institutions) to protect their cultural interests. Understandably, some of the schools run by religious communities or caste groups offer religious instruction to their wards: the Muslim *madrasas*, the Christian convents, and the Brahman/Lingayat *matthas* are typical illustrations. Often they combine religious instruction with general education offered in other schools.

The government schools – or schools run by its allied agencies like the board, corporation, or municipality – are by definition secular in nature. Similarly, the private grant-in-aid schools (other than those protected under the minority rights) are expected to be neutral to primordial considerations. However, both in government schools and private grant-in-aid schools there is a discernible majoritarian orientation. While this is understandably a function of the demographic composition of the school population, it puts the secular ethos under strain and creates an uneasy feeling among the students and teachers belonging to the minority communities.

India is a multi-religious country, and a home to all known major religions in the world. The resulting demographics of religion and inter-religious relations have significance for our understanding of school-community relations. The nature of school-community relations would expectedly vary as between a community that is characterised by religious homogeneity (minority or otherwise) and that which is diverse in its religious composition. Lack of sensitivity to the primordial orientations of the community adversely affects both the educational process at the school and the community relations at large.

Irrespective of the level and type of school, a key factor that has a bearing on school-community relations is the heterogeneity of the students and teachers, the two key human elements in the schooling process. Apart from religious differences, caste and class hierarchies may be significant in the community. The continuing exclusion and oppression of ex-untouchable caste groups by upper and/or dominant caste groups is well known. Under compulsions of democracy, differences and hierarchies can create contestations and conflicts in the community, and this can have serious consequences for school-community relations. Those studying community participation in schools are well aware of this.

In understanding the school-community relations, with reference to the school *per se*, the distinction between two foci needs to be drawn: the *intra-mural* (classroom) and the *extra-mural* (playground). The *classroom* constitutes the main arena for most of the formal educational activities of the school. The child spends most of its school hours inside the classroom and some children are made to spend a significant portion of the time outside the school (at home or in tuition classes) for reinforcing what has gone on in the classroom. Generally, parents too place considerable, if not exclusive, emphasis on classroom transactions and their outcome as reflected in the child's educational performance and achievement. Hence, the significance of classroom and the transactions taking place there, both formal and informal, for our understanding of school-community relations.

Speaking of classroom transactions, it is necessary to problematise the formulation and delivery of school curriculum. One recalls here the thrust of what was advocated as the 'new directions for the sociology of education' in the early 1970s (see M.F.D. Young 1971b; see also Karabel and Halsey 1977a: 52–61). Nell Keddie has highlighted two aspects of 'classroom knowledge' about which we could raise questions: 'what knowledge teachers have of pupils, and what counts as knowledge to be made available and evaluated in the classroom' (1978: 133). 'This', according to him, 'involves casting as problematic what are held to be knowledge and ability in schools rather than taking either as given' (ibid.). In India, this has been dealt with by Avijit Pathak (2013/2002) and Padma Sarangapani (2003); it needs to be explicitly built into our understanding of school-community relations.

The playground is the second arena that must be considered in understanding school-community relations. The *playground* constitutes the main arena of most of the informal educational activities of the school. It is true that in many schools the playground is conspicuous by its absence. The open area around schools, and the street in the case of many schools in urban areas, becomes the locus of out-of-classroom activities – co-curricular, extra-curricular, and non-curricular – of the students. It is here that the social and cultural life of the community directly impinges on the life of students. The extra-mural life of the students has a significant bearing on the intra-mural transactions and the overall outcome of the schooling process. This dimension has not received much attention from the social scientists; this too needs to be explicitly built into our understanding of school-community relations.

The Community: The Metamorphosis of a Concept

In the foregoing discussion on the nuances and implications of the multiple empirical referents of the concept of school for an understanding of the school-community relations, the meaning of the keyword 'community' was taken for granted. The term 'community' was used as if it is has been a static concept about whose meaning there is consensus. We should hasten to clarify that this is far from being so. The concept underlying the term community, which has been in the English language since the fourteenth century (Williams 1976: 65–66), has undergone metamorphosis over time, especially during the last century or so, and is devoid of any accepted definition today. This has serious implications for our understanding of school-*community* relations.

In their one-time classic textbook, *Society: An Introductory Analysis*, R.M. MacIver and Charles H. Page write:

> Whenever the members of any group, small or large, live together in such a way that they share, not this or that particular

> interest, but the basic conditions of a common life, we call that group a community. The mark of a community is that one's life *may* be lived wholly within it. One cannot live wholly within a business organisation or a church; one can live wholly within a tribe or a city. The basic criterion of community, then, is that all of one's social relationships may be found within it (1962: 8–9; emphasis in original).

MacIver and Page were clear that communities '*need not be self sufficient.* Some communities are all-inclusive and independent of others. (...) But modern communities, even very large ones, are much less self-contained' (ibid.: 9; emphasis in original). They further clarified that

> We may live in a metropolis and yet be members of a very small community because our interests are circumscribed within a narrow area. Or we may live in a village and yet belong to a community as wide as the whole area of our civilisation or even wider. (...) Communities exist within greater communities ... (ibid.).

What is important, when it came to the *bases of community*, MacIver and Page highlighted the centrality of 'locality' and 'community sentiment'. 'A community always occupies a territorial area', but locality, 'though a necessary condition, is not enough to create a community. (...) There must be the common living with its *awareness* of sharing a way of life as well as the common earth' (ibid.: 9 and 10; emphasis in original).[2]

In their delineation of the concept of community, MacIver and Page, no doubt, were influenced by the best-known distinction between *Gemeinschaft* (community), based on *Wesenwille* (natural will), and *Geselllschaft* (society or association), based on *Kürwille* (rational will) drawn by the classical German sociologist Ferdinand Töennies (1957). The general idea underlying this distinction has been part of the typological tradition in sociology from Emile Durkheim (mechanical and organic solidarity) through Max Weber (types of action orientation), Charles Horton Cooley (the primary and secondary groups), Robert Redfield (the folk-urban continuum), Howard Becker (sacred and secular societies), Pitirim A. Sorokin (familistic, contractual, and compulsory relations) to Talcott Parsons (the pattern variables of action orientation).

Sociology, however, has moved far away from the conception of community referring to spatio-temporal entities, in which face-to-face interactions are by definition important.[3] The definitional criterion of the concept of community now revolves around 'identity', which has to do more with imagined commonalities even among people who may not be personally acquainted (Anderson 1983), than with face-to-face interactions among people living in physical contiguity. (Of course, face-to-face interaction can solidify and reinforce community identity.) Accordingly, we have such expressions as religious communities, caste communities, linguistic communities, diasporic communities, etc. – all hinging on 'consciousness of kind' in narrow reference group terms.

It must be observed, however, that the concept of community defined in terms of face-to-face interaction in a spatio-temporal context is nevertheless meaningful in village India.[4] The family, let alone the individual, being an autonomous unit is still new or non-existent in most villages in the country. Perhaps it is with reference to schools in villages that one can speak of school-community relations as per the conventional paradigm. It is in this context that the debate on community participation in primary education becomes important and meaningful.

Community Participation in Schools

It is a well-established fact that, while attempts have been made to spread education by expanding primary schools in rural areas and to meet the public commitment to providing a school within one kilometre of walking distance from every village, schools have not become entrenched as formal social institutions in villages across the country. The response to educational efforts in the rural areas is far from satisfactory. The problems besetting rural education are well known to be discussed here. There is a belief that government-directed educational effort at the school level, with its emphasis on uniformity and its lack of sensitivity to community sensibilities, makes schooling an alienating experience for children.

In the mid-1980s, The National Policy on Education–1986 (Ministry of Human Resource Development 1992) recommended empowering the communities for the management of schools at the local level. This is sought to be achieved through appropriate institutions at the district, sub-district, and panchayat levels –

such as the district education board, village education committee, etc. – so that community members can play an active role in the management of primary education. The District Primary Education Programme, implemented in different districts, has been described as 'an exercise in decentralised planning and disaggregated target setting to encourage and promote local initiatives in primary education' (Verghese 1996: 13). It is hoped that all such initiatives in community participation in primary education will contribute to the increase in the rates of enrolment and decrease in the rate of drop-outs from schools. This idea got fillip with the 73rd and 74th Constitutional amendments.

There are various shades of meaning attached to the phrase 'participation', and Sheldon Shaeffer summarises these as follows:

> (a) the mere *use* of a service ...; (b) participation through the contribution (or extraction) of resources, materials and labour; (c) participation through 'attendance' ..., often implying passive acceptance of decisions made by others; (d) participation through consultation on a particular issue; (e) involvement in the delivery of a service, often as a partner with other actors; (f) involvement as implementers of delegated powers; and (g) most completely, participation in real decision-making at every stage – identification of problems, the study of feasibility, planning, implementation, and evaluation (cited in Govinda and Diwan 2003: 15).

With reference to school-community relations, all these meanings seem to suggest that participation lies in 'exhorting generally reluctant community members to take active interest in the education of their children' and/or 'liberalising the otherwise rigid administrative framework to make way for participation of community members in educational management' (ibid.). Evidence, however, points to the fact that the problem of community participation in schools is 'much deeper and complex' than what theoretical literature on the subject seems to suggest.

Anjali Noronha distinguishes between two different kinds of community 'involvement' (participation) in schools: (i) spontaneous or generic kind of involvement, and (ii) political involvement. The *spontaneous* kind of involvement 'exists and evolves in society' and includes: '(a) parents being partners in their children's education by supporting them at home; or (b) parents and community leaders showing interest in schools by contributing time or resources to support school development, solve problems of space or facilities, or lend a helping hand in school matters' (2003: 100). The *political* involvement takes the form of '(a) playing a watchdog role – supervising and keeping an eye on the teacher; (b) controlling the use of resources and their deployment; (c) raising issues for larger educational change; or (d) influencing the curriculum and the way it is implemented' (ibid.).

Besides the government-sponsored programmes of community participation in primary education, including the total literacy mission and Sarva Shiksha Abhiyan, there have been experiments in alternative education, for example, the Shiksha Karmi and Lok Jumbish experiments in Rajasthan. The experience of community participation in school education – in Bihar (see Kantha and Narain 2003), Karnataka (see Mohan, Dutt, and Antony 2003), Kerala (Tharakan 2003), Madhya Pradesh (see Noronha 2003; see also Govinda 2003), and in Rajasthan (Ramachandran 2003) – so far is mixed. Whatever success that has been achieved in this regard seems to be associated with mobilisation of the community for social causes, as in the case of the Kerala Shastra Sahita Parishad (Tharakan 2003: 50–51).

An examination of the community participation experiment in the larger context of school-community relations as suggested above is necessary. For instance, it can reveal why village education committees, that are supposed to function as school governing bodies, have done well in some cases and have become dysfunctional in others. Such an analysis will also problematise the community, which appears to have been taken for granted in policy framework for 'community participation'. Who represents the community? Whose interests do they represent – the dominant castes/classes or that of the oppressed?

Viewed from the perspective of school-community relations, it is easy to understand the need for defining community participation in 'the specific context of primary education' (Ramachandran 2003: 56). In the absence of such contextualisation, 'community participation' will remain a misused and misunderstood word in development jargon (ibid.). Since foreign funding agencies (including the World Bank), besides the government agencies, are talking about and advocating 'community participation' as a panacea for the ills of school education, and coming as this prescription does in the wake of the process of liberalisation, its legitimacy is also suspect. This is particularly so considering that the idea 'is being propagated vigorously when the public sector is being condemned for its "inefficiency", privatisation is being generally promoted and, under the World Bank-IMF conditionalities, the social sector is experiencing major cuts' (S. Saxena 2003: 76).

Sadhna Saxena cautions policy makers, educationists, and social scientists to be cautious on community participation as a policy prescription: 'Given the fractured state of our social polity on the lines of class, caste, religion, region, gender and ethnicity, presided over by an overtly bureaucratic state', she fears that '"community participation" can very easily acquire dangerous and retrogressive forms' (2003: 97). She, therefore, emphasises the need to 'deconstruct and spell out' the concept of 'community participation' rather than 'oversimplify' it (ibid.).

Epilogue: A Note on Methods

How do we go about studying school-community relations? Obviously, there is no one best method for studying a complex subject such as school-community relations. It is, no doubt, tempting to suggest 'triangulation' as the appropriate methodological strategy. We have massive data on school education from various large-scale surveys and periodical reports on programmes. We also have additional insights resulting from small-scale, localised studies using the interview method and focus group discussions. What we seem to lack are detailed investigations of diverse aspects and of the complexities of human social interaction in the context of schools.

The use of the ethnography for researching school-community relations may be emphasised here. The significance of ethnography lies in the fact that it treats the familiar as strange and to 'make' rather than 'take' problems for investigation (see Hammersley and Atkinson 1983). This is well illustrated by Michael F.D. Young's compilation of essays on the new sociology of education (see 1971b). Ethnography is the qualitative method *par excellence*. Qualitative methodology provides scope for the reformulation of the research problem and yields insights that would be missed in a survey research. Thus, theory, as B.G. Glaser and A.L. Strauss (1967) would have it, becomes 'grounded' in data.

Among the various facets of school-community relations that ethnography as a qualitative method can explore, classroom practices; social construction of schooling, discipline, and social control mechanisms; school subculture; status passage; oral culture of the extra-mural arena; language codes; patriarchy and gendered socialisation; perceptions and understandings of boys and girls of the capabilities and future destinations; community orientations to school and education; community involvement in school and school-related activities; the role dynamics of the teacher; etc. are important. Ethnography of the school is thus the quintessential method for a better understanding of school-community relations (see Thapan 2014).

Before concluding, it may be noted that the study of school-community relations cannot be exhausted from within the perspective of any one discipline. Introducing the last of the posthumous volumes of Karl Mannheim, *An Introduction to the Sociology of Education*, W.A.C. Stewart wrote that:

> At the risk of being cloven by a sociological spade or a psychological pick, I would say that if every any study was inter-disciplinary it is education. It is liable to serious distortion if any particular scholar gets his magnifying glass on just a part of it (1962: ix).

This is true of the study of school-community as well.

Notes

1. In an essay, published first in 1949, Brookover and Gottlieb included four points as being essential for 'an understanding of the community educational system and its integration in the total life of the community' (1970: 9). These are '(i) the delineation of the community as it affects school organisation, (ii) analysis of the educational process as it occurs in the non-school social systems of the community, (iii) the relationship between the school and community in the educational function, and (iv) demographic and ecological factors of the community in relation to the school organisation' (ibid.: 8).
2. The emphasis on 'locality' and 'sentiments' can be found in many older textbooks in sociology. For example, according to Inkeles,

> A community exists (i) when a set of households is relatively concentrated in a delimited geographical area; (ii) their residents exhibit a substantial degree of integrated social interaction; and (iii) have a sense of common membership, of belonging together, which is not based exclusively on ties of consanguinity (1965: 68).

3. For discussions on the concept of community in Indian social sciences, see Jodhka (2001), R. Kaur (2001), and Upadhya (2001).
4. As Inkeles notes,

> The example most commonly used, most familiar, and most directly accessible, is that of the peasant village. In such a village the peasants and their families usually live in fairly close proximity, and their common residence area is clearly demarcated and known to them. Most of the villagers' interaction is with other residents of the same village. The inhabitants will commonly consider themselves of the village, know its name, acknowledge their membership in the community, and be defined by and treated by those from other communities in accord with the standing of the village from which they come (1965: 68–69).

4

Education in India

From Colonial Bondage to Neo-colonial Dependency

This chapter examines the impasse in Indian education in terms of the concepts and premises of the dependency theory and of the colonial-neo-colonial model. As such, it also carries with it an implicit critique of the modernisation theory, which has viewed the impasse as a problem *sui generis* that can be resolved through tinkering and rectified through readjustments. Part one traces the origin and development of English education through the colonial period. And part two examines the implications of the 'inherited structure' as a neo-colonial dependency in the educational realm in the post-Independence era.

I
Past Revisited

> The real power of those who built colonial empires lay less in their guns than in the educational systems they introduced: 'the gun coerces the body but the school bewitches the mind'.
>
> **Sheik Hamidou Kane**

The earliest attempt to impart English education in India can be traced to the missionary activities following the establishment of the East India Company and the measures adopted by Warren Hastings as early as 1773. The protracted controversy that had been generated by these initial efforts was finally resolved by William Bentinck, barely a month after Thomas Babington Macaulay had penned his (in)famous Minute (on 2 February 1835). This policy was reaffirmed by Charles Wood's Despatch of 1854, and with minor modifications continued throughout the British rule.

Historians of education have now adequately laid bare the fact that the spreading of English education was not an act of 'disinterested magnanimity'. On the contrary, it was the outcome of a complex combination of motives: religious – proselytising urge; moral – to inculcate new values in the spirit of western liberal Christian concepts; administrative – to staff the vast and elaborate bureaucracy; economic – to familiarise the Indians with the modalities and values of the capitalist economic system, and also to develop in them a taste for British products; and, not the least, political – to consolidate and maintain their dominance in the country.

The British, however, did not embark on a programme of mass education. What they were concerned with was evolving a small class of English-educated Indians, who may act, in Macaulay's words, as 'interpreters between us and millions whom we govern – a class of persons Indian in blood and colour, but English in tastes, in opinions, in morals and intellect' (in Sharp 1965: 116). This class was expected to filter down to the masses the knowledge and values it had acquired and internalised. This, it was hoped, would eventually stabilise the Raj.

The system of education that the British introduced was modelled after the system prevalent in their Mother country. This was particularly so as regards higher education. The striking feature of this educational transplantation was English, which was not only taught as a language, but also became the medium of instruction. While the secondary-school-leaving examination was conducted only in English till 1937, English was exclusively used at the university stage right through the colonial period. For those aspiring for official positions, professional status, or leadership roles, knowledge of English became indispensable.

In conformity with the aims of their educational policy, most of the educational institutions established by the British were colleges and high schools, and they were located mostly in urban centres. With scant attention given to primary schooling, especially in the rural areas, the educational system became top-heavy.[1] Only 12.2 per cent of the population of British India was literate in 1941!

With the adoption of English as the medium of instruction the vast mass of people were progressively estranged from the administrative, judicial, and commercial institutions established by the British. Since they were vitally affected by these emergent institutions and were not able to understand the modalities of their operation, they were forced to depend upon those who were English-educated. This coupled with the fact that English was the language of the ruling class bestowed unprecedented prestige on the English-educated Indians. These 'brown sahibs', because of their link up with the economic and political interests dominated by the British, were alienated from the masses.

Though modelled after the University of London, the Indian universities were nowhere near it in terms of the quality of the education imparted. The content of this education was biased in favour of languages and the humanities and against science and technology as well as vocational training. The excessive emphasis on the mastering of English as a language often eclipsed the purpose of education: it encouraged mechanical learning through memorising and discouraged inquisitiveness and an experimental bent of mind (A. Basu 1978: 61). There was a simultaneous devaluation of the indigenous languages, and a sad neglect of their development.

The curriculum of English education was in tune with the colonial economic and employment policies. All higher appointments in almost all the services were in effect reserved for the British. Added to this was the absence of (or, in fact, hostility to) any policy of industrialisation. This meant limited opportunities for qualified and trained Indians, excepting perhaps in the lower echelons of the bureaucracy and in teaching. English education thus created a large number of 'unemployables'.

Another point needs clarification here. There is a popular belief – held even by many educated Indians – that the educational system in vogue before the colonial conquest was the unorganised *gurukula*. The purpose of this, it is said, was to impart instruction in the Vedic lore to a privileged minority of the upper-caste males. It is further believed that the British brought in the broad-based educational system with universalistic criteria of enrolment.

However, a close scrutiny of the archival evidence, especially the reports and minutes penned by the British themselves, explodes this myth.

At the time of the renewal of the East India Company's Charter in 1813, the Court of Directors had instructed the Provincial Governors to institute inquiries into the indigenous education prevalent in their provinces. The Provincial Governors, in turn, instructed the Collectors under them to survey the state of education in their districts. Based on the reports of the various Collectors, the Governors presented minutes from 1826[2] onwards which prove indubitably that not only were indigenous schools and colleges widespread in the eighteenth century, but also the sex and caste composition of the student body was highly egalitarian.

Expectedly, the later British writers have tried to controvert the findings of the reports of their predecessors. Philip Hartog's attempt to find fault with Adam's report and dub it as a 'legend' is a typical illustration of the denigration of the pre-British system of education in the country (see Hartog1939). While steering clear of this controversy, suffice it to say that pre-British India was not 'dark', but instead could boast of a system of education which was as widespread as it was broad based.

The establishment of the empire and the pursuit of the colonial economic and political policies, in general, and the educational policy, in particular, from somewhere around the first quarter of the nineteenth century dealt a death blow to the indigenous system of education.[3] Henry Hardinge's policy of giving preference to the English-educated among Indians in government appointments drove the last nail into the coffin of indigenous education.

It is true that the destruction of the indigenous system of education would not have been complete without the support, active or passive and direct or indirect, of the Indians themselves. Many of the early generation of English-educated Indians reposed faith in English education. Raja Rammohun Roy and Mahadev Govind Ranade thought that it heralded an 'Indian Renaissance'. The Roys and their like not only protested against the establishment of any oriental oriented educational institutions, but also vociferously demanded the expansion of the English system.

We shall now turn to the 'filtration theory' embodied in the policy enunciated by Macaulay and endorsed by Wood. According to this theory, 'education was to permeate the masses from above'.

Metaphorically expressed, 'drop by drop from the Himalayas of Indian life useful information was to trickle downwards, forming in time a broad and stately stream to irrigate the thirsty plains' (Mayhew 1926: 92). In retrospect, we cannot but feel that Macaulay lacked sociological foresight; he assumed only those things that were in accord with his convictions and failed to anticipate the unexpected unwanted consequences that might emerge. The filtration theory turned out to be a mirage.

In England itself academic education had been elitist. The educational system introduced in India also carried with it its elite bias. Because of the initial advantage of their high status, the benefits of English education also accrued to the upper-caste groups – the Bengali Kayasthas, the Tamil Brahmins, and the Marathi Chitpavans – and the well-to-do, that too in the urban areas. Thus emerged the first generation of indigenous English-educated industrial, commercial, political, and intellectual elite in India.

The English-educated Indians, contrary to Macaulay's expectations, showed the least enthusiasm for spreading education and western ideology among the masses. On the contrary, they used their education for what the system – not Macaulay – wanted them to use it, namely, for obtaining employment and other material gains in the emergent order. What was conceived to operate as a filter thus became a wedge which progressively widened the gap between the English-educated elite and the masses.

Although in the shorter run English education did contribute to the political stability of the Raj, in the longer run it proved to be the undoing of the British stranglehold on the country. The educated class became more and more vocal in its criticism of the Raj. The Sedition Committee, which investigated the revolutionary conspiracies in India, reported in 1918 that most of the conspirators were educated young men. As it turned out, almost all the leaders in the forefront of the nationalist movement belonged to the English-educated elite (Seal 1968).

Macaulay's Minute was, no doubt, regretted in retrospect, but its directives having been implemented, it seemed too late to reverse them. In formulating their educational policy for tropical Africa and South Asia, however, the British were careful not to repeat the 'mistake' committed in India of indirectly encouraging the growth of political consciousness and nationalist sentiments.

II
Continuing Past

> The beginning of all colonial situations did generate a number of myths. So does their end.
>
> **Remi Clignet**

While the English-educated elite changed from being 'zealous co-operators' to 'freedom fighters', they could not transform themselves to accomplish the historic task of liberating the society. Their colonial hangover and their growing alienation from the masses steeped them in contradictions. This has had significant implications for the post-Independence socio-political developments.

An increasing number of scholars working on the developmental problems of the Third World have recognised neo-colonialism as a viable concept in an exposition of such a situation. Of course, neo-colonialism is a complicated concept, subsuming under it a complex network of relations between the developed and the Third World countries, and the motivations of the parties involved. The illusion of independence in the Third World countries, the awareness of this illusion on the part of those on whom these countries are dependent, the inability of these countries to break with this dependency, and the colonial legacy in the structure and values of their key institutions are some of the facets of this syndrome.

Education is one of the crucial agencies through which the ex-colonisers and other developed countries exercise control and obtain influence over the former colonies and other developing countries. It has been aptly described as the 'fourth dimension' of foreign policy (Coombs 1964). Educational neo-colonialism, however, does not operate uniformly or to the same extent, in all the developing countries. Much, to be sure, depends on the configuration of the historical forces and the socio-economic situations prevailing in the former colonies at the time of their gaining formal independence.

Unlike other ex-colonies, at the time of her Independence, India had a growing system of English education. This colonial heritage expanded phenomenally after Independence, but it remained largely intact in its structure and organisation. With the rapid expansion of the educational system the associated problems multiplied and the crisis attendant upon it accentuated over the years.

Was not the political leadership aware of the need for a new system of education to realise the dream of a new India? Certainly. As Jawaharlal Nehru, the then Prime Minister of India told an educational conference in 1948:

> Whenever conferences were held in the past to form a plan for education in India, the tendency as a rule was to maintain the existing system with slight modifications. This must not happen now. Great changes have taken place in the country and the educational system must keep pace with them. The entire basis of education must be revolutionised (quoted in Naik 1965: 13).

But what has actually materialised is only 'moderate reformism'.

Part of the explanation for this state of affairs lies in the very nature of the nationalist movement. It was not a radical revolution premised upon mass involvement and directed towards changing the fundamental institutions and cultural values of society. It was rather a movement led predominantly by the English-educated bourgeoisie, which took charge of the country's destiny after Independence. Being heavily influenced by western liberal ideology and its ethos, this bourgeoisie not only retained the institutions and values that had been introduced by the colonial masters, but also imported other from Britain and elsewhere. And education was the easiest to fit into this scheme.

One must, no doubt, grant that the social institutions, cultural values, and patterns of behaviour implanted and nurtured with the help of economic sanctions and political force over a prolonged period of two centuries of colonial rule are hard to be radically transformed in the course of a few decades. But cultural inertia can hardly be a perpetual excuse. On the one hand, the colonial bent of mind has resulted in acquiescence and complacence. On the other, it has generated a feeling that the colonial institutions are superior cultural outposts for the so-called modern society, nay, worse still, the belief, that there is no feasible alternative.

The failure to make a radical departure from the past lies not in inertia but in the absence of a political will on the part of the leadership, traceable to a vested interest in the *status quo*. The English-educated indigenous elite, which holds considerable power because of its privileged place in the system, functions as the salesman of the English system of education. In what follows, we shall examine the implications of educational neo-colonialism.

Politics of Foreign Aid and Collaborative Research

The illusion of independence in many a developing country is sustained by the 'friendly' assistance by its former colonisers or other developed countries. That foreign aid contains in reality elements of neo-colonialism making for the perpetual dependence of the developing countries has been sufficiently exposed now. But the crucial question is, what makes us dependent upon foreign aid from government and private foundations for our educational development?

Colonial hangover apart, the cost of radically changing the educational system in terms of time, money, and psychological implications, is generally high in any country, and it is magnified in a developing country, which has to adjust scarce resources among competing demands. To this if we add the absence of a sense of direction among the policy makers, the task of planning for educational change understandably becomes most difficult. Considering this, the logic underlying the expansion of the existing system rather than radically changing it becomes clear.

Among the various educational projects undertaken with foreign assistance or collaboration in the country, the establishment of several institutions, the provision of scholarships for students to study abroad, the constitution of joint commissions on textbooks, the nutritional and health programmes for school children, and the exchange of scholars deserve special mention. The educational activities of the British Council, the United States Educational Foundation in India (renamed in 2008 as United States-India Educational Foundation), the Ford and Rockefeller foundations, the various missionary societies, etc. are well known. It only needs to be emphasised that such foreign aid is intertwined with the foreign policy and economic interests of the donor countries and tends to perpetuate dependence.

Scholarly attention has been drawn to how the research areas and priorities in the developing countries are directly and indirectly influenced by the developed countries to promote their own interests (see Kabra 1976: 22). This process is furthered by the collaborative research undertaken at the behest of the developed countries. The disclosures made by the Public Accounts Committee of the Fifth Lok Sabha in this regard are shocking and startling.[4]

What is more disconcerting is the espionage through such collaborative research. H.S. Verma's case study (1974) of one of the apex institutions in the country illustrates the stranglehold of this mechanism. G.D. Berreman (1981: 203–12) has exposed the ulterior motives of research by foreign scholars by revealing the involvement of the United States Department of Defence in 'The Himalayan Border Countries Research Project'. That such espionage through collaborative research has the support of some of the Indian scholars, who criticise any attempt at curbing such activity, is most distressing and deplorable.

English and Intellectual Neo-colonialism

An essential prop for the maintenance of the dominance of Britain and other English-speaking industrial countries, particularly the USA, through foreign aid programmes and other means, is English. Even after six decades of Independence, the problem of English in Indian education has eluded a solution and has not been faced squarely by the policy makers (see Jayaram 1993).

At the primary level – as in the colonial period – the regional language/mother tongue is the widespread medium of instruction. The effort to switch over from English to the regional language at the secondary level is neither complete nor satisfactory. At the tertiary level, and more so in professional education, English still reigns supreme as the medium of instruction. In several universities where English has been replaced by the regional language as the medium of instruction at the college level, English is taught as a compulsory language. English remains the predominant, if not the exclusive, library language.

Of course, the importance of English in Indian education has been defended and emphasised on practical, administrative, and even political grounds. But set against the goal of building a 'democratic-socialist' order enshrined in the Constitution, the case of the regional language appears to be stronger. What are the negative implications of the continued dominance of English in Indian education?

Excluding the large majority of the people who are out of the purview of any kind of education, as A.R. Desai (1967: 119–22) observes, there are two classes of educated people growing in the country: those educated in the English medium and those educated in the medium of mother tongue/regional language. The former constitute 'a higher class of citizens', 'a new class of elite', which is closer to all the strategic decision-making positions. Counterposed to this is the latter class of elite, occupying a subordinate position in the hierarchy of offices. The latter elite are at a disadvantage in securing higher positions demanding an advanced knowledge of English. The net consequence of this dualistic system of education is the consolidation and perpetuation of super-elite in the country.

The continued dominance of English in Indian education and the Anglophilia of its intellectuals has oriented intellectual life in the country towards its former colonisers and other English-speaking developed countries. This is due to two interrelated reasons. First, the major share of the world's knowledge is now produced and refined by the USA, UK, and other developed countries. And second, English has become the chief, if not the sole, language for the communication and dissemination of this knowledge.

The intellectual dependency arising from language has serious implications. Most of the books required by the developing countries are imported. In spite of having a long history of indigenous publishing and a large publishing industry, India imports a large number of books, the vast majority of which are in English. This necessarily drains valuable foreign exchange reserves besides stunting the growth of the indigenous publishing industry. Moreover, given the nature of books which are imported, one wonders whether they are relevant to or in the interests of the country's cultural Independence.

The publishing industry in India itself suffers from the linguistic weight of English. India occupies the third position, after the USA and UK, in terms of the number of English titles published. Nearly 46 per cent of the books published in the country in 1979–80 were in English. More than half the newspapers circulated are in English, and an even higher proportion of intellectual journals appear in that language. This is really amazing considering the fact that only about three to four per cent of the Indian population is literate in English (Baldridge 2002), as compared to approximately 35 per cent literate in all other Indian languages put together.

Another manifestation of this intellectual dependency and academic neo-colonialism is reflected in the craving of Indian scholars to publish their research work abroad. This, a symptom of 'xenophilia', may be due to the prestige such publications carry or because of the snobbery of the scholars concerned. The publications of some scholars, even when they are done in India, are oriented to 'an invisible jury' abroad.

Philip G. Altbach has observed that the international arrangements controlling the flow of knowledge, such as copyright agreements, commercial publishing practices, and so on 'work in the interest of the major publishing countries and to the detriment of the developing nations' (1975: 11). In view of such advantages as a long-standing expertise, advanced technical know-how, backing of foreign capital, a worldwide distribution network, and considerable prestige, the British and American publishers completely dominate the publishing scene in India.

Foreign aid programmes in the area of publishing have not been as much in the interest of the recipient countries as they are in the interest of the donors. Special mention should be made here of the Indo-American Textbook Programme of the 1970s. Under this Programme, more than one thousand American books in English were reprinted in India and more than four million copies were distributed at subsidised prices. This Programme did make available on a large scale and at a cheaper rate many of the difficult-to-get and expensive books to the Indian students. But it cannot be gainsaid that many of the titles, especially in the social sciences, were not relevant to the Indian situation and they reflected the ideological biases of their American authors.

Brain Drain

Another anomalous and stultifying consequence latent in English education in India is brain drain, that is, the flow of its educated people to other countries. Such a flow is essentially an outcome of the personal strategy for self-advancement encouraged by the system of higher education in the country. The magnitude of brain drain from and its cost to India are alarmingly high. The developed countries of the West are the major beneficiaries (see Reddy 1974).

The nature, causes and implications of brain drain have been well researched (see ibid.; Kabra 1976). Suffice it to emphasise here that the system of education in India, introduced by the British for their own ends, and continued with only minor modifications after they formally left the country, seems to be responsible in no small measure in facilitating the debilitating brain drain.

Education in India, both in its structure and content, is oriented to the developed countries of the West, and it is offered in the medium of an international language, namely, English. The students are socialised to internalise the values and ideology of those societies. Not surprisingly then, the doctors, engineers, and others educated in the country seem to fit into those societies with the greatest ease.

Is Dependence Inevitable?

In brief, the achievement of political independence by India has not resulted in the emancipation of its educational system from colonial bondage. On the contrary, the educational system along with its wider socio-economic framework has been transformed into a complex and wide-ranging phase of neo-colonial dependency with grave implications for the future development of the country.

In this context, it has often been asserted, though implicitly, that an element of dependency of the ex-colonies on their former colonisers and other developed countries is an integral part of the modernisation process in the post-colonial phase. The modernisation approach posits a dual system model of society, wherein development involves a transition of the society from the traditional to the modern phase; and, underdevelopment is only a failure to develop at the expected pace. This approach presumes development to be a unidimensional process, whereby a developing or an underdeveloped society moves towards the ideal of a developed society. The developed society is identified with the industrially advanced society of the West governed by the capitalist politico-economic and socio-cultural institutions and ideologies. That is, it is geared to the reproduction of the capitalist society of the West in the ex-colonies and other developing countries.

This line of thought would imply that neo-colonialism is not the outcome of any sinister overt policy of domination by the developed countries of the West. Rather, it is only a by-product of the modernisation process embarked upon by the developing countries. This message is spread by social scientists of the developed countries and is shared by many of their counterparts in the developing countries. Apart from hiding the ugly head of imperialism, this ideology fosters an illusion of development in the developing countries.

This is not the place to go into the modernisation *versus* dependency debate. However, the major advance of the latter theory over the former is certain: that is, the recognition that development and underdevelopment cannot be conceptualised in terms of a dualistic model of individual societies or self-contained nation states. Rather, development and underdevelopment are reciprocal conditions taking place in the context of a global system of capitalist accumulation (see Frank 1981). Seen in this light, a reanalysis of the political economy of growth in India on the lines of the dependency theory becomes imperative.

Conclusion

Having had its origin in the policies of the establishment of British colonialism, the English – or the 'modern' – system of education grew on the ruins of the indigenous system destroyed by the same policies. Nourished by English-educated elite, this system of education not only survived political independence, but also expanded phenomenally, succumbing to neo-colonial dependency in the process. While during the pre-Independence period the educational system was oriented to Britain, in the post-Independence era it is not oriented to India. The more the system expands the more its crisis deepens.

The much talked about radical restructuring and reorientation of the educational system in the country is, no doubt, exigent. But the question is 'which way?' The answer to this profound question, which is as of now unavailable, or at least not clearly formulated, has to be based on an appreciation of the socio-historical bases of our educational crisis. It has also to recognise the fact that 'decolonisation, or liberation, demands personal and societal struggles which go far beyond lowering one flag and raising another' (Carnoy 1974: 22).

Notes

1. 'In the education budget for 1879–80, 68 lakhs of rupees were allotted thus: 11.5 lakhs for 16,06,216 primary school pupils, and 56.5 lakhs for 3,08,868 students in high schools and colleges' (Edwardes 1967: 240). 'At the turn of the century three out of four villages were without a school, and less than one-fifth of the boys of school-going age were in schools' (A. Basu 1978: 59).
2. For Madras, see Sharp (1965); for Bombay, see Parulekar (1951); for Bengal, see Adam (1941); and for Punjab, see Leitner (1973). See also Thomas Fisher's 'Memoir' in A.N. Basu (1952: 1–143) and Dharmpal (1983).
3. The following extract from the Report of A.D. Campbell, the then Collector of Bellary, dated 17 August 1823, is eloquent about the real cause of the degeneration of the indigenous system of education:

   I am sorry to state, that this is ascribable to the gradual but general impoverishment of the country. The means of the manufacturing classes have been of late years greatly diminished by the introduction of our European manufactures in lieu of the Indian cotton fabrics ... the transfer of the capital of the country from the native governments and their officers who liberally expended it in India, to Europeans ... has likewise tended to this effect ... Thus greater part of the middling (*sic*) and lower classes of the people are now unable to defray the expenses incident upon the education of their offspring ... Of the 533 institutions for education now existing in this District, I am ashamed to say that not one now derives any support from the State ... Considerable alienation of revenue which formerly did honour to the State, by upholding and encouraging learning, have deteriorated under our rule into the means of supporting ignorance (cited in A.N. Basu 1952: 181–83).

   That divesting the indigenous educational institutions of their financial support and state patronage, consequent upon the destruction of village self-government in 1816, was their prime destroyer is also revealed by the following plea of F.W. Robertson, the then Collector of Rajamundhry, dated 19 September 1823:

   In those villages under my immediate management where there are no schools, I have found the inhabitants very willing to have such (schools) established among them, but some assistance from government will be necessary to set things going, say a monthly allowance of 2 rupees to each teacher, the scholars to make up the remainder. I shall be prepared to address your Board more fully upon the subject should this proposal meet your approval (in Dharmpal 1983: 191).

Of course, the proposal never met with approval.

4. The utility of some of these (collaborative research) ... seems to be only doubtful or potential, whereas the primary data obtained from these projects are likely to be of vital importance to foreign governments interested in developing techniques of chemical, biological, bacteriological, herbicidal, and anti-subversive warfare (Public Accounts Committee 1974: 184).

Part II

Education and Economy

5

Education, Employment, and Economy

Issues and Perspectives

The most significant contribution of sociology as a critical discipline in the closing decades of the twentieth century has been its exposure of the empirical inadequacy and ideological underpinning of the 'modernisation theory'. The 'ideological child of the Cold War', as P.W. Preston (1982: 72) appropriately describes this theory, which dominated the social sciences for nearly three decades after World War II, coloured the vision of social scientists in regard to the problems of development and gave a misleading direction to their intellectual efforts (see Madan 1983: 26–56). Of the several facets of this theory, the one which forms the focal point for this chapter is the sedulously propagated view that education is the chief 'missing component' of economic development of the 'underdeveloped' countries, and that 'investment in human capital' will by itself contribute to economic growth and effect an improvement in income distribution.[1]

A detailed examination of the 'investment in human capital' thesis is beyond the scope of this chapter. To say that economic development presumes a minimum standard of literacy on the part of the labour force, and that education produces the 'know-how' of development and the trained workers who operate the economy is to state the obvious. But from this to argue that 'the more education the better' will be naive. John Vaizey's appraisal of the attempts at measuring the role of education in economic growth suggests that they have led to fallacious results (1972).

The evidence from the developing countries, in general, and from India, in particular, is categorical in showing that 'education seldom rises above the socio-economic and socio-political situation in which it is embedded' (Kamat 1985: v). Far from functioning as the prime mover of socio-economic transformation, education merely reinforces the existing – and also creates new – rigidities and resistances to such transformation. The expanding but fragile educational system seems to foster a negative attitude to any form of manual work, accelerate urban-ward migration of educated rural folk, and contribute in umpteen ways to what S. Bowles et al. call 'the legitimation of the social division of labour' (1975–76).

An exhaustive review of the crisis confronting India's educational system and its submergence in the socio-economic crisis conditions in which the large majority of her people exist is a fit subject for a multi-volume exercise. Such an exercise can hardly be attempted, even briefly, in a short chapter like this. This chapter confines itself to a delineation of one aspect of it, namely, the mismatch between education and employment. While this mismatch is a problem faced by most capitalist countries in the West also (see Watson 1983b), it is most poignantly apparent in some of the poorest countries. The case of post-Independence India, with its third largest educational system in the world and its six decades of experience of planned programmes of democratic-socialist development, yields rich insights into this problem.

Unemployment: Magnitude and Consequences

The concept of employment, as also its corollary unemployment, is a complex one, subsuming under it several aspects, quantitative as well as qualitative. It 'cannot be defined in terms of physical activity as such' as it has inevitably to be related to 'some notion of the "value" of the work' (Sen 1975: 3, 5). Intriguingly enough, the problem of measurement of (un)employment has received surprisingly little attention in economic theory.[2] The figures obtained from different sources about the quantum of unemployment, employing different concepts and methods of measurement, expectedly vary widely. The problems of reliability and interpretation notwithstanding, the challenging reality behind the statistics, however obscure and enigmatic they may be, can hardly be exaggerated, and much less denied.

Between 1956 and 1978, the number of unemployed shot up from 5.3 million to 38.6 million (see Table 5.1),[3] that is, by 628.30 per cent. The number of unemployed has increased by 1.51 million per year. While the number of jobs generated increased from 7.0 million to 32.0 million in the same period (that is, at an average of 1.14 million per year), the backlog of unemployment shot up from 3.3 million to 26.6 million (that is, at an average of 1.06 million per year).

Table 5.1 Employment Generation in the Plans

(Figures in millions)

	First Five-Year Plan	*Second Five-Year Plan*	*Third Five-Year Plan*	*Annual Plans*	*Fourth Five-Year Plan*	*Fifth Five-Year Plan*
Backlog of the unemployed	3.3	5.3	7.1	9.6	12.6	26.6
New entrants	9.0	11.8	17.0	14.0	32.0*	44.0*
Total (1 + 2)	12.3	17.3	24.1	23.6	44.6	70.6
Employment generated in the Plan	7.0	10.0	14.5	11.0	18.0	32.0**
Unemployment at the end of the Plan	5.3	7.1	9.6	12.6	26.6	38.6

Note: * Estimated; ** Calculated.

Source: Adapted from Puttaswamaiah (1977: 125).

The number of registered unemployed (only a fraction of the actual total) increased from 3,35,000 in 1951 to 3,01,31,000 in 1986, a nearly ninety-fold increase in thirty-five years. An analysis of the activities of employment exchanges between 1956 and 1986 (see Table 5.2) shows that while registrations have increased considerably neither the vacancies notified nor placements effected have kept pace with them. Thus, the number of applicants on the 'live register' of the employment exchanges has grown at an alarming rate of 129 per cent year.

Table 5.2 Impact of Employment Exchanges

(Figures in thousands)

	1956	*1986*	*Net Increase*		*Increase Per Year*	
			Number	*Percentage*	*Number*	*Percentage*
Registrations	1,670	5,473	3,803	227.7	126.8	7.6
Applicants placed in employment	190	356	166	87.4	5.5	2.9
Applicants on the live register	759	30,131	29,372	3,869.8	979.0	129.0
Vacancies notified	279	616	319	107.4	10.6	3.8

Source: Adapted from Ministry of Information and Broadcasting (1987: 545), and Economic and Political Weekly, 22 (40), 3 October 1987, p. 1674.

[The employment exchange data for 2008 are as follows: the number of registrations, 53,15,700; the number of placements, 3,04,900; the number of applicants on the live register, 3,91,14,900; and the vacancies notified, 5,71,000 (adapted from Ministry of Information and Broadcasting 2010: Table 6.7, p. 138)].

The Planning Commission (1981: 214, 217, 206) estimates based on the 32nd Round of the National Sample Survey (1977–78) are more revealing. The rates for 'usual', 'weekly', and 'daily' status unemployment for urban areas were 8.8, 7.9, and 10.3 per cent respectively. The corresponding percentages for all-India were 4.2, 4.5, and 8.2 respectively. Furthermore, 'the usual status unemployment rose progressively from 2.28 per cent in the case of illiterates to 3.6 per cent at the primary level, 15.2 per cent at the secondary level, and 15.8 per cent at the level of graduates and above' (ibid.).

Based on the 'live register' statistics of the employment exchanges, the Planning Commission has observed that 'more than 50 per cent of the job-seekers are educated' (ibid.: 206), including many with a university degree. Between 1953 and 1978, unemployment of the educated increased over thirty-seven times (see Table 5.3). Over these twenty-five years the share in unemployment of beneficiaries of the successive higher levels of education has also risen. This shows that unemployment has penetrated into hitherto protected sectors of the educational system.

Table 5.3 Unemployment among the Educated

(Figures in thousands)

Year	*Matriculate*		*Undergraduate*		*Graduate*		*Postgraduate*		*Total*
	Number	*%*	*Number*	*%*	*Number*	*%*	*Number*	*%*	
1953	125	76.68	17	10.42	21	12.88			163
1958	283	72.53	45	12.33	37	10.14			365
1963	560	75.78	111	15.02	68	9.20			739
1968	810	61.88	324	24.75	157	11.99	18	1.38	1,309
1974	2,278	54.58	1,086	26.01	746	17.87	64	1.53	4,174
1978	3,262	53.94	1,533	25.68	1,124	18.59	104	1.70	6,047

Source: Adapted from Raza et al. (1985: 138–39).

While studies are unequivocal in showing that 'an increasing percentage of recent graduates is likely to remain unemployed' (see Dhar et al. 1976: 10–11), the incidence of graduate unemployment is the highest among the graduates belonging to arts, followed by science and commerce faculties (see Raza et al. 1985: 141–42). They together constituted over 90 per cent of the unemployed graduates in the late 1960s and continued to constitute over 85 per cent of the unemployed graduates in 1977–78. If we add unemployed graduates from the education faculty (9.9%) this percentage crosses 95. Engineering graduates who formed 6.5 per cent of the unemployed graduates in 1968–69 constituted only 1.7 per cent in 1977–78. Medical graduates have formed around 1 per cent of the unemployed graduates during this period.

Presenting the unemployed as a percentage of the graduates in a particular faculty, we get a slightly different but revealing insight. According to the 1971 Census, the incidence of unemployment among arts/humanities, science, and commerce degree holders was 13.1, 16.5, and 13.9 per cent respectively. The incidence of unemployment among technical (engineering) and technical (vocational) degree and diploma holders was 12.8 and 21.8 per cent respectively. The incidence of graduate unemployment was high for agriculture (11.4%) but low for veterinary science (5.5%) and medicine (allopathy) (4.2%). If, as noted earlier, arts graduates form the largest proportion of the unemployed graduates (45.9% in 1977–78), it is obviously because there are more students in the arts faculty (43.8% in 1977–78) than in other faculties.

To the foregoing statistics if we add the dimension of what J. Robinson (1937: 62, 84) termed 'disguised unemployment', the problem would appear to be graver still. Under conditions of shortage of vacancies, unemployed persons are driven to 'inferior' occupations characterised by low productivity, and their labour is thus wastefully utilised. As will be discussed later, such a phenomenon is not unknown in the case of educated persons in India and it is referred to as 'qualification escalation' and 'degree devaluation'.

Paradoxically, while millions among the educated are unemployed or underemployed, there are any many jobs waiting to be done because people with requisite 'education' and training are not available. In a country characterised by rampant unemployment, it is disquieting to note that many vacancies remain unfilled for want of suitable candidates. Though the exact educational qualifications required for these vacancies are not clearly known, based on the *Employment Review* published by the Union Ministry of Labour, Raza et al., point out that 'maximum skill shortages are noted in the technical and professional occupations at the higher level and in the occupational category of craftsmen and production workers' (1985: 143). This aspect of the education-employment mismatch is a clear indication of a lack of perspective planning of education vis-à-vis the humanpower requirements of the country.

The education-employment mismatch and its implications are not a special outcome of the post-Independence period. Their roots can be traced to the colonial times and their darkest picture was during the depression period in the 1930s. It was easy then to place the blame squarely on the British rulers. But, if the same situation persists in an aggravated form even after four decades of Independence, it is obvious that things have not been moving in the right direction. The blame for this must be shared by the politicians, planners, and social scientists.

There is often a tendency to identify unemployment with poverty. This is a consequence of laying stress on the income aspect of employment, as 'employment is an important means of generating and distributing income' (Sen 1975: 38). Moreover, as E. Liebow has observed, unemployment does not strike at the labour force randomly. It is directional and selective; 'it strikes from underneath, and it strikes particularly at those at the bottom of (the) society' (1972: 1).

Notwithstanding this, A.K. Sen makes out 'a good case for keeping "poverty" as a concept distinct from "unemployment", without of course assuming them to be independent of each other' (1975: 38). It is important to note, as Liebow (1972) has stressed, unemployment can mean 'spiritual' as well as 'material' deprivation. An unemployed person can be spiritually deprived even when he is materially sound. As far back as 1857, in his *Critique of the Gotha Programme,* Karl Marx spoke of labour ultimately becoming 'not only a means of life but life's prime want' (Marx and Engels 1970: 19). Work is the medium through which an individual expresses himself and obtains an identity. This is what Sen calls the 'recognition aspect' of employment (1975: 5–6).

What does it mean to be unemployed? The socio-psychological effects of unemployment have not yet been explored adequately. K. Watson has drawn attention to 'the underlying tensions and sense of grievance, injustice and frustration that can so easily eat into a person's psyche as he comes to terms with being unemployed at a very young age, and, in many cases, with being unemployable' (1983a: 7). Unemployment can turn an individual into 'a caricature of himself, giving him the appearance of being stupid and lazy with no concern for the future' (Liebow 1972: 3). Such an individual learns 'to live with his failure by lowering life goals and by other rationalizing measures which effectively remove him from ordinary society' (ibid.: 4). Such social withdrawal would mean that society ceases to have any claim on the loyalty of such individuals. Thus, from the society's perspective, employment would ensure bringing large masses of people, who are at present on the fringes, right into the national mainstream.

Solutions: An Assessment

Employment Generation and Humanpower Planning

Obviously, the most straightforward strategy for reducing the incidence of unemployment, in general, and unemployment among the educated, in particular, is the creation of jobs and relating university places to the humanpower requirements of the economy. But this is more easily said than done. It has been observed that a majority of the people are employed in the public sector, and their proportion has increased from 59.03 per cent in 1967 to 64.76 per cent in 1974. In absolute terms, employment in the public sector rose from 9.63 million in 1967 to 17.3 million in 1985, that is, by 79.6 per cent, giving an average of 0.43 million or 4.4 per cent per year. The increase in employment in the private sector during this period has been meagre, that is, 0.52 million (or 7.6%), giving an average of 0.5 million or 0.8 per cent per year.

Of those employed in the public sector in 1985, 19.3 per cent were in central government service, 36.4 per cent in state government service, 31.9 per cent in quasi-government service, and 12.4 per cent in the service of local bodies. Between 1975 and 1985, though there was an increase in employment in absolute terms in the central government, the state governments and local bodies, their share in the total public sector employment decreased marginally (by 3.9, 0.5, and 2.7 percentage points respectively), whereas the quasi-government share has increased by 7.0 percentage points. In fact, over 43 per cent of the total increase in public sector employment is accounted for by the rise in employment in quasi-government service.

It must also be noted that, excepting in the State of Maharashtra, Karnataka, and Gujarat, a majority of the graduates are employed in the government or quasi-government sector, and, by and large, they are reported to be working as clerks. A study of occupations desired by graduates registered in employment exchanges, reported that 94 per cent of arts, science and commerce graduates sought clerical occupations (Dhar et al. 1976: 12–13).

In brief, there is an excessive dependence on the public sector as the employer, and whatever employment has been generated over a period of time is in this sector. The role of the private sector has not been noteworthy. Based on the figures of the National Rural Employment Programme, it has been worked out that Rs 5,000 will be required to create a job (see Dubashi 1983: 83). It is estimated that, to provide jobs for the teeming unemployed, it would need about Rs 60 billion a year (Rs 40 billion for the rural sector and Rs 20 billion for the urban sector). In addition to this, provision has to be made for the usual leakages, the requisite administrative infrastructure, and sizeable investment in primary industrial sectors to provide the materials required to feed the programme. If the present rate of growth in employment is any guide, one cannot be optimistic about being anywhere near the solution to the problem.

Even granting that the requisite resources for such a programme could be made available, humanpower planning would still pose a serious problem. The question is not merely one of creating jobs, but of creating the type of jobs essential for the socio-economic development of the country. But in a society where the economy is without direction in spite of being excessively centralised, where political decisions are governed by socio-political pressures and demands of populism, and where the planners lack both vision and conviction, humanpower planning tailored to the needs of the country will be difficult to achieve.

A reference may be made to the role of employment exchanges, which have been set up to provide placement assistance to people. It is true that the number of exchanges (720 in 1985) is small considering both the size of the country and the number of unemployed, and that they do not specifically cater to the educated among the unemployed. To overcome these bottlenecks employment information and guidance bureaux have been set up in most universities (80 in 1985).[4] These bureaux are expected to provide vocational guidance to students and also assist them in placement. But the material and technical deficiencies of these bureaux render them virtually ineffective and students obviously do not utilise their services (see Dhar et al. 1976: 80). While students from the better-off families make independent efforts to obtain jobs, those from the poorer sections are quite at sea.

As a facile solution to the unemployment problem it has been demanded by many student organisations that the government should give unemployment dole, as is done in some countries in the West. Such a scheme of public assistance to the unemployed is feasible and relevant when the scale of unemployment is small and manageable and the problem of unemployment is a transitory one. But, under conditions of chronic and rampant unemployment, such a scheme is unthinkable. In the longer run such public assistance cannot arrest the demoralising consequences of unemployment. For aught we know it may even aggravate them.

Reduction of Enrolment and Selective Admission

In the absence of an immediate prospect of a rapid rise in the demand for qualified people, the best remedy, it has been suggested, would be to curtail their supply. This implies a stringent policy of reducing enrolment and selective admission at the collegiate level, as also minimising the element of public subsidy and raising fees. The need for selective admission has been voiced vigorously since the State Education Ministers' Conference in 1959. Besides bringing down the quantum of unemployment among educated persons, this policy is supposed to yield certain economic and political advantages. Economically, it is expected to free resources for alternative investment, change the social attitude in favour of semi-skilled jobs, and alter the consumption pattern of the people. Politically, it is expected to arrest alienation and subdue campus unrest. The Education Commission (1964–66) too recommended this policy.

The main beneficiaries of the present system of top-heavy education (secondary and tertiary sectors appropriate about 60 per cent of the educational expenditure) belong to the top 30 per cent of the income groups who occupy about 70 and 80 per cent of the places in the secondary and university stages respectively. Other things remaining the same, selective admission to higher education would certainly reinforce the class bias in favour of the better-off sections of society.

Besides raising questions about the basis and method of selection, the policy of selective admission will have to be reconciled with the aim of achieving equality of opportunities and the programme of protective discrimination. Be that as it may, selectivity would neither be practicable nor desirable until alternative avenues of employment and training are made available to those who are denied higher education.

The critical plank on which such policy recommendations rest is the unbridled growth in enrolment at the tertiary level. In absolute terms, the enrolment in higher education increased from 2.59 million in 1961 to 5.92 million in 1981, which works out to an increase of 128.6 per cent over two decades. This is indeed low as compared to the increase in enrolment at the secondary stage (283.3%) and only marginally high as compared to the increase in enrolment at the primary and middle stages (117.9%). As a percentage of the population covered in the relevant age-group (17–23 years), the enrolment in institutions of higher education constitutes only 6.8 per cent, and this has hardly increased by 1.7 percentage points over two decades. If with less than 7 per cent of the 17–23 age-group being enrolled in higher education there are problems, imagination boggles to contemplate what will happen if higher education is 'brought within easy reach of all' as envisaged by the government.

More important, according to estimates of the 32nd Round of the National Sample Survey (1977–78), only 2.1 per cent of the total labour force in the country has qualification of 'graduation and above'. Of about seven million added to the labour force annually only about half a million are 'higher educated'. That is, only one out of fourteen persons added to the labour force is a graduate (see Agarwal 1985: 66).

Thus, the real problem is not with the expansion of higher education *per se*, but with its unplanned nature. One feature of this unplanned expansion of higher education, which is its most glaring aspect, and is, therefore, invariably criticised by all, is the too literary and liberal character of higher education. It is sometimes argued that the products of such an educational mill are unemployed because they are unemployable. Part of this is explained by the vague motivation on the part of our youth entering college and the occupational aspirations and defeatist attitudes it breeds.

As early as 1961, V.K.R.V. Rao's survey of Delhi graduates had revealed that the bulk of the alumni who pass through the university are thinking of jobs rather than independent livelihood, and that the university education is primarily regarded as a passport to salaried employment (1961). A similar finding has also been arrived at by a survey of 1,200 college students in five universities by T.N. Dhar et al. (1976: 36). Another significant trend revealed by most studies and surveys of students of higher education is their predisposition for government service. A major reason for this overwhelming preference is the job security and prospects for career advancement that government service is reputed to provide.

Based on an investigation of a sample of 641 employees working in the Life Insurance Corporation of India and the State Bank of Hyderabad, S. Parmaji (1979) has made some interesting observations. He found that 'job aspiration levels generally escalate' and 'inclination to soil hands in non-white-collar jobs decreases' with years of education. Education also tends to progressively wean away people from self-employment. Moreover, the dissatisfaction of clerical workers increases and their efficiency decreases with an increase in education. Parmaji also confirms the predominant pre-entry aspirations of the respondents (93%) in favour of salaried white-collar jobs. In brief, while our higher education does not evidently prepare students for any specific occupation, it mentally prepares them for salaried white-collar jobs, which form only 8.7 per cent of the total occupational structure'.

Vocationalisation of Education

It is in this context that the suggestion for much more vocationalisation at the secondary stage is made. The '10+2+3' pattern of education had envisaged 'alternative avenues' through vocationalisation of education even at the higher-secondary stage. But, in spite of all the experiments tried so far, the enrolment in vocational courses at the secondary stage is estimated to be only about 9 per cent of the total. Lack of a clear perception of the subject, inadequate data in regard to employment opportunities and humanpower needs at the 'middle' level, paucity of trained instructors, lack of interest on the part of private entrepreneurship in the area, and the high cost involved have been identified as the major hurdles in the vocationalisation of education by the standing committee of the Central Advisory Board of Education.

It must also be mentioned here that vocationalisation of education alone will not solve the problem. Firstly, there are not sufficient vocational employment opportunities, and what is more, as noted earlier, the incidence of unemployment among technical (vocational) degree and diploma holders (21.8%) is very high compared to even arts/humanities graduates (13.1%). Thus, it is doubtful whether indiscriminate expansion of vocational education, which would necessitate greater financial inputs, and may at the same time lead students into a blind alley, is indeed advisable. For the time being, the expansion of vocational education should be restricted to those areas where assured humanpower needs do exist and are ascertainable. This should not, of course, be taken to be a defence for the irrelevant education that is being imparted at present. The point is simply that the remedy should not be worse than the disease.

Devaluation of Education

The increasing availability of people with educational credentials in relation to the availability of jobs has resulted in a constant escalation of educational qualification for jobs without any necessary relation to more effective job performance or sophistication demanded by the economy. The educational inflation vindicates Ronald Dore's contention that 'people's ideas as to what qualifications fit what jobs do tend to change over time' (1976: 4).

Attempts have been made to measure the devaluation of education approximately in terms of a lower actual wage obtained by an educated person in relation to what he would be expected to get in ideal conditions. B.L. Agarwal (1985: 68) quotes Panchmukhi's estimation of the devaluation of education to be 5.8 per cent between 1954 and 1974, and 6.9 per cent between 1964 and 1974.[5] If the experience requisite for jobs is also taken into consideration, the devaluation for the latter period rises to 11.0 per cent. Such devaluation is noticed in twenty-two out of twenty-eight job categories examined. 'Maximum' (10% or more) devaluation is observed in the case of the educational categories of arts, science, commerce degrees, and engineering diplomas, 'medium' (5 to 10%) with reference to engineering degrees, and 'minimum' (below 5%) in the case of medical degrees.

Why do employers allow qualifications to escalate? May be, as Dore feels, 'they are simply unquestioning victims of the widespread myth that education "improves" people' (1976: 5) and so they get more for their money if they employ over-qualified people. But, more plausibly, faced with the situation of selecting from among a large number of candidates for a small number of jobs, they find in degrees and certificates an easy sieve. This also legitimises selection and rejection of candidates for choice jobs. To be brief, the phenomenon of escalation of qualification lays special emphasis on the function of education as a social sorting and grading mechanism.

Contrary to expectation, the fact that the problem of unemployment of the educated persons is worsening year after year has not caused a set back to the rising demand for education.

Dore has generalised that 'the paradox of the situation is that the worse the educated unemployment situation gets and the more useless educational certificates become, the *stronger* grows the pressure for an expansion of educational facilities' (ibid.: 4; emphasis in original). According to him, if one finds that the education s/he had acquired does not get her/him the job on which s/he has set her/his sight, then s/he will try to get *more* education. In fact, her/his chances may improve. As it has been found, the mechanism of 'qualification escalation' ensures that once one is in the 'modern-sector-qualification range' a higher educational qualification fetches a job quicker, but not necessarily better, although the chances of earning more later are bright.[6]

Thus, the 'thirst' for education is linked largely to the acquisition of educational credentials with the hope of getting better jobs, or some job, and has nothing to do with a disinterested desire for knowledge. This thirst is easily quenched as higher education is very highly subsidised. Given the stark inequality of opportunities for education at this level, the more the public exchequer spends on higher education the more few benefit at the cost of most.

The steady but certain decline in the equation between education and employment, the accentuation of degree devaluation, the rising incidence of unemployment of the educated, and the diluting mobility significance of higher education have grave implications for the sponsored mobility of the scheduled castes and tribes (see Chapter 8). The ever-shrinking employment opportunities sound the warning that there is a physical limit to the feasibility of upward social mobility for these categories through education. They mostly depend upon the government for jobs and government jobs cannot be created *ad infinitum*. The incidence of unemployment among the educated is already quite high even among the scheduled castes. So, in course of time, even individual mobility would be difficult for the scheduled castes.

It is true that the Indian polity has put up with the unemployment problem for several years now and may continue to do so for some more years. But this is no reason to be complacent about the problem. It is highly regrettable that as part of the strategy for legitimisation of democratic rule people's ambitions and expectations are being whipped up since Independence, while the prospects of realising them have been consistently receding. As a result of the frustration of expectations there is a growing undercurrent of discontentment. Higher education, no doubt, functions as a 'cooling-out' mechanism. But, the process of 'cooling' also results latently in the accumulation of 'heat', which may well explode the entire system.

It is well known that student indiscipline is growing in frequency and intensity, and not a little of this is related to the increasing disenchantment of the students with the education they are receiving. Agitations are observed to occur more often in degree programmes where unemployment is the greatest. 'More than 80 per cent of such agitations come from BAs and only 16 per cent from professional students' (Dhar et al. 1976: 15). Such agitations cannot always be dismissed as manifestations of 'juvenile delinquency'; rather, they should be viewed as the danger signal of a simmering crisis. It will be imprudent to assume for ever that the unemployed do not have an effective political clout.

Brain Drain

Another facet of the education-employment mismatch, which, in view of the mounting problem of unemployment of the educated persons, has been viewed as a blessing in disguise, is the exodus of a large number of educated and trained personnel from the country.[7] In the mid-1970s, it was estimated that 6.1 per cent of the engineers and technologists graduating every year left our country. This figure is only a national average and in case of some prestigious institutions like the Indian Institutes of Technology the export figure is reckoned to be as high as 25 per cent.[8] Similarly, it is estimated that about 1,500 physicians and surgeons leave the country annually, which means that ten out of 106 medical colleges, each with an investment of about Rs 28 million and an annual recurring expenditure of Rs 0.8 million, are being run in India exclusively for the benefit of other countries. Each doctor leaving the country means a loss of Rs 0.33 million.

These official figures on brain drain grossly underestimate the magnitude of the problem. They relate only to those who have settled down abroad on immigration visas. If we add to their number those who enter the developed countries as students and then get their status altered as immigrants, the number of highly educated emigrants would shoot up considerably and the consequent loss would be enormous. While not all those who migrate are endowed with superlative brains, it can hardly be denied that a substantial proportion of them do constitute our best brains, with exceptional abilities and professional skills. Thus, we are in an ironically paradoxical situation of having created talents which we are unable to retain. The mediocrity of our research is to be understood in this context.[9]

Not all the scientists, technologists, and doctors who go abroad permanently settle down there. But to expect that most of them would return and those who do so will be a boon to our developmental programmes is only an illusion. Of the 7,586 scientists enrolled in the Indian Abroad Register of the Council of Scientific and Industrial Research (CSIR), only 49.5 per cent have returned to India (this is despite the majority of the migrating scientists not having registered with CSIR). In medicine, the percentage of returnees is even less, that is, 40.4.

Many of the returnees would have spent the most creative period of their life abroad. Therefore, the education, training and experience with which they return cannot be expected to be of much use to the country. In view of the vast chasm in the socio-economic and organisational environment between the country from which they return and their motherland, many of them may even turn out to be square pegs in round holes.

Brain drain, no doubt, brings into the country remittances from the settlers abroad. The inflow of foreign exchange through such remittance is a precious source of strength to the balance of payments in a country faced by chronic shortage of foreign exchange. But this hardly compensates either the loss of lost opportunities to the home country or the great value of the services emigrants render to the host countries.

Why do our scientists, technologists, and doctors become 'intellectual gypsies'? Reasons such as the lack of opportunities for earning commensurate with educational qualifications and talents, absence of facilities to work, lack of recognition of excellence, the stranglehold of bureaucracy, and so on are *post facto* rationalisations. While surplus production of humanpower in specialist categories is sure to enhance brain drain from the country, a mere quantitative reduction in the number of the highly educated may not help to contain it. This, among other things, calls for a rethinking on the qualitative aspects of higher education.

Delinking Degrees from Jobs

An important measure of educational policy contemplated by the government is the delinking of degrees from jobs. Though this idea has been toyed with off and on for a long time (see Jayaram 1985a) it has remained a cliché. It is *inter alia* expected along with a National Merit Examination Scheme to reduce the scramble for university seats, raise the standards of higher education, match jobs and skills, cut down 'educated unemployment', and avoid wastage of scarce resources. A critical review of the facts of the case, however, seems to indicate that delinking degrees from jobs is not a panacea by itself, and may even prove to be counterproductive.

Based on Union Public Service Commission reports, Agarwal (1985: 54–59) has observed that the share of graduates who qualified at the Indian Administrative Service (IAS) and allied examinations dropped from 29 per cent in 1971 to less than 20 per cent during 1975–80, while that of postgraduates and above increased from 71 to more than 80 per cent during the same period. The success ratio (number of candidates qualified/number of candidates appeared) at these examinations in the final selection dropped down much faster in the case of graduates (from 1/27 in 1971 to 1/64 in 1978) than in the case of postgraduates and above (from 1/8 in 1971 to 1/17 in 1978). (The introduction of a preliminary examination in 1979 improved the success ratio of graduates to 1/14 and that of postgraduates to 1/8). Moreover, the success ratio of first-class holders is three to five times higher than that of others, and their share has increased from 39 per cent in 1971 to 55 per cent in 1980.

In case, following the scheme of delinking degrees from jobs, the floodgates are opened and matriculates and non-matriculates are also allowed to appear for the IAS examination, their share may not be more than 2 per cent, and the success ratio would probably be around 1/1000 (ibid.). This can hardly stand the test of cost-benefit analysis, even assuming that the selectors will be able to cope with the huge horde of applicants.

Delinking of degrees from jobs would not necessarily reduce the pressure for university seats. In recruitment to jobs based on competitive examinations requiring an advanced academic knowledge, irrespective of whether the degree or certificate acts as an eligibility criterion, prospective competitors will tend to go to college or university or such other institutions to enhance their chances of passing the examination. If the competitive examinations now in vogue are any indication, they are at best 'a mirror image' of university examinations.

Concluding Remarks

The foregoing analysis makes it clear that the issues arising from the education-employment mismatch and their relation to the socio-economic framework are complex and multifaceted. Allowing the present state of affairs to continue would certainly aggravate the crisis. But attempting to tackle it by tinkering with the educational system is sure to make confusion worse confounded. An appropriate strategy would be to launch a simultaneous two-pronged attack by way of employment generation, on the one hand, and streamlining the educational structure and content, on the other. This would also call for a major reorientation of the socio-economic policies and priorities.

Unemployment, including that of the educated, is often held by development theorists to be a manifestation of the low rates of economic growth. T.N. Madan has argued well as to 'why we should repudiate visions of the future based on the notion of growth as an unlimited good' (1983: 40–41). Considering the limited resources of various kinds, it is a future with which India would never catch up. And, even if she can mobilise all her resources, should she continue to tread the same path, knowing fully well its limitations as experienced by the advanced capitalist societies?

The reasons for the failure of the conventional development approach are clear enough from the experience of the World Employment Programme (see Emmerij and Ghai 1976), and should help us in planning our future strategy. The conventional approach hinges on the urban-based 'modern sector' which is highly capital-intensive and generates relatively few jobs. However, in view of the consumption culture it engenders and the resulting rise in the cost of living, it enhances the demand for employment.

The rise in the demand for 'modern sector' jobs is related to the relatively high wages paid to them. This stimulates urban-ward migration and expands 'the urban informal sector'. Moreover, the 'modern sector' considerably drains resources, so that more and more people are forced to find a livelihood in the impoverished 'traditional rural sector' and the 'urban informal sector'. That over 48 per cent of the population lives below the poverty line of rural per capita expenditure of Rs 65 per month and urban per capita expenditure of Rs 75 per month at 1977–78 prices (see Planning Commission 1981: 16) should shock the conscience of a nation taken for a ride by the 'developmentalists'.

In addition to prompting us to look for alternative paths for achieving economic self-sufficiency and equitable distribution, and pointing to the urgent need for rationalisation of the wage-structure, the new development and employment policies should grapple with the question of appropriate technology and socio-political context (see Sen 1975: v and vii). It is well known that the microchip technological revolution, while it can take due credit for the miracles it has been able to bring about, has slackened the demand for unskilled and semiskilled labour, both in civil service and in manufacturing industry.

Such a reorientation of developmental strategy and employment policy will raise questions about the long-term educational implications. It is much easier to dub the present education as being irrelevant than it is to indicate what type of education is relevant. In any case, education should certainly not be defined narrowly as a preparation for a livelihood, much less for some specific job as per some ill-designed humanpower development plan. All-round development of human personality, the fuller realisation of human potentialities, and establishing a harmony with the immediate environment are often suggested as aims of education. These are vague and sound utopian, but any search for alternatives in a situation which is in reality hopeless may not yield anything better.

As Preston has it, 'development' is essentially 'a politico-ethical notion and not a technical one' (1982: 17). Any plan of action in relation to employment and education would, therefore, have to ultimately depend on a vision of the kind of society that we would like to create. The national debate on the 'desirable society' which Mahatma Gandhi initiated has unfortunately withered in the political game of winning and retaining power.

Notes

1. For a compendium of pro-educational arguments and their bibliography, see Schultz (1963); see also the book of readings edited by Blaug (1972).
2. On the measurement of unemployment in India, see Sen (1975: 115–34).
3. Statistics cited are drawn from several sources, the chief among them being the *Census of India,* the various issues of *Education in India* published by the Ministry of Education, the various issues of *Employment Review* published by the Ministry of Labour, and *India 1986: A Reference Annual* published by the Ministry of Information and Broadcasting. For more recent analysis, see Acharya and Mohanty (2010).
4. In 2008, there were in all 968 employment exchanges (including university employment information and guidance bureaux) (Ministry of Information and Broadcasting 2010: 138).
5. For a more recent analysis of degree devaluation in higher education, see A.K. Singh (2006).
6. Blaug et al. (1969: 4) observed the average waiting period for a graduate to be about six months and for a matriculate to be seventeen months during 1966–67. Dholakia (1977: 29) quotes a survey conducted by the University Employment Bureau of Gujarat which shows that the average waiting period for a graduate is about nineteen months and for a matriculate about twenty months during the year 1973–74.
7. For an analysis of this problem in the mid-1980s, see Jayaram (1985b). See also Glaser (1978) for a comprehensive bibliography and findings of a multi-national comparative survey on brain drain.
8. According to Ms Suella Pipal, American Consul at Madras, in 1984, *all* the chemical engineering graduates from the Indian Institute of Technology Madras went to the United States of America for employment or study (*Indian Express,* Bangalore, 28 September 1985, p. 5).
9. 'In 1977, there were 10 countries with more than 5,000 publishing scientists. Among them India ranked eighth with 8,120 scientists. Yet their total contribution to international scientific journals was a measly 0.3 per cent' (*India Today,* 8 (21), 15 November 1983, p. 4). For a more recent analysis of the predicament of research in the country, see Jayaram (2007).

6

Beyond Demographic Dividend

Some Aspects of the Sociology of Youth in India

> The wine of youth does not always clear with advancing years; sometimes it grows turbid.
>
> **Carl Gustav Jung**
>
> (Epigraph is quoted from Robert Andrews [1987: 295])

In the current literature on economic development we frequently come across the concept of 'demographic dividend', which is also termed 'demographic bonus', 'demographic gift', or 'demographic window'. Empirically, this concept refers to the rise in the rate of economic growth due to an increase in the share of working-age people in a population. The working-age (15–59 years) population, as of now, largely consists of youth (15–34 years). Given the nature of the age-structure transition in China and India, the two most populous countries in the world, this dividend is expected to largely accrue to these two countries. There is no gainsaying that population is more than mere numbers; it is the

---

Revised and expanded version of a paper presented at Symposium II: 'Globalisation, Youth, and Challenges of Reconciliation in Transitional Societies', held as part of the 34th All India Sociological Conference, University of Rajasthan, Jaipur, 27–29 December 2008. My sincere thanks are due to Professor Uttam B. Bhoite, President and Professor Ishwar Prasad Modi, Secretary, Indian Sociological Society for inviting me to participate in and present a paper at the Symposium and to Professor Jacob Aikara for useful comments on the text of the original presentation.

quality of the youth that will determine the extent to which India can garner the demographic dividend. Viewed thus, youth as a population category warrants urgent sociological attention in India. This chapter[1] discusses some of the substantive and conceptual issues in the sociology of youth in India. As a prelude to this discussion, it analyses the demographic trends in the country and their socio-economic implications.

Demographic Trends and their Socio-economic Implications[2]

According to the Census of India, while the proportion of population in the 0–14 age-group declined from 41 per cent in 1961 to 35.3 per cent in 2001 (that is, by 5.7 percentage points), the proportion of population in the age-group 15–59 increased from 53.3 per cent to 56.9 per cent (that is, by 3.6 percentage points) during the same period. The proportion of those above 60 years of age also increased from 5.6 per cent to 7.4 per cent (that is, by 1.8 percentage points) (see Tables 6.1 and 6.2, and Figure 6.1). In terms of absolute numbers, the increase in the 15–34 age-group population is even more dramatic: from 174.26 million (31.79%) in 1970 to 354.15 million (34.43%) in 2000. The youth segment of the population is projected to peak at 484.86 million in 2030 (see Table 6.3). Excepting China, no other country will have such massive youth population.

Figure 6.1 Age Structure Transition in India, 1961–2050

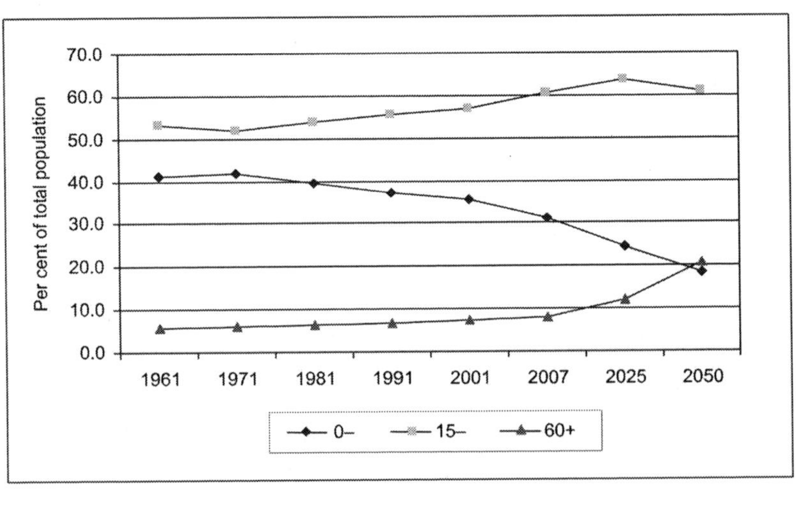

Table 6.1 Age Distribution (in%) of Population, India, 2005–2050

Age Group	*Year*									
	2005	*2010*	*2015*	*2020*	*2025*	*2030*	*2035*	*2040*	*2045*	*2050*
Total Population	*(11,34,403)*	*(12,20,182)*	*(13,02,535)*	*(13,79,198)*	*(14,47,499)*	*(15,05,748)*	*(15,54,182)*	*(15,96,719)*	*(16,31,920)*	*(16,58,270)*
	100	*100*	*100*	*100*	*100*	*100*	*100*	*100*	*100*	*100*
0–4	11.2	10.4	9.6	8.8	8.0	7.3	6.7	6.5	6.2	5.9
5–9	11.0	10.2	9.6	8.9	8.3	7.6	7.0	6.5	6.3	6.1
10–14	10.8	10.1	9.5	9.0	8.5	7.9	7.4	6.8	6.3	6.2
15–19	10.1	10.0	9.4	8.9	8.5	8.1	7.7	7.1	6.6	6.2
20–24	9.2	9.3	9.3	8.9	8.5	8.2	7.8	7.4	7.0	6.5
25–29	8.3	8.5	8.6	8.7	8.4	8.1	7.9	7.6	7.2	6.8
30–34	7.3	7.6	7.8	8.0	8.2	8.0	7.8	7.6	7.4	7.1
35–39	6.5	6.7	7.0	7.3	7.5	7.8	7.7	7.5	7.4	7.2
40–44	5.7	5.9	6.1	6.5	6.8	7.1	7.5	7.4	7.3	7.2
45–49	5.0	5.2	5.4	5.6	6.0	6.4	6.8	7.2	7.1	7.1
50–54	4.3	4.5	4.7	4.9	5.2	5.7	6.1	6.5	6.9	6.9
55–59	3.1	3.8	4.0	4.2	4.5	4.8	5.3	5.7	6.1	6.6
60–64	2.5	2.6	3.2	3.5	3.8	4.0	4.4	4.9	5.3	5.8

Cont'd...

Cont'd...

65–69	2.0	2.0	2.2	2.7	3.0	3.3	3.6	3.9	4.4	4.8
70–74	1.4	1.5	1.6	1.7	2.2	2.5	2.7	3.0	3.4	3.8
75–79	0.9	1.0	1.1	1.1	1.9	1.7	1.9	2.1	2.4	2.7
80–84	0.4	0.5	0.6	0.7	0.7	0.8	1.1	1.3	1.5	1.7
85–89	0.2	0.2	0.2	0.3	0.3	0.4	0.5	0.6	0.8	0.9
90–94	0.05	0.07	0.08	0.1	0.1	0.1	0.2	0.2	0.3	0.4
95–99	0.01	0.01	0.02	0.02	0.02	0.04	0.04	0.05	0.07	0.09
100+	0.001	0.002	0.003	0.004	0.004	0.006	0.007	0.009	0.01	0.01

Source: Data up to 2000 are from United Nations Population Division (2004) and from 2010 through 2050 are from United Nations Population Division (2006).

Table 6.2 Age Structure Transition in India, 1961–2050

Year	*Population by Broad Age Groups*		
	0–14	*15–59*	*60+*
1961	41.0	53.3	5.6
1971	42.0	52.0	6.0
1981	39.5	53.9	6.5
1991	37.2	55.4	6.8
2001	35.3	56.9	7.4
2007	31.2	60.7	8.1
2025	24.5	63.5	12.0
2050	18.3	61.0	20.7

Source: Data up to 2001 are from various census reports, and from 2007 through 2050 are from United Nations Organisation (2007).

Table 6.3 Youth Population (15–34 years) in India, 1970–2050

	Year								
	1970	*1980*	*1990*	*2000*	*2010*	*2020*	*2030*	*2040*	*2050*
Total population (in million)	548.16	683.32	846.42	1,028.61	1,220.18	1,379.20	1,505.75	1,596.72	1,658.27
Youth (15–34 years) population	174.26	227.89	293.71	354.15	431.94	475.82	487.86	474.22	441.10
Percentage of youth (15–34 years) to total population	31.79	33.34	34.70	34.43	35.4	34.5	32.4	29.7	26.6

Source: Data up to 2000 are from United Nations Population Division (2004) and from 2010 through 2050 are from United Nations Population Division (2006).

This demographic fact has important implications for the labour market. On the basis of projections prepared in 2002 by the Registrar General, Government of India, Table 6.4 presents data on the net increase in labour force from 2006 to 2031. It is observed that the country's labour force, which was 472 million in 2006, is expected to be around 526 million in 2011 and 653 million in 2031. It is noteworthy that the 'growth rate of labour force will continue to be higher than population growth rate till

2021. The net increase in labour force between 2006 and 2011 would be 53.6 million persons or 11 million annually' (Premi 2008: 9). According to the Indian Labour Report, 300 million youth would enter the labour force by 2025, and 25 per cent of the world's workers in the next three years would be Indians (cited in Times News Network 2008a: 14).

Table 6.4 Total Labour Force and New Entrants, India, 2001–2031

(Figures in thousands)

	Year						
	2001	*2006*	*2011*	*2016*	*2021*	*2026*	*2031*
Total	4,18,705	4,72,390	5,25,960	5,76,225	6,23,208	6,69,466	6,53,252
Growth rate (%)		2.41	2.15	1.83	1.57	1.43	–0.49
Net increase		53,685	53,570	50,265	46,983	46,258	–16,214
Entrants		79,419	83,781	85,487	87,662	92,655	1,60,513
Exits		25,734	30,211	35,223	40,679	46,397	1,76,727

Source: Premi (2008: 8).

The significant increase in the proportion of the working-age population and the youth segment of the population is, no doubt, due to the decline in fertility rate over the decades. However, the phenomenal increase in absolute numbers is certainly the outcome of high fertility rates in the past. If we can reap the demographic dividend, in retrospect, the failure of the 'family planning programme' has been a blessing in disguise! The declining fertility rate, to be sure, will change the demographic scenario in the decades to come, when increase in old-age dependency will be a reality to contend with.

The United Nations Population Division (UNPD) projections show that, while in absolute numbers the youth segment (15–34 years) of the Indian population tapers off after 2030, as a proportion to the total population it tapers off from 2010 itself. Though this tapering off is marginal (from 35.4% in 2010 to 34.5% in 2020 to 32.4% in 2030) in the next three decades, it will be swift in the decades to follow (to 29.7% in 2040 to 26.6% in 2050). Even so, the youth segment of the population will be a massive 441.1 million in 2050 (see Table 6.3).

Since a majority of the youth knock on the doors of the labour market right by the age of 15, the youth segment of the population will also have to be considered in relation to the larger working-age (15–59 years) population. The UNPD analysis and projections offer valuable insights on this. Although the percentage of the 15–34 age group reaches its peak (35.4%) in 2010 and tapers off from then onwards, the percentage of 15–59 age group reaches its peak (64.6%) only in 2035, and tapers off gradually over the next 15 years to 61.6 per cent in 2050 (still marginally higher than what it was in 2005, that is, 59.5%) (see Table 6.2).

Thus, the demographic predictions are loud and clear: that the promise of demographic dividend will not last long, in any case beyond 2050. So, how can we take advantage of this in the short term, say till 2025, and make provision for the expected increase in old-age dependency after that? There is a prime concern here: will the burgeoning numbers of youth be absorbed by the economy? If not, the promise of the dividend would turn out to be a burden, a worrisome one, too! Globalised economy, no doubt, has been generating new avenues of employment, but recession that has set in the United States of America and elsewhere has adverse implications for India, too (see Times News Network 2008b).[3] If we are to believe the economists, it will take at least 5–10 years before there is a positive turnaround. Incidentally, the remarkable rate at which our economy has grown in the last few decades does not seem to hold much promise either, as it has been critiqued as 'jobless growth'.

To be sure, whatever employment that is generated demands a variety of knowledge, skills, and capabilities on the part of the people; only those in possession of these knowledge, skills, and capabilities will be able to benefit from the opportunities that become available. In this context, Abusaleh Shariff, the chief economist at the National Council for Applied Economics Research, New Delhi has observed:

> India's disadvantage is its unskilled, uneducated workforce which could undermine its global competitive strengths and expose the economy to the risk of stagnation. The growing mismatch between the nature of educated manpower and the demands of newly established companies will pose a serious challenge within the next decade (2007: 12).

The Indian Labour Report rightly states, 'Youth unemployability is a bigger crisis than unemployment, as poor quality of skills show up in low incomes rather than unemployment' (Times News Network 2008a: 14). Thus, enhancing the capabilities of youth and making them employable in a changing economy must be a priority. It is in this context that post-secondary education assumes significance.

It must be noted that, despite the massive growth in 'higher education', barely 7 per cent of the 18–24-year-old age group is currently enrolled in higher education institutions, 'which is only one-half of the average for Asia' (National Knowledge Commission 2007: 48). Unrealistically though, the National Knowledge Commission hopes to raise this percentage to 15 by 2015 (ibid.). It is also relevant here to note the types of courses in which the enrolment has been taking place. Analysing the data for 2001–02 (K. Kaur 2003: 366) reveals that those enrolled in arts (46.1%), science (19.9%) and commerce/management (17.9%) together accounted for nearly 84 per cent of the students in higher education. Among the rest, 6.9 per cent were enrolled in engineering and technology, 3.2 per cent in law, 3.1 per cent in veterinary science, and 1.3 per cent in education. Increasing enrolment in conventional liberal education courses to meet the so-called 'targets' would guarantee the creation of more unemployables (or 'educated unemployed'), something that the Indian Labour Report worries about.

The Survey (61st Round) on employment and unemployment situation in the country, conducted during July 2004–June 2005 by the National Sample Survey Organisation (1961; see also M.K. Singh 2006), found that the rate of unemployment was higher for the educated persons as compared with their uneducated counterparts: among graduates 187/1,000 men and 386/1,000 women in rural areas, and 207/1,000 men and 370/1,000 women in urban areas are unemployed. The Survey also found that 'at the all-India level, for rural male graduates the worker-population ratio was 836 in a thousand as against 797 for the same group in urban areas. The corresponding rates among females were 364 and 307 in a thousand' (M.K. Singh 2006: 8). Furthermore, while these rates reduced by 16 and 21 percentage points for youth males in rural and urban areas respectively, it reduced by about 8 percentage points for youth females both in rural and urban areas.

Thus, the Survey observed that, both in rural and urban areas, the unemployment among the educated was higher than that among those whose education level was lower than secondary.[4]

Reaping demographic dividend calls for huge human resource investments in youth; merely adding numbers to the existing system will only aggravate the situation. The annual growth rate of public expenditure on university and higher education, however, has fallen over the last three decades or so. As a proportion of total government expenditure, the share of higher education declined from 1.57 per cent in 1990–91 to 1.33 per cent in 2001–02. Considering the trends in per student expenditure – from Rs 7,676 in 1990–91 to Rs 5,873 in 2001–02 (in 1993–94 prices) – the decline in public expenditure on higher education would appear even more drastic (Tilak 2004: 2160).[5] Given this, the National Knowledge Commission's hope that 'government support for higher education should be at least 1.5 per cent, if not 2 per cent of GDP, from a total of 6 per cent of GDP for education' (2007: 55) may remain just that (Jayaram 2009: 105).

Youth as a Sociological Category

It is conventional in demography to define 'youth' in terms of age-grades as referring to those persons who are in the age range of 14 to 35 years, that is, from just after the commencement of 'teenage' to the onset of adulthood. It thus refers to the long period of transition from childhood to adulthood. Convenient as this age-based identification of the demographic category of youth may appear, there is neither consensus nor uniformity in enumeration across countries or social science studies as regards the age ranges adopted for the delineation of 'youth'. To the extent that the differences in the identification of youth are socio-culturally rooted, we can well imagine the difficulty in defining youth as a sociological category.

It is beyond the scope of this chapter to go into the problems of defining youth; I have discussed them at length elsewhere (Jayaram 2000b). Suffice it to state here that 'youth' is not a homogenous sociological category: there are significant differences in terms of region, religion, caste, class, and gender. Equally significant analytically is the nature and extent of dependence/independence that the category of population that we identify as youth experience. The transition from 'dependence' to 'independence' in socio-economic terms is expressed as 'youth transition'. To capture this, we need a decomposed and nuanced analysis than what the demographic characterisation of youth as an age-grade would permit.

Sociologically speaking, 'youth' is a construct. This becomes apparent once we appreciate the inherent limitations of accepting the demographic definition of youth in terms of age-grade, howsoever heuristically convenient and useful it may be. To 'understand' the reality of youth, sociologists perforce have to develop a contextually defined analytical construct or an 'ideal type', as Max Weber would have it, of youth. This analytical construct/ideal type may less or more overlap with the demographer's age-grade, but it may not and need not so overlap. What is more important, the analytical construct of the sociologist must be sensitive to the ethno-social construct of youth, that is, the construct that a given people have of youth.

Furthermore, as a construct, 'youth' has two dimensions: processual and collective. The former refers to youth as a *phase* in the development of individuals, and the latter refers to youth as a *group* in society. In reality, these two dimensions are related. But, depending on the objective of one's research, either of these can be privileged in focus. In either case, the study of youth interests more than one discipline, disciplines beyond the conventional boundaries of social sciences. Nevertheless, no discipline can capture all aspects of the reality subsumed under the rubric 'youth'. As an area of study, youth is, therefore, trans-disciplinary in nature. My review of literature on youth (see ibid.) suggests that, more than others, sociologists are open to crossing their disciplinary boundary. We can thus take a lead in the trans-disciplinary study of youth. Of course, I am not recommending self-effacement; quite the contrary: the uniqueness of the sociological perspective lies in locating youth in the larger socio-cultural context. It is this uniqueness that I would want sociologists to take advantage of.

What type of data do we need about 'youth' and how do we collect them in order to capture the nuances that are discussed above? I began this chapter by citing some quantitative data drawn from Census and other sources. Such quantitative data on youth are also available in the several rounds of NSSO (National Sample Survey Organisation) surveys and the three rounds of NFHS

(National Family and Health Survey). These quantitative data are helpful in (a) delineating the large-scale trends and (b) cross-region or inter-state variations. Limited as they may, they provide us with some *generalisations* to operate with.

However, quantitative studies are obviously deficient in micro-level insights, and they can hardly help us *understand* the ground-level nuances. Understanding the ground-level reality of youth calls for rich qualitative data from ethnographic studies. Qualitative methodology is catholic in its approach to different sources of data, including the rich source that is available from the field of literature. In combination with sample surveys and quantitative studies, with multifarious sources of data, qualitative studies can enrich the sociology of youth in India.

Some Substantive Issues

The scope of sociology of youth in a diverse country like India is vast (see ibid.), and cannot be gone into detail here. Besides the educational aspects that were highlighted in the previous section, I would like to emphasise four areas on which we could focus our attention. The first and the foremost is youth culture – or, more appropriately, youth subcultures. The extension of the duration of economic dependence on parents among the middle-class children and the early attainment of economic independence among their underclass counterparts provide a study in contrast. Between these two extremes are various categories of youth. Religion, caste/tribe, rural-urban location, and gender constitute the important variables which, in combination, make for the diversity of youth culture. Identity, self-defined and others-defined, is a key element for analysis in the sociological study of youth culture.

The revolution in communication technology has had a profound impact on youth across the world. The number and coverage of the media have increased informational density and brought more and more people under their influence. Not much is known about how the growth of literacy and education have affected youth in the rural areas. Similarly, research on the impact of the virtual reality created by the cyber world is in its nascency. Free floating of and easier access to a variety of information facilitated by the IT (Information Technology) Revolution has facilitated networking, mobilisation and movement of youth as never before. All this warrants sociological attention.

Karl Mannheim's classic essay 'The Problem of Generations' (1952: 276–320) had established 'generation' as a factor as important as 'social class' or 'gender' in the explanation of individual and group differences in culture, interests, and behaviour. Mannheim's use of the term 'generation' to describe cohort processes,[6] it must be noted, is different from the term 'generation' as used in kinship analysis to describe relationships. Following this, 'generational conflict' was a popular theme in the early work on the sociology of youth (see Jayaram 2000b). Is the generation gap closing? What is the nature of generational conflicts? Have there been significant changes in parent-child relationship over the last half century? What are the differences in generational relations which we find across regions and religions, classes and class, and gender? These questions should interest sociologists in this era of globalisation and consequent changes.

Generational conflict apart, the term youth often evokes the image of an angry young person: not surprisingly, unrest is often viewed as coterminous with youth; passion and rebellion are identified with youth. And rebellion is often accompanied by violence. Student unrest, a recurrent theme in the sociology of education in the 1960s through 1980s, is no more talked about! They were in the forefront of important political changes both in India and elsewhere. Is it that the students are no more characterised by unrest or unrest among students has lost its interest for sociologists? All the same, there is unmistakable evidence that a substantive section of those engaged in extremist ideologies and activities of various types, including terrorism, are in the category we call youth. What does this portend? The interface between youth, on the one hand, and extremism and violence, on the other, deserves our serious attention as sociologists.

It is well known that today's youth was yesterday's children; today's children will be tomorrow's youth. Accordingly, the sociology of youth shares an indefinite border with the sociology of childhood. That is, a sociological understanding of youth by necessity takes into consideration some of the basic issues concerning childhood and the transition from childhood to adolescence. Pressures of a competitive world, reinforced by parental ambitions for children, resulting in the rising incidence of teenage suicides in urban areas are a matter of concern. But more serious are the realities of 'missing childhood' (resulting in child labour) and 'shortened childhood' (resulting from early loss of innocence) contributing to the early onset of youth. So a meaningful sociology of youth would take into consideration the issues of childhood, a stage from which their subjects emanate.

Conclusion

I began with the idea of demographic dividend. This idea highlights the importance of the demographic category called youth and how it is important to invest in youth for reaping the benefits in a globalising world. But a closer examination revealed that, sociologically, youth as a category is heterogeneous and it needs the careful attention of sociologists than what its demographic analysis would suggest. As the epigraph from the Swiss psychologist and psychiatrist Carl Gustav Jung (1875–1961) has it, 'The wine of youth does not always clear with advancing years; sometimes it grows turbid' (cited in Andrews 1987: 295). The sociology of youth can help diagnose the conditions under which the wine of youth grows turbid and suggest what can make it clear with advancing years.

Notes

1. Some of the ideas in this chapter were initially presented in my Keynote Address to the 8th International Conference on Asian Youth and Childhoods held at Lucknow, 22–24 November 2007.
2. The statistical data cited in this chapter come from two sources: the Census of India and the United Nations Population Division. I am grateful to Professor M.R. Narayana of the Institute for Social and Economic Change, Bangalore and Professor S. Siva Raju of the Tata Institute of Social Sciences, Mumbai for providing me with these data, and to Professor T.V. Sekher of the International Institute for Population Sciences, Mumbai for help with a citation.
3. A study conducted by Manpower India, a human resources consultant group, has revealed that 'the Employment Outlook', a measure of keenness of employers to hire fresh staff, is down by 24 per cent over the last quarter and by 27 per cent on a year-on-year basis. The figures are the worst since the third quarter of 2005. However, 'India still seems to have the second most optimistic numbers internationally'. Of the thirty-three countries surveyed,

only Peru has more optimistic numbers than India' (Times News Network 2008a: 14).

4. The rate of unemployment among youth (15–29 years) at different levels of education are as follows: not literate, 0.8 per cent; up to primary, 2.8 per cent; middle school, 5.7 per cent; secondary, 9.7 per cent; senior secondary, 12.7 per cent; diploma/certificate, 18.8 per cent; graduate, 19.7 per cent; and post-graduate, 18.6 per cent (cited in The Times of India 2009: 2).
5. It is significant to note that the Government of India's discussion paper on 'Government Subsidies in India' (1997) classified elementary education as a 'merit good' and higher education as a 'non-merit good' warranting a drastic reduction of government subsidies. The Ministry of Finance has since reclassified higher education into a category called 'merit 2 goods' which need not be subsidised at the same level as merit goods (Tilak 2002: 12).
6. A generation may be defined as 'a social cohort whose collective experience of history is shaped by a significant event or events, and whose memory is constructed around recurrent rituals and significant places ...' (Abercrombie et al. 2000: 150).

Part III

Education, Emancipation, and Social Change

7

Education, Inequality, and Social Change

Education is neither a single commodity nor a homogenous service. On the contrary, it forms a continuum, both in terms of quantity and quality. In terms of the former, it may vary from one to about twenty years and, as regards the latter, there exists a hierarchy of educational institutions with respect to the quality of education imparted to the students. These two aspects of the continuum of education do not operate separately; rather they coincide and superimpose themselves upon each other. Analytically, the higher, professional, and better quality education in urban areas, on the one hand, and the lower and poor quality education in rural areas, on the other, form the extremes of this continuum.

In most societies, the distribution of education, in terms of both quantity and quality, is highly uneven. It seems to correspond directly to the profile of stratification and inequality in them. Inequality in opportunities for education is found not only with reference to individuals and social categories, but also in terms of regions and territorial aggregates such as rural and urban areas.

Urban-Rural Disparities

That our educational system is patently urban biased in the matter of location of facilities, allocation of finance, and content of curricula is now well established. Most institutions of higher learning, as also the better equipped schools, are concentrated in urban areas. The awareness of their existence and utility is also greater there. Consequently, admission to these institutions tends to be almost entirely biased in favour of students from urban areas, though the urban population is small in comparison with the rural.

There is no valid or compelling reason for educational facilities to be concentrated in urban areas. On the other hand, the aforementioned trend, apart from providing definite practical and technical advantages to the urbanites, also acts as a barrier for the rural people. Latently, this has the effect of insulating the educational facilities from being observed by the latter. In matters of cost, adjustment, and complexes, urban people have a decisive edge over their rural counterparts, who will have in addition to surmount the problems arising from their migration to cities to pursue education. The rural rich alone seem in these circumstances to come closer to urbanites in the matter of higher education (Kamat 1972).

The urban bias in the educational system is sometimes defended on the ground that in the potential progress of developing societies the city plays a dynamic multiple role, as it is the focal point for change and progress (Bauer 1956: 55–56), and that such a bias is not entirely absent even in the industrially advanced countries of the West (Roberts 1973: 142). Yet another and stronger rationalisation comes from the advocates of technical efficiency and economic tenability, which, according to them, necessitates educational facilities to be developed as a part of an urban-industrial complex. But these arguments are untenable as they go counter to the role of education as a solvent of inequalities, a role which is much lauded throughout the world.

The inevitable consequence of the urban bias in our education has been the gross and unrepentant neglect of lower education whose importance in a country wherein the majority of the population is illiterate and lives in rural areas can hardly be exaggerated (see Borkotoky and Unisha 2014). Not only is rural education neglected, it is also suffering from serious ills in its present state. Much of the educational neglect at the lower levels can be traced to the present policy of breakneck expansion of higher education in urban areas. A.K. Sen appropriately remarks:

> While viewing one of the most tantalizing growth-pictures of higher education that has ever been seen in the world, it is worth bearing in mind that the average cost of educating an undergraduate in arts and science for one year is the same as educating 22 students in a primary school for one year. The cost of giving someone one year's teaching at the MA level equals that of schooling 41 primary students in equivalent terms (1971: 255).

It is not as though such an anomaly has completely escaped the attention of academicians and planners. Past experience has shown that at the point of planning policy the greatest stress is laid on universal mass education, with special emphasis on the education of women, of scheduled castes and tribes, and in rural areas. But, at the point of execution and performance, the achievements are in the realm of higher education, especially those of men, of higher stratum people, and in urban areas.

According to Sen, what accounts for this shift from policy to performance lies in a mixture of two reasons: 'First, there are upward biases in the Government's method of estimation of the educated manpower requirements for economic growth, and, second, the Government has been remarkably responsive to political pressures for quantitative expansion of higher education' (1971: 257). The former is a responsibility of the economists working in the field of education, and could be rectified in the light of facts. However, the blame for the latter must be squarely placed on the governmental machinery succumbing to political and communal pressure groups.

Incidentally, the fantastic rate of growth of higher education in cities has been accompanied by explosive problems like 'educated unemployment', student unrest, decline in standards, etc. which have a definite bearing on the social structure. However, these issues are beyond the scope of this chapter. Our concern here is with the extent to which non-academic and socio-economic factors influence enrolment of students in higher and professional education, and the role of higher education in stabilising status structure in urban India.

Bearing of Caste and Socio-Economic Status

It is found that higher education, which is a passport to high occupational and social status, is virtually the monopoly of a select stratum of urban society. The institutions of higher learning are highly selective as far as the socio-economic background of the students is concerned. Students in such institutions are predominantly drawn from among the higher strata families characterised by high educational, occupational, and income backgrounds.

Although the independent significance of caste in bestowing social status has become weak, caste still continues to be a significant factor influencing admission to urban higher education. It is observed that Brahmins, who were the traditionally privileged caste group and who were the first to respond to modern education, still seem to be the 'dominant caste' in the field of education, being the single majority caste group in various institutions of higher learning. This is in spite of the various attempts, both formal and informal, to counter their predominance. In the words of Edward Shils, 'no other country can quite match this picture of a continuing intellectual tradition carried so long by a single section of the population' (1961: 21).

Of course, since Independence, some non-Brahmin castes have found their way into the field of education. But it is only the dominant among them who have benefitted from the educational expansion as also from the formal measures to break the Brahmin monopoly in education. At least a part of this trend is explained by the political power which they have been able to wield and exploit. The progress of education among the lower castes, especially among the scheduled castes, seems to be painfully slow and halting. While the government has taken up the cause of ameliorating the educational situation among the scheduled castes and tribes, the response has been far from satisfactory (see Karlekar 1975; Chitnis 1977, 1981). There seems to be a very long way to go before the educational situation of the scheduled castes and tribes is ameliorated.

It is also observed that, despite the rapid expansion in their education, women are still at a disadvantage compared to men (see Mazumdar 1975). The availing of the benefits of the rapid expansion in higher education by women is chiefly confined to those belonging to the higher social strata and upper caste groups in urban areas. However, the elimination of inequality of educational opportunities on sex lines would remain an insignificant issue until the question of the relevance of the education of women is satisfactorily answered.

School Systems and Inequality

Inequality of educational opportunities does not take place solely or abruptly at the level of higher education. In fact, the initial unequal selection takes place at the school level itself, and higher education merely reinforces it. An overwhelming majority of the students in higher education have had English medium education and that too in privately managed schools. The 'public' schools, a very small number in the Indian school system, contribute disproportionately to the ranks of higher education.

It should be noted that the social background of students operates as a selective factor in their admission to qualitatively different types of educational institutions. Alfred De Souza (1974: 236–46) has found that it is exclusively the children of the urban upper strata who avail of 'public' school education.[1] The same seems to be true of English medium education also. Thus, the public schools and English medium education help to 'institutionalise complementary continuation of family socialisation' of the privileged few and stabilise their status at the higher level (Levitas 1974: 53; see also Jayaram 1978).

Myth of Merit and 'Tadpole Philosophy'

Advancing meritocratic arguments, some may altogether deny inequality of educational opportunities as an issue. Since schooling would, according to them, ostensibly be open to all, one's achievement of higher education or absence of it could be portrayed as a result not of her/his birth and background, but of her/his efforts, ability, and talents. This is what Robert H. Tawney calls the 'tadpole philosophy':

> It is possible that intelligent tadpoles reconcile themselves to the inconveniences of their position, by reflecting that, though most of them will live and die as tadpoles and nothing more, the more fortunate of the species will one day shed their tails, distend their mouths and stomachs, hop nimbly on to dry land, and croak addresses to their former friends on the virtue by means of which tadpoles of character and capacity can rise to be frogs (1964: 105).

It is true that in higher education merit cannot be completely ignored either in principle or in practice, as the relevance of higher education demands efficiency on its part. This is rendered impossible even otherwise by the fact that the number of applicants with requisite merit far exceeds the number which the educational system can effectively accommodate. However, research in the area of social determinants of academic achievement has conclusively shown that the so-called 'merit' is itself influenced by certain non-academic and socio-economic factors. Consequently, the resulting meritocracy, instead of cutting across the ascriptive factors, inequality, and stratification, as had been speculated by Michael Young (1961) in his satirical analysis of the rise of meritocracy over a century in England, tends to superimpose itself and reinforce them.

Thus, the justification of the existence and perpetuation of a meritocratic system, in which admissions are said to be based solely on 'merit', and which individualises failure (Bernstein 1961: 308), seems to be a clever strategy for 'social closure' (Parkin 1974: 7–8) and elite perpetuation. It legitimises inequality and makes its continued existence acceptable as a kind of safety valve (see Parkin 1972: 49; Bourdieu 1973: 71; Entwistle 1978: 11).

How the meritocratic principle makes the mechanism of social reproduction has been outlined by Pierre Bourdieu with great insight, and he is worth quoting in full here:

> By giving individuals educational aspirations strictly tailored to their position in the social hierarchy, and by operating a selection procedure which, although apparently formally equitable, endorses real inequalities, schools help both to perpetuate and legitimize inequalities. By awarding allegedly impartial qualifications (which are also largely accepted as such) for socially conditioned aptitudes which it treats as unequal 'gifts', it transforms *de facto* inequalities into *de jure* ones and *economic and social* differences into *distinctions of quality*, and legitimates the transmission of the cultural heritage. In doing so, it is performing a confidence trick. Apart from enabling the elite to justify being what it is, the ideology of giftedness, the cornerstone of the whole educational and social system, helps to enclose the underprivileged classes in the roles which society has given them by making them see as natural inability things which are only a result of an inferior social status, and by persuading them that they owe their social fate (which is increasingly tied to their educational fate as society becomes

more rationalised) to their individual nature and their lack of gifts. The exceptional success of those few individuals who escape the collective fate of their class apparently justify [sic] educational selection and give [sic] credence to the myth of the school as a liberating force among those who have been eliminated, by giving the impression that success is exclusively a matter of gifts and work. Finally those whom the system has 'liberated' – teachers in elementary, secondary and higher education – put their faith in *L'ecole liberatrice* at the service of the school which is in truth a conservative force which owes part of its power of conservation to that myth. Thus by its own logic the educational system can help to perpetuate cultural privilege without those who are privileged having to use it. By giving cultural inequalities an endorsement which formally at least is in keeping with democratic ideals, it provides the best justification for these inequalities (1974: 42; emphasis in original).

Inequality, Elite Education, and Status Retention

Most people today find it difficult to deny the existence of educational inequalities, especially in the face of mounting evidence confirming it. To the liberals, such inequalities are 'passing phenomena, holdovers from an earlier, less enlightened era, which are rapidly being eliminated' (Bowles 1977: 137). Some may still defend it on the ground that it need not reflect prejudice or deliberate neglect of subordinate groups by the superordinate ones (see, for example, Anderson and Foster 1964: 1–18). And the ubiquity of such inequalities may tempt some apologists for capitalism to conclude that it is inevitable for efficiency. This is necessarily a naive functionalist standpoint, and it is incumbent on us to remind ourselves in this context of Alexis de Tocqueville's warning not to confound the familiar with the necessary: '... what we call necessary institutions are often no more than institutions to which we have grown accustomed ...' (quoted in Merton 1968: 91).

The ubiquity of social inequality (Tumin 1969), its stubborn and remarkable resistance to change (Goldthorpe 1973: 6), its assumed functional indispensability (Davis and Moore 1945; Dahredorf 1969a), the inherent irreconcilability of equality with liberty (Holmes 1985: 7), and the supposedly psychological ill-equipment of people for equality (J. Wilson 1966: 165), may induce a docile complacency about the whole problem of inequality. What is more, the desire for equality may even be dubbed a romantic illusion, the pursuit of which for its own sake being 'more than impractical and self-defeating' is 'morally objectionable' (Joseph and Sumption 1979: blurb). We would do well, therefore, to bear in mind Tawney's admonition about 'the religion of inequality':

> It may well be the case that capricious inequalities are in some measure inevitable, in the sense that, like crime and disease, they are a malady which the most rigorous precautions cannot wholly overcome. But, when crime is known as crime, and disease as disease, the ravages of both are circumscribed by the mere fact that they are recognised for what they are, and described by their proper names, not by flattering euphemisms. And a society which is convinced that inequality is an evil need not be alarmed because the evil is one which cannot wholly be subdued. In recognizing the poison it will have armed itself with an antidote. It will have deprived inequality of its sting by stripping it of its esteem (1964: 56).

The conclusion seems to be irresistible that our educational system is elitist and inegalitarian and strongly reinforces and gives impetus to the working of what is called the 'Mathew principle', that is, that 'to him that hath, shall be given, and he shall have more abundance' as declared in St Mathew's Gospel (13:12). A striking illustration of this phenomenon is the high subsidisation of higher education by the government which benefits the affluent sections of society to the detriment of its poorer sections. P.J. Foster's assertion that 'the coexistence of gross inequalities of access to advanced schooling with relative "openness" in absolute profiles of representation can occur in those societies where the socio-economic profile of the population is broad at the base but extremely constricted at the apex' (1971: 24) seems to be true of the Indian context too. In the absence of distributive justice in education, the claim of equality of educational opportunities turns out to be a myth.

With widespread inequality in opportunities for education, resulting from the operation of socio-economic and cultural factors, education seems to have failed as an effective equalising factor. Instead, the evidence points to the long-term strategies –

widely understood and employed in certain strata – by way of choice of schools and colleges intended to help the next generation to retain or transcend the parental level of income, wealth, and status. In brief, higher education is found to have contributed to the stabilisation and perpetuation of ascribed status or to 'status retention' (see Jayaram 1978, 1987a).

Such a trend, instead of showing any signs of decline, has gained momentum with the rapid expansion of education and industrialisation in the country. This seems to confirm Raymond Boudon's theorem that 'other things being equal, and under broad conditions, educational growth as such has the effect of increasing rather than decreasing social and economic inequality' (1974: xi).

It is not argued here that education has not contributed at all to the process of upward social mobility in urban areas. The presence of first-generation students in schools, in general, and colleges, in particular, will not sustain such a claim. Part of the little mobility that can be and is seen is sponsored by the government as part of its measures for ameliorating the status of the scheduled castes/tribes and other backward classes. And part of it has been the outcome of the strategy of the economically dominant groups of converting their status parameter, that is, from landholding and economic assets to education. However, considering the phenomenal growth of higher education in the last six decades or so, the extent of such mobility appears to be only marginal.

In this connection, the conceptual distinction between social mobility through the supply of vacant statuses and by the interchange of ranks, outlined by Seymour Martin Lipset and Hans Lennart Zetterberg (1966: 565) seems to be meaningful. One will have to grant that some people from the lower strata are more educated and better employed now than they were a few decades back, partly because of the widening of opportunities in education and occupation, and partly because of the policy of protective discrimination. But it remains a stubborn fact that the relative advantage of the upper strata and the informal barriers to the higher status occupations have not only persisted but also become strengthened. 'All in all, what education has helped to achieve is a limited embourgeoisement of certain segments of the population' (Kamat 1985: 18).

While a general trend in status retention is observed throughout, this seems to be markedly so at the highest levels of occupational status. In other words, while access to higher education is selective, the selectivity seems to be more pronounced with regard to the prestigious professional courses like medicine, technology, management, etc. If the students in higher education are a select group, the medical students are elite within it (see Jayaram 1987a: 20–35). A tendency for occupational inbreeding or self-recruitment in medical education can be discerned. Such self-recruitment contributes to the crystallisation of stratification through time.[2]

It is relevant to point out here that the structure of the educational system itself contributes to a great extent towards such a tendency. Some of the complex formalities of the educational system which are primarily designed to effectively contain the burgeoning demand for higher and professional education, in fact, act as social bottlenecks, necessarily favouring the elite and higher echelons in the stratification pyramid. This is one of the notable ways in which the educational system directly reinforces the prevailing stratification and rigidifies it further.

Other than inequalities in opportunity for education, there is an important factor limiting the mobility role of higher education in urban areas. That is, 'peoples' ideas as to what qualifications fit what jobs tend to change over time' (Dore 1976: 4). The generation of employment in the country has been inordinately slow as compared to the output of people with educational credentials. Hence, there is an increasing availability of people with educational credentials in relation to the availability of jobs, a phenomenon described as 'educated unemployment'. This has resulted in a continuous escalation of educational qualifications for jobs without any necessary relation to more effective job performance or sophistication demanded by the economy. Other things remaining the same, a more 'qualified' person (that is, one possessing higher/more degrees) is more likely to be appointed for a job though it does not require such a high qualification. Such an educational inflation or degree devaluation has diluted the mobility potential of education in relation to occupation. In brief, along with 'a hardening of social arteries', there has been 'a secular decline in the mobility significance of education' (Saberwal 1978: 243).

Private Enterprise and Educational Inegalitarianism

The existence of the private sector in education not only reflects the basic division of society, but also perpetuates social inequality contingent on such a division. In India, the private enterprise in education[3] has got considerable fillip due to the scarcity of higher and better quality educational facilities resulting from the government's inability to meet the ever-increasing demand for them. This sector is largely capitalistic in orientation and operates strictly according to the principles of market economy. It generally caters to the affluent sections and the 'middle-class mobiles' in the urban areas. The charging of capitation fees, collecting donations, etc. are all part of the functional logic of this sector.

The fact that private educational institutions instead of removing or at least lessening inequalities tend to perpetuate them has been shown by various studies on the social composition of such educational institutions and the social character of those who control the private sector in education[4] (see B.G. Desai 1967: 29–32; Madan and Halbar 1972; Di Bona 1974: 158–59; Seshadri 1976: 225–29). John Vaizey rightly remarked 'even if a wholly egalitarian ethic prevailed in the public sector, the provision of private facilities would always tend to restore the inequality prevailing in the economy as a whole' (1968: 51). The survival of private education with state patronage and protection, and the resistance to a comprehensive reorganisation of education, could be viewed as part of a strategy of the privileged to transmit their privilege to their children (Westergaard and Resler 1975: 284).[5] This seems to be a disquieting problem, notwithstanding the contribution that the private sector has made to the cause of education in the country.

Mobility Myth and Conservative Ideology

That such an educational system with potentialities of stabilising social status and perpetuating inequality is not peculiar to India, but is true of both the developed and the developing countries, is very well documented empirically (see Jayaram 1987a: 18, fn 4). Nevertheless, it seems to be a generally accepted view, as Boudon (1974: 3) has pointed out, that industrial societies are largely meritocratic, and that the level of educational attainment is one of the major determinants of status and a major factor of social mobility in such societies. It appears that such a faith is largely due to what is termed the 'mobility myth', which is an element of the capitalist ideology (Levitas 1974: 59). This myth has been succinctly outlined by Ivan Reid as follows:

> Social mobility is seen as a necessary characteristic of industrialised society, both economically – changing technology and production demand a redefinition of occupations – and culturally – democracy has a value set aiming towards an open, meritocratic society. Educational qualifications can be viewed as a relatively neutral criterion for occupational entry once educational opportunity has been extended, even minimally, to the whole society. The functions of the educational system are to provide people with the qualifications and aspirations to meet society's occupational needs. Built into the system is the assumption that people will, or should, want to be upwardly mobile. Underlying such reasoning is, then, the belief that social mobility is a desirable characteristic of society and that the educational system exists to promote and facilitate it (1978: 243).

At the same time, this myth provides society with a useful complacent belief in the openness of society through the educational system.

This, 'the educational blind alleys of social mobility', as Stanislav Andreski (1974: 24) calls it appropriately, is necessarily an illusion. People may *feel* that they could move up the hierarchy and this may provide them with some psychological satisfaction. Functionalists are prone to look for the functional significance of such an illusion for the maintenance of social stability (see, for example, Levy Jr 1966: 785–86). If sociology of education has not been able to completely explode the above myth, and to project the educational system as obstructing social mobility, limiting educational opportunity and achievement, subscribing to 'social closure', and in general contributing to social and cultural reproduction, it is because 'the sociology of education, like education itself, operates within a set of cultural values' (Reid 1978: 244).

The Way Out?

Since we are educating now to reap the benefit twenty years later, the present inegalitarian and elitist system of education will have profound effects on social structure for decades to come. This certainly breeds anxiety and, to one with some sociological imagination, the question of *the way out* becomes significant. Even otherwise, the intrinsic faith in education itself would necessitate a search for alternatives.

Of late, there has been mounting criticism, both in the developed and the developing countries, of the role of educational institutions, recognising the need for radically restructuring society. In the 1960s, Jonathan Kozol (1967) and J. Herndon (1968) demonstrated that the big city schools in America were unable to educate the underprivileged children. In the 1970s, the criticism turned radical to the extent of rejecting the institution of schooling itself. According to the radical thesis, the school is manifestly incapable of educating all children and is instead latently dysfunctional in that it perpetuates class privileges and turns out generations of acceptors of the *status quo*. Thus, to Everett Reimer (1971) the 'school is dead' and to Paul Goodman (1971) compulsory schooling is 'compulsory miseducation', and so Ivan D. Illich (1973) vociferously seeks the 'deschooling society'. All these radicals, including their compatriot Paulo Freire (1972a and 1972b), emphasise the need for alternatives in the form of 'education without schools' (see Buckman 1975).

While it is amply possible to disagree with this radical view of education,[6] it will be hardly realistic to ignore it, in view of its relevance for the educational situation in India which harbours a serious malady behind the facade of statistics on educational growth. A comprehensive critique of our educational system on the above mentioned radical lines is yet to come. The much vaunted 'radical reconstruction of education' has only been widely discussed while what has actually been effected is 'moderate reformism' (Naik 1965: 16). It is observed that all the commissions on education, including the more comprehensive Kothari Commission, 'have operated essentially *within* the fundamental framework of the present system, however far reaching some of their recommendations may *look*' (Saran 1971: 239; emphasis in original).

Evidence from abroad where such attempts as 'protective discrimination', 'intervention programmes', 'compensatory education',[7] etc. have been made at reforming the situation from within reveal that tinkering with the educational system will not enable a society to equalise the life chances of its citizens (see Bernstein 1973; Boudon 1974; Carnoy and Levin 1976; Bowles 1977).[8] These efforts failed because, as Samuel Bowles has argued, they 'sought to eliminate educational inequalities without challenging the basic institutions of capitalism' (1977: 149–50). Thus, to those who pin their hope on changes in the government policy to equalise education the experience of Britain (see Little and Westergaard 1964) and the United States of America (see Bowles 1977: 150) does not offer any comfort. At best government policy can only scratch the surface of inequality, as much of the educational inequality has its origin and base outside the limited sphere of state power.

In this context, it is necessary to point out that *formal* equality of opportunity is essentially a conservative notion (Bourdieu 1974: 37): 'It is a sort of entrepreneurial businessman's or bourgeois concept which is something quite different from, and indeed incompatible with, egalitarianism' (Hobsbawm 1975: 37). And 'as a recipe for social engineering it merely makes for mobility within the *status quo*', says Harold Entwistle (1978: 9). Viewed thus,

> ... it almost seems that the word equality is an accidental occurrence in the phrase (or, perhaps, cynically included to exploit its emotive overtones), where everything really hangs on the word 'opportunity' which, in turn, seems logically inconsistent with the notion of equality. When the emphasis is upon opportunity, the implication is that outcomes will be unequal. He who is offered and seizes an opportunity receives a bonus, something which the others haven't got ... (ibid.).

We are, therefore, obliged to conclude that *formal* equality is fallacious in conception as well as unjust in reality.

In brief, the argument that a formally egalitarian education compensates for inequalities generated elsewhere in the system is patently fallacious (Bowles 1977: 144) and equality of *opportunity* without equality of *conditions* is a sham (Crossland 1962; Halsey 1973: 95). If it is conceded, as it must be, that educational inequalities are rooted in the basic institutions of society, a far-reaching, thoroughgoing egalitarian transformation of society seems to be the only way out.

Notes

1. Tawney aptly remarks: 'A public school ... is not a school that is easily accessible to the public, but a school that the great majority of the public are precluded from entering' (1964: 77–78).
2. As stated by Parkin, 'stratification implies not simply inequality, but a set of institutional arrangements which guarantee a fairly high degree of social continuity in the reward position of family units through the generations' (1972: 14).
3. According to the Ministry of Education and Social Welfare (1978: 22–87, Table III), in 1970–71, 73.9 per cent of all colleges for general education and 51.8 per cent of professional colleges of degree and postgraduate level were in the private sector. Private enterprise in school education is confined to high/higher secondary and pre-primary levels: 66.2 per cent of the former and 73.1 per cent of the latter are privately managed. Private enterprise is the least enterprising in primary and middle levels of schooling: only 16.1 per cent of the former and 26.1 per cent of the latter are privately managed.
4. Private control over education is far more pervasive than what either its domain or legal authority would suggest. Based on an intensive study of seven colleges in Kanpur, Nirmal Singh (1983) has examined the nature and consequences of the resulting 'siege' of public education by private control.
5. With most states in the country reducing the Right to Education Act – which reserves 25 per cent of seats at the elementary level in private schools for children from economically weaker sections – to a farce, 'inclusive education and equal opportunity to all children remain nothing more than fond hope' (Rangan 2014: 26).
6. For an incisive critique of the radical tradition in educational theory, see Barrow (1978). For a critique of deschooling from a Marxist perspective, see Gintis (1972).
7. For a critique of 'compensatory education', see Bernstein (1974a).
8. For a critique of protective discrimination in education as a strategy for social change in India, see Chapter 8.

8

Education and Protective Discrimination

The policy of protective discrimination as a strategy for social change is a specific expression of the liberal ideology. This ideology advocates social change in a piecemeal fashion, within the existing framework of social institutions, and prescribes non-violent, constitutional, legal, and administrative solutions. The Constitution of India, which is premised upon this ideology, declares the society to be open and assures equality of opportunity to one and all in all realms. 'The claim of the individual to welfare is sacred and irrefutable' in such a constitution, and it 'partakes of the character of a natural right' (Marshall 1971: 38).

This has special significance to the members of the scheduled castes, who have been traditionally oppressed and are consequently underprivileged. They are, in theory, liberated by the Constitution, and they can now climb up the social ladder and stake their claim to higher status and the accompanying privileges. However, in view of the prevalence of market conditions and their past background and present predicament, they will not be able to compete with those of the other sections. To overcome the impediments in their upward social mobility, they need some prop. The state has, therefore, assumed the role of a generous donor and bears the responsibility for providing the necessary help to uplift them in the form of protective discrimination.

Of course, it is conceded that not all the members belonging to these castes can be emancipated through such state generosity in the realisation of individual rights. Hence, the policy of protective discrimination necessarily concentrates on few members of these castes. It is presumed that the initial beneficiaries – the 'elite' among the scheduled castes – would act as catalysts for social change among their less fortunate brethren. The essence of their own social mobility is expected to percolate to those who are below them, and in due course the whole community, it is hoped, will catch up with the rest of society. Since the process of such sponsored, non-violent, and piecemeal change is by nature gradual, the emancipation of these castes is necessarily a long-drawn process, spread over several decades and generations. In brief, the philosophy of the welfare state, the ideology of social mobility, and the theory of downward percolation constitute the postulates of the policy of protective discrimination.

Of the various facets of this policy, the one which has acquired maximum prominence is education. Education is expected to equip the scheduled castes to overcome their caste-defined confinement to low-status occupations by promoting occupational mobility among them and improving their standard of living. Educational institutions are expected to function as melting pots for obliterating caste differences and to facilitate the cultural integration of the scheduled castes with the upper-caste Hindus. Moreover, education is expected to generate a climate for change by changing social attitudes and aspirations on the lines of liberalism and humanism.

Thus, education is regarded as both the foundation and the vehicle for the emancipation of the scheduled castes. With educational institutions functioning as social elevators and as melting pots of social alchemy, education becomes a painless and conscience-relaxing solvent of social inequalities and the main instrument for introducing a new era free from the curse of the underprivileged. Not surprisingly, more than fifty per cent of the funds for the welfare of the scheduled castes has been allocated to implement an elaborate programme of scholarships, hostel facilities, and reservation of admission to educational institutions to secure the educational advancement of these castes.

How far has the programme of protective discrimination been successful in realising its objectives? Has it brought about occupational mobility among the scheduled castes, and if so, what is the nature of this mobility? To what extent and in what direction have the educated and the mobile among them changed their outlook and aspirations? What are the consequences, both structural and attitudinal, of the policy of protective discrimination? Based on the all-India report of the study commissioned by the Indian Council of Social Science Research on the progress and problems of education among the scheduled castes (Chitnis 1981; hereafter called the national study)[1] and gleaning relevant findings from the Twenty-sixth Report (1978–79) of the Commissioner of Scheduled Castes and Scheduled Tribes (1980; hereafter called Commissioner), as also from other studies, we shall examine some of these questions.

Education, Mobility, and Social Change

The national study (Chitnis 1981: 12–37, 38–72) has revealed that the overwhelming majority of the scheduled caste students come from backgrounds that may be considered disadvantageous for education. That most of them happen to be the first generation entrants to colleges or high schools in the family would indicate positive returns from the investment on the education of the scheduled castes. A majority of them aspire to study up to graduation and do not consider themselves bound to their traditional occupations, and they display a tendency to move out of the caste-defined confinement to low-status occupations. These findings seem to reflect a trend in and orientation towards upward social mobility among the scheduled caste students.

In the absence of data on the differential access to education between the scheduled castes and non-scheduled caste youth from comparable socio-economic backgrounds, it is difficult to determine if the progress of the former is exclusively due to protective discrimination. Nevertheless, the mobility aim behind the policy of protective discrimination seems to have been, apparently at least, partially achieved.

About their social outlook and attitude, the national study (Chitnis 1981: 73–106) shows that the students continue to be conformist and traditional on the issue of marriage. They have a pronounced tendency for homophily and a diffident self-image (this seems to be more so in those states in which the provisions for the uplift of the scheduled castes are relatively better). That these reactions of theirs are found not to be rooted in their experience of ill-treatment or discrimination would point to the failure of educational institutions to function effectively as instruments of social change. The majority of students have a poor exposure to mass media and a low level of politicisation.

Trend Towards Dependence

The purpose of protective discrimination being the elimination of the criteria by which the scheduled castes are defined, the continuation of the same would be self-defeating by definition. To make use of a metaphor, 'protective discrimination is a "crutch", and in the long run no substitute for a healthy leg' (Dushkin 1972: 216–17). An important aim of the education of the scheduled castes is to develop in them self-reliance and an attitude of independence. But it is found that the students invariably feel that the various facilities that are provided to them are useful but inadequate (Chitnis 1981: 107–44). They invariably prefer the secure reserved jobs in government service, thereby betraying their diffidence about being selected for jobs without the assistance of reservations.

Thus, the scheduled caste students, instead of being fired by a zeal for change, seem to be willing to depend on official programmes and policies for their advancement. In view of the poor level of politicisation among them, there does not seem to be any prospect of organised action on their part either. The data seem to confirm the oft-repeated complaint that the policy of protective discrimination has a tendency to perpetuate itself and to breed a sense of utter and permanent dependence on the part of the scheduled castes, crippling and crushing their initiative.

Education and Selectivity

As regards the academic life of the students (ibid.: 38–72), a majority of them have gone through their education without suffering gaps and breaks, have no problems of comprehension, and are hardworking. Considering that most of these are first-generation students, this is commendable indeed. But this would also mean that 'in spite of the massive facilities for the education of the scheduled castes it is only the brighter amongst them, the good performers, who make it to high school and college' (ibid.: 70).

Data reveal that though the growth in enrolment ratio in absolute terms among the scheduled castes is noteworthy, they are still lagging far behind other communities (see Table 8.1). While the growth in school enrolment among the scheduled caste children in the 6–11 age-group is indeed appreciable, the growth in the 11–14 age-group is not so. This indicates a lot of wastage of education among the scheduled castes (see Commissioner 1980: 164).

Table 8.1 Enrolment Ratios to the Corresponding Age-group

	Classes I–V (age-group 6–11)			*Classes VI–VIII (age-group 11–14)*		
	1973–74	*1974–75*	*1977–78*	*1973–74*	*1974–75*	*1977–78*
Scheduled Castes	68.9	67.1	75.5	22.1	22.7	25.5
Scheduled Tribes	59.3	59.7	66.1	15.7	15.7	17.7
Other Communities	90.7	87.6	85.7	40.4	40.2	42.0

Source: Commissioner (1980: Part I, p. 163).

A closer analysis of enrolment in absolute terms over a period of time substantiates this (see Table 8.2). Of the 65,20,000 students who had registered in standards I–V in 1968 only 12,16,000 (that is, 18.7%) were enrolled in standards VI–VIII in 1973. This means that the rest, constituting an overwhelming majority of 81.3 per cent of the enrolees in standards I–V in 1968 had dropped out. Similarly, of the 11,19,000 students enrolled in standards VI–VIII in 1968–69, only 5,75,000 (that is, 51.4%) enrolled in standards IX–XI in 1973.

Table 8.2 Progress of Enrolment of Scheduled Caste Students in Schools (in Lakh)

Year	*Classes I–V*	*Classes VI–VIII*	*Classes IX–XI*
1968–69	65.20	11.19	4.58
1973–74	68.36	12.16	5.75

Source: Kirpal (1978: 167).

Whatever may be the explanation for the low participation rates of these castes, there seems to be no room for complacency about their educational situation. What is the fate of those – the majority – who drop-out and discontinue their education, many even before acquiring functional literacy, is a question that the proponents of liberal ideology do not seem to be serious about. Is it that they are blinkered by the statistics on 'achievements' in terms of enrolment and expenditure? Or is it that the mobility ideology individualises failure and drops the drop-outs as irredeemable?

Where Sponsored Mobility Fails to Come Off

With reference to certain courses of study, the intended sponsored mobility fails to come off. Generally, the scheduled caste students tend to get enrolled in general degree rather than vocation-oriented diploma courses and they tend to move away from science and technology to commerce and arts courses (Shah and Patel 1977; Chitnis 1981: 249). As far as their enrolment in professional and other higher courses is concerned, the Commissioner has found the position to be 'rather deplorable':

> The co-efficient of equality[2] in enrolment of scheduled castes which was 29.3 in 1964–65 for all professional courses increased to 39.0 in 1974–75. This is insignificant considering the fact that during the year 1974–75 out of every 100 students enrolled in professional and other higher courses, only about 4 belonged to these castes. For some courses like agriculture, commerce, law, nursing and physical education, the co-efficient among these castes in 1974–75 was as low as 35.6, 36.3, 35.6, 32.9 and 27.4 respectively (1980: 7).

In several professional courses, the seats reserved for the scheduled castes are not filled for want of suitable candidates. Even when some attempt is made to enrol the scheduled caste students into these courses, the result has not been encouraging. A study team of the Commissioner investigated the admission pattern and academic performance of the scheduled caste students at the Jawaharlal Nehru Medical College in Raipur (Madhya Pradesh) during September 1979 (ibid.: 177). It was revealed that while all the candidates, including those belonging to the scheduled castes, are required to appear for an entrance test for admission to the college, the State Pre-Medical Test Board had lowered the minimum percentage of qualifying marks for the scheduled caste candidates to as low as 35. Since very few of the candidates belonging to these castes could secure even this percentage, it was sometimes reduced to as low as even 15 so that more reserved seats could be filled.

A review of the performance of the scheduled caste students in the College from 1964 to 1973 revealed it to be unsatisfactory. Out of forty-two students admitted during these years, four took four and a half years to pass the final examination, six took five to six years, six took six to seven years, seven took as long as seven to eight years to pass the examination. While three were rusticated, two migrated to other colleges. Furthermore, fourteen of them were reported to have left their studies leading to a lot of wastage. All this was in spite of the special coaching given to these students during the first year of the course.

Turning to technological education, in 1973, the government stipulated that 15 per cent of the seats in the various graduate courses in the Indian Institutes of Technology should be reserved for the candidates belonging to the scheduled castes. Besides the admission through the Joint Entrance Examination, till 1978, the scheduled caste candidates who had secured more than 50 per cent marks in the qualifying examination were also directly admitted. The cut-off value of the marks to be obtained by these candidates in the entrance examination was fixed at approximately two-thirds of that prescribed for the other candidates. In 1978, of the 41,857 candidates who appeared for the entrance examination, only 1,401 (that is, 3.3%) belonged to the scheduled castes and tribes. Out of the 1,919 candidates who qualified, only eleven (that is, 0.6%) belonged to these groups. However, based on the minimum marks fixed for direct admission 153 scheduled caste/tribe candidates were offered admission, out of which 132 joined the Institutes (ibid.: 179).

The experience of a batch of thirteen scheduled caste/tribe students admitted to the Institute at Bombay in 1973 provides a good example of what promise such institutions hold for the scheduled castes:

> At the end of Special (Preparatory) Course, four students left the Institute. The remaining nine students were promoted to the First Year. Of these, one left at the end of the First Year. Two out of these eight students fared very badly and withdrew for a Semester. The remaining six registered for Second Year but one of them, who had not been performing well, was asked to leave later in the Semester. Of the remaining five students, two were on probation, i.e. their performance was much below the prescribed standards. Thus, out of 13 students admitted in 1973, only three students seemed to be giving an average performance. The rest were borderline cases (Kirpal 1978: 168–69).

Not surprisingly, from the academic year 1979–80 direct admission of scheduled caste/tribe candidates has been stopped and they are admitted to the Institutes, as all others, only through the entrance examination. It is learnt that, in 1979, only eighty-eight scheduled caste candidates were selected for admission on the basis of the entrance examination against 246 seats reserved for them.

According to V. Kirpal, the future of the scheduled caste students absorbed through the reserved seats in the Institutes is bleak. This has serious socio-economic and psychological repercussions. Besides being a wastage of resources, 'the feeling of not having been able to "make it" will shatter whatever little confidence they have and render them misfits in society' (ibid.: 169). Perhaps the same could be true of the scheduled caste students in other professional courses (see Rao 2013).

Nature and Implications of Mobility

Studies have shown that the growth of education among the scheduled castes has not been uniform and that the various educational facilities are unevenly distributed. The capacity to utilise the privileges has tended to vary from one sub-group to another (Patwardhan 1973; Commissioner 1980). The national study (Chitnis 1981: 319–26) found that, in all the states, a few castes dominate the sample to the exclusion of others, which means that the educational facilities are disproportionately utilised. Numerical strength coupled with such factors as urban residence, the social and occupational position of the caste in the traditional hierarchy, a tradition of occupations that provide for independent business, and experience of organised political effort seem to explain the unique advance of some castes.

Protective discrimination in education seems to function effectively as a sieve for catching the most able and discarding the rest. While a small elite among the scheduled castes has benefitted from protective discrimination, the remaining large majority has lagged behind. Consequently, the mobility that is witnessed among the scheduled castes through education is not spread over the whole community, but is confined to particular caste groups and, within these groups, to particular individuals.

Not only is the spread of mobility limited and the unit of mobility the individual, but also the distance traversed, in general, is not very long as is to be expected. Given the trend towards increasing under-representation of the scheduled castes at successively higher levels of education, towards their clustering around liberal science degree courses and that too in inferior and less prestigious institutions, and towards their performing poorly in education, the likelihood of their equipping themselves for prestigious and highly paid jobs remains remote.

What are the implications of the nature of mobility that is being channelled through protective discrimination in education? According to Dushkin, the policy of 'protective discrimination as a whole seems to have fostered the growth of a "new class"' (1972: 212). That the students covered by the national study constitute only a minority and not the mass (who do not enter or who stagnate or drop-out of the educational channel having entered it) points to the role of education in the formation of an elite class among the scheduled castes.

The processes of elite formation and consolidation among the scheduled castes have simultaneously created and widened the gap between the elite and the elite-in-making in urban areas, on the one hand, and the mass of their fellowmen living in rural areas, on the other hand (Isaacs 1965; Dushkin 1972). Considering the type of reference group behaviour entailed in the process of individual social mobility undergone by the elite among these castes, it is hardly surprising that there is an increasing alienation among them from the rest of their fellowmen.[3] Thus, what is expected to function as a percolator becomes in reality a wedge. What is more saddening is that, with their positive reference group members unwilling to accept them as equals, the mobiles among the scheduled castes are rendered 'marginal men' (Isaacs 1965; Patwardhan 1973).

Will the Policy Work?

Education, no doubt, has the effect of weaning people away from their traditional occupations. But once weaned what are the alternative jobs in which they will be employed? It was observed that, while the scheduled caste students tend to move away from the traditional occupations, they invariably prefer jobs in government service. Since most of them are getting such education which would not qualify them for any profession or throw open avenues for self-employment, they have to depend upon the government for jobs. The state of our economy being what it is, how many jobs can the government create? There is already a heavy backlog of unemployment, and not an insignificant percentage of this backlog is constituted by the educated (see Chapter 5). The incidence of unemployment, including those of the educated, is quite high even among the scheduled castes (see Tables 8.3 and 8.4).

Table 8.3 Work Performed by the Employment Exchanges in Respect of Scheduled Caste Applicants during 1978

Registrations Made	*7,26,033*
Placements effected	68,187
Number of reserved vacancies notified	64,019
Number of reserved vacancies filled	32,665
Number on the live register at the end of the year	14,79,035

Source: Commissioner (1980: Part II, p. 8).

With a steady but definite decline in the equation between education and employment, there has already set in a situation of educational inflation or degree devaluation, which is sure to accentuate in due course. This will definitely dilute the mobility significance of education even for the scheduled castes. Furthermore, the ever-shrinking employment opportunities indicate a physical limit to the possibility of mobility through education. That is, in course of time, even individual mobility would be difficult for the scheduled castes.

Table 8.4 Scheduled Castes on the Live Register of Employment Exchanges as on 31 December 1978, Classified by Educational Level

Educational Level	*Number*	*Percentage*	*Number*	*Percentage*
Below matriculate (including illiterate)			8,94,710	60.49
Matriculates			3,54,710	23.98
Persons passing higher secondary (including intermediate/undergraduate)			1,53,821	10.41
Graduates (including postgraduate)				
a. Arts	49,997	65.96		
b. Science	8,882	11.72		
c. Commerce	9,047	11.94		
d. Engineering	366	0.48		
e. Medicine	687	0.91		
f. Agriculture	667	0.88		
g. Law	202	0.27		
h. Education	5,281	6.97		
i. Others	665	0.88		
Total of 4			75,794	5.12
Grand Total			14,79,035	100.00

Source: Commissioner (1980: Part II, p. 10).

Even assuming that this trickle of individual mobility will continue, with the same conditions of operation, it would at least need a few centuries before the whole mass of the scheduled castes is put on the mobility channel. The amelioration of the vast majority of those who have remained outside school, either having not entered it or dropped-out after having entered it, and those who would either not enter it or would drop-out if they enter it, would remain substantially unaffected.

Sustenance of a Pipe-dream

What explains the sustenance of the ideology of sponsored mobility? As far as the scheduled castes are concerned, the policy of protective discrimination and the implied social mobility and development offers a rationalisation of their predicament by way of what R.H. Tawney calls 'the tadpole philosophy' (1964: 105).[4] The actual possibility of social mobility for the exceptional few, combined with the individualisation of failure, becomes the primary illusion of an entire class. It legitimises inequality, making its continued existence acceptable as a kind of safety value and cooling down any stress that may be generated (see Parkin 1972: 49). It diverts attention away from the full extent of the problem and its roots in the overall socio-economic framework.

In the light of this, it is easy to understand how the palliative of protective discrimination and the illusion of social mobility created by it are adopted by the ruling class to wean away and absorb the ablest elements among the scheduled castes. Thus, protective discrimination is an effective instrument of social control of groups which could otherwise prove to be potentially disruptive (see Jayaram 1981a: 14).

That the policy of protective discrimination is an effective instrument for buying peace is now well known. It was with the help of this policy that peace was bought from the depressed castes before Independence and more so at the time of drafting the Constitution of independent India. The continued anxiety to ensure this peace is seen in the uniform and unquestioned extension of the policy, six times beyond the initially stipulated period of ten years, without a comprehensive review of the results of its implementation so far.

Realising this, other 'dominant' caste groups have started demanding the shelter of the policy of protective discrimination. The innumerable committees and commissions charged with the investigation of the problem of backwardness have been dismayed at the large number of petitions and deputations proclaiming backwardness in order to be listed for benefits (see Dushkin 1972: 218; Government of Karnataka 1975). Knowing fully well the implications of the pressure potential of these groups, both the central and the state governments have extended the cover of the policy to other caste and community groups.

For instance, in Karnataka, of the 205 castes that the Backward Classes Commission appointed by the state government could distinguish, 197, constituting about 45 per cent (excluding the scheduled castes and tribes, who form another 14%) of the population were declared backward (Government of Karnataka 1975). With the exception of the concessions shown in the matter of eligibility requirements for admission to educational institutions and employment, virtually all the other benefits enjoyed by the scheduled castes are now extended to other 'backward' castes, classes, and communities as well. A similar situation exists in other states also. The extension of the special concessions and privileges to other castes and communities has virtually done away with the uniqueness of the scheduled castes. Thus, in addition to being perpetuated, the policy has been extended to a point where it loses its *raison d'être*.

Is Caste the Factor?

How the caste factor impinges on the educational situation of the scheduled castes is not clearly established. In fact, 'the disadvantages suffered by scheduled caste students at school and college do not seem to be substantively different from those suffered by others who are economically or culturally disadvantaged', states the author of the national study (Chitnis 1981: 165). To the extent that caste is subsumed under class, she opines, as far as education is concerned, 'it may be more advantageous to merge their cause with that of other disadvantaged sectors' (ibid.).

Presuming that caste is significant independently of class, the constitutional and administrative label 'scheduled castes' suggests too much of a homogeneity. That this is not so is confirmed by the inter-state and inter-caste variations in the educational progress and problems of the scheduled castes reported by the national study (see also Wankhede 2001).

Epilogue: Education for Social Transformation

The class nature of the scheduled caste problem has been analysed and it has been emphasised that the scheduled castes share a position of chronically inadequate material circumstance with many others in the existing socio-economic framework (see Jayaram 1981a). An overwhelming majority of the scheduled castes (about 90%) live in villages, mostly as landless labourers faced with irregular employment, onerous work, and low wages. But for the stigma of untouchability, they are not unlike the other rural proletariat. The socio-economic conditions of a majority of the urban scheduled castes, by and large, are on a par with those of the lowest social stratum in urban areas (Rajagopalan 1978).

Poverty, illiteracy, and ill-health are not exclusive to the scheduled castes and are to be found in every group irrespective of caste or religion:

> The tacit assumption that a man is comfortable or depressed because he belongs to a particular caste, and that these conditions are perpetual, is wrong. In some parts of the country, Brahmins are discriminated against because they are considered solely responsible for the centuries-old discrimination against the Harijans and other castes. Is turning caste system upside down an answer to the problem? Or, is it the transformation of the class basis of the caste system, which would weaken the latter's exploitative potency, which is needed? (Jayaram 1981a: 14).

It must be emphasised here that the structurally determined 'class' is more fundamental than the subjectively evaluated ephemeral notion of 'status'. What the scheduled castes need along with other exploited and oppressed sections of the society is collective emancipation from the structurally determined class position rather than the individual upward social mobility on the status scale within the *status quo*. That such class emancipation cannot take place *sui generis*, that is, from within the existing socio-economic framework and with the policy of protective discrimination alone, is being slowly realised. Formulating the problem for the *Seminar* on reservations, André Béteille (1981: 13) points out that, without a radical change in the structure of Indian society and a corresponding change in the mental horizons of people, there can be no real or meaningful change in the conditions of scheduled castes and of their class brethren. Intoxicated as it is with liberal ideology, is the ruling class willing to – or more appropriately, capable of – bringing about such a radical transformation is a moot question.

Ignoring this question for the time being, an important prerequisite for such a transformation is the recognition that it can come about only through a process of education whose aim is what Paulo Freire calls 'conscientisation' (1972b: 15). Conscientisation refers 'to learning to perceive social, political, and economic contradictions, and to take action against the oppressive elements of reality' (ibid.). This implies that, using education as the bedrock of social regeneration, people can be awakened to their suppressed and deprived conditions. A small section of the people getting higher education and becoming individually mobile does not help spread conscientisation; rather it would act as a wet blanket on conscientisation, keeping social awareness forever in swaddling-bands.

It is true that the spread of literacy and oracy through lower levels of education can play an important role in bringing about social transformation. But it is precisely at this level that the present system of schooling has failed. At the snail's pace at which the rate of literacy is growing it would take many more decades to reach a significant level. How long will it take for the oppressed sections in rural areas to reach the general level of literacy is anybody's guess.

Let alone the physical limits, the present system of education, premised as it is upon mobility ideology and welfare state policy, cannot be expected to undertake the historical task of social transformation. In fact, it seems to be an effective instrument for the maintenance of the *status quo*. This points to the need for a discussion on alternatives to the present system of education in the country.

While there is a lot for us to learn from the experience of countries like the People's Republic of China, as also from the educational thought of Paulo Freire, Ivan Illich, and company, we have no ready solutions to be derived from them. At the same time, since a radical alternative to the present system of education would upset the apple cart, the ruling class will certainly not take the initiative to search for it. The onus for solving it, therefore, falls on those who are committed to the emancipation of the oppressed as a collectivity.

Notes

1. This study surveyed a sample of 3,644 high school students (in fifteen states) and 3,263 college students (in fourteen states) belonging to the scheduled castes with the help of a standardised questionnaire.

2. Co-efficient of Equality =

$$\frac{\dfrac{\text{Enrolment of Scheduled Castes / Tribes}}{\text{Total Environment}}}{\dfrac{\text{Population of Scheduled Castes / Tribes}}{\text{Total Population}}}$$

   If the co-efficient of equality is 100, the enrolment of scheduled castes/tribes is in proportion to their population. If it is less than 100, it indicates that their enrolment is less than proportionate to their population (Commissioner 1980: 7).
3. In a recent study of 'pay back tendency' among dalit elites in five cities – Mumbai, Pune, Nashik, Nagpur, and Aurangabad – of Maharashtra, Prahlad G. Jogdand found that the beneficiaries of the reservation policy do not help out their community (see Srivastava 2014: 4). Asked 'Who benefit from these "creamy layer" elites?', Jogdand responded, 'Their children, mostly' (ibid.).
4. See Chapter 7 for a brief outline of this philosophy.

9

Value-Oriented Education and the Oppressed

> It would be better for men to be deprived of education than to receive their education from their masters; for education, in that sense, is no better than the training of cattle that are broken to the yoke.
>
> **Thomas Hodgskin**[1]

A majority of the oppressed do not *actually*[2] enter the school; a majority of those who do so drop out of it even before reaching the fourth standard and a small minority passes through the school mill spread over ten years; and only a microscopic minority reaches the carrot of occupational and professional status held out to those who complete collegiate education. Viewed in the light of these facts the debate about value-oriented education may seem irrelevant with reference to the oppressed sections of our society.

However, even the few among the oppressed who do get schooled have to pass through the state school system and even the 'sincere' effort at schooling those 'formally' enrolled has to be within its framework. Since this schooling is for a life fifteen or twenty years later, its value orientation is sure to have profound implications for society, in general, and the oppressed, in particular. It is this which makes exigent an examination of the meaning of value-oriented education of the oppressed.

The thesis that an ethical life demands some degree of effort and preparation is generally justified in the name of social order. Émile Durkheim (1956: 61–90), the classical French sociologist, characteristically expressed this when he observed that the major function of education is to inculcate some kind of moral discipline without which no society could survive. This thesis and its underlying rationale are particularly appealing now when social and political disorder is escalating and the moral fabric of society is wearing out alarmingly fast.

Whether moral or value-oriented education is a panacea for the degeneration a society is facing is questionable. The belief that it is so is grounded in an inadequate appreciation of the socio-economic roots of this degeneration. To expect a social reconstruction through sermons on ethics in the form of value-oriented education, and that too in the absence of any sincere attempt to resolve the socio-economic contradictions, is moonshine.

Also, the presumptions that morality can be taught as any other school subject and that the values imparted through the curriculum would be automatically internalised by the students are naive. In fact, a person can go through the whole process of schooling without really understanding a single idea in the sense of integrating it with his pre-existing experiences. This commonly happens to those whose native experiences and culture are not the same as those of the educated and the dominant classes who construct and impart their curriculum. This is what is expressed in the popular cliché that education is alienating.

Be that as it may, it is not the ineffectiveness of value-oriented education as the key to moral regeneration which is alarming; rather, it is the potential for indoctrination that such an education is fraught with. At a time when a large and complex contradiction-ridden society fails to confront the stresses that threaten it, and when violent repression is known to be counter-productive in the longer run, those steering the society, in their own self-interest at least, will have to turn to non-repressive mechanisms of 'gentling the masses'.

The school, as an 'ideological state apparatus' (Althusser 1971), is an obvious agency to be utilised for the desired process of domesticating the younger generation. This inevitably bewitches the mind, impairs critical thinking, contains radicalism, and curbs dissent. The resulting intellectual emasculation makes people accept the logic of the system under which they exist and facilitates their conformity to it.

How does all this matter to the oppressed? There is a hierarchical school system in the country reflecting and perpetuating social inequality. The schools vary in terms of the sources of finance, machinery for social control, medium of instruction, social milieu, process and direction of socialisation and, not the least, the class clientele. At the top of the hierarchy are the so-called 'public' schools – schools from which 'the great majority of the public are precluded from entering' (Tawney 1964: 78) – and their slightly faded versions in private/convent English-medium schools. At the bottom are the majority of the ill-maintained (more so in rural areas) vernacular-medium schools run either by the government itself or with its aid by private managements.

The former category of schools caters mainly to the children belonging to the ruling class, professional elite, and some middle-class mobiles. By and large, they raise their own funds and, consequently, enjoy relative autonomy in their functioning. But these generally exclusive and inaccessible schools do not pose a major threat to the dominant classes or to their establishment. On the contrary, they serve their interest by socialising successive generations of civil servants, army officers, professional elite, and managerial magnates who have, as is to be expected, internalised the values necessary for their dominance in the existing order.

On the other hand, the 'state' schools, which depend almost entirely on the public exchequer, cater to the oppressed by way of realising the statutory objective of universalising elementary education. These schools, no doubt, provide a schooled and differentiated labour force for the economy. But, given the worsening crisis due to socio-economic contradictions, they also constitute the breeding ground for discontentment and a mass base for potential unrest and a threat to the establishment.

In a study of political socialisation of school children, Ehsanul Haq (1981: 160) has delineated a positive relation between poverty, on the one hand, and non-conformity and militancy, on the other. Viewed in this light, it is easy to understand how value-oriented education can become an instrument for soothing discontent, enforcing conformity, and nipping in the bud any revolutionary mobilisation of the oppressed.

The ideology of value-oriented education also raises the key ethical issue of the justification of the values that are intended to be imparted. Values cannot be supported or refuted by reference to facts the way facts can be. They can be validated or rejected only by reference to other values. That is, value-oriented education presumes the need for a framework for the choice and evaluation of values.

Another related issue arises from the fact that values are embodied in a culture and are socially rooted. The promotion of certain values through the curriculum cannot *per se* represent the interests of all the sections of society. As Basil Bernstein says, 'how a society selects, classifies, distributes, transmits and evaluates educational knowledge it considers to be public, reflects both the distribution of power and the principles of social control' (1971: 47). Thus, the questions that arise are whose values are going to be embodied in value-oriented education and with what consequences?

A closer examination of our Constitution reveals its class character. Notwithstanding this, one would expect the government to use the Constitution as the framework for deriving the values to be embodied in the curriculum. Instead, we have heard persons in authority talking about identifying the 'uniquely Indian values'.[3] Such a search would, by inference, imply that the government is disillusioned with the values enshrined in the Constitution, which among others include equality, social justice, and freedom of opinion. In fact, it is these values which are most important for the oppressed in the present order, and substituting them with values 'uniquely' Indian would have pernicious consequences for the oppressed.

The quest for 'uniquely Indian values' would also call for a return to traditional standards of morality and excellence and, what is more, with an emphasis on didactic teaching. In its programme to Indianise teaching, the Working Group set up by the government to review teachers' training programme (in the light of the need for value-orientation) (see K. Joshi 1983) recommended that teachers should be exposed to ancient Indian concepts of psychology, spirituality, and esotericism! Such a 'rape of reason' through value-oriented education is sure to reinforce the current wave of revivalism. The resulting absence of a vision of a society looking forward could make revivalism a device for the retrogression of the oppressed.

Value-oriented education is advocated, plausibly enough, not as protecting the interests of particular classes or groups (which they, in fact, are), but as the only basis for a just and orderly society for all. To the gullible, unwary, and uncritical, such a stance has a far deeper consequence. The facts that the schooling of the oppressed is controlled by the state predominantly, that the state is the handmaid of the dominant classes and groups, and that the move is for a search for 'uniquely Indian values' outside the Constitution, would assuredly result in value-oriented education fostering a 'culture of silence' among the oppressed.

Apart from these, value-oriented education has certain latent consequences which are detrimental to the oppressed. Value-oriented education, especially the ethical component in it, is sure to be a shadowy counterpart to religious instruction. Considering the great pressure to which secularism is currently subjected to in a multi-religious country like ours, one can well imagine the consequences of such religious indoctrination in the name of value-oriented education.

Moreover, in the zeal for value-oriented education, its advocates seem to have overlooked the problem of consensus in values in a pluralistic society which is in a flux. One need not labour hard to realise that the possibility of arriving at a consensus on prime values in the present state of religious and cultural diversity is fortuitous. And any explicit effort at listing values to be embodied in the school curriculum will definitely give rise to social tensions. In both these cases social polarisation and conflicts may take place in ways which are divisive of the oppressed and harmful to them in the long run.

In any successful programme of education, teachers play a pivotal role. Presuming that it is possible to teach anything to any child, can it be taught by any teacher? A cursory look at the data on the socio-economic background of our school teachers confirms that, by and large, they belong to the dominant sections rather than to the oppressed. These teachers have as much a vested interest in the present system as those who manipulate, direct, and control it. As such, what would be their predisposition to the oppressed and the latter's emancipation can be anybody's guess.

The report in the press about a school in Mehekar village in Amravati District in Maharashtra where the seventh standard students allegedly tore off pages from a book containing a lesson on Dr B.R. Ambedkar following an order from their teacher, according to whom Dr Ambedkar was an untouchable and not a fit topic for instruction in the school, is a pointer.[4]

A few teachers from among the oppressed sections could be expected to act as catalysts in bringing about a critical awareness among their brethren. But, if the Report of the Working Group noted above is any indication, even these few teachers will be made instruments of manipulation in the hands of the dominant classes. As to the others, the proposed teachers' training programme would only provide legitimacy to what they have already been doing.

In brief, the context in which the need for a value-oriented education has been conceived and the direction in which it is likely to move seem to confirm the suspicion that value-oriented education would be a subtle tool for containing any possible disruptive behaviour on the part of the oppressed and submerging them in a situation in which critical awareness and response are practically impossible.

An ideal society focuses on the promotion of 'the good of *every* human being and of the *whole* human being'. No society moves towards such an ideal on its own. Society is changed by human beings. To the extent that there is as much a vested interest in maintaining the *status quo* as there is in bringing about a change, social conflict is real and inevitable.

The oppressed sections of the society who are in effect defenceless should be inculcated with values which would strengthen them to face such a realistic social conflict. This implies two interrelated things. The oppressed should be helped to perceive the social, political, and economic contradictions in their existential situation. And, being conscious of such contradictions, they should be prepared to deal critically with the oppressive elements of reality. A prime requisite for bringing about change towards an ideal society through such 'conscientisation' (Freire 1972b: 15) is the promotion of the confidence of the oppressed in their own power.

This has certain implications. The vision of a schooling system should necessarily grow out of the vision of an ideal society for the oppressed, and at the same time it should also be the most powerful agency in realising that vision. Equally important, '"the fight for state power" and (for) "educational change" are not mutually exclusive acts, the one to be preceded or followed by the other; they are mutually necessary aspects of the same political process' (Frith and Corrigan 1977: 264). And, a 'pedagogy of the oppressed' must be 'forged *with*, not *for*' the oppressed in the incessant struggle to regain humanity (Freire 1972b: 25).

Unfortunately, neither the social nor the educational development in the country is taking place in this direction. The talk about radical reconstruction of education, as also the call for social revolution and eradication of poverty, in the last six decades has remained only slogans. What has been achieved, in fact, is only moderate reformism.

One aspect of this reformism is the notion of 'quality of opportunity'.[5] This notion has made the oppressed the object of humanitarianism and the implied 'false generosity' has foisted an illusion of amelioration upon them. At best what this can achieve is in making access to classes more open to each generation of competitors, especially to those who had hitherto been deprived of it. But it leaves totally untouched the bases of classes themselves. And, if the oppressed are 'unable' to benefit from the state generosity, the blame is squarely placed upon them by individualising failure. This has a fatalistic consequence for the oppressed.

Obviously the school cannot be expected to function as a liberating force within the existing socio-economic framework. The onus for evolving and practising a 'pedagogy of the oppressed' thus falls on those who are genuinely committed to the emancipation of the oppressed as a collectivity. Considering the role that education can play in bringing about a revolution or preventing it, one is reminded in conclusion of the need to 'rescue education from the influence of the ruling class', recognised by Karl Marx and Friedrich Engels (1976: 502) as early as 1848.

Notes

1. Epigraph quoted in Simon (1960: 215).
2. This is as against the fictitious enrolment by school authorities to satisfy the government.

3. Some of these values, according to them, are tolerance, purity, renunciation, search for knowledge (rather than for power), and adherence to duty.
4. *Indian Express,* Bangalore, 15 February 1984, p. 1.
5. As Entwistle notes,

   It almost seems that the word equality is an accidental occurrence in the phrase (or perhaps, cynically included to exploit its emotive overtones), where everything really hangs on the word 'opportunity' which, in turn, seems logically inconsistent with the notion of equality (1977: 9).

10

Education and Emancipation

The Saga and Ideology of Dr B.R. Ambedkar

> To educate untouchables is, in a profound sense, to liberate them.
>
> **Oliver Mendelsohn and Marika Vicziany** (1990: 284)

Introduction: Education, Leadership, and Emancipation

That education is a *sine qua non* for the emancipation of a chronically exploited and inhumanly oppressed section of society has come to be accepted as a sociological axiom both by academics and policy makers.[1] The realisation of the need for education of such suppressed groups, and of education's potential in emancipating their members, can come about exogenously or endogenously. The nature and significance of the sources of such realisation are varied.

In India, the exogenous realisation of the importance of educating the depressed classes[2] has come about as part of an

I dedicate this chapter to the memory of the late Professor C. Parvathamma of the Department of Sociology, University of Mysore, at whose instance its ideas were originally articulated. I thank Professor R. Govinda and Professor Avinash K. Singh for their kind invitation to write them up as a paper for presentation at the Anil Bordia Memorial Policy Seminar on 'Education and Social Empowerment: Policies and Practices', National University of Educational Planning and Administration, New Delhi, 16–17 December 2013.

enlightened policy perspective. Its roots can be traced to the influence of the western liberal ideology to which the social reformers and the leaders of the freedom movement were exposed as a part of their education and cultural socialisation. Its culmination is to be found in the constitutional provisions relating to the education of the depressed classes and the various educational programmes formulated and implemented by the successive governments and their agencies.

How sincere the external agencies are in their concern for the educational advancement of the depressed classes is a moot question. But it is certain that the educational efforts on the part of the external agencies assume the form of a conscious intervention in a given socio-economic and cultural situation. They are perceived and reacted to by the depressed classes accordingly. The objectives of the educational programmes and the sincerity with they are implemented as experienced and interpreted by the depressed classes, no doubt, distort the scenario.

On the other hand, the endogenously generated realisation of the need for and the importance of education on the part of the depressed classes in the amelioration of their socio-economic and cultural conditions could be expected to result in a better appreciation of the educational objectives. This may, in turn, be expected to enhance the demand for more and better educational facilities for their wards. And, in the long run, all this may result in the fruition of the emancipatory objectives of education.

Of course, it could be argued that the endogenous and exogenous sources of realisation operate dialectically and dynamically, so that each of them reinforces the other. While these two sources of realisation are *not* mutually exclusive, their inter-bearing in a socio-historical situation is too complex to permit easy grasping, let alone the gauging of their relative significance. Nevertheless, the qualitative significance of the endogenous source of realisation, given the quantitative inputs of the endogenous, can hardly be gainsaid. Indeed, no socio-economic programme can be expected to succeed if the people at whom it is directed do not accept it in the spirit in which it is conceived and appreciate its intrinsic worth.

However, the endogenous realisation does not come about among all, or even most of the members of the depressed classes, who are remarkably heterogeneous themselves. Its origin and spread is a protracted process. Paradoxically, sometimes the external agencies themselves try to foster such a realisation through propaganda and awareness-building campaigns. Given the background of the nature of social relations between members manning the external agencies and the depressed classes, the moves of the former may be suspect in the eyes of the latter, or it may imply a new mode of the latter's subservience to the former.

It is in this context that the role of the endogenous leadership of the depressed classes becomes crucial. However, if this leadership is itself uneducated, then it may not be helpful in leading these classes to deliverance. That is, in the ultimate analysis, the emancipation of the depressed classes depends upon the committed and enlightened leadership of the educated among them. Such a leadership can awaken consciousness among their uneducated brethren, fight for their educational rights and facilities, and may even bend the exogenous agencies towards this end.

It should, however, be pointed out that there is no guarantee that the enlightened leadership will always be in control of the depressed classes. What use the educated members of these classes will put their education to? How far does the objective of their emancipation guide their attitudes and actions? How do they respond to the initiatives and programmes of the external agencies? What reactions do they provoke and crystallise in the wider community? And what prospects are there for the total emancipation of the depressed classes? The answers to these questions, which one inevitably encounters in the educational route to the emancipation of the depressed classes, can only come from detailed empirical research.

In examining the nature and significance of the endogenous realisation of the need for and importance of education for the emancipation of the depressed classes with reference to India, one has perforce to focus on the saga and ideology of Dr Bhimrao Ramji Ambedkar (1891–1956). Ambedkar perhaps had the highest academic credentials for an Indian in his days, and to this day, as for that matter. His academic laurels included MA, PhD, LlD, DSc, DLitt, and Bar-at-Law;[3] none of this was honorary, but all of them were earned by him the hard way (see Box). He championed the cause of the depressed classes with so much zeal and determination as no other leader of these classes has done or will ever do. And the cornerstone of his emancipatory strategy was the unbridled faith that he reposed in education.

The Educational Saga of Ambedkar[4]

Ambedkar was born on 14 April 1891 at Mhow, near Indore, into the Mahar caste, one of the populous 'untouchable' castes. His ancestral family in Ambavade village in Mandangad taluk in Ratnagiri district of the erstwhile Bombay Province (now in Maharashtra), was of some consequence as it had 'the honour of keeping the palanquin of the village goddess' (Keer 2009: 8). Both his grandfather, Maloji Sakpal, and his father, Ramji Sakpal (1848–1913), had served the British army.

Compared to the cultural standards of the mass of the depressed classes, Ambedkar's kin circle was certainly characterised by 'high' culture. His maternal grandfather and maternal uncles were Subhedar Majors in the army. They belonged to the Kabir Panth, and discussed its philosophy and theology. His father was an intensely religious person who was interested in the spiritual development of his children. He had an excellent command over the Marathi language and an abiding interest in the works of Marathi saint poets. He was a trained teacher, who knew English, and had served as a headmaster in the military school. And, he was very much concerned with the social problems of his day.

Thus, Ambedkar had a good start in the first school of life, namely, family. He immensely benefitted from his father's command over language and familiarity with literature. As Dhananjay Keer puts it succinctly, Ambedkar 'derived from his father his painstaking spirit, his forceful mental energy, and his intense interest in the welfare of his society' (ibid.: 12).

Ambedkar began his primary education along with his elder brother Anandrao at Daopoli when he was five years old. He completed it and entered the Government High School at Satara,[5] where his father had secured a job in the military quarters. He finally completed his high school education at the Elphinstone High School, a leading institution in Bombay (now Mumbai), to which city his father had moved after completing the assignment at Satara.

It was during his school days that Ambedkar painfully realised what the stigma of untouchability meant. At school he was treated indifferently and was humiliated often. He was made to sit in a corner of the classroom on a piece of gunny bag, which he carried to the school. Some teachers would not touch his notebooks. He was forced to take up Persian as the second language, as the Sanskrit pandit refused to teach Sanskrit to 'untouchables'.[6] And, the curse of untouchability was not confined to the school premises alone.

Considering the cultural legacy that he had inherited from his illustrious father, it is no wonder that young Ambedkar vowed to devote himself to free his brethren from the inhuman yoke of social slavery. He came to view his intellectual exercises as an attempt to educate people to overcome the constraints imposed by the caste system. In his Preface to *Who Were the Shurdras?*, he defined the objective of the treatise as one 'of educating and thereby preparing the *Shudra* fully for ... (the) sacred task' of destroying the *Chaturvarna* system, which has been the primary bane of their degradation (1946: xxii).

Ambedkar passed his matriculation examination in 1907,[7] and since this was an extraordinary achievement for a Mahar, it was celebrated by the community at a public meeting. One of the speakers at this meeting was Krishnaji Arjun Keluskar (1860–1934), a high school teacher, scholar, and social reformer. Keluskar, a Brahmin, had been impressed by the studious habits of Ambedkar, whom he used to meet in the evenings in a public garden. He encouraged Ambedkar's academic endeavours and shaped his future life in many ways, of which two deserve special mention.

Keluskar lent young Ambedkar books and presented him with a copy of his new booklet, *Bhagwan Gautam Buddhache Charitra* (in Marathi, on the life of Gautama Buddha) (1898). This little gift enkindled Ambedkar's interest in Buddha, of whose teachings he made a systematic study later on (see Ambedkar 1957), led him to advocate conversion to Buddhism, and made him become a Buddhist himself toward the fag end of his life.

More important, knowing the difficult economic circumstances of Ambedkar's family, Keluskar helped him to prosecute his college education. Keluskar took Ambedkar to Maharaja Sayojirao Gaekwad (1863–1939) of Baroda (now Vadodara), who had a few days earlier announced his intention to help 'any worthy Untouchable in the prosecution of higher studies' (Keer 2009: 21). The Maharaja granted him a monthly stipend of 25 rupees, which was a big sum in those days.

Ambedkar joined the Elphinstone College, Bombay, where he was helped by Professor Muller. He passed the Bachelor of Arts degree examination of the University of Bombay in 1912. After a brief and unhappy stint in the service of the Baroda State, and again upon Keluskar's initiative, Ambedkar was awarded a scholarship for higher studies in the United States of America by the Maharaja of Baroda in June 1913. This was, indeed, 'an epoch-making event', 'an event of enormous magnitude for an Untouchable' (ibid.: 26).

In July 1913, Ambedkar joined the Columbia University in New York. Here he came under the tutelage of Professor Edwin Robert Anderson Seligman (1861–1939). He took up political science, moral philosophy, anthropology, sociology, and economics as subjects for his study. In June 1915, he obtained the Master of Arts degree with a dissertation on *Administration and Finance of East India Company*. A year later, in June 1916, his doctoral thesis titled *National Dividend in India: A Historical and Analytical Study*[8] was accepted by the Columbia University.

During his stay at Columbia University, Ambedkar also came into contact with the great American educationist and pragmatic philosopher John Dewey (1859–1952). It was perhaps Dewey's philosophy of instrumentalism which might have led Ambedkar to undertake a critical analysis of concrete social problems and search for practical solutions for them. Ambedkar 'fully endorsed Dewey's emphasis on education as a means to change the world and not merely to understand it' (Lokhande 1977: 10).

After an extremely successful career at the Columbia University, in October 1916, Ambedkar joined the London School of Economics for the degree of Master of Science (Economics) and Doctor of Science (Economics), and the Greys Inn for Law. Unfortunately for him, the end of Baroda benevolence meant that he had to return to India. After serving the Baroda State for a brief period, and doing odd jobs for some time, Ambedkar was, in November 1918, appointed Professor of Political Economy in the Sydenham College of Commerce and Economics, Bombay.

Keen to complete his unfinished studies in London, Ambedkar saved money from his salary and, in March 1920, he resigned his job and went to London. 'Surely any ordinary man in his place would not have bothered to study further after being MA, PhD and having a nice job of professorship at a salary of Rs 450 per month ...' (Ahir 1990: 10). In June 1921, Ambedkar was awarded the degree of Master of Science (Economics) by the University of London for his thesis titled *Provincial Decentralisation of Imperial Finance in British India.* In October 1922, he was called to the Bar. He also spent three months at the University of Bonn, Germany, studying economics.

Financial constraints and domestic compulsions forced Ambedkar to return to Bombay in April 1923. A few days later he submitted his thesis *The Problem of the Rupee,*[9] for which he was awarded the Doctor of Science (Economics) degree by the University of London. As Keer notes, 'a long laborious industry, iron will and conquering intellect won at last a great victory' (2009: 49).

It should be emphasised here that a crucial factor responsible for Ambedkar's unprecedented academic achievements was his singular devotion to studies. It has been observed that during his school and college days 'he used to get up at two o'clock at night as he found the early morning hours most suitable for attentive studies' (Ahir 1990: 6). Keer records Ambedkar's college mates in New York recalling with pride 'how Ambedkar seized every possible hour for his study for which he said he had been given a life's opportunity' (2009: 28). 'For eighteen hour a day went on the endless digging for knowledge and this continued for months together' – so describes Keer, Ambedkar's *Dnyana Yadnya* (ibid.: 28–29).

Ambedkar's singular devotion to studies and his unstinted commitment to purpose is revealed by his solemn refusal to be drawn into politics during his student days. A frequent visitor to Columbia University Library during Ambedkar's stay in New York was Lala Lajpat Rai, the great nationalist leader from Punjab. Ambedkar attracted Rai's attention and the latter asked him to join the political party which he was organising in America to help India. While Ambedkar was not averse to politics, he politely declined Rai's invitation on the ground that he was in America for pursuing higher studies and he wanted that mission to be fulfilled first (see Ahir 1990: 8).

Ambedkar was a bibliophile and a voracious reader. He had an insatiable desire for possessing books, and browsing through the second-hand bookshops was his favourite leisure-time activity. M.S. Gore draws attention to the fact that Ambedkar 'had stinted himself even in days of economic hardship as a student in London, in order to buy books' (1993: 209). Gore doubts, 'except for Nehru ... whether there was any one else in that generation of leaders who loved books more' (ibid.). Ambedkar was keener to read books other than what the curriculum wanted him to. This explains how he turned out to be a bright scholar who was penetratingly insightful as he was enormously versatile.[10] No wonder, M.N. Roy described Ambedkar as 'one of the finest flowers of the twentieth century renaissance' (quoted in Lokhande 1977: 250).

For all his academic achievements and scholarly contributions, Ambedkar was remarkably humble. He never forgot his benefactors who were responsible for what he turned out to be. This is evident from the fact that he dedicated his *The Problem of the Rupee* respectfully to his parents as a token of 'my abiding gratitude for the sacrifice they made and the enlightenment they showed in the matter of my education' (1927). Similarly, his book *The Evolution of Provincial Finance in British India* was dedicated to the Maharaja Sayojirao Gaekwad of Baroda with the inscription 'my gratitude to his help in the matter of my education' (1925).

Education for Emancipation

Ambedkar was acutely conscious of the educational backwardness of his people.[11] Reflecting on his own experience, he recognised that education was a great means to forge their progress. Education, he believed, was important not only because it would help them qualify for government jobs, 'but it was equally essential for gaining an awareness of the social and political environment in which they functioned, and which they had to fight' (Gore 1993: 209). He exhorted his followers to give proper education to their wards and he repeatedly emphasised that parents can mould the destiny of their children by getting them educated. In a letter he wrote from New York in 1913 to a friend of his father, he concluded: 'let your mission ... be to educate and preach the idea of education to those at least who are near to and in close contact with you' (quoted in Keer 2009: 27). In fact, in his later politically active life he came to attach so much importance to education that he gave it primacy in his slogan for action, namely, 'educate, agitate, and organise'. This slogan, which Ambedkar had formulated at the time of founding the Bahiskrita Hitakari Sabha (Depressed Classes Welfare Association) on 20 July 1924, 'was repeated in different ways and with newer emphases through many years of political travail' (Gore 1993: 214).

Ambedkar took an abiding interest in the dissemination of education among his people.[12] Beginning in June 1928, he started many hostels at Panvel, Poona (now Pune), Nasik, Sholapur, Thane, and Dharwar (now Dharwad). To organise school education of his people on a sound basis, he established the Depressed Classes Education Society on 14 June 1928. The Society collected donations and grants, provided students with boarding and lodging facilities, and met their other academic requirements. The Society, thus, contributed a lot to the promotion of school education among the children of the depressed classes.

Ambedkar's ultimate ambition, however, was to provide higher education to the depressed classes on par with the advanced sections of society. This ambition was grounded in his strong belief, expressed succinctly in his speech on the occasion of the foundation stone laying ceremony of Milind Mahavidyalaya, that it was only higher education which would help to remove from his unfortunate brethren:

> that inferiority complex which has stunted their growth and made them slaves to others, to create in them the consciousness of the significance of their lives for themselves and for the country of which they have been cruelly robbed by the existing social order (quoted in Ahir 1990: 141).

Moreover, he knew that higher education was indispensable for them to qualify for positions of power and prestige in the administration.

Ambedkar's ambition started taking shape in July 1945 with the founding of the People's Education Society by him, and the establishment of the first college, the Siddarth College, under the Society's auspices in 1946. As a Labour Member in the Viceroy's Executive Council (1942–46), Ambedkar persuaded Viceroy Lord Linlithgow and his Cabinet colleagues to grant assistance to this college which had been established with the explicit purpose of benefitting the downtrodden classes. Today, the People's Education Society, which runs scores of colleges catering to thousands of students, about one-third of whom hail from the

Buddhist and the scheduled caste families, is a standing monument to the crusading mission of Ambedkar as a great educationist (see Ahir 1990: 142).

In this context, it must be observed following Barbara R. Joshi that, since the untouchable community had not been allowed to develop a tradition of education, Ambedkar's extraordinary educational achievement and self-development represented 'a major departure from conventional mores and became another key element in a new philosophy' (1982: 51). In fact, Joshi's discussions with scheduled caste college students revealed that 'these ideas are still influential, even where Ambedkar is known only through oral folklore' (ibid.). The salutary example of Ambedkar's achievements is also highlighted by a college student interviewed by Owen M. Lynch:

> 'Parents hold up Dr Ambedkar as a model to children and tell them how he became educated by his own efforts and worked hard ...' This model is continually reinforced in the many songs and poems which have been composed about Ambedkar and his deeds (1972: 109).

Thoughts on Educational Strategy

Ambedkar did not pen a compendium of his educational thought, nor are his views on educational policy presented cogently in a single book or paper. His views on educational policy in general and on the education of the depressed classes in particular are spread over his various writings, speeches, letters, etc. Based on his speeches and interventions in the debates at various legislative forums, let us briefly outline the policy perspective on education as envisaged by him.

Ambedkar emphasised the need for state intervention in education in the form of increased expenditure in this vital area. Intervening in the debate in the Bombay Legislative Council on grants for education, he argued 'that unless we spend a sufficient amount of money, to see that every child that enters a school reaches the fourth standard, what we have already spent upon him is of no purpose whatsoever' (reprinted in Government of Maharashtra 1982: 40). According to Ambedkar, 'it is only fair that our educational expenditure should be so adjusted that we should spend on the education of the people as much as we take from them in the form of excise' (ibid.).

An important reason for Ambedkar's emphasis on the need for the government to spend more on education was to ensure that education is not the exclusive preserve and privilege of any caste, class, or community. He wanted to ensure that it is brought within the reach of everyone. This is particularly important in view of the widespread inequalities in access to education in terms of caste and class. As long as inequality of educational opportunities was rooted in the unequal status and progress of different castes and communities, Ambedkar argued, equalising opportunities will not be of any avail. He believed 'that equality of treatment of people who are unequal is simply another name for indifferentism and neglect' (in Government of Maharashtra 1982: 42).

In a later work, *Mr Gandhi and the Emancipation of the Untouchables* (1943), Ambedkar tried to elucidate the sociological principle that equality of opportunities without equality of living conditions can hardly be expected to result in equality of outcomes. Whether an open competitive system for recruitment into the public service is socially justifiable, he observed, depends upon the nature of the educational system. 'Is it sufficiently democratic? Are the facilities for education sufficiently widespread and sufficiently used to permit persons from all classes to come forth to compete?' (reprinted in Government of Maharashtra 1991: 417). He noted that, in India, the answer to both these questions is negative:

> Higher education in India is a monopoly of Hindus and particularly of high caste Hindus. By reason of Untouchability the Untouchables are denied the opportunity for education. By reason of their poverty higher education necessary for higher posts in the public service ... is not within their reach. The state will not take the financial responsibility of giving them higher education ... so that to ask the Untouchables to rely upon the results of competitive examination for entry into the public services is to practice a fraud upon them (ibid.: 417–18).

Ambedkar, therefore, contended that if the depressed classes 'are to be brought to the level of equality then the only remedy is to adopt the principle of inequality and give favoured treatment to those who are below the level' (Government of Maharashtra 1982: 42). Thus, early on, Ambedkar consciously reposed faith in the liberal strategy for the emancipation of the downtrodden through the policy of protective discrimination. He ensured that this ideological element was finally enshrined in the republication Constitution of India, and it has become an effective instrument of social welfare in the decades following Independence.

Ambedkar was critically conscious of what he was pleading for while demanding representation for the depressed classes in the legislative bodies associated with education. For instance, intervening in the debate in the Bombay Legislative Council on the Bombay University Act Amendment Bill, he emphasised the 'necessity for the representation of communities which are not intellectually advanced, on the Senate of the Bombay University' (ibid.: 50) and clarified that such a representation is not sought in the Academic Council or Syndicate, 'bodies which are to be manned by experts' (ibid.: 52).

Ambedkar was critical of the general policy of giving scholarships to the students from the depressed classes. According to him, given the chronic poverty background of their families, the parents have tendency to use the scholarship amount to meet domestic expenses. As such, the goal of education will not be achieved. He was, therefore, in favour of diverting the scholarship amount towards building hostels. During the debate on grants for education referred to earlier, he noted that 'a hostel ... weans the boy from evil surroundings. It provides effective inspection. And when a hostel is managed by private agency, it will mean some saving of money to Government' (see ibid.: 44).

While emphasising the need for protective discrimination, Ambedkar also recognised that it cannot be a permanent measure. It was only a crutch, and not a substitute for healthy legs. He remonstrated with his people that 'if you believe in living a respectable life, you believe in self-help which is the best help!' (quoted in Keer 2009: 60). Whenever he addressed students he made it a point to tell them that they should view the opportunity for education as 'a challenge thrown to them by the orthodoxy which believed in the myth created by Manu that the untouchables were incapable of learning' (Ahir 1990: 141).

Reform through Education Versus Political Action

The fact that Ambedkar was fired by a liberalist reformative zeal for the uplifting of the depressed classes does not mean that he was agreeable to set it in the mould of a gradual process of painless change. He tried to combine it with 'a deeply personal sense of the urgency of social action for this cause' (Kumar 1991: 103). The political conditions prevailing in the 1930s provided him with the base and scope to rise as a political leader.

Being entangled in the domain of turbulent politics, Ambedkar's attention was diverted from the education of the depressed classes. Keer notes that 'there was something in Ambedkar that motivated him ... to astonish and electrify his great contemporaries and to show that he was an equal of those who ranked the highest on earth. To such an ambitious nature politics is a more congenial field than a social one' (2009: 126).

According to Keer, the change in Ambedkar's strategy should not, however, be interpreted as one of relegating education to the background. Rather, it should be seen as an outcome of his diagnosis of the Indian situation. Thus, since Ambedkar thought 'that by investing his people with political equality and political power the problem of their education would be automatically solved through governmental efforts and agencies, he devoted his time and talent more to securing political rights than to securing education uplift' (ibid.).

In Retrospect: A Critique

Notwithstanding the sincere and herculean efforts of Ambedkar to seek emancipation of his people through education, it can hardly be gainsaid that the change has not been as radical as he himself would have expected it to be. It is true that a small section of the depressed classes has been upwardly mobile socio-economically, a section whom Lelah Dushkin calls as a 'new class' (1972: 212). But, the overwhelming majority of his brethren, especially those living in rural areas, not only continue to be poverty stricken and illiterate but are also the butt of social humiliation, inhuman oppression, and economic exploitation (see Shah et al. 2006; see also Thorat 2009).

It can, however, hardly be denied that but for Ambedkar's yeoman efforts and the resulting policy of protective discrimination, the depressed classes would not have been able to make whatever progress they have so far achieved. Nor can it be ignored that, towards the fag end of his life, Ambedkar was growing impatient with the pace and nature of change among his people. It is against this background that a critical appraisal of Ambedkar's strategy for emancipation through education becomes relevant.

It is necessary to emphasise that by his early socialisation Ambedkar was a social reformer, by his education and training he was a liberal, and in his political ideology he was a social democrat. Both in India and abroad Ambedkar's education was in the humanities and social sciences rather than in science, engineering, or medicine. During his youth he came under the influence of western liberal values and beliefs, which came to be reflected in his ideas and speeches, and dress and deportment. And his reading of political history and his study of law shaped him as a social democrat in politics, which is evidenced in his political career since the 1930s and in his role as the chief architect of the Constitution.

Of specific importance to our purpose here is one element of the liberal ideology to which Ambedkar committed himself and the state and that is the policy of protective discrimination, especially in the sphere of education. A detailed examination of this policy as a strategy for emancipation is beyond the scope of this chapter (see Chapter 8 in this book). What is, however, necessary to note is that this policy is premised upon the assumption that 'an unjust social order can be treated as a market' (Kumar 1991: 106).

The one point that has been substantiated by sociology since the World War II is that as long as the underlying competitive morality of the market remains untouched, no radical change is possible. In fact, what the policy of protective discrimination does at best is to equip certain individuals of the depressed classes better for facing the competitive scene of the market, and thereby inadvertently validate that morality.

Thus, as Krishna Kumar observes,

> Even though the state ends up improving the lot of a few individuals who would otherwise have no chance of betterment in an unjust social order, it actually perpetuates the social order in which injustice is inevitable for a far greater number of individuals. The state's help creates the hope of individual ascent among members of the lower strata, a hope which apparently acts as an instrument capable of perpetuating the prevailing social order (ibid.).

One aspect of the educational component of the policy of protective discrimination highlighted by Kumar deserves special consideration. That is, the arguments for equality in the realm of education, as also the indicators chosen for evaluating its effectiveness, have as their referents factors extrinsic to educational experience, such as 'the representation of different social groups at different levels of education system and in the pyramid of the job market' (ibid.: 107). Criteria such as 'the treatment of children from the lower strata at the hands of teachers in actual pedagogic settings' and 'the share of symbols representing the lower strata in the curriculum of schools and colleges' (ibid.), which are intrinsic to the education system are hardly ever used. A closer examination of the evidence would convince that after over six decades of Independence there is hardly anything to cheer about (see Kumar 1991: 107–09; see also Kumar 1989: 59–77; Jayaram 1990: 143–49).

The liberal ideology for the emancipation of the downtrodden has a crucial weakness, that is, it treats the individual as the unit of society. Because this idea was firmly ingrained in Ambedkar's programme of action, he could never reconcile himself with the possibility of mobilising the downtrodden on class lines. In fact, he was averse to the Communist ideology. So, when he became impatient with the pace and nature of change being experienced by his people, the only alternative strategy he could think of was conversion to Buddhism. But then proselytism itself has serious limitations as a strategy for emancipation (see Jayaram 2004).

Another aspect of the critique concerns leadership. Concluding his chapter on Ambedkar's fight for human rights, G.S. Lokhande aptly observes,

> The cretinizing (*sic*) influence of an iniquitous social order eulogistically designated as the oldest civilisation cannot be rid of within the short span of a few decades howsoever earnest be the efforts in that direction. The progress achieved so far is indicative of the tremendous possibilities lying ahead. It is the responsibility of the new generation of enlightened men and women to carry forward the mission of Dr Ambedkar with renewed vigour and determination (1977: 234).

Herein lies a queer irony of history.

Ambedkar emerged as a great leader from within the stratum which was the lowest and most depressed and despised. The facilities were meagre and the hurdles were numerous. He struggled hard and had to depend on the benevolence of others to establish himself. The essence of his own achievements he tried to pass on to his people. And, because of his ceaseless efforts facilities for education came to be available to the depressed classes on an unprecedented scale and they were provided a protective umbrella by the Constitution.

Unfortunately, however, these facilities and protective measures have not produced a second leader of the stature and eminence of Ambedkar (Isaacs 1965), a leader who is not drawn into embourgeoisement, a leader who is not enamoured of political offices, and a leader who will not allow his people to be used for narrow political gains. Rather, as Eleanor Zelliot observes, they seem to have 'inhibited the emergence of a new Mahatma decrying passionately against remaining injustices, or the development of a separatist Untouchable leader capable of building a movement outside the walls of government privilege and patronage' (1972: 93). Worse still, they have 'walled off the continuing problems of the Untouchable from the Indian consciousness' (ibid.).

It is often complained that some clever elements have been capitalising on Ambedkar's name. Since enterprise in education is thriving, and since such enterprise established to supposedly further the cause of the education of the depressed classes carries concessions in various matters and a preferential treatment in grants-in-aid, several educational institutions have sprung up using Ambedkar's name. Considering the principles and causes which Ambedkar espoused, he would certainly not have allowed such misuse and debasement.

One is reminded in this context of the meeting of the Scheduled Castes organisations held at Nare Park, Bombay on 28 September 1952, when Ambedkar 'publicly criticised the organisers of the Building Fund and asked the organisers to submit accounts immediately' (Keer 2009: 444). He even said 'that he had lost faith in the educated men of his community and pinned his faith on the illiterate' (ibid.).

As it has happened to many a great historic figure, perhaps the greatest damage to the cause and struggle of Ambedkar has been the deification of his personality. In the ritualisation of his movement the essence of his mission has been given the go by. The need of the day is thus for another endogenous leader who can stand on the shoulders of this illustrious giant and see the distant objective of all-round emancipation of his people and, taking stock of the existing situation, carve out a path for realising it.

Notes

1. Although education is a 'soft prescription', Mendelsohn and Vicziany aver, 'in the present (non-revolutionary) circumstances it alone can produce *new* men and women' (1990: 284).
2. The phrase 'depressed classes' is used here to refer to those who are officially called 'the scheduled castes'. The term 'untouchables', which is *not* necessarily coterminous with either of these, is used synonymously for convenience.
3. Dr Ambedkar was also conferred Honorary Doctor of Laws degrees by the Columbia University, New York, in June 1952 and the Osmania University, Hyderabad, in January 1953.
4. In outlining this section, I have drawn heavily upon Keer's excellent and the most popular biography of Dr Ambedkar in English (Keer 2009; see also Keer 1982). I have also used Ahir's account of Dr Ambedkar's legacy (Ahir 1990), and the 'Chronology' prepared by Rodrigues (2002: 555–59).
5. It was in this school, impressed by Ambedkar, his Brahmin teacher changed Ambedkar's surname from Ambavadekar (derived from his ancestral village) to Ambedkar (the teacher's own surname) (see Keer 2009: 14).
6. It is noteworthy that in his later life Ambedkar became a scholar of this 'forbidden language'.
7. He secured only 282 out of 750 marks (that is, 37.60%). But, as Keer notes, 'this scoring of average number of marks is not uncommon in case of ambitious boys whose minds are absorbed in subjects other than the texts and who became great in their future lives' (2009: 19).
8. An extension of the thesis was published in 1925 by P.S. King and Sons, London, under the title *The Evolution of Provincial Finance in British India.*
9. This was published in 1927 by P.S. King and Co., London.
10. For a comprehensive bibliography of Ambedkar's works, see Kadam (1991: 132–35) and Rodrigues (2002: 535–40). Rodrigues also

provides a brief guide to Ambedkar's writings (ibid.: 540–46) and biographies (ibid.: 546–47) and secondary writings (ibid.: 547–52).

11. See 'Statement Concerning the State of Education of the Depressed Classes in the Bombay Presidency', submitted by Ambedkar on behalf of the Bahiskrita Hitakari Sabha to the Indian Statutory Commission on 29 May 1928 (Government of Maharashtra 1982: 407–28). In fact, 'in 1920 in the whole of Bombay Presidency with a Depressed Classes population of 16 lakhs, there was only one BA (that was Ambedkar) and six matriculates' (Ahir 1990: 138).
12. Mahatma Jyotiba Phule (1827–90) was the first social reformer to establish a school for the education of the untouchables (Mangs and Mahars) (Lokhande 1977: 228). Ambedkar held Mahatma Phule in so great an admiration that he dedicated his book *Who Were the Shudras?* (1946) to his memory.

Ambedkar: Educational Milestones

1907	Completed Secondary School Leaving Certificate Examination
1912	Passed BA examination, studying in Elphinstone College, Bombay
July 1913	Joined the Faculty of Political Science, Columbia University, New York, assisted by a scholarship from Maharaja Sayoji Rao of Baroda
1915	Completed MA dissertation on Administration and Finance of the East India Company
June 1916	Submitted PhD thesis on National Dividend of India: A Historical and Analytical Study to Columbia University
October 1916	Joined the London School of Economics (LSE) as well as Grey's Inn
1917	Awarded PhD degree by Columbia University; dissertation published by P.S. King and Sons, London in 1925, after suitable revision, under the title The Evolution of Provincial Finance in British India
November 1918	Appointed Professor of Political Economy at the Sydenham College of Commerce and Economics, Bombay
September 1920	Returned to LSE for continuation of studies
June 1921	Submitted MSc dissertation on Provincial Decentralisation of Imperial Finance in British India
1922	Invited to the Bar-at-Law from Greys Inn; submits DSc thesis on The Problem of the Rupee: Its Origin and its Solutions to LSE; departs to Berlin University for studies

Cont'd...

...Cont'd

1923	Awarded DSc degree by LSE; thesis published by P.S. King and Co., London
June 1925–March 1928	Worked as part-time teacher in Mercantile Law in Batliboi's Accountancy Training Institute, Bombay
June 1928–March 1929	Worked as Professor of Law in the Government Law College, Bombay
June 1928	Founded the Depressed Classes Education Society, Bombay
June 1935–June 1938	Worked as the Principal, Government Law College, Bombay
July 1945–1946	Founded People's Education Society, Bombay
June 1952	Conferred Doctor of Laws degree by Columbia University, New York

Source: Adapted from Rodrigues (2002: 'Chronology', 555–59).

11

Ethnicity and Education

On the Educational Backwardness of Indian Muslims

In a pluralist secular polity like India, where social perceptions of and interactions between religious communities are conditioned by layers of historical experience, education provides the arena for both the expression and the understanding of ethnic relations. Based on this postulate, this chapter attempts (a) to examine the problems and prospects of the education of minorities, and (b) to analyse thereby the phenomenon of ethnicity. These twin objectives are sought to be achieved by first focussing on the educational situation prevailing among the 'major' minority religious community of the Muslims, and then contrasting it with that prevailing among the 'minor' minority community of the Christians.

Concepts and Reality

Although the debate on the conceptual framework for the analysis of ethnicity continues, the inadequacy of existing analyses on the subject has been traced to the ambiguities of the key terms 'ethnic' and 'ethnicity'. Hence, it is necessary to place the key concepts in a

---

This is a revised version of the paper presented at the Joint Session on 'Ethnic, Race and Minority Relations: Education and Ethnic Conflict' organised by the Research Committees 04 and 05 as part of the 12th World Congress of Sociology, Madrid (Spain), 9–13 July 1990.

perspective to preclude any inadvertent misinterpretations that might occur during the presentation of ideas.

The concept of 'plural society' was first introduced by J.S. Furnivall to refer to a society which comprised of 'two or more elements or social orders which live side by side, yet without mingling, in one political unity' (1944: 446). This concept has undergone several changes over the decades, and today it describes a nation which is characterised by 'a plurality of cultures and institutions, which are held together by a dominant community by political arrangements which are coercive in their implications' (Naidu 1980: 1–2).

The concept of plural society thus axiomatically implies the existence of two or more ethnic groups, that is, groups of people with common traits and customs. Max Weber described ethnic groups as those which:

> ... entertain a subjective belief in their common descent – because of similarities of physical type or of customs or both, or because of memories of colonisation and migration – in such a way that this belief is important for the continuation of non-kinship communal relationship ... regardless of whether an objective blood relationship exists or not (1965: 306).

In the context of ethnic relations in a plural society, the term 'minority' is often substituted for the term 'ethnic group' (see, for example, Schaefer 1979: 4; Schermerhorn 1978: 13). However, such usage not only restricts the term ethnic group but also deflects the essence of the term minority group. Thus, as Louis Wirth puts it, a minority is:

> ... a group of people, who because of their physical or cultural characteristics, are singled out from the others in the society in which they live for differential and unequal treatment, and who therefore regard themselves as objects of collective discrimination (1965: 309).

In other words, the concept of minority necessarily presupposes a sphere of majority-minority relations. To the extent that these relations are consciously ingrained in the ethos of a people, thus binding them together into a community, and are transmitted as a cultural legacy from one generation to the next, they come under the label of ethnic relations.

The ethnic relations between the majority community and the various minority communities are not symmetrical or uniform, and may also change in the light of the experiences and perceptions of both. What is important to bear in mind, as Ratna Naidu has underscored, is that 'ethnicity is not always an a priori category, but is often created by conflict' (1980: 3–4).

In its ethnic connotation, 'minority' is certainly more than a statistical entity. It is this fact which makes the determination of minorities a sociologically vexing problem. As Myron Weiner et al. aver, 'the question of what constitutes an ethnic group remains as unclear in India as it does in so many multi-ethnic societies where ethnicity itself has been in a state of flux' (1981: 14).

In his study of ethnic groups in India, R.A. Schermerhorn (1978) lists ten ethnic 'minorities': Scheduled Castes, Scheduled Tribes, Jains, Jews, Sikhs, Muslims, Christians, Anglo-Indians, Parsees, and Chinese. He does not regard the linguistic states as minorities because they are only formal units of government and he omits categories like linguistic minorities on the grounds that there are innumerable linguistic groups whose fractionalised nature precludes them from an analysis on a societal basis.

Schermerhorn's contention that only minority groups qualify for the status of an ethnic group has been contested (see Phadnis 1990: 34–35). Ignoring the contentions and counter-contentions about Schermerhorn's identification of ethnic groups in India, it can hardly be denied that Muslims, the followers of Islam, constitute the demographically largest and sociologically most significant minority.

According to the 1981 Census, the population of India (excluding the state of Assam, where the Census was not held) was 665.3 million. The Hindus, formed an overwhelming 82.6 per cent of the population (549.8 million), the Muslims constituted 11.4 per cent (75.5 million) forming the largest minority group. Constituting 2.4 per cent (or 16.2 million) of the population, the Christians were the distant second important minority group. Besides the Muslims and the Christians, only the Sikhs formed over 2 per cent (13.1 million) of the population. Those professing other religions together formed only a minuscule 1.6 per cent.[1]

The sociological significance of the Muslims as a minority group does not rest solely on their numerical strength. Rather, their social construction as a minority in the socio-political history of India is a crucial factor (Saberwal 2006, 2008). Their forefathers were once the rulers of this land; as a community they were at the centre of Partition of the country in 1947; and in independent India they have been one of the main elements in most 'communal riots', either as perpetrators or victims, or both.

As a volatile minority, the Muslims are not comparable to any other minority group, including the Christians who also follow a religion with its origin in an alien land. In J.A. Laponce's classification, the Muslims are essentially a minority 'by will' (1960: 12),[2] which refuses assimilation, seeks to retain its identity, and thus inflicts upon itself a sense of minority status.

It should be pointed out that, in India, contrary to common belief, neither the Muslims nor the Christians constitute a socially homogeneous community. Both are characterised by regional and linguistic variations and highly unequal systems of social stratification with caste-like formations (see Ahmad 1978; Rodrigues 1989). Among both these communities, religion has functioned as an effective ideological apparatus, insulating the contradictions within the community.

A major distinction between the Muslims and the Christians in India worth noting is that while religion 'never imparted a socio-cultural identity to the Christians' (Rodrigues 1989: 254), it fostered such an identity among the Muslims, an identity which was both 'self-defined' and 'other-recognised'. This is explained by the convergence of ethnicity and socio-economic status over a period of time which accentuated ethnic distinction and awareness (see Phadnis 1990: 19). This fact should be borne in mind while discussing and interpreting the differential ethnic responses of the Muslims and the Christians in almost every realm, including education.

Educational Situation among the Muslims

It must be stated at the outset that very little macro-level data are available on the educational situation among the Muslims, or indeed on any religious minority in India.[3] In pursuance of the professed drive against communalism, the post-Independence census operations only recorded the broad count by religion, and do not present data on literacy, education, or occupation according to religion. Systematic, large-scale empirical studies are also conspicuous by their absence. As a result, statements based on flimsy evidence or fleeting observations have passed for analytical generalisations. Much of the literature on the subject has tended to be one-sided and polemical. The uninformed and biased assertions and counter-assertions about the behaviour of the Muslim community have confounded its ethnic problem. Keeping this lacuna in mind, let us try to grapple with the few systematic though small-scale investigations on the problem.

Attempts at collating data on the educational situation among the Muslims in India (see Ahmad 1981; Kamat 1985: 293–301; Kareem 1988; Peer 1991; N.C. Saxena 1989) have invariably shown that at the high school level and higher, the Muslims are at least three to four times behind other communities. The enrolment of Muslim children in primary schools is generally poor, even in those areas where the Muslims constitute a majority. By and large, a significant majority of those enrolled attend Muslim schools or Urdu-medium schools wherever such schools exist. The enrolment of Muslim girls is extremely low. Moreover, the drop-out rate is significantly higher for Muslim students as compared to their non-Muslim counterparts. An all-India survey of 430 schools and forty-four colleges managed by the Muslims (cited by N.C. Saxena 1989: 165–66) found that the percentage of non-Muslim students in such institutions increased with the level of education. This suggests that Muslim educational institutions are not able to attract a sufficient number of Muslim students at successive levels of education.

As compared to the performance of students in general, the performance of Muslim students is poor and unsatisfactory. Significantly, 'the Muslims studying in Hindi medium schools did much better than Muslims who studied in Urdu medium institutions' (ibid.: 164). This seems to imply that either the standard of teaching in Urdu-medium schools is not up to the mark or the students attending them lack the spirit of competition. Whatever progress the Muslims have been able to make in the realm of modern education is confined to the urban areas.

Not surprisingly, the Muslims are reported to have one of the lowest literacy rates in India. The most conservative 'guesstimates' put it at around 10 per cent and the most liberal, at around 23 per cent. In either case, the extent of literacy among the Muslims is far below the average for the country, that is, 36.2 per cent.[4] Within the community, the male-female literacy ratio is said to be a staggering 20:1. In brief, as A.R. Kamat writes, 'for the majority of Muslims, their educational advance is of an order comparable to that of other backward castes among the Hindus' (1985: 297). And, as if in confirmation of this view, the Government of Karnataka has listed the Muslims under the category of 'Backward Communities' for protective discrimination.

It is often argued that only a very small section of the Muslim population looks forward to the charmed realm of professions or government employment through higher education. The projection of the problems of this small section of the community as the problems of the entire community is, therefore, held to be unjustified (see N.C. Saxena 1989: 156–57). This argument is also sought to be buttressed by the fact that even among the Hindus the educational opportunities are unequally distributed. This position is tantamount to generalising the problem of educational backwardness at the societal level and ignoring its religious dimension.

Although such a generalisation is valid from the vantage point of Marxian class analysis, one can hardly ignore the glaring educational backwardness of the Muslims as a minority community *per se*. This position is particularly disquieting in view of the contrasting educational situation among the Christians, as revealed by studies on community organisation among them. Moreover, several studies on the social background of students have also invariably demonstrated that the Christians are comparable to the Hindus, or might even be a shade better, in the realm of education.

Educational Backwardness in Ethnic Perspective

A variety of explanations have been offered for the educational backwardness of the Indian Muslims. Kamat has succinctly summarised these explanations under three main heads. According to him,

> (a) some writers trace it to the religious traditionality and backwardness of those professing Islam, which as a religion is alleged to identify the religious and the secular; (b) some others try to explain in terms of the partition of India and the acute psychological crisis of identity it created for Indian Muslims; and

(c) some other scholars put forward a reason also based on religion, namely, the deliberate neglect of and discrimination against Muslims by the larger (Hindu) society, which professes to be secular but is, in fact, discriminatory whether in education or in educated and literate employment (1985: 299).

These explanations themselves take on an ethnic hue. The first explanation is usually emphasised by Hindu scholars, and even by the secularists among them. The last explanation is a grievance generally voiced by Muslim scholars. The second explanation focuses on a historic event, namely, the partition of India, which marked the culmination of one phase of communalism and the onset of another.

As Kamat rightly points out, while each one of these explanations touches upon 'a specific aspect of reality', none of them by itself grasp 'the core of the problem' (1985: 299–300). The roots of the problem lie in the shaping of the Muslims as a minority and the socio-economic structure of the Muslim community.

The Historical Background

In her insightful work on communalism, Naidu (1980) has convincingly argued that the communal problem in India today has emerged out of the social forces generated by British colonialism and the resultant exogenous process of growth. This process of growth associated with colonialism had an uneven impact on the different regions of the Raj, and the various religious communities and classes therein. 'The communities, classes, sectors or regions which were strategically placed vis-à-vis the colonial economy, modernised first' (ibid.: 25). Extensive evidence dating back to the second half of the nineteenth century (see Hunter 1872) shows that the Hindus[5] first took advantage of the process of modernisation initiated by the British, while the Muslims lagged far behind.

It must be borne in mind that the Muslims have not always been educationally backward everywhere in India. Studies by scholars such as Paul Brass (1975), Francis Robinson (1975), and Anil Seal (1968) have revealed that, even at the turn of the century, in many areas governed by the British, literacy and school enrolment among the Muslims were comparable to, if not higher than that, among the Hindus. It was only in those areas 'where the

Muslim population was mainly agrarian and extremely poor, that they were lagging behind considerably also in education' (Kamat 1985: 298).

Thus, in order to understand the changing educational fortunes of the Muslims and the emergence of the communal problem, it is necessary to refer to the serious socio-economic imbalances introduced by the onset of the colonial economy in India. The operational logic of colonialism necessitated the initiation of an exogenous process of 'development', which, unlike its endogenous counterpart, drew into its ambit different regions, communities, and classes 'at extremely disparate rates'. As compared to both the Hindus and the Christians, the Muslims entered the developmental process rather late and even then not effectively. The communal problem in India, as in many other Asian countries, is held to a great extent to be the 'result of such time lags in the entry of different communities into the modernisation process' (Naidu 1980: 26; see also De Bary et al. 1963: 587–90).

It is not as if the colonial rulers did not recognise the need to adopt special measures to promote western education among the Muslims (see Hardy 1972: 80–91). Following its Resolution on Muslim Education dated 13 June 1873 (quoted in Philips 1962: 180–83), the then Government of India encouraged western education among the Muslims. But these efforts bore little tangible fruit.

It is significant that the community of Indian Muslims, with a tradition of literacy and education, was not only apathetic but often explicitly hostile to western education, which alone was the 'open sesame' to employment and other economic opportunities. The special distaste for English among the Muslims of Bihar is recorded in the Minutes of a Lieutenant-Governor of Bengal (dated 19 November 1858), noting that the Office of the Inspector of Schools at Patna was described as '*sheitanka dufter khana* – the devil's counting house' (quoted in Misra 1961: 158). 'English education was, in fact, misconstrued by them as an attempt on the part of the government to convert the province to Christianity' (ibid.: 159).

Naidu has summarised the cultural logic underlying the differential responses of the Muslims and the Hindus as follows:[6]

> There remained a tradition among Indian Muslims of a sense of superiority of learning imparted within the limits of their own

> cultural norms. The result was that when the British brought some of the fruits of the Renaissance to the Indian subcontinent, the Muslims were too proud to be in a vulgar hurry to savour it. The Hindus, on the other hand, not having scaled great cultural heights in the immediately preceding period and long suppressed by the Muslim invasions had a more open mind. They quickly learned the English language, and then the sciences and technology, and equipped themselves with the skills that gave them relative advantage over the Muslims in adjusting to the impending systematic changes in the subcontinent (1980: 32).

Some enlightened Muslims such as Abdul Latif, Syed Amir Ali, and Syed Ahmad Khan recognised the importance of western education for the development of their community under changing conditions. They not only advocated the introduction of western education, but even took steps to foster it among their brethren. But their moves were strongly opposed by conservative elements within the community, especially by the *ulama* at Deoband (see Hasan 1979: 25–26). In fact, Syed Ahmad Khan was dismayed that he was accused by some as 'being disloyal to the culture of Islam, even to Islam itself' (quoted in De Bary et al. 1963: 744).

With the theological orthodoxy reigning supreme and the community clinging tenaciously to cultural traditions bound with its religion, the main form of education which the Muslims received was the traditional curriculum which was imparted in *madrasas* and *maktabs* (Hasan 1979: 24–25; see also Alam 2013). No wonder that the Muslims lagged behind in modern scientific, technical, and professional education even as they continued with their traditional education. Their educational backwardness was gradually reflected in their declining representation both in the professions and in government service during the colonial era.

It is true that the Muslim response to western education was not uniform throughout the country. As compared to Bengal, the situation was far better in Uttar Pradesh and Punjab. This, according to Naidu (1980: 33), is explained by what B.B. Misra termed the principle of 'minority effect', that is, in the pre-Independence Indian states wherever the minority community had the least concentration, they were more urban, more educated and more vigorous as a community as compared to the states where they were numerically in the majority.

The adverse impact of the colonial economy on the indigenous trading and artisan classes, and the indifference and hostility of the Muslims towards the advantages of the opportunities created by it, isolated and marginalised them in the changing economy. The socio-psychological consequences of such an isolation resulting from their late and halting entry into the modern sector are double-edged. As Naidu has observed, 'just as some communities were in the *lead* in modernisation due to their strategic position vis-à-vis the colonial economy, other communities lagged in modernisation due to their strategic position vis-à-vis the pre-colonial feudal economy' (1980: 26; emphasis in original). She emphasises this point as one which exacerbates the communal problem, 'for it is fed on memories of past splendour or humilities, as the case may be, and dreams, in a psychological sense, of breaking even' (ibid.).

By 1931, the impact of the colonial economic, political, and educational policies on the communal situation in the country had become perceptively grave. The Muslims began to give expression to their fear of the threat of being displaced. A sense of insecurity and the shadow of communal tension implicit in it fell over the whole society. It was experienced even in areas which had enjoyed a composite Hindu-Muslim culture for over centuries and where economic symbiosis between the members of the two communities necessitated co-operation between them (ibid.: 39).

With neither the Hindu intelligentsia nor the Congress leadership – which was at the forefront of the freedom struggle – being seriously worried about such a fear complex on the part of the Muslims, and with the already entrenched Muslim elite being concerned only with preserving their position by exploiting the sentiments of the indigent sections of the community, the inevitable occurred in August 1947: the partition of the country and the creation of Pakistan.

But the partition of India did not solve the communal problem for either the Muslims or the government of independent India. It is necessary to emphasise the demographic fact that there are more Muslims in India than in Pakistan. The migration to Pakistan of a substantial section of the educated upper, middle, and lower-middle classes among the Muslims only increased the vacuum of Muslim participation in the modern sector and depleted the leadership which could have shaped an ethos for the onward march of the community in a secular political scenario. On the other hand, the migration of the educated Muslims from the modern sector to Pakistan did little to improve the educational situation of Muslims there (see Wheeler 1970: 37–90).

Post-Independence Scenario

It has been an ordeal for the secular leadership of India to bring an 'economically backward' but 'politically volatile' community into the mainstream of national life. To allay any fears among the Muslims (or other minorities for that matter) of the threat of displacement, the Constitution of India guarantees the educational and cultural rights of the minorities (see Sharma 1973). In addition, in several states, the Muslims are given preferential treatment in the areas of education and employment.

But it can hardly be gainsaid that the efforts of the government to elevate the Muslims cannot be expected to be successful unless the Muslims themselves as a community make a mark in the realm of education and, through it, in the professions and higher echelons of the bureaucracy. Furthermore, it is also incumbent on them to emerge from their insular religious outlook if only to set aside the aspersions on their loyalty to the nation, which the Hindus are naturally prone to cast after Partition.

However, the continuing formation of middle and lower-middle classes among the Muslims, a process which is a *sine qua non* for the spread of literacy and education in the community, is retarded. One obvious reason for this is that, having lagged behind other religious communities for decades, the Muslims find it extremely difficult to compete with non-Muslims who have established a lead by taking advantage of the new opportunities as soon as they were thrown open.

No systematic effort has been made on the part of either the government or the Muslim leadership to convey to the community either the historical causes for its educational backwardness today, or the need for and the means of emerging from its present educational impasse. Thus, the community is deluded into believing that it is being discriminated against. Discrimination on religious grounds in a communal scenario as prevails in India cannot entirely be ruled out. But, the Muslims' perception of discrimination as the sole or primary explanation for their educational backwardness can only result in self-deluding despair.

Urdu: The Language Question

Scholars working on ethnicity in India, as also in other South Asian countries such as Pakistan and Sri Lanka, have identified language as a critical ethnic group marker. And, when, a language is appropriately or inappropriately identified with a religion, it assumes tremendous value as an ethnic symbol. While discussing the educational and cultural situation prevailing among the Muslims in India, a reference to the contentious language Urdu is necessary (see Brass 1975; Kamat 1980; Peer 1988: 184–242).

According to the 1981 Census, there were 35.53 million Urdu-speaking people, forming 5.34 per cent of the total population of India or the sixth largest linguistic group in the country, next only to those speaking Hindi, Telugu, Bengali, Marathi and Tamil.[7] However, unlike these latter groups which are concentrated in one or two states, Urdu-speakers are scattered all over India, as also widely dispersed within each state. It is only in Uttar Pradesh that the Urdu-speaking population forms over 10 per cent of the total population.

As a consequence of the wide dispersal of Urdu-speakers, 'Urdu is not the state-language in any state except in Jammu and Kashmir where the majority of people, some 53 per cent, in fact, speak Kashmiri' (Kamat 1985: 294). Except in Andhra Pradesh, in certain districts of Bihar, and only recently in Uttar Pradesh, Urdu is not even recognised as a second official language. This is unlike the other languages listed in the Eighth Schedule of the Constitution, with the exception of Sindhi and Sanskrit.

Even assuming that Urdu is spoken exclusively by the Muslims (which is certainly not the case), in 1971, only 46.58 per cent of the Muslims claimed Urdu as their mother tongue. A large majority of the Muslims in Assam, Gujarat, Jammu and Kashmir, Kerala, Rajasthan, Tamil Nadu, and West Bengal have claimed the language of the state rather than Urdu as their mother tongue. It is only in Andhra Pradesh, Bihar, Madhya Pradesh, Maharashtra, Karnataka, and Uttar Pradesh that the ratio of Urdu-speakers to the state's Muslim population is more than 50 per cent (ibid.). But, even in these states, all those who speak Urdu are not necessarily Muslims. In other words, Urdu is a language that has been used by both Muslims and Hindus in many parts of north India, from the Mughal period down to the present day.

In the light of the foregoing facts, it is intriguing how Urdu has come to acquire a religious-cum-political nuance in discussions on Muslim ethnic identity. According to Kamat, this is explained by the Perso-Arabic origin of several words in the Urdu vocabulary, the close relationship of its script to Arabic (the language of the Koran, the sacred book of Islam), and its historical association with the erstwhile Muslim rulers (ibid.: 295). It is not only the Muslims who identify Urdu as their language;[8] such an identification is also claimed by many non-Muslims.

It is in this context that we should understand the Muslim grievance about the government's indifference to and neglect of Urdu. Although this grievance is voiced primarily with reference to the status of the language in official parlance, it is not without wider educational and cultural ramifications. Muslim educational conferences often complain about the neglect of Urdu-medium schools and the teaching of Urdu as a language, and the non-availability of Urdu textbooks for many subjects. Closely related to this is the complaint about 'the pronounced cultural bias in the curricula, their exposition in the prescribed textbooks and in actual teaching by non-Muslim teachers' (Kamat 1985: 300; see also Sharma 1978: 26–27).

Education of Christians: Case in Contrast

The Christians offer a study in contrast to the Muslims, especially with regard to ethnicity and education. While this chapter does not specifically focus on the issues in the education of Christians *per se*, it is nevertheless necessary to record some of the contrasting features.

Christianity, like Islam, has a long history in India that dates back to the first century CE. But the spread of this religion (mainly through proselytism), the introduction of doctrinal specificities, and the peculiarities of rites and rituals of western Christians took place primarily during the colonial era. Unlike the spread of Islam which was by and large directly associated with and directed by the Muslim rulers, the spread of Christianity was never the avowed political mission of the British colonialists. They only provided an umbrella for the missionaries who concentrated on the task of spreading the religion, while at the same time subtly attempting to demarcate the spheres of religion and state power.

Of the various spheres of activity on which the Christian missionaries in India put an indelible stamp, education is certainly the foremost. They established, generally as an extension of the Church, schools and colleges over the length and breadth of the country, many of which rank among the best even today.

Unlike the Muslims, the Christians did not have any cultural or religious inhibitions in accepting western education. A large number of Christian boys and girls received education in the missionary institutions. Thus, along with the Brahmins and other upper-caste Hindus, the Christians too were able to get ahead in the sphere of education and thereby take advantage of the emerging economic opportunities in modern India. This explains the favourable educational situation of the Christians as compared to that of the Muslims, and even to that among the Hindus. Despite this, however, the educational situation of later converts from the lowest castes has hardly improved (see Rodrigues 1989: 268).

It is necessary to recall Valerian Rodrigues' significant observation that, in India, religion 'never imparted a socio-cultural identity to the Christians' (1989: 254). This is in contrast to the experience of the Muslims who did develop such an identity for the socio-economic and political reasons mentioned earlier. In the light of this, it is not difficult to understand why the Christians, unlike the Muslims, neither experienced a crisis of loyalty, nor had their loyalty questioned by the Hindus.

In other words, Partition did not have a significant impact on the ethnicity of the Christians. Nevertheless, they have benefitted considerably from the Constitutional provisions safeguarding minority rights, provisions which were incorporated keeping primarily the Muslims in mind. The frequency with which the Christians have moved the judiciary to safeguard their minority nights in the realm of education would give the impression that they have been able to derive the best from both worlds – secular and religious minority – in a complex and confused ethnic situation.

The phenomenal success of a small Christian minority in the realm of education, as compared to the halting advancement of the large Muslim minority, can also be explained by elucidating an economic postulate of the principle of 'minority effect' referred to earlier. As Naidu puts it, the 'opportunities open to a minority seem also to be related to its size' (1980: 33). She quotes the economist A.M. Khusro, who found that 'the majority gets opportunities roughly proportional to its population, a small minority more than proportional and a large minority less than proportional to its numbers' (ibid.).

Finally, the efforts of the Muslim leadership (including invoking the constitutional guarantees for minorities) have been primarily directed at safeguarding the religious interests of the community and at resisting any felt assaults on its socio-religious identity. But, in the case of the Christians, as Rodrigues (1989: 260–61) has argued with reference to the Catholic hierarchy in the Dakshina Kannada district of Karnataka, their educational institutions (as also other institutions such as hospitals) are the key instruments through which the Church hierarchy wields its clout in the society at large, apart, that is, from being the principal means of socio-economic advancement for its members. This is so because most of these institutions, especially the English-medium schools and colleges, cater to the elite and well-off sections of society, irrespective of their religious affiliation.

Conclusion

The various explanations offered for the educational predicament of the Muslims seem to apply, by and large, to the similar predicament of the neglected sections of other religious communities as well; for instance, those below the poverty line, women, and scheduled castes and scheduled tribes. This would suggest the mobilisation of the Muslim minority along with other underprivileged sections of the population as a way out of their socio-economic predicament. But, considering the stranglehold of the religious orthodoxy on the Muslim community and the 'false consciousness' fostered by their religion, the possibility of such a mobilisation cutting across religion is indeed remote. Rather, with the politicisation of the ethnic problem, politicians of every hue, including the leftists, find in religion and the minority issue a political trump card.

The majority Hindus believe that every government has 'pandered' to the demands of the minorities, thus ignoring their rights. They often voice the feeling that, in India's secular democracy, it is the majority which has suffered by being called to upon to make all manner of sacrifices for the insatiable minorities.[9] This sentiment has certainly gained strength over the last six decades and has hardened inter-ethnic relations.

Be that as it may, protective discrimination as a strategy for social amelioration has certain limitations (see Chapter 8 in this book). On the one hand, the avenues of government-sponsored mobility have narrowed and, on the other, the significance of education in terms of mobility has waned. At best, over a period of time it can bring about individual mobility for a small section of the minority population while social awareness among the large majority of them would continue to remain in swaddling-bands.

Furthermore, protective discrimination and constitutional provisions in favour of the minorities, and the Muslims' demand for the preservation of Muslim Personal Law has placed the community in an incongruous situation. The desire to be treated as a separate and distinct community can hardly go hand in hand with the desire of its individual members to be treated equally with others in matters of education and employment (N.C. Saxena 1989: 179). This dilemma has been well summarised by Gopal Krishna:

> Community recognition and assertion is needed for certain purposes, and anonymity is desired for others. The gains from community assertion are far from obvious, though they seem to be of considerable psychological import, while the cost to individuals arising from lack of anonymity is tangible and immediate (1982:117).

Nevertheless, as the problem is aggravated by the sense of insecurity on the part of the Muslim community consequent upon the partition of the country, as also the suspicion to which they are subjected by certain sections of the majority community of Hindus, it is a problem that has to be tackled, at least for a while longer, primarily in ethnic terms. This necessarily implies that serious and sincere efforts will have to be made not only to reduce ethnic inequalities, but also to convince the Muslim minority that this is indeed being done.

In the ultimate analysis, however, the impetus for the educational progress of the Muslims has to come from within the community itself. M.R.A. Baig (1974), a reputed Muslim intellectual, has traced the roots of the community's stagnation to the general orthodoxy which is imposed upon it by the intermingling of religion and socio-economic issues. Thus, it cannot be denied that the immense responsibility of carving out a progressive worldview in order to draw the Muslims into the mainstream of national life and ensure their progress within it lies with the leadership of the community itself. And, the quintessential element of this progressive worldview has to be modern education.

Notes

1. Over the next two decades the proportion of the Hindus has declined by 2.1 percentage points and those of the Christians and the Sikhs by 0.1 percentage point each; the percentage of the Muslims increased by 2 percentage points. According to the 2001 Census, India's population was 1028 million. Of this Hindus constituted 80.5 per cent (827.6 million); Muslims, 13.4 per cent (138.2 million); Christians, 2.3 per cent (24.1 million); Sikhs, 1.9 per cent (19.2 million); and those professing other religions together formed 1.9 per cent (19.5 million) (Census of India 2001b).
2. According to Laponce (1960), the distinction between 'minorities by will' and 'minorities by force' is based on the attitudes adopted by a minority in its relationship with the majority community. A minority which refuses assimilation is a minority by will (typically, the Jews in Germany) and a minority which desires assimilation but is refused is a minority by force (typically, the Blacks in the United States of America).
3. The *Handbook of Muslims in India,* edited by Basant and Shariff (2009) examines the status of Muslims in contemporary India by focussing on their socio-historical background, demographics, and educational and socio-economic conditions; it also looks at policy options to improve their condition.
4. A reanalysis of census data by C.A. Abdussalam has revealed that, in seven out of nine Muslim majority districts, the level of literacy is well below the national average. The two exceptions are Malappuram in Kerala and Lakshadweep (Kareem 1988: 9–13).
5. Even among the Hindus, it was the Brahmins and other upper castes with a heritage of literacy and a tradition of learning who first took to English education and the fruits it offered. This fact explains their continued dominance in the realm of education (see Chapter 7 in this book).
6. A similar statement is also made in De Bary et al. (1963: 589).
7. According to the 2001 Census, there were 51.53 million Urdu-speaking people, forming 5.01 per cent of the total population

of India, and their position vis-à-vis other linguistic groups in the country remained the same (Census of India 2001a).

8. According to Hussain, 'the learning of Urdu is not only vital culturally but also a religious necessity for the Indian Muslims' (1965: 219), while Mujeeb even contends that 'the survival of Indian Muslims in a culturally recognizable form is generally linked up with Urdu' (1967: 561). The fact that the identification of Urdu with Islam is firmly entrenched in the minds of Indian Muslims is also revealed by empirical studies (see, for example, Peer 1988: 212–23; Srinivasan 1981: 81).
9. This line of thinking is often buttressed by the fact that in the North-Western Provinces and Oudh in the 1850s (see Misra 1961: 388; Seal 1968: 304) and in the Nizam's Hyderabad in the 1930s (see Naidu 1980: 38), the representation of Muslims in governmental positions was far greater than their share in the population.

Part IV

University, Teachers, Students

12

The Decline of the University as a Public Institution in India

The success of any large-scale democratic polity and its efforts at sustained economic development is contingent upon the effective functioning of its public institutions. In a democracy, public institutions such as schools and universities, hospitals and banks, legislatures and courts, the civil service and the army – as different from private institutions like families, extended kin groups, and religious communities – are expected to contribute to the common good irrespective of caste, creed, or religion. As such, in multi-religious and socio-culturally heterogeneous societies like India, public institutions have an even greater role to play.

Almost all the public institutions currently functioning in India were originally introduced there by the British rulers as part of the colonialist modernisation project.[1] These institutions were modelled after their counterparts in Britain, and they were intended to serve the economic and political interests of the British and help them consolidate their rule in the country. All the same, both in their 'morphological forms' and in 'the values that (gave) them meaning and legitimacy' (Béteille 2000: 154), these

This is a revised version of a paper presented at the seminar on 'Public Institutions and Social Transformation in India and Sri Lanka', jointly organised by the India-Sri Lanka Foundation and Indian Council of Social Science Research, at Colombo on 18–20 October 2007.

new institutions differed from those existent in the country. They were premised upon universal normative structures and legal-rational considerations.[2] So much confidence was reposed in the efficacy of these institutions that they were adopted, with little or no modification, by the state managers after India became independent.

It is sixty-seven years since India attained Independence and sixty-four years since she adopted the republican form of government. But for the brief dark interregnum of the Emergency era, her track record as a functioning democracy has been remarkable. Within the democratic framework she has been negotiating significant socio-economic changes and addressing a plethora of socio-political movements. Taking a long-term perspective of six decades, it is hard to deny that the India of today is significantly different from the India on the eve of her Independence. In retrospect, one is tempted to ask: what has become of the British-implanted public institutions that India inherited and adopted at the time of Independence? This question assumes greater sociological significance considering that these institutions did not have organic roots in the native society. In this chapter an attempt has been made to answer this question with reference to one of these public institutions, namely, the university.[3]

The Historical Background

The foundation for the university as a public institution in India was laid by the British colonial regime in the mid-nineteenth century (Ashby and Anderson 1966: 54–146). The initial educational efforts of the Christian missionaries and the East India Company generated a protracted controversy between the 'Anglicists', commending a western course, and the 'Orientalists', favouring an indigenous direction. William Bentinck finally resolved this controversy in favour of the Anglicist orientation, barely a month after Thomas Babington Macaulay had penned his (in)famous *Minute* (on 2 February 1835). Charles Wood's *Despatch* (of 19 July 1854) reaffirmed his policy. Upon the recommendation of the Committee appointed on 26 January 1855, the first three universities were established at Bombay (now Mumbai), Calcutta (now Kolkata), and Madras (now Chennai) in 1857.

Modelled after the University of London (established in 1836), these pioneer universities were largely affiliating and examining bodies with very little intellectual life of their own. They lacked, what André Béteille has called, 'corporate identity' (2000: 159). All the universities that were subsequently established, including those in the princely states of Mysore (1916) and Hyderabad (1919), developed in an isomorphic fashion set on the pattern of the original universities.

The British educational implantation in India, as noted earlier, was conceived to serve the economic, political, and administrative interests of the British and, in particular, to consolidate and maintain their dominance in the country.[4] It emphasised English, which not only was taught as a language, but also was made the exclusive medium of instruction in higher education. The content was biased in favour of languages and the humanities, and against science and technology.

It is not as if the British rulers did not realise the problems associated with such an educational implantation or its adverse consequences for the colonised society. Yet, it was only during the early years of the twentieth century, thanks to the initiative of Lord Curzon, the then Viceroy of India (1898–1905), that efforts were made to 'rescue the original concept of the university from its corrosive narrowness' (Tickoo 1980: 34).[5] Several inquiries were instituted during the last three decades of the colonial rule, but 'hardly any of their major recommendations were translated into university policy or practice' (ibid.).

Thus, the legacy of the university system inherited by India at the time of her Independence was already crisis-ridden. As an integral element of colonial underdevelopment, it was 'anaemic, distorted and dysfunctional'. Low level of enrolment, 'liberal' nature of education, 'enclavisation' of the institutes of higher learning, and spurious modernisation were its festering features (see Raza et al. 1985: 100–09). While the obsolescence of the inherited university system, by and large, persisted, the system itself underwent such a phenomenal expansion as never before seen in the world. At the time of her Independence (in 1947), India had twenty universities and 496 colleges catering to 2,41,369 students. After a massive expansion of the university system during the next sixty-two years, by the end of 2009 it had

496 universities and university-level institutions and 29,951 colleges catering to almost twelve million students.

Thus, India today has the third largest university system in the world (behind China and the United States of America). It is also noteworthy that this system has a history of 150 years. It has been producing graduates and doctorates in science and technology, arts and humanities, medicine and law, etc. in thousands every year, making India the second largest repository of university credential holders, and the fourth largest science and technology workforce in the world.

The University as a Public Institution

As a public institution, the university is ascribed a purpose, and it carries a meaning, not only to those who directly participate in it, but also to those who are indirectly affected by it. Accordingly, every university sets for itself a vision and mission and draws up a roadmap to realise its vision and accomplish its mission. All universities, at the time of their establishment, have a statement to this effect. But as they grow and age, there develops a disjunction between their vision/mission statement and what they do and what happens in their precincts. And, in many a case, the university just begins to drift and go moribund.

While the strain towards such disjunction and drift is noticeable across the board, obviously, not all universities experience it uniformly or in the same fashion. This is because the universities vary widely on several parameters. The nature of the disjunction and drift experienced by any university, therefore, is a subject for empirical analysis. This chapter does not undertake such an analysis. Rather, focussing on the strain towards such disjunction and drift, it seeks to discuss the decline of the university as a public institution in India generally. The discussion here will be substantiated by instances drawn from the life of specific universities.

As a public institution, a university is expected to (a) produce and refine knowledge and transmit it from one generation to the next, (b) train successive generations in the vast variety of skills required for the sustenance of the society, (c) certify the acquisition of knowledge and skills by those enrolled into the system, and (d) engage itself in a meaningful way with the community in which it exists. Thus, as the University Education Commission (1948–49) (the Radhakrishnan Commission) described, universities are 'the organs of civilisation' and 'the homes of intellectual adventure' (University Education Commission 1985: 240 and 241).

It is from the foregoing expectations that the university derives its legitimacy and it is to fulfil them that it is endowed with requisite authority. As a public institution, it enjoys legal status and is subject to regulative authority. In India, universities are established either by an Act of Parliament and regulated directly by the Government of India's Ministry of Human Resource Development (MHRD) (the central universities) or by an Act of State Assemblies and regulated by the respective state governments (the state universities).

Besides the central and the state universities, a large number of institutions have been recognised as 'institutions deemed-to-be universities' under the University Grants Commission (UGC) Act, 1956[6] and several university-level institutions (including the Indian Institutes of Technology) have been conferred the status of 'institutions of national importance' by the Government of India. The deemed universities and the institutions of national importance are also empowered to award degrees which, according to the UGC Act, 1956, can be granted only by a university.[7]

Not only are the universities, institutions deemed-to-be universities, and institutions of national importance established following the due process of law or recognised under provisions of duly enacted laws, they are also substantially supported financially by the government. The central universities and several deemed universities get their funds from MHRD (through UGC), and the institutions of national importance, from the respective ministries under which they come. The state universities are financed by the respective governments, though they also get some funds from UGC.

Thus, it is important to emphasise that the university is essentially a public institution in India, and it is under state patronage that it has hitherto expanded. The concept of a purely private university (of the American type) is new in India. The bill to provide for the establishment of private universities, introduced in the Rajya Sabha (the upper house of Parliament) in August 1995, has since lapsed. Meanwhile, invoking the existing legal provisions (for example, the UGC Act, 1956), several private institutions of higher education have been given the 'deemed university' status, but without any financial assistance from the government.

Considering that higher education is a concurrent subject under the Constitution, some states (like Chhattisgarh), had enacted private university acts of their own, and private universities had begun to mushroom in these states. This has, no doubt, attracted the adverse attention of UGC, which only feels helpless. However, in its judgment of 11 February 2005, the Supreme Court of India has held certain clauses of the Chhattisgarh Private Sector University Act, 2002 'unconstitutional' and cancelled the registration of 112 private universities as void (see Thomas and Tiwari 2005). The judicial pronouncement of the apex court of the land has endorsed the university's status as a public institution. In what follows, let us see how the university system has functioned vis-à-vis the expectations from it as a public institution.

Distortion of Objectives and Deterioration of Quality

The Missing Research Orientation

It must be noted that research (that is, production and refinement of knowledge) as an essential part of the university system was not emphasised during the colonial era. The colonial legacy of universities as retailers of knowledge has persisted. As the former Director General of CSIR (Council of Scientific and Industrial Research), R.A. Mashelkar notes, 'Despite the two-fold increase in the number of universities and rise in expenditure on research and development by sixteen times during 1980–2000, the quantum of research has gone down' (cited in *The Navhind Times,* Panjim, 2 September 2002, p. 11). According to the report of The World Bank's Task Force on Higher Education and Society (2000: 124–25), the number of papers in sciences and social sciences from India increased only marginally from 13,623 in 1981 to 14,883 in 1995 (that is, by 9.25% in fifteen years). This is negligible compared to the phenomenal 784.38 per cent (from a meagre 1,293 to 11,435) increase registered by China during the same period.

Mashelkar also cites a report which records India's decline in the number of scientific papers cited in the International Science Citation Index from 15,000 to 12,000 during 1980–2000: whereas India slipped from eighth rank in the world in 1980 to fifteenth in

2000, China improved its position from fifteenth to ninth! In absolute terms, there was, no doubt, an increase in the number of citations of Indian scientific papers – from 56,464 in 1981–85 to 90,162 in 1993–97 (that is, by 59.68%). But this increase appears to be infinitesimal compared to the stupendous increase in the number of citations of Chinese scientific papers for the corresponding period – from 8,517 to 77,841 (that is, by 813.95%) (ibid.). Quoting a CSIR Report, B. Vijayakumar notes that 'In the entire history of CSIR of India, only three out of over 20,000 papers published by the scientists have been cited 100 times against a world average of one in every 250'. He further adds that a paper with 'thousand citation counts' (that is, a paper that has been cited 1,000 times) is either nil or extremely rare (2003: 4 and 5). No wonder, there has been a growing disquiet over the declining quality of science education and research in the country.

While the University Education Commission (1948–49) (the Radhakrishnan Commission), appointed by the Government of India soon after Independence, examined the development of higher education and made proposals for its future expansion and improvement, and reflected on the philosophy of higher education and suggested measures for improving the standards of teaching, it had very little to say about how to reorient the university system toward research, excepting noting the teachers' obligation 'to engage in research' and 'to keep themselves up-to-date in their knowledge' (University Education Commission 1985: 247).

It is in the report of the Education Commission (1964–66) (the Kothari Commission; henceforth the Commission)[8] that we find a well-articulated proposal for reorienting the university system toward research. Perhaps the most important reform that this Commission envisaged was the development of five or six 'major universities' 'where conditions may be provided, both as to staff and students as well as to the necessary equipment and atmosphere, to make first-class postgraduate work and research possible'. The standards of these universities, it was emphasised, 'should be comparable to the best institutions of their type in any part of the world ...'. The Commission was confident that, if given top priority, the idea of 'major universities' can be realised in 10 years (Ministry of Education 1971: 506–07).

Given the large capital expenditure involved and also the delay the process of establishing such universities from scratch would entail, the Commission recommended that UGC should select 'from amongst the existing universities, about six universities (including one of the IITs (Indian Institute of Technology) and one agricultural university) for development as major universities'. It spelt out guidelines for the recruitment of 'an intellectually distinguished group of teachers who will be able to provide the requisite training and make valuable research contributions' and for the enrolment of qualified students who can benefit from the superior training to be given, and recommended the provision of 'adequate facilities and satisfactory conditions of work' (ibid.: 510 ff).

As a supplement to its idea of 'major universities', the Commission recommended the expansion and strengthening of the UGC's CAS (Centres of Advanced Study) scheme. This, the Commission thought, could be undertaken as a preparation to the establishment of major universities, or as a consequence of their establishment. Ideally, 'clusters' of advanced centres could be established in select universities, as had been done in the University of Delhi. Such a cluster of advanced centres, the Commission hoped, would strengthen and enrich one another, and promote interdisciplinary research. Where such clusters are not possible, UGC could begin with the establishment of single centres of postgraduate teaching and research, especially in areas where such centres do not exist (ibid.: 512).

The Commission's eloquent proposal for the establishment of 'major universities' was, however, opposed from all quarters. It was summarily rejected by the Parliamentary Committee and the Vice-Chancellors' Conference. While scholars like Dr D.R. Gadgil,[9] who opposed elitism in all its forms, were extremely critical of the proposal, it did not find favour even with academics who generally favoured a selective approach to higher education (see Naik 1982: 111–13). A rhetorical ground on which the proposal was opposed and rejected was that it was elitist and antithetical to the egalitarian ethos of a socialist-democratic polity. The Commission had anticipated such a criticism of the proposal, and it conceded that its proposal would, at that stage, involve a differentiation between universities. 'This', the Commission held, 'is not only inevitable in an economy of scarcity but is also the only sure and practicable way to benefit all ultimately in the shortest time possible' (Ministry of Education 1971: 509). It went on to argue that 'we must recognise that pursuit of excellence implies and requires a discriminatory approach; and that to provide equal resources to all irrespective of the quality of their performance and potentiality for growth merely promotes mediocrity' (ibid.).

Even those who accepted the principle of selective approach for qualitative improvement argued against the concept of major universities on the ground 'that a *Department*, and not a university, should be taken as the unit, that *all* departments of *all* universities should be eligible for selection as Centres of Advanced Study ...' (see Naik 1982: 113; emphasis in original). They, however, accepted the idea of clustering a number of advanced centres into some selected universities where conditions were favourable. This idea was also endorsed by the Parliamentary Committee which reviewed the Report. While the idea of 'major universities' was shelved, the idea of clustering of centres of advanced study found a place in the National Policy on Education (1968). However, as J.P. Naik, Member Secretary of the Commission, observes, this 'was of no avail and no effective steps were taken to implement the proposal even in this modified form' (1982: 113). In March 1987, there were as many as twenty-five independent Centres for Advanced Study in science subjects, and fifteen in humanities and social sciences. However, the 'prestige and glamour' that the idea of Centres of Advanced Study had in 1966 were lost.

The neglect of university in science policy formulation has often been interpreted as a failure on the part of scientific leadership and management (see Dadhich 2004: 2181). According to Jayant V. Narliker, paradoxical as it may sound, 'the manner of establishment of institutes like the TIFR (Tata Institute of Fundamental Research) ... has been largely responsible for the present decline in the following of basic sciences amongst the students today' (2003: 8–9). The Tata Institute of Fundamental Research was established in 1946 on the eve of India's Independence, and the research institutes and laboratories established after Independence were all based on this model: they enjoyed considerable autonomy and generous funds and facilities, and they were 'decoupled from universities so that teaching undergraduate or postgraduate students should not come "in the way" of the researcher' (ibid.: 9). The catch in this was that the researcher was not only decoupled from university/college teaching, but also from students. 'So while research got progressively to the back seat in universities, teaching became noticeably absent from the research institutions' (ibid.).

Thus, while research got an enormous boost from the creation of such specialist institutes, facilities, and laboratories, the fact that they were developed outside the university system undermined whatever little research potentialities that the universities had by contributing to an 'internal brain drain' of science talent from the universities to institutes and laboratories. One may recall, as Sushanta Dattagupta (2005: 19–20) does with reference to physics, that J.C. Bose worked in Presidency College, before he founded the Basu Vigyan Mandir (now under the Department of Science and Technology [DST]), C.V. Raman was in Calcutta University and the Indian Institute of Science (IISc) (Bangalore) before establishing the Raman Research Institute (also under DST), and M.N. Saha moved from Allahabad University to create the Saha Institute of Nuclear Physics (now under the aegis of the Department of Atomic Energy).

The divorcing of teaching from research by building research institutes outside the university system seems to have had adverse consequences for the former, too. The autonomous research institutions are finding it

> ... increasingly difficult to attract young talent, with the problem that a vacuum is slowly but steadily being created at the younger age of the spectrum. Since it is this young age-group that eventually grows to take up higher responsibilities, scientific projects which proceed in a mission mode ... are experiencing serious humanpower shortages (Narliker 2003: 11).

With research getting progressively to the backseat in universities, 'the very lifeline of science graduates from universities that fed young scientists to (the research) institutions began to get more and more tenuous and is now close to becoming extinct' (ibid.). Thus, the divide between teaching and research has perhaps done the most damage to the universities as centres of creation of knowledge.[10]

Orienting Universities towards Research

In 1985, the new Congress-government proposed to embark on the complex task of 'restructuring the system of education'. Toward this end, in August that year the Ministry of Education (since reorganised as the Ministry of Human Resource Development) presented to Parliament a 119-page document titled *Challenge of Education: A Policy Perspective* (see Chapter 19 in this book). This document placed the utmost emphasis on higher education, and noted that because 'major national inputs have gone to laboratories outside the universities', there has been 'great deprivation in terms of facilities for frontline work' in the university system. It called for correcting this anomaly (Ministry of Education 1985: 49), while at the same time, recommending a moratorium on the expansion of the conventional pattern of colleges and universities and the establishment of new centres of excellence.

The Programme of Action of the National Policy on Education (MHRD 1986) was reviewed by the Acharya Ramamurti Committee (MHRD 1991). The recommendations of the Central Advisory Board on Education that considered the review report were adopted by Parliament in May 1992. The revised *Programme of Action–1992* (see MHRD 1992) laid emphasis on the need for strengthening research. The setting up of Inter-University Centres for providing common facilities for research in key areas of science, support to departments under the scheme of 'Strengthening of Infrastructure in Science and Technology', and the signing of a memorandum of understanding between UGC and CSIR in 1991 for providing scientists in universities access to research facilities in CSIR and vice versa were all the outcome of the New Education Policy 1986 (see MHRD 1992: 66–67).

The revised *Programme of Action–1992* also recommended the establishment of university-industry linkage on 'a priority basis in metropolitan areas, cities and regions with a concentration of industry', and 'inter-institutional links between universities in India and "state of the art" research institutions abroad'. More important, it recommended the constitution of 'a high powered committee', with representatives of DST, CSIR, Indian Council of Social Science Research, Indian Council of Historical Research, etc. 'to assess the quality of research' in the universities. However, not all these recommendations have received the serious attention that they deserve.

Appreciating that teaching without research is sterile, on its part and in accordance with the changing educational policies UGC has been undertaking several schemes to provide substantial support to universities and colleges to strengthen their teaching and research activities. Besides the Centres of Advanced Studies referred to earlier, UGC gives financial support to select well-established departments under the Special Assistance Programme for undertaking academic programmes in specific fields. UGC also extends financial assistance to 'major' (long-term) and 'minor' (short-term) research projects undertaken by individual teachers or a group of teachers or by a department as a whole.

For research to go on and major breakthrough to come about, there should be a symbiotic relationship between research and teaching. As a follow-up of the New Education Policy's revised *Programme of Action–1992*, UGC has established specialised Inter-University Centres as world-class facilities which could be used by university teachers and students. The Inter-University Centre for Astronomy and Astrophysics (Pune), Nuclear Science Centre (New Delhi), and Inter-University Consortium for Department of Atomic Energy Facilities (Indore) are such common facilities. Modern computer-based information centres have been set up at IISc (Bangalore), SNDT Women's University (Mumbai) and M.S. University of Baroda. UGC's Inter-University Centre for Information and Library Network (Inflibnet), Ahmedabad is now providing access to current literature through E-subscription of journals. Such centres, of course, are no substitute to establishing 'research universities', but considering the general state of affairs in the universities, these and similar initiatives are welcome developments.

Perhaps the most significant effort of UGC in the direction of research-oriented universities – à la 'major universities' recommended by the Kothari Commission more than four decades before – is its heavily funded scheme of 'Universities with Potential for Excellence' (UGC 2002–2003: 127–28). Based on the proposals submitted by several universities and presentations made by their vice-chancellors on their achievements and promise, UGC has selected five universities – Jadavpur University, Jawaharlal Nehru University (New Delhi), University of Hyderabad, University of Madras (Chennai), and University of Pune – and given each a fabulous development grant of Rs 300 million for five years.

Deterioration of Quality

How well is the university system performing the functions of knowledge transmission and training in skills? As is to be expected, rapid expansion of higher education in post-Independence India has been at the cost of its quality.[11] The deterioration in quality is most glaring in the state universities in general, and at the undergraduate level in affiliated colleges in particular. This crisis now encompasses the conventional postgraduate courses offered in the university departments, too. These courses are now performing an extended 'baby-sitting' function. This is understandable considering the relatively low unit-cost of running these courses, and that the students entering this stream pay absurdly little toward their education – far less than what students in the private-sector primary schools pay. The unregulated expansion of this sector of education has been invariably identified as the main cause of its quality crisis.

What goes on in the name of higher education in many a state university and college is pathetic. In many institutions, the physical facilities are so deplorable and the library and laboratory facilities are so woefully inadequate that they have earned the sobriquet 'academic slums'. While lack of resources[12] – a general refrain heard in this context – is primarily responsible, we cannot blame it alone. What is serious is that even the prescriptions governing the minimum qualifications for the appointment and promotion of academic staff are violated, the minimum number of working days is not met, the calendar of academic activities, if at all, exists only on paper, and the administration has virtually collapsed. In most universities, student feedback and evaluation of teacher performance are either perfunctory or non existent. All this has adversely affected the quality of education imparted in the universities. Naturally, there is very little in the university system to attract the best talent.

Furthermore, the undue emphasis on certification rather than on teaching-learning process seems to have distorted the orientation of university education. Béteille rightly draws attention to 'the constant threat to the institutional focus of the Indian university from the pressures of certification. Examinations are no doubt important, but when a university subordinates its other concerns to the concern for certification, there cannot but be a loss of institutional focus' (2000: 158). Perhaps there is a good case for transferring the conduct of examinations at the undergraduate level to a Board, as in the case of Secondary or Higher Secondary School Certificate examinations.

Unlike its British counterpart, UGC[13] in India has the responsibility of regulating the quality of education in universities and colleges.[14] However, considering the inordinate number of universities and colleges it is required to oversee, and being endowed with very little power, UGC has been virtually reduced to a fund-disbursing agency, incapable of enforcing its own recommendations. As a step in the direction of quality control in higher education, following the National Policy of Education (MHRD 1986), in 1994, UGC set up an autonomous body called the National Assessment and Accreditation Council (NAAC) (see Stella and Gnanam 2003). The scheme of assessment and accreditation as of now is voluntary, but the idea of an external institution doing this was not received well by universities and colleges. By September 2011, NAAC had assessed and accredited only 159 universities and 4,171 colleges (NAAC 2010: 20). How far this will improve the state of affairs in the university system, even if indirectly, remains to be seen.

Spatial Aspects of the University

The Physical Space

The institutional life of the university needs to be located in physical space; there must be a congenial environment for scholarly interaction among students and teachers. Many universities in Europe and North America are as much known for their buildings and campuses as for their knowledge-generation and academic activities. Some of the European universities – Cambridge and Oxford in England, St Andrews in Scotland, Louvain/Leuven in Belgium, and Heidelberg in Germany, for example – are educational towns. They are abuzz with intellectual and cultural activities. This is what Lord Curzon had in mind when he bemoaned the University of Calcutta lacking 'corporate existence' – 'it is not a collection of buildings, it is scarcely even a site' (quoted in Ministry of Education 1971: 498). Universities that were established since Curzon's time, including the ones in Benares and Delhi, took into consideration the spatial dimension of the university as a public institution. 'The idea that every university must have its own campus has now come to be generally accepted' (Béteille 2000: 158), though not all universities succeed in having a well laid out campus of their own.

It must be noted, however, that physical space (campus), though necessary, does not by itself guarantee a vibrant academic and cultural life. Many a university campus is located far away from the city: Bangalore, Mangalore, Calicut, and South Gujarat readily come to one's mind. Even after 40 years of its shifting to the new campus (Jnanabharathi), the Bangalore University busses its students, teachers, and staff from and to the different parts of the city. Incidentally, for three decades it even ran a transport system for this (which has since been handed over to the Bangalore Metropolitan Transport Corporation)! It was first housed in the century-old Central College (a masterpiece of Gothic architecture) campus in the city centre, and was surrounded by many educational institutions – an arts-and-science college, a law college, an engineering college, a women's college, a commerce college, and a polytechnic. Thanks to the powers that be, a great opportunity of developing a vibrant university campus in the heart of the city was lost.

Whatever may be the logistic reasons for locating the university campus away from the city, unless it is a residential campus, it has invariably resulted in loss of academic vitality of the institution. Many of them become ghost campuses after the classes are over, and in some cases even as early as early afternoon. Even in Goa University, the campus is deserted in the afternoon, as students and teachers, who come from far-off places, are eager to get back home. Thus, interaction between teachers and students is confined to the classroom setting, and no extra-curricular academic or cultural activity is possible. In most universities, even sports as a part of university life is non-existent.

Another facet about the physical dimension needs to be mentioned here. Even when universities put up their own buildings, some at huge cost, the maintenance of these buildings is very poor. 'Peeling walls, broken windows-panes, leaking taps, unswept corridors and filthy toilets meet the eye everywhere, and the sad thing is that teachers and students become so easily inured to the dirt and decay' (Béteille 2000: 166). Financial constraint is the familiar refrain we hear from the university authorities. While financial crunch is certainly a problem, the way the universities expend their scarce resources makes one wonder whether cleanliness and upkeep of the precincts are missing as a cultural value in our universities. The slogans, graffiti, and posters mercilessly defacing the university walls are a living proof of the woeful lack of civic culture in many universities.

The Social Space

In absolute terms, apparently, the opportunity for university education has expanded. Estimates of the participation rate vary from a conservative 7 (National Knowledge Commission 2007: 43%) to a liberal 10 per cent (MHRD 2007: 61, 2008: 16), and the Government of India itself has set a modest target of 30 per cent by 2020. If the rate of growth of enrolment during the last two decades is any indicator, even this modest target appears ambitious (see Parhar 2002). That is, despite the phenomenal increase in enrolment, the vast majority of the youth in the age-group 17–23 years not only remains outside the sphere of higher education, but will remain so for decades to come.

The limited participation rate notwithstanding, the social composition of the university has changed remarkably since Independence. In 1950–51, the percentage of women in total enrolment in higher education was only 10, and this percentage has peaked at 40 in 2004, but there are significant regional variations in women's enrolment in higher education. Thanks to the policy of protective discrimination, there has been a slow but steady increase in the enrolment of scheduled caste and scheduled tribe students. In 2004, the scheduled castes constituted 10.7 per cent of the enrolment in higher education, and the scheduled tribes, 3.7 per cent (cited in Jayaram 2010: 164). Several state governments have extended the reservation of seats for students belonging to backward castes and communities, too. Further, more and more students from the rural background are entering the university.

Thus, there is a noticeable broad-basing of the university as regards its student body. The teacher community too has been undergoing a similar change. An examination of the changing composition of university as a public institution is due. However, the dialectics of cosmopolitanism and parochialism is noticeable in the universities. On the one hand, the university is a forum where students and teachers belonging to different sexes, communities, and socio-economic backgrounds can meet and interact. On the other hand, it is also a site for contestations of symbols and struggle for interests. If sectional interests succeed in influencing academic decisions, as it is noticed in several universities across the country, the university will be doomed as a public institution.

The Political Space

As a self-governing public institution, in a democracy, the university is naturally expected to provide space for some form of politics. The university campus is, in fact, the meeting place for divergent and often opposed views, opinions, and interests. As the highest centres of learning, it was expected that the universities would play a significant role in fostering a political culture to gel with democratic institutions and procedures. Regrettably, they have failed in this, and as a consequence academic politics is today 'all politics and hardly academic' (Béteille 2000: 169). As Béteille rightly observes 'Leaders of teachers' unions have not enhanced their own dignity or the dignity of the university by becoming petty instruments' of political parties. 'And they could hardly protect the autonomy of the university by surrendering their own autonomy to their parties' (ibid.: 168 and 169).

That organisation of teachers is engrossed only with securing better pay, career advancement and easy conditions of work, rather than with scholarship and professional issues is now well known (Jayaram 2003). What is not equally well known is the violent and abusive language used by the teachers in academic bodies. Based on his experience about the Academic Council of the University of Delhi and 'from hearsay about similar bodies in other universities' Béteille feels that the tone displayed by the teachers is 'now marked by a conspicuous, even deliberate, lack of civility' (2000: 167). What is pathetic, 'Many scholars and scientists have begun to feel that it is no longer possible to participate in the decision-making bodies of the university and maintain their self-esteem' (ibid.).

The students emulate their teachers. In many universities student unions function as extensions of the national- or the state-level political parties. They fight elections for representative offices in the university on the financial and moral support of these parties. The party functionaries even address election meetings on the campuses. In campuses where the involvement of political parties is not open, candidates contesting elections get indirect support from politicians. Often, the politicisation of the campus life results in violence, destruction of university property, and suspension of academic activities.

The teachers and students alone are not responsible for the politicisation of the campus. In most states, the autonomy of the university as a public institution is eroded by the aggrandisement of the state. Almost all the states have now enacted legislations to bring the universities under their control. In most state universities, the vice-chancellor and other functionaries of the university are now appointed by the political bosses running the government. Their nominees also sit in the decision-making bodies of universities. No wonder, the New Education Policy (1985) contemplated, though unrealistically, the depoliticisation of the academia.

The Loss of Legitimacy

Since Independence the university system has expanded rapidly, and haphazardly, too. Contrary to the moratorium on the expansion of the conventional pattern of universities, as contemplated by the New Educational Policy (1985), the National Knowledge Commission is recommending the expansion of this system even more rapidly. With little thought being given to the institutional life of universities, many of the old universities are decaying, and the new ones too will follow suit. It is as if each university has a life-cycle: born with euphoria, seeing a phase of growth and then becoming stagnant and moribund.

As Béteille observes,

> An important aspect of the university as an institution is that its individual members – whether students or teachers – should have some sense of it as a whole. Not many persons can say confidently or honestly that they have such a sense about Delhi University today, and in that regard it is now different from what it was forty years ago and what the Jawaharlal Nehru university still is today (2000: 157).

If this is what a senior academic has to say about a university located in the nation's capital, one can well imagine what could be said of universities elsewhere!

Along with the growing loss of its identity as a public institution is the erosion of the credibility and integrity of the university. The pervasive mistrust of the integrity of the academic selection process, with every selection invariably being questioned in courts of law; the umpteen scandals about university affairs reported in the media; the debilitating inbreeding in universities, resulting in mediocrity breeding more mediocrity; the shocking self-assured complacency among the academia; and, not the least, 'the demoralizing effect of the irrelevance and purposelessness of most of what is being done' (Naik 1982: 163) – all these have seriously violated the dignity of the university and undermined its legitimacy as a public institution.

Epilogue

It is hardly surprising that not even one Indian university or institute found a place in a recent academic ranking of top 100 universities and institutions of higher education in the world, and only two institutes and one university found listing under ranks below 200: IISc (Bangalore) (ranked in the bracket 202–301), IIT (Kharagpur) and University of Calcutta (Kolkata) (both ranked in the bracket 404–502) were the top three Indian institutions of higher education in that order.[15] Surely, the university as a public institution is now moribund.

There has been no dearth of suggestions for stemming the rot and improving the state of affairs. Several committees and commissions, including the Kothari Commission in the mid-1960s, have reviewed the situation and offered recommendations. Even in the best political climate, such proposals were rejected on grounds of elitism, and the government was content with tinkering with the system. Considering the economic and political cost of wholesale overhauling, and in view of the compulsions of coalition politics now, radical reform proposals are sure to remain on paper only.

Notes

1. If not on the same scale, similar institutions were implanted by the Portuguese and the French in those parts of India they had colonised respectively.
2. This is not to imply that the administration of these institutions was not influenced by personal or sectional interests. After all, these were institutions of the 'rulers', and not that of the 'ruled'. However, the history of public institutions in colonial India would, by and large, vindicate the integrity with which they were administered. It is not surprising that streets/roads, residential areas, and establishments in many Indian cities and towns are named after the great administrators of public institutions during the colonial era.
3. In writing this chapter, I have drawn on (a) my earlier work on higher education in India (see Jayaram 2003, 2004b, 2006, 2007, 2010), (b) my experience of working in two universities (Bangalore University and Goa University), an institute deemed-to-be university (Tata Institute of Social Sciences, Mumbai), and a research institute (Institute for Social and Economic Change, Bengaluru) outside the university system, and (c) my formal interaction with faculty, students, and administrators in several universities during the last forty years.
4. Higher education in India was intended to evolve a small class of English-educated Indians who may act, in Macaulay's words, as 'interpreters between us and millions whom we govern – a class of persons Indian in blood and colour, but English in tastes, in opinions, in morals and intellect' (in Sharp 1965: 116). It was never their intention to spread modern education among the masses. The British rule gradually supplanted the pre-colonial indigenous system of education consisting of Buddhist *viharas*, Hindu *pathashalas* and *tols*, and Muslim *madrasahas* by stopping financial aid. The Indian urban elite, too, welcomed English education as it was viewed not only as an avenue to jobs but also an instrument for social and political regeneration of India (A. Basu 2002: 168).
5. About the University of Calcutta, one of the three pioneer universities in the country, Lord Curzon observed: 'How different is India! Here the university has no corporate existence ... it is not a collection of buildings, it is scarcely even a site. It is a body that controls courses of study and sets examination papers to pupils of affiliated colleges' (Ministry of Education 1971: 498).

6. These institutions either specialise in some area of knowledge or are heirs to a tradition. They are not expected to grow to be multidiscipline universities of the general type.
7. The Indian Institutes of Management, which are also national-level institutions, are not vested with the power to award degrees, though their 'fellowships' are treated on par with university degrees.
8. The Kothari Commission was the first commission in India's educational history to look comprehensively at almost all aspects of education and to evolve a blueprint for a 'national system of education' (see Ministry of Education 1971). The Ministry of Education, which processed the Report, obliterated it by treating in a piecemeal fashion selected aspects of what was conceived to be a package deal (Naik 1982: 31–32).
9. In his Convocation Address to the University Poona (1966), Dr Gadgil used the choicest epithets to describe the proposal: 'favours "elitism"', 'grandiose', 'no relevance to an improvement of existing conditions in our universities and colleges' but will 'surely worsen these conditions', 'monstrous idea that I am prepared to risk the misunderstanding' (quoted in Naik 1982: 111–13).
10. What is said about the disjunction between universities (teaching) and institutes (research) with reference to science would hold good for social sciences, too. This is confirmed by a report on the social science research capacity in South Asia commissioned by the Social Science Research Council, New York in 2001 (see Chatterjee 2002).
11. Lacking any objective measurement of higher education standards over a period, it is, no doubt, difficult to determine precisely the nature and extent of deterioration. Nevertheless, there is no denying that India's standards compare unfavourably with the average standards in educationally advanced countries. The Education Commission had drawn attention to this as early as the mid-1960s (see Ministry of Education 1971: 66). No wonder, then, that degrees awarded by Indian universities are not regarded by many foreign universities as equivalent to their degrees; employers in India, including the government agencies, are wary of these degrees; and the students are resorting to 'shadow education' or private tuition conducted through 'coaching classes'.
12. There has been a drastic cut in public expenditure on higher education: between 1980–90 and 1994–95, the share of higher education in development (plan) expenditure decreased from 12.6 per cent to 6 per cent, whereas the same in maintenance (non-plan)

expenditure declined from 14.2 per cent to 11 per cent (Tilak 1996). Overall, the allocation for higher education, which had peaked at 28 per cent in the Fifth Five-Year Plan (1974–97), has steadily declined in the successive Plans to just 8 per cent in the Tenth Five-Year Plan (2002–07), which is the same as the allocation in the First Five-Year Plan (1951–56). As a proportion of total government expenditure, the share of higher education declined from 1.57 per cent in 1990–91 to 1.33 per cent in 2001–02. Considering the trends in per student expenditure – from Rs 7,676 in 1990–91 to Rs 5,873 in 2001–02 (in 1993–94 prices) (by 23.49%) – the decline in public expenditure on higher education would appear even more drastic (Tilak 2004: 2160–61).

13. The University Grants Commission (UGC) was established by an Act of Parliament in 1956 as a centralised authority vested with the power to provide funds and to set and coordinate standards of higher education (A. Singh 2004). It was modelled after the British UGC (established after World War I, since abolished).
14. The standards of academic performance in professional education are coordinated and regulated by statutory bodies such as the Indian Medical Council, the All India Council of Technical Education, the Bar Council of India, the Dental Council of India, the Pharmacy Council of India, and the Nursing Council of India. The Indian Council of Agricultural Research looks after agricultural education. These bodies were created by different ministries of the central government, and the lack of coordination among them is a problem. The question of jurisdiction between these bodies created by acts of Parliament and the universities established by acts of Parliament or state legislative bodies has often been agitated before courts of law. The National Knowledge Commission (2007: 53) has recommended the abolition of these bodies and the establishment of an Independent Regulatory Authority for Higher Education.
15. This ranking was based on a study of 2,000 universities and institutions of higher education across the world undertaken by the Institute of Higher Education, Shanghai Jiao Tong University, Shanghai, China. On the methodology of ranking adopted by this study, see http://ed.sjtu.edu.cn/rank/2004/top500list.htm. As of now, there is no official ranking of institutions of higher education in India. Some news magazines have attempted such a rank of colleges, but their rankings are populist and lack methodological rigour.

13

Confucius and the Guru

The Changing Status of the Academic Profession in China and India

with Philip G. Altbach

Being late starters in the sphere of modern higher education, developing countries find themselves in a difficult situation: on the one hand, they need to catch up with the rest of the world, particularly the advanced ones in the West; on the other, they confront the inexorable changes wrought by massification and globalisation and their ever increasing integration into the world economy. The dilemmas involve serious policy challenges given that a growing proportion of the world's higher education students are located in developing countries: by the mid-1990s, forty-four million of the world's eighty million students in higher education were in developing countries – despite the fact that only 6 per cent of the population in these countries attained post-secondary degrees, while 26 per cent in high-income countries had similar qualifications (The Task Force on Higher Education 2001: 111, 115). This part of the world is experiencing the highest rate of expansion of higher education.

Established in 1898, modern Chinese higher education has expanded rapidly over the last 100 years. There are now

> more than 3,000 universities and colleges – including 1,225 regular full-time universities and colleges, 686 adult higher education institutions, and 1,202 new private universities and colleges. The system encompasses 13 million students over 1.45

million staff members, 5,54,000 of whom are faculty members (Min 2004: 53–54).

In India, modern higher education was established as early as in 1857 as part of the British colonial enterprise. At the time of Independence (in 1947), however, there were only twenty universities and 496 colleges catering to 2,41,369 students. During the next fifty-five years, India built up a massive system of higher education. In 2001–02, there were 323 university-status institutions (178 state and eighteen central universities, eighteen medical and forty agricultural universities, fifty-two institutions 'deemed-to-be universities', twelve institutes of national importance, and five institutions established under state legislature acts), 13,510 colleges, and about 900 polytechnics. The system now employs 3,50,664 teachers and caters to about 82,75,000 students (though estimated to be covering hardly 8 per cent of the population in the relevant [17–23] age-group) (Jayaram 2006).

By examining the developments in China and India, the 'Asian giants' in higher education (Altbach and Umakoshi 2004), this chapter will discuss the problems and prospects of the professoriate in developing countries.[1] These two countries together account for more than one-third of the world's population. China recently overtook the United States of America as the country with the highest enrolments, while India ranks in the top five. With their well-developed higher education systems, including some excellent research universities, both countries differ from many developing countries (Altbach 1998). The conditions China and India share with many other developing countries include the large number of low quality institutions, sometimes difficult conditions for study, and shortage of funds at all levels. The main focus of this chapter is to explain the changing position of academics in these countries today, the implications for higher education. This chapter will deal with such issues as constricting employment opportunities, deteriorating career prospects and working conditions, and changing role expectations.

The Changing Context of Higher Education

Both in China and India, and in developing countries generally, higher education has traditionally enjoyed considerable patronage.

However, over the last two decades, higher education has been thrown into a vortex of change, inevitably impacting the academic profession. China has undergone a pronounced shift from a command economy to a market economy (albeit while still within the socialist framework) and from a predominantly bureaucratic culture to a competitive corporate culture. In India, the stimulus for change has come with the 1990 adoption by the government of structural adjustment reforms influenced by the World Bank and the International Monetary Fund.

The structural change in the Chinese higher education system since the 1990s has centred on the large number of state-driven mergers. In 1998, China's 1,022 regular public higher educational institutions enrolled 10,83,600 students. Total enrolments at higher learning institutions including adult education institutions, amounted to 62,31,000. During 1992–95, more than seventy public (state-run) institutions merged into twenty-eight universities, and over 100 institutions set up cross-institution consortiums. As of 2000, a total of 612 higher education institutions merged into 250. Operationally, these changes – heavily influenced by western ethos and practices – have significantly impacted the academic profession, which hitherto carried the stamp of traditional Chinese cultural values and norms. The introduction of the 'post system' in academic appointments, in contrast to the existing 'title system', represents a case in point. This new system reflects the mover from a predominantly bureaucratic to a competitive corporate culture in Chinese higher education.

Another reform of the Chinese higher education – particularly noteworthy, considering the unwavering socialist foundation of the Chinese state – consists of the introduction of *minban* (non-state-run) or private universities and colleges. By the beginning of 2001, about 2,000 institutions existed in this new sector in Chinese higher education, though 'with a lower level of student enrolments and a less stable faculty' (Chen 2003: 108). The employment and service conditions at these institutions are different from those in the public institutions.

In India, structural adjustment has meant a scaling back of state patronage and a simultaneous privatisation of higher education. However, the government itself is confused and has been dithering about the policy to be adopted on this matter. State investment in education in India has always failed to meet the needs of 'education for all'. Structural adjustment has meant a drastic cut in public expenditure on higher education: between 1980–90 and 1994–95, higher education's share of the central government's five-year plan expenditure decreased from 12.6 per cent to 6 per cent; whereas the same in non-plan expenditure declined only from 14.2 per cent to 11 per cent (Tilak 1996). Overall, the allocation for higher education, which had peaked at 28 per cent in the Fifth Five-Year Plan (1974–97), has steadily declined in the successive plans to just 8 per cent in the Tenth Five-Year Plan (2002–07), which is the same as the allocation in the First Five-Year Plan (1951–56). The annual growth rate of public expenditure on university and higher education, which was 13.1 per cent between 1980–81 and 1985–86, fell to 7.8 per cent between 1980–81 and 1995–96 (Shariff and Ghosh 2000: 1400). Thus, the state, which had hitherto been the dominant partner in funding higher education, is finding it increasingly difficult even to maintain the same level of funding for higher education.

The gradual withdrawal of the state from higher education in India has been accompanied by its inability to address the need for reforms within the conventional higher education. The National Policy on Education (1985) and the Programme of Action (1986), and their review by the Acharya Ramamurti Committee (1991) were all pre-structural-adjustment reform initiatives. Neither the phenomenal fall in the demand for conventional graduate courses, nor the remarkable spurt in the demand for course in such areas as computer science and information technology, biotechnology, and management studies, was anticipated.

The unwillingness and inability of the state to invest in the new areas of education explain the growth of private institutions. These institutions, also referred to as 'self-financing institutions', are of uneven quality – ranging from a small number of centres of excellence to roadside teaching-shops. These new entrants to the arena of higher education raise questions of autonomy and accountability (since they do not depend on state funding), on the one hand, and issues concerning teachers (like qualifications and recruitment, career options, pay and working conditions, etc.), on the other. Thus, private initiatives in higher education are fraught with serious implications for the academic profession.

Both in China and India, the general context of higher education has been undergoing change. While in the Chinese case the transition has been regulated, in the Indian case it is one of gradual withdrawal of state patronage in an unregulated market. What do such scenarios mean to the academic profession in the respective countries? What are the conditions and prospects of employment relations for academia?

China: Unfinished Reform and Professorial Uncertainty

Problems of Overstaffing and Understaffing

For almost fifty years, since the beginning of the socialist system of planned economic and social change, teachers were appointed in China under a 'tenure system'. Under this system, once hired, the academic as well as auxiliary staff were provided with what the Chinese called an 'iron rice bowl', that is, a secure job for life. All teachers received more or less the same salary regardless of their qualifications and contributions. Over the decades, this system of appointment resulted in problems of overstaffing, incompetence, and inefficiency. In 1998, the faculty-student ratio was 1:11.2. While the problem of overstaffing cuts across the system of higher education, it is particularly concerned with the non-teaching or auxiliary staff, rather than the teaching staff.

The problem of overstaffing has worsened with the merger of higher education institutions. The rationale for mergers was to produce economies of scale, delegate more administrative power to the local authorities, and render institutions more comprehensive. 'If a smaller, less-renowned institution merges with a larger, prestigious one, the new entity usually takes the name of the latter as well as its standards for faculty appointments' (Chen 2003: 109). Given their generally lower level of competence, with mergers, faculty members from the smaller institutions are obviously placed in a disadvantageous position.

Mergers have also resulted in the downsizing of the professoriate: some positions are eliminated with their corresponding staff and some faculty are retrenched or reassigned or forced to find work at other institutions or in other professions. For example, 'After Central Technical Arts College was merged with Tsinghua University in 2000 ... only 6 of the 12 English teachers at the former were retained in the English Department of

Tsinghua University. The rest were forced to find work at other institutions or in other professions' (ibid.). It is not surprising, therefore, that while the teachers at smaller institutions are generally unenthusiastic about the mergers, their students welcome it.

While overstaffing exists throughout higher education, almost every institution also suffers from a shortage of competent faculty. The latter has to do with the expansion of higher education, which has accelerated since the early 1990s:

> The number of first-year students at regular higher learning institutions increased by 47.3 per cent, from 1.084 million in 1998 to 1.597 million in 1999. Enrolments at adult learning institutions increased by 15.7 per cent, from 1.001 million to 1.158 million, and the number of graduate students increased by 17.6 per cent. Total student enrolment doubled between 1990 and 1999. The gross enrolment rate of the 18 to 22 age cohort increased from 3.9 per cent in 1992 to 9.1 per cent in 1997, to 10 per cent in 2000, and is expected to rise to 15 per cent in 2005 (ibid.).

For the professoriate, the fact that institutions now have more students than they can handle has led to an increase in class-size and workload. Without the help of teaching assistants, the quality of teaching is an obvious casualty. Not surprisingly, most professors follow what the Chinese call the 'duck-feeding' method – teachers delivering monologues and students taking down notes passively; a system with minimal interaction between the teacher and the taught. The most acute understaffing is reported in the local vocational and adult learning institutions, which have also experienced rapid expansion during the last decade, and in institutions located in small cities.

Understaffing is compounded not only by relatively low salary levels but also by the lack of opportunities for professional development. As Weifang Min notes, 'while basic salaries of university faculty were comparable to those of other professionals with similar educational qualifications, faculty remuneration was lower because of larger bonuses given to employees in companies, especially in joint venture firms' (2004: 75). Many well-qualified, competent faculty members are dissatisfied with their jobs, and tend to leave them as and when they get the opportunity. That is, the professoriate is affected by 'brain drain'. For the same reasons, teaching does not attract the best talents from universities. In fact, research universities affiliated with the Ministry of Education or other ministries suffer from the same weakness. Furthermore, under the conventional tenure system it is not easy to remove the incompetent teachers either.

The laws enacted by the State Council determine the qualifications for teaching positions. The Teachers' Qualification Law of 1995 stipulates the minimum qualification of a master's degree for faculty below the age of 40. In fact, the qualification levels of teachers are still low: in 1999, only 5.4 per cent of faculty held a doctoral degree, and 24 per cent a master's degree. The system permits pronounced inbreeding, with senior faculty and administrators tending to employ their own students. Very little mobility exists in the academic profession, which gives the many underqualified teachers who entered a low-salary but high-security job little incentive to work hard. Many of these staff have retired or have been pushed out in the process of modernisation.

From 'Title System' to 'Post System'

Recognising the importance of quality higher education in a rapidly globalising world, the Chinese government has embarked upon a programme of reform in structure and orientation. The main objective of this reform is to make the system of higher education internationally competitive, and the strategy is to raise the quality of the faculty. Now at the experimental stage, once the programme of reform is implemented across the institutions of higher education, it will have profound impact on the professoriate. While the Chinese government and the ruling elite have the power to implement the reform, their commitment to systemic and sustained reform remains an open question.

A hallmark of higher education reform in China, signifying a radical change in the system of recruitment for academic profession, has been the implementation of a 'post system' in the place of the conventional 'title system' of tenured employment. In 1998, the Ministry of Education introduced the post system of academic appointments on an experimental basis in two universities – Peking University and Tsinghua University. Each of these universities was given a special annual grant of 1.8 billion Yuan or US $ 222 million for three years. Twenty-five per cent of these grants were earmarked for faculty development.

Academic positions are divided into three categories (A, B, and C in the descending order), with each category containing three ranks. Above the top category (A) is the special category of internationally known scholars. The rank-related subsidy is predetermined and divided into two parts: only 70 per cent is paid to a faculty member each month, and the remaining 30 per cent is paid after a faculty review at the end of the year.

Xiangming Chen lists four main objectives of this reform:

> (i) to break away from the 'all-tenure' system with its 'iron rice bowl syndrome'; (ii) to separate one's title from one's rank so that competent people can be hired for the right posts even if they do not have a certain title; (iii) to link one's salary with one's post, thus widening the gap between different salary scales; and (iv) to downsize the faculty by reassigning surplus people to other jobs (2003: 113).

Unless they are competent enough, no teachers, including full professors, will be selected for the category they desire. Thus, teachers who are not competent enough will get only the basic salary for their title and no subsidy. The performance appraisal of teachers also has a provision for punitive action for non-performers, and three professors at the prestigious Tsinghua University were reportedly dismissed because of negative evaluations and 'poor performance'.

Since 2000, the post system has been implemented in other universities including Fudan University and Shanghai Transport University. Shandong Agriculture University abolished the title system, and the savings resulting from expenses earlier incurred on superfluous personnel were diverted to increase the support for faculty with posts.

The post system and the associated rank-related subsidies are reportedly motivating the faculty to work harder than under the former title system. It is also expected to enhance the professional development of the faculty and commitment to their work and institution. Considering the generally low basic salaries under the title system, the financial position of teachers with proven qualifications and capabilities has steadily improved. This has been a welcome development considering that the cost of living has risen over the decades, whereas the rise in the basic salary has not been commensurate.

However, for the vast majority of the teachers, who are by and large less qualified and less competent, this reform has meant closed doors. Their salaries being low and the cost of living rising, many of them are forced to look for additional job outside the university. Those who have been laid off due to downsizing as a result of the introduction of the post system have reached the end of the road. Of course, the downsizing has affected the administrators, auxiliary staff, and Party officials more than faculty members. For the university leadership, the reassignment of surplus staff and faculty has been a great challenge.

As noted earlier, attracting competent people and improving faculty capabilities have been on the agenda of reform. The Ministry of Education, other ministries, and institutions have carried out several recruitment campaigns. Awards, both in kind and in cash, have been instituted to improve the competence levels of the faculty. Opportunities for advanced study and research are being extended to competent faculty. Model programmes – such as the 3-T (top talents, top university set-up, and top scientific achievement) initiative of Shanghai 2nd Medical University – have been instituted. Even overseas teachers have been invited to teach and do research in some Chinese universities.

The Growing Private Sector

These reforms in higher education have all addressed the public universities. Besides the public sector, China now has a rapidly growing private sector in higher education that is entirely financed by non-governmental sources. Since the early 1990s, about 2,000 private institutions have been established mostly in the 'practical fields of study'. While the Ministry of Education oversees the establishment of private higher education institutions, it prescribes no hard and fast rules about the number, title, ranks, or salary of the faculty.

Accordingly, private higher educational institutions offer a different model for faculty appointments, namely, the contract system. Teachers are appointed on contract for a given term, usually one year. In some cases full-time teachers are hired on monthly contracts or are paid by the hour. Part-time teachers are, as a rule, paid by the hour. Faculties at these institutions, irrespective of their specific contractual appointments, are generally not provided benefits in addition to their salary. Even so, the faculty salaries at private institutions are higher than those in their public counterparts.

It must be noted that a majority of the faculty at private institutions are part-time appointments. These institutions tend to hire as full-time teachers retired professors from public universities. Moreover, except for the few institutions accredited by the Ministry of Education, private institutions do not provide opportunities for promotion. These institutions maintain high teacher-student ratios. The teachers find themselves called upon to help the institutions with multiple tasks like accounting, counselling, etc. in addition to teaching.

Continuity and Change

The reform measures in higher education, no doubt, have produced some positive results. The efficiency and effectiveness of teaching and research have improved. The criteria for appointment and promotion have become more fair and transparent than before. Apparently, however, while the old problems are being solved or dealt with, new ones emerge. The persistence of the mentality associated with the old title system causes dissatisfaction and resentment among faculty, who now feel deprived because of reforms. Tensions have also arisen among different institutions, as for example, between prestigious research universities (such as Peking University or Tsinghua University) and less-well-known universities and institutions. Obviously, prestigious institutions have a competitive edge over the others.

The fact that the programme of reform draws on western ethos and practices raises questions about its compatibility with traditional Chinese cultural norms. In a country where traditional culture advocates 'peace, harmony, and contentedness', the new system, premised upon competitive efficiency, has engendered social tensions. The new system, which has introduced ranks and pecuniary differences among faculty, contradicts the idea of 'social justice' hitherto emphasised by the socialist ideology. Realising the adverse implications of such tensions, attempts, both formal and informal, are being made to contain them.

The size and diversity of China's higher education system make it difficult to generalise about the academic profession. This chapter examines mostly academics in the relatively high-prestige sector of an increasingly differentiated academic system. This discussion focuses less attention on the large number of academic staff, many with only bachelor's degrees, who are teaching in provincial institutions, or are part-time teachers. This chapter also does not point out some of the basic realities of many universities, including limited academic freedom, especially in the social sciences, and a governance system that gives limited power and autonomy to the professoriate.

In China, rapid expansion of higher education, a desire by the Chinese government to improve the qualifications of academic staff, growing institutional diversity, and accountability-based management are all creating a changing environment and increased pressure on the academic profession.

India: The Declining Profession

Declining Employment Prospects

The unbridled expansion of higher education in India during the 1970s and 1980s had resulted in an unprecedented demand for teachers. Responding to this demand, India has experienced a sixteen-fold increase in the number of teachers in higher education over a period of five decades; the total number now stands at 3,21,000. This development does not, however, indicate a state of healthy growth, strength, or vitality of the academic profession. Not only has the prospect of employment as a college or university teacher diminished, but security of employment, once taken for granted in the academic profession, is also becoming more problematic. As early as 1983, the National Commission on Teachers (1985) found that only 70.7 per cent of university teaching staff and 68.5 per cent of college teachers enjoyed permanent employment with all statutory benefits. Other faculty and staff constitute 'temporary' (with no guarantee of continuation) or ad hoc (appointed as a leave replacement for a short period of time) lecturers. New categories of teachers, such as 'part-time' lecturers (who teach for a specified number of teaching hours per week) and 'guest' lecturers (who help the college or department 'to complete portions of the syllabus') have been added. Such teachers are paid on an hourly basis, and they do not enjoy the other privileges that accompany a permanent or even a temporary or an ad hoc appointment.

The decline of employment prospects in the academic profession relates to the combined effect of structural adjustment reforms and the market forces operating within higher education. The expansion of conventional arts and sciences courses seems to have outstripped the demand for them by students, with some colleges (most Indian first-degree students study at colleges affiliated to a university) facing a severe decline in enrolments. For some private colleges assisted by grant-in-aid from the government, it has even become difficult to find workloads for teachers in these disciplines.

Most state governments have imposed an embargo on the recruitment of teachers. This has meant a freeze on the establishment of state-supported colleges, a downsizing in the number of permanent teachers at existing colleges, and most effective use of resources by redeploying teachers through a policy of transfers. In addition, most state governments have also introduced 'voluntary retirement schemes' (giving incentives to teachers to retire from permanent service before they reach the compulsory retirement age). State governments are contemplating lowering the retirement age for college and university teachers. Not surprisingly, temporary part-time teachers have become a standard feature of higher education in India.

The downsizing of the academic profession through freezing of recruitment, redeployment of excess staff, appointment of guest lecturers, etc. is now a pan-Indian phenomenon. Moreover, this trend is not confined to the conventional liberal arts and sciences colleges, but has affected some technical education institutions too. However, in such fields as computer science, information technology, and biotechnology, where the expansion has been most rapid, there is a dearth of qualified teachers. Medical education suffers from the most acute teacher shortage.

The bulk of the teaching community, however, is engaged in general education. Employment opportunities here have almost dried up, and those seeking entry into the profession have been employed on a part-time or ad hoc basis. That existing teachers find it difficult to get adequate workloads does not augur well for the academic profession. State policies of downsizing the profession will likely adversely impact the already low morale and commitment of teachers.

Traditionally, a preserve of the higher social strata, the academic profession has enjoyed a prestigious reputation. However, the rapid expansion of higher education, combined with state policy of protective discrimination, has altered the social profile of the profession. A significant proportion of the candidates belong to the scheduled castes, scheduled tribes, and other backward classes. The new entrants into the academic profession, in many cases the first generation in their caste and community groups to have acquired postgraduate qualifications, basically lack exposure to the cultural moorings of the profession and are confused about the ethos of a profession in decline. Women still constitute only about one-fourth of the teachers in higher education, although in some fields as the humanities and social sciences their numbers are higher, yet lag in academic leadership roles.

Parochialism and inbreeding have become integral practices in higher education. Educational institutions run by minority religious communities have always shown preference for candidates belonging to their own religion or sect, and similarly those dominated by particular caste groups have shown bias in favour of their caste fellows. Universities and state governments also prefer candidates from their own geographical region. In fact, the adoption of the state language as the medium of instruction in many colleges and universities precludes eligible candidates from outside a given state.

The University Grants Commission (UGC), the national government's main funding and regulatory agency for higher education, supports inter-institutional mobility of teachers to help infuse fresh blood into a system that would otherwise become stagnant and induce cross-fertilisation among the different institutions. While inbreeding inhibits mobility, other impediments also exist. Moving from one institution to another reduces one's chances of promotion, which discourages lecturers and readers from leaving the institution in which they are working. State government regulations covering teachers' retirement benefits are rigid, making senior teachers wary of moving out of the state in which they are working.

Deficient Professional Preparation

Studies on college teachers have invariably emphasised the sad deficiency of academic preparation of the people entering the profession and their declining commitment to it. This lack of qualification, no doubt, has a lot to do with the deplorable standards of master's and doctoral level education. For decades most master's degree holders could easily find employment at colleges, or even at universities, with absolutely no training or orientation to teaching, and with doubtful aptitude for the vocation.

To ensure proficiency in the subject and aptitude for teaching or research on the part of candidates aspiring to become teachers, UGC introduced the scheme of the National Eligibility Test (NET). Many state governments have been permitted by UGC to conduct State Eligibility Test, which is treated as equivalent to NET. As a screening mechanism, NET is a step in the right direction. Despite these efforts, standards of post-baccalaureate education remain generally low. Professions, such as architecture, law, and medicine require their prospective recruits to undergo a specialised period of internship. Even a high school teacher needs to obtain the bachelor of education degree. To become a lecturer at a college or university, however, no prior training or experience is necessary.

While this anomaly is recognised by many, educators do not agree as to the additional qualifications that should be required for entry into the academic profession. Insistence on a research degree (PhD or MPhil) has become counterproductive. The rush for enrolment in doctoral programmes, following the UGC's decision in the 1970s to make a PhD the minimum qualification, has resulted in a deterioration of the quality of doctoral research at universities.

Regardless of the importance of qualifications and screening at the point of entry into the profession, the need for post-induction training and periodical professional enhancement can hardly be exaggerated. Stating in 1987, UGC established at least one Academic Staff College (ASC) in each state with the mandate to improve standards of teaching through 'orientation courses' (focussing on pedagogy and social relevance of education, for new entrants into the profession) and 'refresher courses' (providing up-to-date information on the content of various disciplines, for those already in the profession as lecturers).

The Academic Staff Colleges conduct programmes to orient the new entrants into the profession and to improve the knowledge and skills of those already in it. To instil a sense of seriousness, an element of compulsion has also been introduced. Those entering the profession are required to attend an orientation course before they complete their probation. Teachers in service must attend two refresher courses to become eligible for career advancement or promotion. As with all initiatives carrying a compulsory element, the original objectives underlying the establishment of ASCs are lost and the courses have been ritualised.

The dwindling recruitment to permanent posts at universities and colleges has reduced the enthusiasm for orientation courses. However, the situation concerning refresher courses differs given the large number of teachers seeking career advancement and the ASC's facilities are limited. To meet the demand for such courses, UGC has been providing grants to departments at universities without ASCs to organise refresher courses. In addition to the ASC refresher courses, universities departments and disciplinary associations have organised 'self-financed' courses. Most refresher courses, whether they are organised by ASCs or university departments (UGC-sponsored or self-financed), are conducted as a formality and they generally lack the advanced academic orientation expected for them.

Besides ASCs, UGC established the College Science Improvement Programme and the College Social Science and Humanities Improvement Programme to enhance the quality of teachers. Permanent teachers desirous of acquiring doctoral qualifications receive paid leave for two or three years under the Faculty Improvement Programme (FIP). Teachers interested in pursuing research are offered grants for minor and major research projects. Financial assistance is extended to teachers to attend seminars, symposia, and workshops. Promising young teachers with a research proclivity are offered funds under the Career Award Scheme, and the renowned among senior teachers are given National Associateship.

While they are expected to improve the quality of teaching and thereby benefit students, these human resource development schemes do not seem to have yielded the expected results. Most teachers do not avail themselves of the opportunities for professional development. Even those teachers who have made use of

FIP or other facilities have at best obtained only a research degree, but not implemented their advanced training in the classroom. Some teachers who have participated in FIP are reported to have spent time on activities other than research. Similar complaints have been raised about the provision of sabbatical leave for university teachers. Not surprisingly, UGC has now become more restrictive in awarding the FIP fellowships.

Career Prospects and Working Conditions

While professional development and teaching performance have seldom concerned teachers or their associations, the issues of salary, career prospects, and service conditions have always ranked high on their agenda. In fact, the teachers have often blamed inadequate salaries and unattractive career prospects for the deterioration in the status of the academic profession. In absolute terms, if not in relative terms, with the revised pay package promulgated by UGC in 1998, teachers obtained the best deal ever, especially considering the nature and extent of their workload and the little accountability that is demanded of them.[2] While the UGC pay package has been accepted in principle across the country, significant variations exist in its implementation by different states.

The academic profession has traditionally been pyramidal in structure, with more lecturers than readers and more readers than professors. This has meant that irrespective of the academic achievements and professional development, after a specified span of service, the teaching faculty was destined to stagnate. To offer opportunities for vertical mobility to teachers at multiple stages in their career, UGC has incorporated a career-advancement scheme based on the professional development of teachers. While this scheme is well thought out, its implementation cannot be taken for granted, especially considering the failure of the merit promotion scheme that has been ended.

The UGC pay package fixed the retirement age for university and college teachers at 62. While UGC is categorical that 'no extension in service should be given', it has allowed the universities the option to re-employ a superannuated teacher up to the age of 65 years in certain cases. However, only the central universities (those directly funded by the central government) have accepted the recommendation to set the retirement age at 62. State governments have retained the existing retirement age (58 for college academic staff and 60 for university academic staff), as they fear that it would lead to agitation by government employees demanding a similar revision of the retirement age. Given the growing unemployment rate among the educated, it would be indefensible for any state government to raise the retirement age. More important, when state governments have meagre resources for higher education and are consciously pursuing a policy of downsizing the number of teachers (including through early retirement incentives), raising the retirement age would be unthinkable.[3]

The UGC's new pay package also set the number of teaching days and the workload of teachers. A minimum of 180 'actual teaching days' per year has been stipulated for universities and colleges. Universities are to devote seventy-two days and colleges sixty days for admission formalities and the evaluation of students. The workload of full-time teachers has been fixed at not less than forty hours a week for thirty working weeks (180 teaching days) in an academic year. Of these, sixteen hours of direct teaching have been set for lecturers and fourteen hours for readers and professors.

These regulations have received unenthusiastic acceptance by the academic profession and based on past experience are sure to be observed more in theory than in practice. For instance, university and college calendars formally include the official number of 'working weeks' and 'teaching days' and the stipulated duration of vacations. However, in connivance with the teachers unions, some universities have cleverly introduced mid-term holidays called as 'breaks' rather than 'vacations'. There is little accountability with regard to the required number of teaching days. With delayed admissions, innumerable official and unofficial holidays, and strikes by students, teachers, and the non-teaching staff, the loss of working days is quite high.

State governments imposed specific workloads on grant-in-aid colleges to ensure that teachers would have a certain number of 'direct teaching' hours – a policy necessary for downsizing the number of teachers and redeploying or firing excess teaching staff. Fearing downsizing of staff, however, some university departments have inflated the workloads by creating dummy timetables.

Whether the number of direct teaching hours (sixteen hours per week for lecturers and fourteen hours for readers and professors) is a pedagogically sound norm does not seem to concern the academic profession or UGC. Of concern, instead, are the issues of teacher truancy and absenteeism, since rather than regularly teaching the classes allotted to them, many teachers are not even on site at the institution for the stipulated five hours a day. Attempts by concerned vice-chancellors, principals, and department heads to police teachers have not yielded the desired results.

Performance Appraisal

Evaluation of the performance of its members is sadly lacking in the academic profession. Traditionally, the quality of teaching has not been a criterion for teachers to be recognised and rewarded. In practice, promotions have been based almost exclusively on seniority in service. The lack of objective indicators of performance may well undermine the effectiveness of a career advancement scheme.

Some states (for example, Karnataka) have instituted annual 'best teacher' awards, although they provide little motivation or incentives to improve teachers' performance. It is true that good performance by the students in the examination may provide some credit (and satisfaction) to teachers, either directly or indirectly. However, poor student performance is seldom used as a basis to admonish or punish teachers. Except at a few top universities and the Indian Institutes of Technology and Indian Institutes of Management, peer review or student evaluation of teachers is virtually non-existent in most colleges and university departments. Any proposal for such forms of review or evaluation would be vehemently opposed by teachers unions.

The National Policy on Education envisaged the creation of an open, participative, and objective system of teacher evaluation. It even contemplated laying down 'norms of accountability', 'with incentives for good performance and disincentives for non-performance'. Subsequently, UGC announced a format for 'self-appraisal' by teachers, both at the time of entry into the profession and annually thereafter. However, this process has either not been initiated or has been perfunctory. In response, UGC has now made 'consistently satisfactory performance appraisal reports' mandatory for career advancement.

Academic Autonomy and Professional Organisation

Barring a few rare exceptions, academic autonomy is reasonably secure in India. In fact, the instances of teachers abusing it are plenty, and these take many forms, such as non-performance of role obligations (teaching and research), resisting change in curriculum and pedagogy, indulging in malpractice in evaluation, and others. This calls for governmental intervention, just as it raises the question of professional obligation of teachers.

Private tutoring by college teachers is one issue that has attracted critical attention of governmental authorities and members of the public alike. The rise of 'shadow education' conducted through 'coaching classes' is closely related to the falling standards of formal education. With the existing colleges being unable to teach effectively and the students wanting to sharpen their competitive edge, private tuition has become a vital supplement to classroom instruction and is thriving. Since teachers involved in coaching classes are, by and large, formally employed in colleges on a full-time basis, private tuition raises the question of professional ethics.

The University Grants Commission has always been critical of the college and university teachers engaging in private tutoring, but has not been able to do anything about it. State governments have been ambivalent about private tutoring: while in principle, they are opposed to it, some states have introduced special coaching classes for students belonging to the scheduled castes, scheduled tribes, and other backward classes. Others have issued administrative orders banning private tuition and coaching classes conducted by regular teachers, but find it impossible to implement the ban. Teachers' organisations are silent over the whole issue.

After a prolonged period of political apathy, the teaching community has been gradually politicised. This trend started in the mid-1970s. That this politicisation coincided with the decline of the profession is a matter of concern. It is not that academia has become an arena of party politics or ideological battles, though in some universities even this has happened. Rather, 'the politics of scarcity' has more direct bearing on the academic profession now than ever before, and is the main motivating force for professional militancy. To date, however, teachers' unions have not been especially effective in improving conditions for the academic profession.

Practically, every university has one or more teachers' unions, euphemistically called organisations or associations, to distinguish themselves from the working class trade unions. The growth in the number of such unions does not necessarily denote a healthy development for the profession. There has been fragmentation of organisation and often conflicts among them. Such proliferation of teachers' unions through a process of fragmentation and segmentation has weakened the teachers' movement and hindered their professionalisation. Studies on unionisation of teachers have revealed that it 'does not necessarily ensure their collegial participation or promote professionalisation among them' (Jayaram 1992: 161–62).

Teachers' unions are generally weak. Even the All India Federation of University and College Teachers Organisations (AIFUCTO) does not command the mass support it once did. Given the middle-class focus on working conditions, salary is the only issue on which teachers can be mobilised. On a closer review it appears that whatever strength teachers' unions manifest is not due to any intrinsic qualities, but due to the soft attitude of the government towards them. It is amazing that even when teachers go on prolonged strikes, the principle of 'no work, no pay' has seldom been applied to them.

The pattern of agitation by teachers is by now well established. It consists of protest rallies, mass or relay hunger strikes, marching to chief/education minister's house, abstention from work, and finally the boycott of examination work. Going by how the government has dealt with strikes by much stronger unions of employees in the telecommunication, postal, insurance, and banking sectors during the last decade or so, teachers cannot take the material success of their strike for granted. Let alone an all-India agitation, even state-level agitations are running out of steam.

The Decline of the Professoriate

With the structural adjustment reforms and liberalisation of the economy, the state is gradually shedding its responsibility for higher education. The University Grants Commission has been virtually reduced to a mere fund-disbursing agency, incapable of enforcing its own recommendations. Educationally, the Indian university system has progressively become marginalised. Being outside the purview of UGC and to a large extent of the state governments, the emerging private educational sector may be more successful, but it is too early to assess this.

The decline of the academic profession, which was noticed over a quarter of a century (see Shils 1969), is now almost complete. Entering the profession with no prior professional preparation other than a postgraduate degree, assured of tenure, doing unchallenging work without much accountability, teachers in colleges and universities have been largely reduced to the lowest common denominator. Every laudable policy to improve the situation has been merely ritualised. It is true that the situation is better in some centres of excellence, the institutions of national importance, and a few university departments and colleges. They are, however, drops in an ocean of mediocrity.

Ironically, the improvements in pay scales and career prospects have come at a time when the profession is at a low ebb. Teachers are largely happy with the pay package, but they are also worried about the gradual withdrawal of state support for higher education. In the meantime, both politicians and the general population have the common view that college and university teachers are a pampered lot, probably being paid more than they are worth. Without question, the profession of the guru has fallen from its pedestal.

Conclusion: The Professoriate at a Crossroads

In both China and India, the academic profession is in an uncertain transitory phase. In China, the academic profession is caught between the push and the pull of a state-centred socialist ideology and the old bureaucratic control, on the one hand, and the socialist market economy and the new corporate culture, on the other. The professoriate in China faces the challenge of deciding what to keep and what to discard from its traditions, what to adopt and what to modify from the trends of modernity from the West, and how to decentralise an excessively centralised system without creating chaos. In India, with the state gradually withdrawing from the sphere of higher education and dithering about long-term policy, the academic profession faces an uncertain future.

In China, reform measures for public universities and the new private sector in education have brought about greater academic autonomy, attention to quality, and increased transparency in the career advancement of teachers, though the old forces of central planning and official interference are still at work. In India, the partial loss of traditional job security has been accompanied by the diminishment of academic autonomy. In both China and India, there is an increased emphasis on quality, something that was largely ignored under systems of state control and patronage. The emphasis on quality should at least partially be credited to market forces and the internationalisation of higher education.

Notes

1. In preparing this chapter, the authors have drawn heavily on Chen (2003), Jayaram (2003), and Min (2004). For more recent analysis of the academic profession in India, see Jayaram (2012, 2013).
2. To arrest the flight of talent from teaching profession, since 1 January 2006, the salaries of university and college teachers have been upwardly revised steeply and a revised career advancement scheme has been put in place (see Jayaram 2012).
3. Following the introduction of the new pay scales in 2006, in central universities and centrally funded higher education institutions, the age of retirement for faculty is now fixed at 65, with a provision of re-appointment for five more years in exceptional cases. The state governments, however, have not followed suit: the retirement age for university and college teachers varies from 60 to 62 (see Jayaram 2012).

14

Teachers and Unionism

with G. Sivaramakrishnan

The debate over the distinction between professional and non-professional occupations has been both protracted and prolix. Since the notion of 'profession' is at best an 'ideal type' (Vollmer and Mills 1966: vii), the contention whether particular occupations are professions or not is ill-conceived and sterile. 'Hughes has rightly pointed out that the significant question to ask is not whether or not they are professions but to what extent they exhibit characteristics of professionalisation' (Jackson 1970: 5).

Persons pursuing an occupation, after assessing their occupational situation, come to associate in a professionally meaningful fashion. Such professional organisations may vary in terms of their goals, organisation structures, and strategies of operation. They promote professionalisation of the occupation by contributing towards professional identity, solidarity, autonomy, and status. They foster the welfare and security of their members, facilitate exchange of information, and evolve and promote codes of conduct. Some of them even openly operate as direct pressure groups in the formulation of public policy.

According to George Strauss, 'occupational associations form a continuum, from the learned society (which exists only to advance knowledge) at one extreme, to the economically oriented unions at the other' (quoted in Vollmer and Mills 1966: 184). Ideally, a teachers' organisation is expected to fall at the former extreme of the continuum and contribute to the professionalisation of teaching. This chapter seeks to understand where along this continuum the college teachers' organisations in India lie.

The report of the Education Commission (1964–66) has envisaged the following as some of the functions of teachers' organisations:

- to secure for their members, individually and collectively, their rightful status – social, economic, and professional;
- to safeguard their professional interests and to secure satisfactory conditions of work and service;
- to secure the professional growth of teachers through refresher courses, seminars, publications, library service, and research;
- to work for the improvement of education in response to the challenge of the ever-changing socio-economic situation;
- to improve the teaching of subjects through the establishment of subject-teachers associations; and
- to establish a professional code of conduct for teachers and to ensure that it is followed by members (Ministry of Education 1971: 114).

That teachers' organisation may provide an opportunity for teachers to participate in the affairs of the profession, serve as a liaison between teachers, on the one hand, and the administrators and the public, on the other, and assist in legislative campaigns has been recognised (Dutt 1970: 9–11). Thus, it would be difficult to exaggerate the importance of teachers' organisations for the effective functioning of teachers as professionals.

It is both interesting and important to study teachers' organisations, since teachers constitute a key element in the academic equation and their organisations affect not only themselves and the educational system in which they are working, but also the wider society. The problems involved in organising teachers, the nature and functioning of some teachers' organisations, the prospects of their organisations developing into a teachers' movement, and the implications of all this for the professionalisation of teaching, are some of the issues dealt with in this chapter.

The chapter is divided into five sections including this introduction. Section II briefly sketches the history of teachers' organisations in the country. Section III presents data on the experience of one college teachers' organisation obtained through an intensive study of the Bangalore University College Teachers Association.[1] Section IV presents some empirical data on the teachers' perspective of their organisation. These data were obtained through the administration of a questionnaire to 170 (about 15%) randomly selected teachers working in the under-graduate arts, science, and commerce colleges in Bangalore. Section V ties up the main findings and examines their implications. The picture of teachers' organisation presented thus may not be statistically representative of the country. Nevertheless, we do hope that it will provide some acquaintance with the important and hitherto neglected area of higher education.[2]

II

The Origin and Development of Teachers' Organisations in India[3]

From State to National Level

Teachers' organisations in India have a long history, lengthier than that of the trade union movement. The earliest effort in the direction of organising teachers in the South was the founding of the Women Teachers Association in Madras in 1890. Five years later the Madras Teachers Guild, an organisation representing both male and female teachers was founded. Fourteen years later, in 1909, the first federal organisation affiliating teachers associations was formed. It is known as the South India Teachers Union. This has developed into a strong and well-knit organisation with branches all over South India.

The first efforts at organising teachers in the North were perhaps the formation of the Non-Gazetted Educational Officers Association of Uttar Pradesh, and also of what is now the Association of the Heads of Anglo-Indian Schools in India at Allahabad in 1920. The Uttar Pradesh Secondary Education Association (now, UP Madhyamik Shiksha Sangh) and the Uttar Pradesh Adhyapak Mandal were founded in 1921. During the 1920s the teachers' movement reached the take-off stage and spread to other states and provinces. Among the important organisations that came to be established during this period, mention may be made of the All Bengal Teachers Association, Bihar Vernacular Teachers Association, Bihar and Orissa Secondary Teachers Association, Central Provinces and Berar Teachers Association, Bombay Presidency High School Headmasters Conference, and Baroda Secondary Teachers Association.

The need for bringing together, at the national level, teachers of all grades and categories was felt by Shri D.P. Khattry and Professor P. Seshadri. The former founded the All India Federation of Teachers Associations (renamed in 1933 as the All India Federation of Educational Associations), of which he remained the Secretary till his death in 1946. Today, this is one of the few federations in the world with a broad base, including in its membership teachers of all categories, educators, and associations concerned with the promotion of education throughout India.

Since Independence, there has been a phenomenal growth of teachers' organisations in the country. According to a survey made by the All India Federation of Educational Associations in 1966, there are seventeen all-India and sixty-five state-level organisations of teachers (Dutt 1970: 8). There are also numerous local organisations. The All India Federation of University and College Teachers Organisations is the only organisation of university and college teachers at the national level. This Federation has been in existence for more than three decades now and claims a membership of nearly two lakh teachers through its affiliated organisations. Of the sixty-five state-level organisations noted earlier, eighteen are specifically organisations of university and college teachers, the most powerful among them being the West Bengal University and College Teachers Association, the Delhi University Teachers Association, the All Orissa Teachers Association, the Bombay University Teachers Union, and the All Kerala Private College Teachers Association.

Multiplicity and Fragmentation

While the multiplication in the number of teachers' organisations does indicate the spread of organisation in the profession, it does not necessarily denote a strong and healthy growth. Multiplicity and fragmentation of organisations has been a conspicuous feature of the development of teachers' organisation in India. G.S. Aurora (1970: 13) highlights two significant axes of internal divisions in teachers' organisations: geographical and professional. To these may be added the process of segmentation within any one level. For example, there are ten prominent organisations of university and college teachers in Karnataka. They are:

1. The Mysore University Private College Teachers Association, which is perhaps the oldest of the teachers' organisations in the state.
2. The Bangalore University College Teachers Association, which is 'practically' an organisation of private college teachers under the jurisdiction of Bangalore University.
3. The Karnataka Government College Teachers Association, which is an organisation of teachers in the government colleges spread over the state.
4. The Karnatak University Teachers Association, which is an organisation of teachers in the university and colleges under the jurisdiction of Karnatak University.
5. The Mysore University Teachers Association, which is an organisation of postgraduate teachers of the University of Mysore.
6. The Bangalore University Teachers Council, which is an organisation of teachers in the colleges directly managed by the Bangalore University.
7. The Karnataka State College Teachers Association, which is an organisation intended to encompass teachers in all the colleges (including junior colleges) and universities in the state.
8. The Hyderabad-Karnatak College Teachers Association.
9. The Karnataka State Engineering College Teachers Association, which is an organisation of teachers in engineering colleges in state.
10. The Association of Teachers of the University of Agricultural Science.

Thus, college teachers in Karnataka are organised at state or local levels, as postgraduate or undergraduate teachers or both, as employees of government or private or university-managed colleges, and based on the faculty of study. The proliferation of teachers' organisations through a process of fragmentation and segmentation weakens the teachers' movement and also hinders the professionalisation of teaching.

III

The Bangalore University College Teachers Association

The Bangalore University College Teachers Association (henceforth BUCTA or the Association) was born along with the Bangalore University which was carved from the University of Mysore in 1965. In the first few years, the Association represented the University and college teachers in Bangalore. With the birth of the Karnataka Government College Teachers Association and the Bangalore University Teachers Council to protect the interests of teachers in government colleges and the University-managed colleges respectively, the membership of the Association dwindled and its representative nature waned. Now, though constitutionally the Association is open to all college teachers in the Bangalore University area, excepting those working in junior colleges, it has in effect become an organisation of the private college teachers. Despite this, BUCTA is still the most representative and powerful organisation of college teachers in Bangalore. Even though no legal recognition is accorded to it, the Bangalore University and the state government have recognised this Association for all practical purposes. Its President is included in the State Advisory Committee on Education and s/he is a member of the Joint Consultative Committee under the Directorate of Collegiate Education.

In the first decade of its existence the Association consisted of seven office bearers: one President, three Vice-Presidents, two Secretaries, and one Treasurer. But, with the promulgation of the Common Universities Ordinance in 1976, the jurisdiction of Bangalore University was extended to include colleges in three more districts (Bangalore Rural, Kolar, and Tumkur), and this necessitated a change in the constitution of the Association. According to the constitution of BUCTA, as amended in 1976, there are eleven officers. In addition to these officers, there is a Managing Committee consisting of one to three representatives elected from each college based on its membership strength. Normally, the Managing Committee meets once a month. Apart from this, the officers meet frequently.

Activities and Leadership

Initially, BUCTA was primarily a 'cultural organisation'. It conducted teacher seminars and student debates, arranged film shows, and organised social service camps. The Association also conducted an opinion poll on the Report of the Khosla Committee about kissing in films! The first President of the Association was the principal of a renowned private college in the city, who later became the Vice-Chancellor of the Bangalore University. The second President was a professor in a University-managed college known for his liberal views. Though the Association threatened twice to launch agitations pressing for the fulfilment of certain demands, there was no agitation as such during the first five years. Thus, the activities taken on by the Association in its earlier years may be described as largely cultural and the line of its approach as 'soft'.

It was around 1971 that the activities of the Association gathered strength and grew to be more specifically focussed on issues relating to the occupation of the members. At this juncture, a member of the Managing Committee emerged as a key leader. This leader, with a commitment to Marxian ideology, with a broad perspective of the workers movement, in general, and the teachers' movement, in particular, and with inexhaustible energy for the cause of teachers, started advocating a stiff line of approach. With his entry, the Association was energised and its outlook changed. A number of agitations aimed at obtaining better rights and working conditions for teachers were launched. The Association's name frequently appeared in newspapers, especially through this leader's letters to the editors.

Internally, this leader was instrumental in the amendment of the constitution of BUCTA to provide for the direct election of office bearers at the annual General Body meeting. Thereby, the principals of colleges were indirectly prevented from becoming office bearers of the Association. This was an important accomplishment in the development of the Association, as the so-called 'agents' or 'stooges' of the management were kept out of the Association and prevented from scuttling it from within. Moreover, this was also expected to improve the involvement of teachers in the functioning of the Association in general.

Simultaneously, this leader, along with a few others, was responsible for founding the Federation of College Teachers Associations in Karnataka in 1974. In the same year, BUCTA was affiliated to the All India Federation of University and College Teachers Organisations, and it started developing contacts with similar organisations in other states. This leader was elected as the General Secretary of the State Federation and a Vice-President of the All India Federation.

This leader, who continued to function actively in BUCTA for a long time, may be called on 'ideologue', stands in contrast to others, especially to another leader who is equally serious and hardworking but a liberal-minded person, who may be called a 'stoic'. Being a founder member, the latter was a Vice-President of the Association for a few years and later became its President. While he too was totally committed to the cause of teachers, he did not seem to have tenacious views on socio-political matters, let alone being committed to any ideology.

Both these leaders hailed from the same college and belong to the same department, the stoic being its head. The partnership of these two leaders had been of immense importance to the Association. The stoic's participation in the struggles of the ideologue and the latter's influence on him remarkably changed his attitude towards unionism among teachers and on methods of agitation.

This account of the development of the Association illustrates how the orientation of a teachers' organisation may change and how it may become militant when an ideologue leader emerges from within the membership at the appropriate juncture. In marked contrast to the industrial unions, where militancy is found to be the quality of the outside leadership (Weiner 1963: 98), militancy in a teachers' organisation has been found to be a product of the committed leadership from within.

Membership Strength

While a strong, committed, and active leader is one element in the efficacy of an organisation, its strength is essentially determined by the extent to which it is complete in membership. The organisational property of completeness, which is distinguished from the property of size (measured by the number of members), is defined as the proportion of potential members to actual members. 'Correlatively, this means that groups of the same absolute size may have markedly different degrees of *social power,* according to whether they encompass all potential members or varying proportions of them .... The more nearly complete the group, the greater the power and influence it can exercise'

(Merton 1968: 342–43; emphasis in original). It is the recognition of the relationship between completeness and power that prompts organisations to enlarge their membership to include as large as possible a proportion of the potential membership (ibid.: 343). This is especially so when the organisation is voluntary.

It is difficult to present an exact picture of completeness of membership in BUCTA. While we have information about the membership over time,[4] the corresponding figures of potential membership are not easily available. However, on a rough estimate, over the years, nearly 80 per cent of the potential members have been members of the Association.

In accepting the completeness of membership of BUCTA as indicative of its strength as an organisation, it is necessary to understand the way in which this membership is enrolled and renewed. The annual membership drive is a tough job for the office bearers. Every year, before the annual General Body meeting, the Managing Committee members from various colleges are asked to enrol and renew membership in their colleges. These 'active' members have to persuade their not-so-active colleagues to pay the Rs 10 membership fee and enrol or renew their membership.[5] They are sometimes hard put to convince their colleagues of the utility of a teachers organisation and of the wisdom of paying the membership fee. Sometimes the membership fee appears to be felt as a 'levy', and many of the teachers seem to enrol only to oblige their 'active' colleagues. Not unexpectedly, a majority of those who are thus persuaded to enrol or to renew their membership seem to consider that they have fulfilled their 'duty' by paying the membership fee, and may sit back and leave it to the office bearers to get their problems solved.

The experience quoted earlier suggests that 'completeness' of a membership thus enrolled does not necessarily guarantee complete involvement on the part of the members. In fact, one anticipates involvement to be poor in a situation wherein membership starts with such indifference.

Poor Involvement and Participation of Members

Involvement on the part of its members is a prerequisite for the successful development of any organisation. There are various indices of measuring this involvement: the attendance of members at the meetings of the organisation, the readiness of the members to sacrifice for the collective interest of the organisation, expectation of the members from the organisation and their reactions to the gratification or otherwise of these expectations, etc. are some of the salient ones.

Attendance at the annual General Body meetings of BUCTA – important gatherings to approve the report of the Secretaries and the statement of accounts, apart from electing the office bearers – is very small.[6] The members of BUCTA seem to believe that their obligation to the Association is confined to enrolment to membership and payment of membership fee. In fact, they seem to look upon membership as an insurance policy so that their problems, if any, will be solved by the Association. The gravity of the situation is tersely expressed in the report of the Secretaries for the year 1972–73: 'Let us remember that membership of our Association does not amount to taking out an insurance policy .... We are afraid our Association is not that strong. It becomes strong through the participation of its members'. That teachers consider the membership of the Association as a sort of insurance is clearly brought out by the report of the Secretaries for the year 1973–74: 'To rush to the office bearers of the Association in a crisis or for getting some personal grievances redressed and then to ignore the Association is most unbecoming of the members. The Association loses its strength and integrity if this practice is perpetuated'.

While this is understandable in the case of ordinary members, surprisingly, even some of the Managing Committee members have very little real involvement in the activities of the Association. Records reveal that every year there is a line or two in the report where the Secretaries complain about the thin attendance at the Managing Committee meetings. In spite of repeated reminders, many colleges fail to send representatives to the Managing Committee meetings. Many colleges have a problem finding someone who is 'willing' to represent the college at these meetings.

While the involvement of teachers in general in the activities of the Association is poor, it is particularly so on the part of women teachers. The representatives of the ten women's colleges in Bangalore University are conspicuous by their absence at the Managing Committee meetings. On the whole, women take little interest in the activities of the Association. Since they constitute nearly 45 per cent of the membership, their non-participation affects the Association seriously.

The following illustration indicates the quality of the involvement of the members, and the precarious situation it creates. Though BUCTA has a membership of nearly 1,000 teachers, it is not able to field its own candidates for elections to the Senate and the Academic Council of the University. When this matter was raised once or twice at the Managing Committee meetings, the leaders, eager to mask the weakness of the Association, replied that the Association did not sponsor candidates because it was difficult to choose a nominee. The truth of the matter seemed to be that the Association did not sponsor candidates because the chances of their getting elected were very poor. In fact, when in 1973 five members of the Association – two of whom were prominent leaders – did contest the elections to the Academic Council, as its unofficial candidates, the result was disastrous. Except for one leader who got narrowly elected, all the others were defeated by a wide margin.

Thus, the Association presents an enigmatic situation. On the one hand, it has deeply committed leaders who hold a broad socio-political perspective and are devoted to the cause of the organisation as a major movement. On the other, it has members who value the organisation from the narrow perspective of the immediate gains that it can bring them. They seem to subscribe to it as they would to an insurance company, expecting the office bearers to take the total responsibility for 'covering the risks'. In order to win the support of their apathetic membership, the leaders exert themselves to solve the problems of individual members. But, more often than not, the members conveniently forget the organisation after their individual problems are solved. Thus, the members are prepared to support their leaders only to the extent of their personal gains. They do not share the broader vision of the leadership.

All this points to the strange but real situation where the leadership of BUCTA is exploited by its members. This is quite surprising and is in glaring contrast to the oft-repeated complaint that organised elements are being exploited by self-seeking ambitious leaders and politicians (see Weiner 1963: 234).

The Association in Action: Tactics for Success

The successes that BUCTA has gained may be traced to at least three different factors. Firstly, it must be conceded that success has been possible because the Government of Karnataka has never really taken a rigid stand on the teachers' demands. Secondly, although the members have not been actively involved in the activities of the Association, its leaders have diligently lobbied and negotiated with officials concerned. This has enabled them to win many of the demands of the teachers. Lastly, the Association has, when cornered, used or at least threatened to use the most powerful weapon available in the Indian university system, namely, refusal to undertake the examination work of the University.

Boycott of examination work by teachers throws the entire academic schedule out of gear and literally paralyses the University. Thousands of students are affected. Their parents are agitated, and editorials on the situation appear in newspapers. Ad hoc citizens' committees are formed to settle the issue. Appeals are made to the government to consider the demands of teachers sympathetically and resolve the deadlock. Simultaneously, appeals are made to teachers. As members of a 'noble' profession they are implored to withdraw their agitation in the interest of students. The situation becomes explosive. Eventually, the government agrees to meet the demands of teachers half way. The Association, in turn, issues a press statement suspending the agitation in response to the public opinion and in view of the assurances of the government. This sequence of events was noticed when BUCTA boycotted the annual and the supplementary examinations of the Bangalore University in 1974 and 1977.

Displacement of Target

Significantly, no teachers' organisation in Karnataka has ever struck directly against the private colleges.[7] While the tactics of crippling examinations may be understood in the light of the fact that every organisation evolves and employs the techniques best suited to serve its ends, the fact that BUCTA directs its agitation against the University and the government and not against the managements who run colleges may, in a sense, be considered to be a reflection of the weakness of the Association and its members.

As noted earlier, BUCTA is an organisation of teachers employed by private colleges in Bangalore. Before the introduction of the scheme for direct payment of salaries by the government to all teachers in the private-aided colleges in November 1977, many irregularities were reported in the payment of salaries to teachers in these colleges. Private managements have also been accused of indulging in unethical and exploitative practices like retrenchment of temporary teachers before the summer vacation, non-confirmation of teachers, and imposition of excessive teaching loads. They have been criticised as being totally undemocratic in their functioning. The Association has been fully aware of the pathetic condition of teachers in these colleges, and may be expected to fight private managements on these issues. However, it has never ventured to do so. Instead, it fights the government and the University: processions are taken to the residences of the Chief Minister and the Education Minister, relay hunger strikes are organised in front of the State Assembly, and the Association threatens to or even boycotts the examinations conducted by the University. On one occasion, when the Association gave a call for mass casual leave for a day, the private managements were assured that the agitation was not directed against them!

The logic behind this curious displacement of the target of agitation is simple. Any direct action by private college teachers against their managements will invite disciplinary action. In the absence of statutory protection of their service conditions, the private college teachers have to be careful about agitating against their employers. It is easier to agitate against the government, an anonymous entity which anyone can attack. It is easier to boycott the examination work of the University, for such a boycott attracts widespread public attention without exposing the teachers to any specific punitive action.

IV

Teachers Speak

The data from our sample survey of 170 college teachers offer yet another vantage point for understanding the working of teachers' organisations. This section presents some data from the survey indicating what the teachers have to say about their relationship with and participation in organisations.

Membership

A significant majority of 82.4 per cent of the 170 teachers covered by the survey are members of one or the other of the three organisations: BUCTA, the Karnataka Government College Teachers Association, and the Karnataka State College Teachers Association. While 15.3 per cent are not members of any organisation, 2.3 per cent have not replied to the question. A teacher may hold membership of more than one organisation, and 26 per cent of the respondents are members of two organisations: BUCTA or the Karnataka Government College Teachers Association and the Karnataka State College Teachers Association.

Of the 140 teachers who hold organisation membership, 114 (81%) are members of BUCTA, fifty-one (36%) are members of the Karnataka State College Teachers Association, and twenty (14%) are members of the Karnataka Government College Teachers Association. Of the 133 private college teachers, 114 (85.7%) are members of BUCTA, the organisation that mainly represents their interest. Of the thirty-seven government college teachers 20 (54%) are members of the Karnataka Government College Teachers Association which particularly presents their interests.

Two points emerge from this. First, while the majority of the teachers hold membership in teachers' organisations, they are relatively more predisposed to membership in a local organisation (namely, BUCTA) than to a state level organisation (namely, the Karnataka State College Teachers Association). This suggests that teachers are more concerned with their immediate problems, which they feel are effectively handled by the local than the state level organisation. Secondly, the predisposition towards membership is relatively more pronounced among the private (86%) compared to the government (54%) college teachers. This is probably due to the better service and working conditions prevalent in the government colleges compared to their private counterparts, and also due to the absence of exploitation similar to that found in private colleges. Incidentally, the Karnataka Government College Teachers Association is a state level organisation, and transfer of teachers does not affect the membership at all.

A sex-wise analysis of membership reveals that male teachers (87%, n = 99) are relatively more disposed to membership compared to their female counterparts (76%, n = 71). Conversely, the percentage of non-membership is nearly double among the female teachers (21%) compared to their male counterparts (11%). Of the twenty-six non-members, fourteen have put in service of two to seven years and ten of them are female. This corroborates our earlier observation that the involvement of female teachers in organisational affairs is very weak and highly discouraging.

Interesting reasons have been advanced by the twenty-six teachers for remaining eligible non-members. Six of them are new entrants to the profession and they are either not aware of the organisations or are yet to enrol as members. While these teachers are favourably disposed towards membership, there are others who are either indifferent or negatively inclined. Indifference is expressed in their short and casual answers: 'not interested' or 'never felt the need to become a member'. Motivation not to become a member is clear in answers like 'the organisations are indifferent towards local candidates and their grievances', etc. There are some who do not disclose their attitude towards membership, but who explain their position in statements such as 'the higher authority [principal] is not a member' or talk of private managements which 'do not like their staff being members of any organisation'. One female teacher quipped that she would like to 'avoid entanglement in staff politics'.

Seeking the Help of the Association

With a view to knowing something about the readiness with which teachers approach their organisations and the faith that they repose in it, they were asked: 'Have you ever approached your organisation for any help?' Of the 140 teachers who are members of teachers organisation, only eighteen (13%) said that they have approached their organisations for help. The nature of the help sought from the organisation by these teachers falls into two categories. Some teachers have approached the organisation with fairly specific problems such as payment of salaries, provisions for certain allowances, matters relating to promotions, and retrenchment. Others, possibly the Managing Committee members, have approached the organisation for somewhat more general demands like abolition of the cadre of demonstrator, gazetting the post of lecturers, introduction or implementation of new pay scales, and getting certain rules of grant-in-aid amended.

The response of the organisation is reported by most of them to be helpful and sympathetic. One teacher is glad that the organisation 'contacted our management and got us... allowances'. But three teachers have pointed out that the response of the organisation is one of silence or helplessness. Some teachers have defended the inability of the organisation to solve their problems by passing on the buck to the government, their typical response being that 'the organisation responded immediately and well, but the government is delaying the decision'.

Perception of Objectives and Achievements of Organisation

The members' perception of the major objectives and achievements of their organisation is an important index of their involvement in the organisation. This will tell us the extent to which the teachers are conversant with the affairs of their organisation.

To a question on the major objectives of their organisation, the teachers have responded very poorly. Apparently, this is an exposure of their ignorance. But this may also be because the teachers think that these objectives are too well known to be mentioned. In fact, a few teachers have replied: 'refer to ... Association's charter of demands'. The various responses to the question as to what the organisation seeks to achieve are grouped under eight broad categories as follows:

1. Abolition of the cadre of demonstrator (51).[8]
2. Job security: regularisation of 'local' candidates, preventing illegal retrenchment, etc. (47).
3. Better pay scales and conditions for promotion: implementation of new pay scales, time-scale promotion, triple benefit scheme, creation of supernumerary readership, and prompt payment of salary (110).
4. Gazetting the post of lecturers (22).
5. Improvement in working conditions: reduction of workload, leave and other facilities (21).
6. Voice for teachers in the formulation of courses and syllabi: representation of teachers in Boards of Studies, enabling them to have a say in syllabus-making, etc. (1).

7. Restoring the age of retirement to 58 years (5).
8. Increased representation for teachers in academic bodies of the University, such as the Syndicate, the Senate, the Academic Council, etc. (6).

It is seen that the organisational objectives of obtaining better pay scales and promotions are perceived to be the most important. Abolition of the demonstrator's cadre (which has since been done), and job security are demands perceived to be next in importance. Demands such as democratisation of administration, increased representation to teachers on academic bodies of the University, etc. are seldom perceived. Thus, the teachers seem to be more concerned with the immediate material problems than with academic, let alone, distant ideological problems. This points to the fact that teachers' organisations are based on a crude form of 'economism'.

As regards the major achievements of their organisation, the response of teachers is disappointing. Some of the demands such as time-scale of pay and time promotions which were still under consideration by the government at the time of the study are listed as achievements of the organisation. A few have taken this opportunity to ridicule the working of the organisation. One teacher sarcastically remarks 'conducting a seminar on the syllabus' as a major achievement of the organisation, and another is scathing in his criticism that the organisation has achieved 'Nothing ... [It] has no guts!'

It must be said to the credit of the organisations concerned that, due to the persistent efforts of their leaders, many things have been achieved. Most of the major demands such as the abolition of the demonstrator's cadre, implementation of the triple benefit scheme in private colleges, setting up of an appellate tribunal, and introduction of staffing pattern have all been conceded by the authorities concerned. It is, therefore, surprising that the teachers should give such a poor picture of their perception of the achievements of their organisation.

Opinions about the Functioning of Organisation

In order to understand teachers' assessment of their organisation, they were asked: 'Do you think your organisation is functioning well?'. A significant majority of 80 per cent of the 140 teachers who are members of an organisation have answered that their organisation is functioning well and only 11 per cent of the teachers have replied in the negative.

The sixteen teachers who thought that their organisation is not functioning well were further asked to substantiate their assessment. Five of them have found fault with the organisation itself and five with the teachers' response to the organisation. Those who have criticised the organisation have pointed out that 'the organisation is not strong and it lacks guts to agitate' because 'the office bearers are too white-collared'. Those who have blamed the members have pointed out that 'the teachers are indifferent and uncooperative' and they think of 'the organisation only when they are in difficulty' and 'expect the organisation to do everything for them just because they have become members'. Two teachers have held the nature of demands of the organisation as responsible for its failure, whereas one has held 'the interference of the vested reactionary political elements' to be responsible for this.

Perception of Others' Response to Organisation

The perception of teachers about the response of other teachers, the management of private colleges, and the government towards their organisation determines to some extent their own response to the organisation. The following are the responses of the teachers to a structured question asking them to state their impressions regarding whether other teachers, the government, and the managements of colleges react 'favourably', 'indifferently', or 'unfavourably' to their organisations.

A very high percentage of teachers (78%) have reported that other teachers are favourably disposed towards the organisations. As compared to this, only 31 per cent say that the government is favourably inclined and even fewer (24%) say that managements are favourably inclined. The respondents feel that teachers who are not favourably disposed believe that they are indifferent (22%). The percentage of those who believe that the government is indifferent (34%) is almost identical to those who believe that the managements are indifferent (32%). None of the teachers thinks that other teachers are unfavourably disposed to the organisations, but 11 per cent of the teachers believe that the government is unfavourably disposed to their organisations, and 17 per cent believe that managements are unfavourably disposed.

In brief, as perceived by our teachers, the attitude of teachers towards organisation is most favourable. The attitude of managements and government is one of indifference or unfavourable, and between the two, the attitude to managements appears to be more unfavourable. Thus, there is some amount of subjective consciousness among the teachers of their objective conditions vis-à-vis the managements and the government. Let us see if this consciousness is developing on trade union lines.

The Views on Unionism

The teachers are divided over the question of teachers' unionism, though the percentage of those advocating it (41%) is somewhat smaller than those who do not (49%). Analysed sex-wise, the percentage of those advocating unionism is relatively higher among male teachers (46%, n = 99) as compared to their female counterparts (32%, n = 71).

Among the reasons advanced for advocating unionism, the effectiveness of collective bargaining and strength in unity are the most important. According to one teacher, 'having hitherto lived in ivory towers, the teachers have allowed themselves to be treated like beggars'. Three teachers have asserted that teachers are wage earners and, therefore, they have the corresponding rights.

Not surprisingly, some teachers are apologetic about favouring unionism. These teachers do not advocate unionism as a right, but plead that they have to resort to it because nothing else works. 'These days only a crying baby gets milk', is their typical response. According to one teacher, 'our government does not appreciate peaceful behaviour'. Only two teachers have favoured unionism on grounds of evoking public sympathy and creating awareness among the teachers.

As many as fifty-three (64%) of the eighty-three teachers who disapprove of unionism for teachers failed to give reasons for their disapproval. One of the reasons invariably given by all the remaining teachers is that unionism is not in keeping with the dignity of their profession (28%). Many of them eulogise teaching as a noble, dedicated, and ideal profession. A second set of reasons points to the adverse consequences of unionism on students, education, and society in general. Some teachers fear that it would harm the interest of students and create indiscipline among them. Five teachers feel that there are other means to redress their grievances. One teacher has expressed the fear that 'public sympathy will be withheld'. Another teacher is worried about the dangers of multi-unionism and inter-union rivalry.

Views on Strikes

The foregoing data regarding the teachers' attitude towards unionism would lead one to anticipate that those who favour unionism would approve of strikes as a strategy for pressing their demands, whereas those who do not would disfavour them. The data do not support this expectation. Of the sixty-nine teachers who have favoured unionism, only forty-two (61%) approve of strikes. As many as twenty-four (35%) do not. On the other hand, of the eighty-four teachers who have disapproved of unionism, eighteen (21%) approve of strikes. This suggests that some of the teachers do not have a clear understanding of unionism and/or of strikes.

On the whole, the data indicate that a majority (54%) of the teachers in the sample have not approved of strikes, whereas 38 per cent have approved of it. Analysed sex-wise, we find that strikes find greater favour among male teachers (48%, n = 99) than among women teachers (24%, n = 71).

Many of those who have advocated strikes are apologetic about their approval of the use of this weapon. They emphasise that they accept strikes only as a last resort (48). They concede that strikes are neither decent nor desirable, but feel that strikes are inevitable when authorities are apathetic and when all other means of resolving problems fail. However, an alternative view point holds that strikes are the best method of drawing the attention of the management, government, and public alike (12). By and large, both categories of respondents seem to accept strikes for purely tactical reasons. Not even a single respondent has asserted that strikes are a legitimate instrument of coercion and a democratically recognised way of expressing demands. The acceptance of strikes apologetically or on purely tactical grounds is not the same as recognising them as a democratic right and an accepted mode of organised action.

A majority of 57 per cent of the ninety-two teachers who have disapproved of strikes have not substantiated their disapproval with reasons. From among the forty teachers who have given reasons, a large number (21) say that 'strike is the most undignified, immature and indecent way of expressing demands. It is not in tune with the dedicated and noble profession of the intellectuals'. Equally frequent (24) are statements which point to the adverse effects that strikes have on students, particularly the fear that they may lead to indiscipline and irresponsibility among them. Obviously, disapproving of student strikes one teacher asked: 'How can a teacher advise his students not to go on strike when he himself does it?'.

Among the other reasons given by the teachers against strikes, mention should be made of the fear that strikes may lead to loss of public sympathy for their cause and the apprehension that they could spoil the image of their profession. Some teachers are afraid that strikes may degenerate into violence and lead to anti-social results. Others merely feel that when other means are available teachers should not indulge in strikes (10).

While the above responses indicate how different groups of respondents feel about unionism and strikes, the general attitude of teachers may be summed up in the following words of an articulate teacher:

> The teaching profession is an ideal profession and teachers handle the richest 'raw material' of the nation, namely, the youth .... A good teacher is one who works in a 'self-effacing' spirit. Our ancestors used the phrase *vidya dana* (gift of knowledge) and not *vidya vikraya* (sale of knowledge). If by organising strikes the teachers themselves set a bad example, the student community, which is already turbulent, will become more explosive and this will lead to a national disaster. Teachers associations are good as long as they are organised for progressive purposes. Teachers have the right to represent their grievances, but they have no right to resort to the politics of blackmail and to hold to ransom the welfare and future of the students for their own benefit.

V

Concluding Comments

In the preceding sections we have examined the organisation of college teachers, first from the perspective of data available on the establishment, growth, and working of BUCTA, a teachers' organisation in Bangalore, and later from the perspective of a sample survey of teachers in Bangalore. In this section we shall try to link up the two perspectives.

Poor Involvement of Members

One of the most striking revelations from both the perspectives is that teachers' organisations are fairly strong or complete in as much as a large percentage of potential members are actually enrolled as members, but they are weak in terms of the *involvement* of the members. To start with, members are indifferent about joining the organisations and, if they do so, it is largely due to pressure or persuasion from organisation leaders who also happen to be their colleagues in the academic profession. Having joined the organisation, they remain indifferent and only marginally involved. Few teachers, other than those who are office bearers and leaders, concern themselves with the activities and affairs of the organisation.

Poor Organisation

In terms of the continuum along which occupational associations may function, referred to at the beginning of this chapter, from learned societies to economically oriented unions, our observations indicate that they do not function as learned societies at all. Teachers' perception of the demands and achievements of their organisation and the nature of help sought by them from their organisation makes it obvious that these organisations are more concerned with the immediate problems of pay or job security than with issues concerning the profession. The teachers' interest in the organisation may, therefore, be characterised as one of economism than that of professionalism. As economically oriented unions, teachers' organisations seem to be fairly effective; not because of the involvement of members, but because of the commitment and the tenacious persistence of their leaders. Our observations do not give us reason to believe that the situation is likely to improve in the near future.

Weak as Unions

The poor involvement of teachers in the activities of their organisations as unions and their negative predisposition towards working-class modes of operation like unionism and strikes, seem to confirm Thorstein Veblen's observation, made at the end of World War I, that teachers would not join unions because of 'a feeling among them that their salaries are not of the nature of wages, and that there would be a species of moral obliquity implied in overtly dealing with the matter' (quoted in Ladd and Lipset 1975: 243).

This is probably even more truer of the Indian teacher. The present-day teacher in India is a by-product of the emergence of the middle class in the latter half of the nineteenth century (see Misra 1961). The upper-caste and middle-class background of the college teachers is very well established (see Gore et al. 1970: 276–312; Chitnis 1974b: 239; Jayaram and Sivaramakrishnan 1976: 69–72). 'There seems little doubt that in various countries those engaged in different forms of non-manual work see themselves in a higher status category', and 'the factors underlying the upward class identification of the white-collar workers inhere in the very nature of a stratified society' (Lipset 1967: 530 and 531). It has been a pronounced tendency among the middle-class and upper-caste people in India to shy away from manual work and the cultural ethos of the working class.

Moreover, the traditional stereotype of teaching as a 'sacred' profession and of the teacher as a *'guru'* or *'pundit'* who is engaged in dispensing knowledge as a sacrament and who is, therefore, above wordly considerations and material gains, which persists in spite of the modern concept of teaching as a secular vocation, seems to preclude the institutionalisation of unionism among teachers. That is, as we have seen earlier, unionism is not regarded as the 'legitimate' or 'customary' way for teachers to act in relation to their employers or to redress their grievances. They are apprehensive of the fact that unionisation would violate some of the traditional conceptions regarding the norms of behaviour expected of them as the high priests of learning and jeopardise their place in society.

Yet another factor contributing to the poor unionisation of teachers is the fact that many of the teachers are women. There is a widely accepted view that women are, by and large, conservative and docile, and as such unwilling to unionise. Data from the perspectives presented in this essay indicate that women teachers are relatively more apathetic to the organisation as compared to their male counterparts. The percentage of non-membership is nearly double among women teachers as compared to men teachers. Women teachers who are members are also less involved in the organisation. They are relatively more negatively oriented to unionism and strikes.[9]

There are various explanations for this. Women teachers are drawn from relatively higher socio-economic backgrounds as compared to the male teachers (Jayaram and Sivaramakrishnan 1976: 69–71). Employment for many of them is not a source of livelihood but a status symbol. Many of them are wives of well-placed, white-collar officers, and it is highly likely that many of the husbands would not like their wives to be 'agitators'.

Furthermore, women teachers are very much less career-oriented (ibid.: 71–72).[10] Even the few among them who would like to take up teaching as a career, may be cautious not to risk their position as entrants into a new role, and consequently reluctant to pitch in with the total commitment required for participation in union activities. The high rates of turnover of female teachers resulting from the fact that they combine teaching with family life or return to teaching after having left it for family reasons, limits meaningful membership and participation on their part.

Position of Leaders and Future of Organisations

It would be pertinent to ask as to how the leaders of the organisations justify economism in a situation wherein the teachers are not particularly inclined to unionise. Economism, the leaders like the ideologue argue, is the first step in the direction of building a teachers' movement. According to them, waging limited struggles for salary increases raises the consciousness of teachers. They believe that, once teachers participate in economic struggles, they will be sufficiently politicised to wage higher level political struggles. One doubts whether there is substance in this claim. Observations suggest that the *petit bourgeoisie* class position of teachers and an ambivalent role context inhibits the politicisation of teachers along class lines.

The situation being what it is, some questions arise. What happens to teachers' organisations once the immediate problems are solved and the demands of economism are met? Do the leaders fix 'new goals' or do they try for an improvement over what has already been achieved? These questions are interesting, but are difficult to answer. From whatever we have observed the indications are that teachers' organisations will die a natural death after their immediate goals have been fulfilled. However much the leaders may try to take the organisations off economism, the organisations seem exclusively to rest on economism, and have little strength to survive if this base is withdrawn.

Another weakness of teachers' organisation is manifest in the displacement of their target of agitation. With the exception of the problems faced by teachers working in government colleges, the problems faced by teachers are mainly with reference to their own private managements. Yet teachers' organisations do not strike work in their own colleges or direct agitations at the private managements. Instead, they use the state government and the university as targets of attack and agitation. The private college teachers dare not protest against their own managements for obvious reasons. In this process, what they should actually fight is indirectly supported.

This should not be taken to imply that the teachers are hand in glove with the private managements, or that their attitude is one of accommodation of interests with the managements. In fact, a majority of teachers feel that the response of the managements to their organisations is unfavourable or one of indifference. This is in marked contrast to the perception of a significant majority that their colleagues' response is favourable. There is some sort of a 'class consciousness' among the private college teachers, and the management is their 'antagonistic class'. But the feeling of antagonism does not surpass a particular limit because the teachers are at the mercy of the management and their own socio-economic background acts as a limitation on what they can do.

However, in teachers' organisations, there is a contradiction in orientation towards organisation between the leaders and their followers. While the aim and perspective of the leaders are broad, those of their followers are narrow and necessarily limited. The followers' interest is one of economism, while some of the leaders like to transcend this. The ultimate consequence is that these leaders get themselves exploited by their followers, in spite of having enough scope for exploiting the followers, especially in view of the latter's indifference. With reference to the organisations where the committed leaders are exploited by their indifferent followers, one may ask why they should get exploited, especially when they are conscious of this exploitation.

The leaders seem to oblige their followers by helping them out of their individual problems with the intention of winning them over to their fold. Unfortunately for the leaders, the teachers seem to follow them only to the extent that their demands of economism are met. In this process is produced a band of frustrated leaders, the intensity of whose disappointment seems to vary directly with their commitment. It is quite possible that some of the leaders are successful and satisfied without having any commitment, ideological or otherwise. This is so because their perspective coincides with that of their followers.

A relevant question that follows is why should the leaders continue to work for the organisation if they are disappointed over the whole situation? Some of the leaders are optimistic that it is still possible to get at least some teachers to their side. Others argue that to the extent that they are able to neutralise the power of their opponent ideologists and prevent them from controlling the organisation, it is worth the sacrifice.

With the rapid growth of white-collar employment, teachers have lost in relative status and income. Being employed in bureaucratic institutions as functionaries or service personnel, they have lost autonomy and authority. More than all this, the gap between the traditional stereotype of their role and profession, on the one hand, and the realities of the present educational and social situation, on the other, seems to be constantly widening. In the light of all this, it is only to be expected that teachers' organisations will develop on trade union lines with economistic commitment on the part of its members.

While teachers' organisations fulfil union-type functions pretty effectively, they cannot hope, at least in the near future, to attain the stature and strength of a trade union. The socio-economic background of teachers, their status image, and the situation of their profession inhibit them from involvement and participation in the activities of their organisations and block the absolute unionisation of teachers. The present status of teachers' organisations does not promise any contribution towards professionalisation of teaching. The prospects of the existing organisations developing into a teachers' movement are also very dim. Nevertheless, a small leadership continues to struggle in spite of an indifferent and ambivalent following.

The peculiar position of our teachers may be aptly summarised in the following portrayal of the white-collar people by C. Wright Mills:

> The white-collar people slipped quietly into modern society. Whatever history they have had is a history without events; whatever common interests they have do not lead to unity; whatever future they have will not be of their own making (1951: ix).

Notes

1. The choice of BUCTA is not fortuitous. Our larger study of college teachers, of which this chapter is a part, was conducted in the colleges under the jurisdiction of the Bangalore University; and this is the Association representing the interests of teachers in these colleges. More importantly, the co-author (G. Sivaramakrishnan) was one of the Secretaries of this Association. This is a unique advantage in that we have an insider's view of the organisation, its working and problems. Moreover, we had access to all the files and records of the Association.
2. That this is a poorly researched area is proved by the fact that in Altbach's twenty-six-page 'Bibliography on Indian Higher Education' (1974: 421–46) there is not even one citation on teachers' organisations. The same is true of Chitnis' fifteen-page bibliography appended to her trend report on sociology of education (1974a: 166–232).
3. The following account of the origin and development of teachers' organisations in the country is mostly based on Franklin (1970).
4. The membership of BUCTA, obtained from its audited accounts, is as follows: 1971–72, 995; 1972–73, 828; 1973–74, 1,000; 1974–75, 647; 1975–76, 516; and 1976–77, 700.
5. Until 1973, the annual membership fee was only Rs 5.
6. The percentage of attendance at the annual General Body meetings of BUCTA is as follows: 1971–72, 13.37; 1972–73, 11.11; 1973–74, 15.50; 1974–75, 16.85; 1975–76, 25.39; and 1976–77, 13.14. The actual attendance is sometimes less than that of the strength of the Managing Committee!
7. One notable exception is the strike by the teaching staff of Sri Jagadguru Renukacharya College of Arts and Science, Bangalore, on 1

April 1974, demanding the reinstatement of one of their colleagues who had been removed on 'flimsy grounds'. The teachers decided to intensify the stir, but the strike was called off following a settlement arrived between the management of the College and its teaching staff (see *Deccan Herald*, Bangalore, 2, 3 and 4 April 1974).

8. The figures in brackets refer to the frequency with which the particular response is cited.
9. Many employers in many fields of work and industry are reported to prefer women workers because, among other things, they are generally less involved in trade unions, agitations, and disputes (see T.A. Baig 1976: 177).
10. This is found to be true of working women in general: Prema Jauhari has found that a majority of working women in her study neither took work seriously nor had developed any notion for a career; and Harsha Tripathi has observed that these women are more satisfied in the role of a homemaker and experience greater self-fulfilment in the role of a mother than in that of a career woman (studies quoted in Kapur 1974: 94).

15

Student Political Activism in India

Political activism among students has been an endemic phenomenon of the educational scene in India. Though it has a long history dating from the freedom struggle, its content and orientation have not remained the same over the decades or in different regions of the country. In the pre-Independence period, student activism had a single definite goal, namely, independence for India, and was intertwined with the country's life and politics. The wave of student agitations since Independence has not always been directly political, but has often been concerned largely with local and non-ideological issues.

What makes student activism a significant social phenomenon in India is its varying socio-cultural appeal and the political complexion which it acquires now and then. Generally, the authorities and the lay public alike have tended to view the restlessness among students as 'indiscipline'. It has, therefore, been described often, even by academics, as merely a problem for the educational and political authorities. However, occasionally, there have been instances of a limited transformation of student activism into articulated movements with far-reaching socio-political consequences.

Students and the Freedom Struggle[1]

As early as the 1880s, students had agitated for the holding of the Indian Civil Service examinations in India also instead of only in England, as it would obviate the need for a long and expensive journey for prospective Indian candidates. But only by the turn of the century did students start responding to specific political issues. The short-lived Young India League, started in 1906 under the stewardship of Lokamanya Bala Gangadhar Tilak, was perhaps the first students' organisation with an explicit political orientation.

The Non-Cooperation Movement led by Mahatma Gandhi in 1920 was the first political struggle in which the students were involved on a substantial scale. The first annual All India Student Conference held in that year provided the requisite coordination to the growing student political movement. The student movement was further intensified following the militant Civil Disobedience Movement of 1930. To provide the student movement a common platform, the All India Students' Federation (AISF) was established in 1936. This Federation, which was conceived as the student wing of the Indian nationalist movement, was radical in its political views. Initially, Communists, Socialists, and Gandhians worked together harmoniously within its fold. Its annual sessions, which were held simultaneously with that of the Indian National Congress, were attended by upwards of 3,000 delegates and the top Congress leaders addressed them.

There were also other important trends in the mobilisation of students. Many Muslim students, who were previously apathetic or pro-Congress, joined the Muslim League-sponsored All India Muslim Students' Federation, an organisation which stood up for Muslim rights and interests. The Hindu right-wing Rashtriya Swayamsevak Sangh (RSS), appealing for the defence of Hindu nationalism and cultural regeneration, also gained strength. Its para-military programme, which laid emphasis on physical training and discipline, was an added attraction. As a counter to the communal extremism of both the All India Muslim Students' Federation and RSS, secular-minded leftists organised the Rashtra Seva Dal. The Dal also sponsored a para-military programme in addition to other cultural and social activities.

By 1938, Indian students had become highly politicised. The ideological sophistication of the nationalist politics had repercussions on the student movement. Factional infighting between the Communists, on the one hand, and the Socialists and the Gandhians, on the other, resulted in the split in AISF in 1940. While AISF became the student wing of the Communists, the Socialists and the Gandhians formed the All India Students' Congress. This inevitable polarisation necessarily weakened the student movement to some extent.

In India, student political activism has been a predominantly male phenomenon, and this was particularly so before Independence. Women formed a relatively small percentage of the student population and the traditional values relating to the status of women discouraged any extrovert protest on her part as being unwomanly. The participation by a large number of women in the 1938 campaign for the release of political prisoners is, therefore, noteworthy (see Chakravarty 1980: 7–10). Following this campaign, some women activists set up a girl students' committee within AISF. Its inaugural conference held in 1940 was the first ever all-India meeting of women students. The resulting awakening challenged the oppressive tradition which had hitherto excluded women from politics.

The Quit India Movement launched in 1942 marked the zenith of the student movement in India. With the Communists supporting the British war effort to strengthen international resistance against the worldwide danger of fascism, AISF withdrew from the scene. But the nationalist students represented by the All India Students' Congress were exhorted by leaders like Jawaharlal Nehru and Jayaprakash Narayan to take an active part in what turned out to be the final assault on British hegemony. These students succeeded in getting most of the colleges closed and disrupting and sabotaging the British Indian administration. They assumed leadership when the senior Congress leaders were imprisoned. They also acted as a link between the movement and those of its leaders who had gone underground evading arrest. Student groups published illegal newspapers and even operated a clandestine radio station.

However, the militancy of the mainstream student movement of 1942 gradually abated and by 1947 it had lost most of its élan. This was mainly due to the disillusionment of the All India Students' Congress (disbanded in 1948) with the Congress leadership for its compromises for securing independence. The disenchantment was complete with the Congress leadership ordering the surrender of arms by the Indian Navy militants who had mutinied in 1946, a mutiny to which the students had extended active support.

According to Philip G. Altbach (1968b: 33–35), several factors contributed to the growth of a militant student movement in the pre-Independence period. Most of the colleges in the country were located in the urban centres. The student community was small and was drawn predominantly from the upper-middle- or upper-class and higher caste families in urban areas. The relative compactness of these colleges facilitated communication between them. The characteristically liberal tradition of education exposed the students to a variety of western political ideologies and many of them were strongly influenced by Fabian Socialism and Russian Communism.

The political rebelliousness of the students was legitimated by the morally imposing authority of the nationalist leaders 'who stood in quasi-paternal and avuncular relationship to the students' (Shils 1968a: 2). But, most important, 'from the beginning, many of the best students were involved in the student political movement, particularly in the left-wing groups, and this helped to make the movement more "respectable"' (Altbach 1971: 210).

With the dawn of Independence, the student movement lost its main *raison d'être*. Not only was there no clear political goal set for the student community, the Congress leadership even urged the students to stay away from politics. In a situation of increasing political opportunities, most leaders became busy carving out a niche for themselves. The emergence of the politics of expediency, opportunism, and compromise eroded ideology and the spirit of self-sacrifice which had characterised the freedom struggle. Before analysing the metamorphosis of student activism in the post-Independence era, a brief description of the socio-political and educational contexts in which it took place is necessary.

Post-Independence Unrest: The Background

India became independent on 15 August 1947 and proclaimed itself as a 'Sovereign Socialist Secular Democratic Republic' on 26 January 1950. The Constitution of India envisages a parliamentary form of government which is federal in structure with distinct unitary features. The country now (in 2014) comprises 29 states and seven union territories organised mostly on linguistic basis. Both at the national and at the state levels the governmental and bureaucratic set-up inherited from the colonial regime has been retained and reinforced. There is a multi-party system functioning, with a mixture of national, regional, and local level parties.

Starting with 1951, the country adopted a modified version of the erstwhile Soviet planning, called the Five-Year Plan, an important feature of which is the attempt to blend the private and the public sectors in what has come to be known as 'a mixed economy'.[2] The government not only became the single largest employer, but also assumed the responsibility for implementing a variety of welfare programmes to bring about an egalitarian society as laid down in the Constitution.

Notwithstanding the repeated protestations to the contrary of the ruling class, the pattern of socio-economic development in India has, by and large, followed the capitalist path. This has created various imbalances – regional, rural-urban, etc. – and has accentuated the disparities between the different sections of the population. With a grossly unequal distribution of the fruits of national development, pockets of very rich people now exist amidst the large masses of the chronically poor.

Since an inordinate social emphasis is laid on wealth and its associated lifestyle values, corruption in various walks of life has become so rampant that it has come to be acquiesced in as a normal phenomenon. The ill-gotten wealth, dubbed as 'black money', has created a parallel economy with its own norms. There is a general sense of dissatisfaction with the pace of change and its direction.

That India has survived as a nation for six decades now is no doubt sufficient proof of the intrinsic tenacity of its basic unity amidst religious, ethnic, linguistic, and cultural diversities. Even so, the weaknesses of her nationhood are apparent in the many fissiparous tendencies witnessed in different parts of the country. Such tendencies as regionalism, communalism, linguistic chauvinism, and parochialism of various sorts could be viewed only as the inevitable outcome of the drifting and unregulated nature of the democratic process that has been operating over the past six decades.

Explosion of Higher Education

On no section of society is the impact of the stresses associated with such a climate of social change as sharp and pronounced as on the student community, especially in the context of a phenomenally expanding area of education.[3] The number of universities increased from twenty in 1947 to 130 in 1985, in which year there were in addition sixteen 'deemed universities' and eleven 'institutions of national importance'. The number of arts, science, and commerce colleges increased from 542 in 1950–51 to 8,114 in 1984–85. In addition, there were about 500 junior colleges, 3,000 colleges for professional education, and 300 polytechnics. The post-school level student population has increased from some 3,00,000 to about 45,00,000 in the course of thirty-five years.

An important consequence of the unregulated expansion of higher education with an emphasis on equality and wider accessibility has been the mass enrolment of first generation students from rural areas and from socio-economically backward segments of the population. These new entrants lack a clear conception of higher education, and view it only as a passport for obtaining secure jobs in government service. They are not carefully nurtured to receive collegiate education, as they suffer from both linguistic deficiencies – especially the command over English, which is still the predominant medium of instruction at the tertiary level and almost an exclusive library language – and inadequacy of exposure to varieties of fast expanding knowledge.

The rapid expansion of facilities for higher education with a stress on the certification function under conditions of inadequate allocation of funds has meant the growth of substandard institutions and deterioration in the quality of instruction offered by them. Excessive bureaucratisation and authoritarian orientation of the system, decreasing teacher-student contact due to the growing student-teacher ratio, the increasingly impersonal nature of instruction, and the gradual disappearance of organised social life in colleges are all parts of the same syndrome.

Attention is often drawn to the deficient and deteriorating campus environment as a source of discontent among the students. But, even more important, the generation of employment vis-à-vis the expansion of the tertiary level of education has been extremely slow, and the consequent escalation of educational qualification for jobs has inevitably diluted the mobility significance of education in relation to occupation (see Chapter 5). While this by itself has not reduced the demand for higher education, it is nevertheless a certain source of anxiety, frustration, and cynicism among the students, and a potent incentive for their inward restlessness and outward expression of protest.

Students as a Political Class

No wonder then that a large and growing student body with very weak academic orientation and a subterranean sense of alienation is 'a captive audience *par excellence* for political manipulators' (Ross 1969: 255), and a crucial ready base for mobilisation by political parties. It is in this context that the politicisation of students (see Di Bona 1972) and the emergence of students as a new political class (see Rudolph, Rudolph and Ahmad 1971) become meaningful.

As a political class, the Indian students conform to Samuel N. Eisenstadt's description of the 'semi-autonomous and relatively unregulated youth grouping' (1963: 307). Not having assumed major responsibilities of work and family as yet, they are relatively free to respond to suggestion. Their political significance lies in the fact that they are an easily mobilisable section of the population who can increase the size and heat of protest movements by their youthful excitability. They could also be used for securing votes during elections, and for recruiting party cadres. Accordingly, there is a competition among political parties 'to catch them young'.

The political parties extend their patronage to student organisations and their leadership, and take a solicitous interest in student demands and grievances. And, the politically ambitious student activists aspire to become leaders and enter the wider arena of politics by establishing contact with the politicians. The direct link between students and politicians and their parties has become such an accepted fact of campus life that the major student organisations in the campuses are often the student wings of the national or sometimes the regional parties.

Metamorphosis of Student Activism

Since the early 1960s, student agitations have become almost a daily occurrence, and they are no longer news. It is estimated that, in 1966, there were 2,206 student demonstrations, of which 480 were violent. The prominent student agitations till 1968 have been recorded by Altbach (1968b), and the Vishwa Yuvak Kendra (1973: 59–98) has documented fifty-nine student agitations which have obstructed the normal functioning of academic institutions during 1968.

Of the ninety-six instances of student agitations recorded in 1963 analysed by Ross (1969: 13–15), twenty-five had no set purpose, and they seemed to have occurred as 'a release of tensions, or for enjoyment'. The remaining seventy-one were carried out 'to protest against some phase of the educational system, or to protect the students'. This implies that Indian students find it easier to promote collective action in order to protect the interests of 'students *as* students'.

Considering the type of issues involved – such as, for example, dissatisfaction with college administration, increase in fees, dismissal of a popular principal, difficult examination standards, inefficiency of a lecturer, poor conditions of hostel – the rebelliousness of the students would certainly appear to be out of proportion, and fits into Edward Shils' characterisation of such agitations as manifestations of 'juvenile delinquency' (1968b: 3).

An analysis of the series of student agitations in Allahabad (see Anderson and Pant 1970; Di Bona 1972), Benares (see Ray 1977), Calcutta (see Dasgupta 1974), Mysore and Bangalore (see Ross 1969), and elsewhere (see Vishwa Yuvak Kendra 1973) in the 1960s and in Delhi (see Singhal 1977) during the early 1970s reveals that, in the late 1960s, the student agitations gradually started gaining an organised form. However, it was only in 1974 that a student agitation started manifesting characteristics of an articulated mass movement. This movement originated in the western state of Gujarat under the banner of the *Navnirman Samiti* (see Jones and Jones 1977; Sheth 1977). From there it spread to the northern state of Bihar under the banner of the *Chhatra Sangharsha Samiti* (see Ghanshyam Shah 1977). And, later on, it was transformed into a country-wide movement.[4]

This movement was ably served by a leadership which was both experienced and commanded respect. Though started by students, it developed into a broader political movement with the toppling of the Congress (I) government as its target. Also important in this context were the dramatic provocative events of

1974–75 – such as frequent police firings, imposition of President's Rule in Gujarat without dissolving the legislature, the Allahabad High Court judgement annulling the election to the Lok Sabha of Mrs Indira Gandhi, the then Prime Minister, etc. – which provided the necessary momentum to the movement.

Given the course of events, the student movement would have become full-blown. But, the government, finding itself in a precarious predicament, ruthlessly crushed it during the Emergency (1975–77) (see Jayaram 1981b), a period of drastic curtailment of civil liberties which constitutes a black chapter in the history of modern India. Student unions were forcibly converted into docile associations confined to purely cultural activities. Resistance to this suppression was systematically destroyed.

Contrary to expectations, the lifting of the Emergency and the defeat of the Congress (I) in the March 1977 general elections did not bring peace and tranquillity to the campus. While the mainstream student movement had lost its *raison d'être,* the 7,520 incidents of student unrest in 1977, of which 1,146 were violent, resembled those of the agitations of the early 1960s. But for the student movements in Assam, Gujarat, and Punjab, the student agitations in the rest of the country since the 1980s have been a continuation of the legacy of the 1960s.

Nature and Form of Unrest

Myriad explanations have been offered for the ferment in the student world, from 'high jinks', at one end, to acute politicisation of the academia, at the other. Some of these are (a) generation gap, (b) erosion of the hierarchical structure of the society, (c) status of students as marginal elites in society, (d) emotional strains imposed on youth by modern society, (e) academic maladjustment and consequent failure, (f) failure of education in socialisation, (g) student alienation, (h) economic uncertainty, and (i) contrast between affluence and poverty generating resentment.

As regards the forms that the unrest takes, expression of resentment (both verbal and written); boycott of classes and walkout from examination halls; demonstrations, rallies, and courting arrest; strikes, *dharnas* and *gheraos*; damage to public property; and assault and intimidation are found to be salient. As Shils (1968a: 5–6) has observed, the students invariably attack minor or unconnected symbols like principals, vice-chancellors, district administrators, police officers, post offices, street lights, public transport buses, etc. rather than the pivot of the system, namely, the government or the regime.

Even when the unrest focuses on a political issue – as for example, in Orissa during 1964–65 or in Tamil Nadu in 1965 – the focus does not persist in the absence of a sustaining and cogent ideology. Such unrest is generally ephemeral and fades away when the issue around which it is organised ceases to exist or loses its glamour. The span of a student 'generation' too is short, lasting hardly two to five years and depriving it of stability and continuity. In any given generation, students do not also constitute a homogeneous entity.

Politicisation of students and the intervention of political parties no doubt give some momentum and continuity to politically oriented student movements. However, unlike in the pre-Independence era, when students were involved in 'regime politics', that is, challenging the legitimacy of the British political order, in the post-Independence period, they have been involved in the politics of interests, issues, and programmes (see Rudolph, Rudolph and Ahmad 1971: 1657). But for the short-lived exceptions of Naxalite students (wedded to the policy of the annihilation of class enemies) in the late 1960s in Bengal and in the early 1980s in Andhra Pradesh and Kerala, and the contemporary secessionist student extremism in Punjab, they have not challenged the legitimacy of the existing political order as such. This perhaps explains the displacement of targets and the ephemeral nature of student agitations precluding the possibility of their becoming perennial movements. Student upheaval, except during the freedom struggle and briefly during the 1974 movement has not also been a uniform pan-Indian phenomenon, either in its complexion or in its manifestation. Persistent student disturbances have been confined to the few states of Uttar Pradesh, Bihar, West Bengal, Orissa, Gujarat, Madhya Pradesh, and Assam. In contrast, students in South India have been, by and large, passive and fairly docile. These regional differences are partly explained by the variations in the political climate of the states or regions, their overall cultural traditions, and the extent of the socio-economic hardships experienced by the local population.

The vast majority of students, especially women students, are apolitical and keep out of political agitations (see Ross 1969:

233 ff; Ray 1977: 192–96; Pattnaik 1982: 102). In a study of student politics in Delhi University, T.K. Oommen (1974: 789) found that over 83 per cent of the student leaders came from the faculties of humanities, social sciences, and law. Similar findings have been reported for the Allahabad and Benares Hindu Universities (see Anderson and Pant 1970: 941; Ray 1977:196). It would appear that students enrolled in courses of vague job values are relatively more prone to activism than their counterparts in courses with clear vocational goals and a more or less assured future.

The active few, who have earned the sobriquet 'professional students', show a pronounced desire for political careers (see Robert C. Shah 1968; and Oommen 1974: 790), and view campus politics as a stepping stone to the politics of the adult world. It is they who function as the agents of political parties for mobilising the larger community of students. As many as 67 per cent of the student leaders in Delhi University interviewed by Oommen (1974: 791) confessed to be having contacts with party leaders, and a little more than one-third of them met these politicians every week. For this reason, politicisation of the campus has come to be viewed as a crucial factor in student unrest in India. This is a singular feature which distinguishes Indian universities and colleges from their counterparts in most other countries.

Some General Observations

An examination of the dynamics of student political activism in India for over a century now reveals a pattern of rhythmical swing between growth and decline of student movements. In view of the vastness of the country, the sharp regional differences, the growing heterogeneity of the student community, the absence of an exigent goal capable of maintaining the sustained interest of the students and having the potential for their immediate mobilisation when necessary, and the ephemerality of the student population as a political class, there have been only two nation-wide movements: The first was a part of the country's freedom struggle, and the second, against the authoritarian and repressive Congress (I) government in 1974. In both the cases, the movements lost their *raison d'être* once their initial aims were achieved, and petered out thereafter as the political bosses behind them lacked the vision and the will to harness the latent student power for realising the larger aims of nation-building.

On the other hand, there have been many regional or local level movements, which, while generally being short-lived and not always successful in achieving their avowed goals, have nevertheless evoked significant political response. Notable among them are the anti-Hindi agitation in Tamil Nadu (and elsewhere in South India) during the 1960s (see Barnett 1976), the anti-reservation policy agitation in Gujarat in 1980 (see I.P. Desai 1981), and the anti-'foreigners' agitation in Assam during 1979–85 (see Guha 1980). The last one is noteworthy in that the Asom Gana Parishad, of which the All Assam Students' Union was a leading component, was voted to power in the state assembly elections in 1986.

Notwithstanding the politicians' interest in student affairs and the student leaders' interest in politics, student agitations, by and large, steer clear of political controversies. Most often their aim is 'the correction of particular grievances', and when they do 'concern themselves with institutional reform, it is usually to oppose it'. The student agitation in India would, therefore, appear to be conservative in orientation despite 'the violence of the means used to express its protests' (Shils 1968a: 6). But even so, it draws attention to the inadequacies of the educational as well as the social systems.

The reason why the pressure tactics which the students resort to are often coercive and violent is not far to seek. Aileen D. Ross has observed that students in India are 'in the advantageous position of being able to release their frustration without incurring severe penalties' (1969: 251). This is so because of the relatively better socio-economic background to which the students in the urban campus belong, as also their ambivalent status which makes them, in the eyes of authorities, a liability to be handled with indulgence. Activities which when indulged in by other categories of the population invite severe punishment are tolerated and excused in the case of students as 'natural aggressiveness' or 'youthful excitability'. The resulting diminution or even lack of the fear of retribution from the authorities encourages the students to repeatedly resort to coercive and violent tactics. Furthermore, student agitations or movements, especially if they succeed in evoking some favourable response from the authorities, result in a sense of power among the students.

Prospective Trends

It is extremely difficult to forecast the future trends in the political activism of Indian students for the country as a whole. Reflecting on the nature and orientation of student agitations in the early 1960s, Ross had prophesied that

> as student protest becomes better organised, as the students begin to gain a more powerful and respected position, and as the educational system changes to meet more of the students' needs, the number of spontaneous outbursts and the instances of violence will gradually diminish (1969: 268).

The continuation of the 1960s' type of agitations has falsified this prophecy.

Similarly, Shils (1968a), a close observer of the Indian educational scene till the mid-1960s, had categorically denied that student activism in India has any constructive content or definite direction. But the 1974 movement, as also the movements in Gujarat and Assam since then, have discounted this conclusion. In fact, under certain socio-economic and political conditions, student agitations are found to get transformed into articulated movements (see Jayaram 1981b), and the potential for political action by Indian students has been amply demonstrated. Currently, no organised student movement is in evidence. It is, however, certain that it will be extremely difficult to depoliticise the student community and its leadership in the foreseeable future, because of the rapid politicisation of practically all spheres of life in Indian society since Independence.

The University Grants Commission has time and again emphasised that politicised student unions have no place in higher education. Leaders of several political parties keep advising students, though not convincingly or sincerely, to keep themselves away from politics. But, having experienced the mutually profitable relationship, neither would the politicians want to give up their hold on the students nor would the students cease to look up to their political patrons. The Commission and other such educational authorities can hardly muster the administrative will or the political support to implement their policy of de-politicisation of student unions. One will not, therefore, be surprised if the objective of de-politicisation of teachers and students contemplated in the government's 'new' education policy (see Chapter 19) remains a pious hope.

Notes

1. For a detailed account, see Philip G. Altbach (1968a, 1968b: 25–40).
2. The Planning Commission was the brain child of the first Prime Minister Jawaharlal Nehru. It has been in existence from 1951 and has formulated twelve five-year plans and two annual plans. In his Independence Day speech to the nation, delivered on 15 August 2014, Prime Minister Narendra Modi announced the scrapping of the Planning Commission (*The Times of India*, Mumbai, 16 August 2014, p. 1).
3. The data here are drawn mainly from Ministry of Information and Broadcasting (1987: 69–70) and Association of Indian Universities (1985).
4. For a recent revisiting of the *Nav Nirman Andolan* of Gujarat, see Varsha Bhagat Ganguly (2014).

Part V

Political Aspects of Education

16

Multiculturalism and Education

The Indian Experience

> Education is the influence exercised by adult generations on those that are not yet ready for social life. Its object is to arouse and develop in the child a certain number of physical, intellectual and moral states which are demanded of him by both the political society as a whole and the special milieu for which he is specifically destined.
>
> **Émile Durkheim** (1956: 71)

Worldwide, 'multiculturalism' has been gaining prominence on the academic agenda of social sciences. To be sure, the idea underlying the concept of multiculturalism is not novel; it can be traced to the now out-of-fashion concept of 'plural society', originally conceived by J.S. Furnivall in 1939 and developed by other scholars (see Furnivall 1948; M.G. Smith 1965: 66–91). However, the context of the changing contours of ethnic and socio-cultural groups vis-à-vis politico-geographical boundaries has given new currency to this concept and its underlying ideology.[1]

For more than 50 years, India has celebrated and trumpeted its ethnic, cultural, religious, and linguistic plurality or 'multiculturality'. 'Unity in diversity' has been a familiar and

---

This is a revised version of the Keynote Address delivered at The International Conference on Globalisation and Multicultural Perspectives in Education, organised by the School of Educational Studies, Universiti Sains Malaysia, Penang on 3–4 December 2003.

'overworked cliché' (Dube 1992: 29), used not only by politicians in India but also by her intellectuals. However, it is only since the mid-1980s that the reality of multicultural existence has been formulated and advanced as an explicit ideology. The making of an 'ism' (an ideology) of multicultural existence is something more than a mere semantic shift. Essentially, it underscores the emergent reaction to the metamorphosis of nationalism in India.

Nationalism in India, as it has been conventionally understood in social sciences, referred to the movement that emerged as a reaction to the British (and more generally, the European) colonialism. It was primarily articulated and spearheaded by the Indian National Congress. It is not surprising that the exit of the British in 1947 saw political power being transferred to the Congress. The nature of this political nationalism and its centralising tendency has been the subject of analysis and interpretation by social scientists of various ideological hues.

The concern with this type of nationalism is now passé. As if reflecting this, the political fortunes of the once mighty Congress party have also dwindled. More important, the country is now engaged in reinventing the nation, and this process is willy-nilly directed by a fuzzy and controversial brand of religion-based 'cultural nationalism' (euphemism for 'Hindu nationalism') advocated by the Bharatiya Janata Party (BJP) and its allied quasi-political organisations. In fact, the rise of BJP since the mid-1980s has been inversely related to the fall of the Indian National Congress,[2] and this change has come about through the medium of democratic elections.

As an ideology, multiculturalism in India is essentially a reaction to, or the antithesis of, the inevitably 'majoritarian', possibly exclusivist, and potentially intolerant tendencies inherent in 'cultural nationalism'. It stands for an inclusive socio-political space for the plurality of ethnic, religious, and cultural groups inhabiting the geopolitical area that is India. The juxtaposition between nationalism (be it 'political' or 'cultural') and multiculturalism constitutes the political ferment that will determine the form India takes as a nation-state.

It is in this background that we have to understand India's experience of the interface between multiculturalism and education.[3] Her proverbial socio-cultural diversities make India a laboratory case for understanding this interface, an interface that will have profound significance for her experiment with nation-building.

Socio-Cultural Diversities: Recognition and Responses

'The People of India' (POI), a comprehensive ethnographic survey launched by the Anthropological Survey of India (October 1985–March 1992), identified 4,635 diverse communities which are 'marked by endogamy, occupation and perception' (K.S. Singh 1992: 23). While *endogamy* (a kinship principle) and *occupation* (an economic-activity category) are objectively observable criteria, *perception* is essentially a socio-psychological phenomenon that characterises a community's identity. In India, this identity has been articulated in religious, linguistic, and ethnic/cultural terms.

According to the 2001 Census, an overwhelming majority of India's people identified themselves as Hindus (80.5%). Muslims (13.4%) constituted the single largest minority group, followed by Christians (2.3%), Sikhs (2.0%), Buddhists (0.8%), Jain (0.4%), and Others (6.6%) in that order. While percentage is a convenient device for comparison, in a country of billion-plus people like India, it does not present the reality in all its magnitude. For example, Muslims, who constitute 13.4 per cent of the population, are 138 million in number; in absolute numbers, India has the largest number of Muslims next only to Indonesia. As many as 385 communities profess various forms of tribal/folk religion (K.S. Singh 1993: 19).

The distribution of people in terms of their linguistic identities is more diverse than in terms of their religion: the POI survey lists 325 languages spoken by various communities; the 1991 Census identified 114 languages and 216 mother tongues with a strength of 10,000 and above; and the Eighth Schedule of the Constitution of India recognises twenty-two languages. According to the 1991 Census, the single largest group of people identified themselves as speakers of Hindi (40.2%), the official language of India. Bengali (8.3%), Telugu (7.9%), Marathi (7.5%), Tamil (6.3%), Urdu (5.2%), Gujarati (4.9%), Kannada (3.9%), Malayalam (3.6%), Oriya (3.4%), Punjabi (2.8%), and Assamese (1.6%) are the other eleven languages spoken by more than 1 per cent of the population.

Concerning these diversities two points need to be made. First, as Yogendra Singh argues, the POI survey affirms that 'the diversity of communities does not reduce the nature of sociological reality of states/union territories. More than 71 per cent of the communities are located within the boundaries of states/union territories' (2000: 46). That is, states/union territories of India are not only linguistic and cultural categories but also sociological ones. This implies that the question of diversities within its boundaries becomes the concern of the state/union territory governments as the case may be.

Second, and more important, neither the recognition of the reality of socio-cultural plurality nor the need for or importance of its effective handling is a recent phenomenon. The British administration in India not only recognised the phenomenal diversity of its colonial subjects, but also initiated the earliest steps for their systematic documentation. Having been essentialised through such documentation, religion, caste, and language became crucial determinants of political life in the decades preceding Independence. The leaders of the nationalist movement had sought, though not always successfully, to relegate these diversities to the background. However, the British, as the history books tell us, skilfully adopted 'divide and rule' as an effective strategy: they sowed the seeds of division and disharmony among communities, or sharpened them where they existed. Partition of India and the creation of Pakistan based on religion were only the logical culmination of the process set in motion by the British rulers. Partition has had a lasting impact on India both internally, in the management of the inter-religious relationship between the Muslims and other religious groups (mainly the Hindus), and externally, in its relationship with Pakistan.

The members of the Constituent Assembly that drafted the Constitution of India after India became independent in 1947 recognised the infinite plurality of her population and consciously adopted explicit provisions for safeguarding their rights to conserve their culture. Through the Constitution of the Republic of India, adopted by the Constituent Assembly on 26 November 1949 and which came into force on 26 January 1950, 'The People of India' resolved 'to secure to all its citizens: *Justice*, social, economic and political; *Liberty* of thought, expression, belief, faith and worship; *Equality* of status and opportunity; and to promote among them all *Fraternity* assuring the dignity of the individual and the unity of the Nation'. Thus began India's experiment in reconciling two apparently contradictory forces, namely, nation-building and multiculturalism.

Since people are the recipients of education as a resource, and the state, as a hegemonic enterprise, seeks to control its distribution, contents and orientation, the experiment to reconcile multiculturalism and nation-building has profound significance for education: on the one hand, this experiment has influenced the developments in the educational sphere; on the other hand, the developments in education have implications for the outcome of this experiment. In what follows, we shall focus on some of the important dimensions of multiculturalism and nation-building as they relate to education in India.

The Federal Dilemma in Education: The Centre and the States

In the language of political science, India is a quasi-federal republic: the country is divided into twenty-nine constituent States (each governed by a democratically elected state government) and six Union Territories (administered directly by the Government of India). There is, however, a strong unitary tendency in the form of the central government (that is, the Government of India), called popularly the 'Centre'. The central government has total control over almost 100 most important matters, including defence and foreign affairs, and shares a 'Concurrent List' of about fifty subjects with state governments, retaining residual powers for any matter not listed in the Constitution. While the state governments control about sixty matters, including agriculture, land revenue, police, and public welfare, they remain clearly subordinate to the central government in most matters and during any emergency interlude.

Under the Constitution of India, education was largely the responsibility of the states, the central government being concerned only with certain areas like co-ordination and determination of standards in technical and higher education. In January 1977, through the 42nd Amendment the central government was empowered to legislate on education concurrently with the states. Though the central government thereby established supremacy over education, the hopes of a national reform in education that this Amendment aroused failed to materialise. With the hegemonic Congress rule at the centre and the gradual deterioration of the relationship between the centre and some states,[4] no government at the centre could take any bold steps in the realm of education confidently.

As it stands today, school education – including primary (the first seven years), secondary (the next three years), and higher secondary (the last two years) stages of schooling – largely remains the responsibility of the states. To the extent that the states are 'cultural regions', encapsulating historical, regional, linguistic, and cultural identities, they are apparently better placed to take care of the diversities of the pan-India level, especially in view of the unitary tendency of the centre. However, no state in India is culturally homogeneous and all need to address multicultural demands articulated by the respective groups, be they linguistic, religious, caste, or ethnic/cultural.

For instance, though the dominant language in a state is the essence of its identity, no state (or even union territory) is entirely homogeneous, and communication within any given state involves more than one language. 'The minority languages in the state range from 5 per cent (Kerala) to nearly 85 per cent (Nagaland) of their respective populations' (S. Krishna 1991: 28). The same is true of religion, and more so of caste. In no state, therefore, is the educational sphere free from claims and contestations concerning recognition and incorporation of diversities, even as each state strives to attain some uniformity across within its boundary. That is, both at the centre and the state levels there is constant balancing between multicultural demands and unitary tendencies in the sphere of education.

The ambits within which the states have to address multicultural demands in school education are, no doubt, limited by the diversities in their respective regions. However, school education is not confined to the jurisdiction of the states. The centre, too, directs and regulates an all-India system of school education under the aegis of the Central Board of Secondary Education (CBSE). There are three types of schools under this system: Kendriya Vidyalayas,[5] Navodaya Vidyalayas,[6] and other affiliated schools. The Central Board of Secondary Education prescribes a standardised common curriculum for all schools under its umbrella. In the formulation of this curriculum, and the preparation of textbooks thereof, the National Council of Educational Research and Training (NCERT, established in September 1961), an organisation that is directly under the control of the Central Government's Ministry of Human Resources Development, plays an important role.

Not surprisingly, the curriculum and textbooks of NCERT have become a bone of contention ever since 'cultural nationalism', which had been hitherto advocated by BJP and its allied quasi-political organisations, came to be implemented by the National Democratic Alliance government led by BJP in 1999 (see SAHMAT 2002; K. Roy 2002). Opposition parties, mainly those with Left leanings, and the self-proclaimed sentinels of secularism have been critical of the so-called 'saffronisation'[7] of education. The matter has been taken up at the highest level of the judiciary, namely, the Supreme Court of India. The states in which parties or coalitions opposed to the BJP ideology are in power have categorically eschewed the use of NCERT curricula or textbooks or selectively used them in their school systems.

Apart from the CBSE school system, the open schooling under the authority of the National Open School (established in November 1989) and the schools affiliated to the Council for the Indian School Certificate Examinations (Indian Council of Secondary Education (ICSE) and the Indian School Certificate (ISC) examinations at the end of Standards X and XII, respectively) and the Indian Public Schools Conference (IPSC, formed in October 1939) are other school systems with an all-India span. While these systems prescribe their own curricula and textbooks, the IPSC-affiliated schools have considerable freedom in using textbooks of their choice.

Although the National Open School is an autonomous body, it is under the constant influence of the central government. Nevertheless, given the extra-mural nature of schooling it offers, and its limited (about 2,20,000 students) and dispersed coverage, its unitary strain has seldom been controversial. The schools affiliated to other all India umbrella bodies such as CISCE and IPSC are invariably run by religious minority groups, especially Christian, or some foundations. These schools generally cater to the elite sections of the population. They enjoy considerable flexibility in what they teach (curriculum) and how it is taught (pedagogy). Considering the elite tag attached to the certificates by these school systems, students from other religious groups seldom have any problem with the religious orientation of these schools.

To provide a new initiative and a special thrust to achieve universalisation of elementary education, the central government launched the District Primary Education Programme in 1994. This Programme envisaged decentralised management, participatory process, empowerment, and capacity building at all levels. It was implemented through state-level registered societies, and the expenditure was shared by the central and the state governments in the ratio of 85:15. The emphasis on decentralisation and participatory processes in the Programme was expected to foster and promote multiculturalism. This Programme was superseded by the Sarva Siksha Abhiyan in 2001.

The situation concerning higher education is more complicated. In India, the term 'higher education' suggests too much of a homogeneity, glossing over the enormous structural and functional diversities within the system. Broadly defined, it includes the entire spectrum of education beyond twelve years of formal schooling. As for their structure, most Indian universities belong to the *affiliating* type, which, besides their own departments of studies, have a large number of colleges affiliated to them. As for their legal status and regulative responsibility, the universities are of three types: the central universities (established by an Act of Parliament, and regulated directly by the central government's Ministry of Human Resource Development) and state universities (established by an Act of State Assemblies, and regulated by the respective state governments), and institutions 'deemed-to-be-universities' under Section 3 of the University Commission Act 1956. Besides, the central government has conferred upon eleven university-level institutions the status of 'institutions of national importance'. Furthermore, there are eight open universities and forty-one institutes or directorates of distance education functioning under conventional universities. In India, the concept of private universities is nascent.

The question of multiculturalism inevitably crops up in the sphere of higher education, too. As in school education, in higher education also, the state governments seek to safeguard their regional interests vis-à-vis the unitary thrust of the central government. The opposition from some states, especially those opposed to the ideology of 'cultural nationalism' propounded by BJP, to some courses of study (for example, astrology and priest craft) proposed to be introduced in universities and colleges is a case in point. But then, the state governments have to contend with multicultural demands faced by the universities established by them. Even so, internally, the state universities tend to be parochial and inward looking, as compared with central universities and national level institutions which are broad based, expansive, and outward looking. We may note, however, that the state universities cannot pursue their parochial ends beyond a particular limit, as they are humiliatingly dependent financially on the central government. Furthermore, ineffective as they no doubt have been, the national-level bodies like the University Grants Commission (UGC, established in 1956) and National Assessment and Accreditation Council (NAAC, established in 1994) try to rein the state universities.

The Language Question in Education: Colonial Legacy and Post-Colonial Dilemma

The earliest attempt to impart education in India, as it exists today, can be traced to the missionary activities following the establishment of the East India Company and the measures adopted by Warren Hastings as early as 1773. The protracted controversy that this generated – between the 'Anglicists' commending a Western course and the 'Orientalists' favouring an indigenous direction – was finally resolved by William Bentinck in favour of the Anglicist orientation, barely a month after Thomas Babington Macaulay had penned his (in)famous *Minute* (on 2 February 1835). His policy was reaffirmed by Charles Wood's *Despatch* (of 19 July 1854), and with minor modifications continued throughout the British rule.

The system of education that the British introduced was modelled after the system prevalent in their mother country. The striking feature of this educational transplantation was English, which was not only taught as a language but also became the medium of instruction. While the secondary school certificate examination was conducted only in English till 1937, English was almost exclusively used at the university stage right through the colonial period. The excessive emphasis on the mastering of

English as a language often eclipsed the purpose of education: it encouraged mechanical learning through memorising and discouraged inquisitiveness and an experimental bent of mind. There was a simultaneous devaluation of the indigenous languages, and a sad neglect of their development.

The spread of national awakening and the growing prospects of independence brought to the fore the question of the national language and the replacement of English by Indian languages in education. A definite result of the nationalist movement and the efforts of the Hindi zealots to impose that language on all non-Hindi-speaking states after Independence has been the 'ideologisation' of Hindi in the six Hindi-speaking states, and the glorification of the respective regional languages in the non-Hindi-speaking states. Linguistic ethnocentrism has now taken deep roots in several states.

In all the states, especially the non-Hindi-speaking ones, there has been considerable on-going controversy about the instruction of languages. The context of the debate on language instruction at the school level is provided by the 'three-language formula', which was adopted as part of the National Education Policy in 1968. According to this formula, every secondary school student must compulsorily learn at least three languages. In the non-Hindi-speaking states these three languages are: one's mother tongue or regional language (L1), Hindi as the national language (L2), and English as a foreign language (L3). In the Hindi-speaking states English will be L2 and one of the modern Indian languages listed in the Eighth Schedule of the Constitution L3. While all the states accepted this policy in principle, it has either not been implemented (as in Tamil Nadu) or been implemented half-heartedly (as in Andhra Pradesh and Karnataka) or as a sham (as in Uttar Pradesh and Bihar).

As can be expected, linguistic chauvinism has adverse consequences for linguistic minorities living in a state, raising questions of constitutional safeguards, just as it opens new arenas of social confrontation. In Karnataka, a prolonged agitation led by the protagonists of Kannada had led the Government of Karnataka in 1982 to pass an Order that made the teaching of Kannada compulsory at the primary school level, and accorded Kannada the sole 'first language' status.[8] This order did not find favour with those who wanted the freedom to choose the language of study, and particularly with the educational institutions run by linguistic minorities, who challenged its constitutional validity. The High Court of Karnataka upheld the contention of these institutions and struck down the Government Order in January 1989.

A status survey of language instruction in the country revealed that, of the 1,652 mother tongues listed by the 1961 Census, only fifty-one languages are spoken by more than 1,00,000 people each. Of these fifty-one languages, sixteen have no script of their own, and only the remaining thirty-five languages are accepted as media of instruction at the school level (see Chaturvedi and Mahale 1976; Chaturvedi and Singh 1981). D.P. Pattanayak hypothesises that the disjunction between the home languages and the school language is responsible not only for wastage and stagnation but also for 'the development of a low self-image and lower achievement all through education in the schools' (1981: xii). This is more piquant considering that, despite the great diversity of languages, the people of India are mostly monolingual.

Concerning higher education, in the mid-1960s the *Report of the Education Commission (1964–66)* emphasised the need 'to move energetically in the direction of adopting the regional languages as media of education ...' (Ministry of Education 1971: 527). However, English has not only persisted but is still the predominant medium of instruction, especially at the postgraduate level and in science and professional courses. The progress in the switch over from English as the medium of instruction, though still insignificant, is better in Hindi than in other regional languages. Even so, such a switch over is mostly confined to arts, education, and to some extent to basic science courses at the undergraduate level. A review of the trends in the medium of instruction in higher education concluded that 'a complete switch over to the regional languages as media of instruction at all levels and in all courses is not a possibility in the foreseeable future' (Jayaram 1993: 112).

Any attempt by the government to force the pace of the switch over to the regional languages as media of instruction is politically resisted through students' agitations and legally stalled by invoking the constitutional guarantees, especially those meant for the linguistic minorities. In May 1971, the Constitution Bench of the Supreme Court of India held that no university in the country could declare a particular regional language as the sole medium of instruction and examination, as it would infringe the rights enshrined in the Constitution.

Systematic data on the preferences of the medium of instruction of students and of parents for their wards are hard to come by. The Review Commission of Universities in Karnataka also 'found widespread preference among students, even from rural areas, for the English medium' (Government of Karnataka 1980: 5). How much is such a preference for English as the medium of instruction characteristic of university students in the Hindi-speaking states is difficult to ascertain. Nevertheless, the pronounced preference for English rather than the regional language as the medium of instruction in some states calls for some explanation. From the point of view of education, easier access to the large body of technical literature, and greater scope for and felicity of communication are often stressed. From the point of view of the students, the perception of more and better employment opportunities, and the possibility of greater mobility within and outside the country seem important. A combination of these two sets of factors seems to infuse among students 'a fear of being treated as an inferior category among the educated, unless the courses are taken in the English medium', and this fear is an important factor in their aversion to the regional language medium (Government of Karnataka 1980: 5).

Selective bilingualism is often advocated as a transitory policy option. The introduction of the regional language as the medium of instruction in one or two subjects/papers, with the option given to the students to answer the examination either in English or in the regional language, is an element of such a policy. While selective bilingualism is apparently a more democratic measure, its consequences are not likely to be necessarily egalitarian. The variety of standards that is inevitable in the transitory period coupled with the fact that command over languages (such as English, for instance) constitutes an important socio-economic and political asset, would result in the emergence of at least three categories of elite, educated respectively in English, Hindi and the regional language medium, and results in differential exploitation of resources by them. Thus, at least in the transitory period, the process is more likely to contribute to the reproduction of inequality across various cultural groups.

Whatever may be the medium of instruction, English can be given up only at grave peril to the educational system in India. This is vindicated by the fact that, even in countries which have been politically and culturally distant from the English-speaking world, ever more people are learning English as a first foreign language. This is being realised even in those states (not only Hindi-speaking ones) in India which had been politically antipathetic till recently to the continuation of English in education in any form, as it is a manifestation of the 'cultural imperialism' of the West. It is interesting that, in spite of the official efforts at banishment of English in these states, and notwithstanding their conscious promotion of Hindi/regional languages there, English has not only survived but even seems to be thriving. English is still the most widely known second language followed by Hindi, and in fact, more Indians want to learn it today than ever before.

Religion and Education: The Minority Rights

It is well known that, in India, the primordial identities and interests rooted in religion and caste have a determining influence on social and political life. During the colonial era, the leaders of the nationalist movement had sought, though not always successfully, to relegate them to the background. The dawn of Independence brought them to the fore, and the adoption of the republican form of democracy converted them into significant pivots around which group interests could be articulated and major confrontations could jell.

Partition of India on the eve of Independence in August 1947, and the creation of Pakistan based on religion, had resulted in a violent turmoil and a permanent cleavage between the majority Hindus and the minority Muslims. Playing the card of political nationalism and adopting a policy of keeping the religious minorities in good humour, the successive Congress party governments at the centre ignored the incipient subterranean majoritarian ideology and assumedly kept the politics of religious confrontation at bay. However, the situation started changing with the decline of the legitimacy of Congress party in the aftermath of the infamous Emergency era (1975–77) and the ascendancy of BJP, a right-wing Hindu nationalist party.

The rise of BJP as the single largest political party has profound significance for the political dynamics of modern India. The success of BJP lies in articulating the nationalist imagination in religious and cultural terms, confirming the strong affinity between 'nationalist imagining' and 'religious imagining' emphasised by Benedict Anderson (1983: 19). To the extent that BJP seeks to articulate the aspirations of the Hindus, nebulous and heterogeneous as their religion may be,[9] and consolidate their religious/cultural identity, the trend towards 'majoritarianism' is discernible.

The trend towards Hindu majoritarianism in a country where the Hindus constitute the overwhelming majority (80.5%) of the population is only to be expected. It is, however, viewed, and justifiably so, with suspicion and apprehension by the minorities. The growing psychology of fear among them is to be understood in this context. Apart from turning communalism, defined as the 'antagonistic mobilisation of one religious community against another' (Ludden 1996: 1), into a perennial problem, the majoritarian 'cultural nationalism' has resulted in contestations over every issue involving religion, including education.

It must be pointed out that, in India, contrary to common belief, neither the Muslims nor the Christians constitute a socially homogeneous community. Both are characterised by regional and linguistic variations and highly unequal systems of social stratification with caste-like formations. Among both these communities, religion has functioned as an effective ideological apparatus, insulating the contradictions within the community. However, a major distinction between the Muslims and the Christians in India worth noting is that, while religion 'never imparted a socio-cultural identity to the Christians' (Rodrigues 1989: 254), it has fostered such an identity among the Muslims, an identity that is both 'self-defined' and 'other recognised'. This is explained by the convergence and jelling of ethnicity and socio-economic status over a period, which accentuated ethnic distinction and awareness (see Phadnis 1990: 19). This fact should be borne in mind while discussing and interpreting the differential ethnic responses of the Muslims and the Christians in almost every realm, including education.

Very little macro-level data are available on the educational situation among the religious minorities in India. As a conscious policy to arrest divisive tendencies, the Census of India no more presents data on literacy, education, or occupation according to religion. Available data on the educational situation among the

Muslims show that at the high school level and higher, the Muslims are at least three to four times behind other communities. The enrolment of Muslim children in primary schools is generally poor, even in those areas where the Muslims constitute a majority. A significant majority of those enrolled attend Muslim schools or Urdu-medium schools wherever such schools exist. The enrolment of Muslim girls is extremely low. Moreover, the drop-out rate is much higher for Muslim students as compared with their non-Muslim counterparts. Not surprisingly, the Muslims are reported to have one of the lowest literacy rates in India.

It is often argued that only a very small section of the Muslim population looks forward to the charmed realm of professions or government employment through higher education. The projection of the problems of this small section of the community as the problems of the entire community is, therefore, held to be unjustified (see Saxena 1989: 156–57). This argument is also sought to be buttressed by the fact that even among the Hindus the educational opportunities are unequally distributed. This position is tantamount to generalising the problem of educational backwardness at the societal level and ignoring its religious dimension. Though such a generalisation is valid from the vantage point of class analysis, one can hardly ignore the glaring educational backwardness of the Muslims as a minority community *per se*. This position is particularly disquieting in view of the contrasting educational situation among the Christians.

Of the various spheres of activity on which the Christian missionaries in India put an indelible stamp, education is the foremost. They established, generally as an extension of the Church, schools and colleges over the length and breadth of the country, many of which rank among the best even today. More important, unlike the Muslims, the Christians did not have any cultural or religious inhibitions in accepting western education. A large number of Christian boys and girls received education in the missionary institutions. Thus, along with the Brahmans and other upper caste Hindus, the Christians too could get ahead in the sphere of education and thereby take advantage of the emerging economic opportunities in modern India. This explains the favourable educational situation of the Christians as compared with that of the Muslims, and even to that among the Hindus.

It is important to note that Partition, which impacted the Muslim ethnicity significantly, hardly affected the ethnicity of Christians. Nevertheless, the Christians have benefitted immensely from the Constitutional provisions safeguarding minority rights,[10] provisions incorporated keeping primarily the Muslims in mind. The phenomenal success of a small Christian minority in the realm of education as compared to the halting advancement of the large Muslim minority can also be explained by elucidating an economic postulate of the principle of 'minority effect'.[11] As Ratna Naidu puts it, the 'opportunities open to a minority seem also to be related to its size' (1980: 33). She quotes economist A.M. Khusro, who found that 'the majority gets opportunities roughly proportional to its population, a small minority more than proportional and a large minority less than proportional to its numbers' (ibid.).

Finally, the efforts of the Muslim leadership (including invoking the constitutional guarantees for minorities) have been primarily directed at safeguarding the religious interests of the community and at resisting any felt assaults on its socio-religious identity. But, in the case of the Christians, as Valerian Rodrigues has argued with reference to the Catholic hierarchy in the Dakshina Kannada district of Karnataka, their educational institutions (as also other institutions such as hospitals) are the key instruments through which 'the Church hierarchy wields its clout in the society at large', apart from being the principal means of socio-economic advancement for the Church members (1989: 260–61).

The problem of Muslim educational backwardness is aggravated by the sense of insecurity of the Muslim community consequent upon partition of the country, as also the suspicion to which they are subjected by the praxis of cultural nationalism.[12] It is a problem that has to be tackled primarily in ethnic terms. This necessarily implies that serious and sincere efforts must be made not only to reduce ethnic inequalities, but also convince the Muslim minority that this is indeed being done. Pursuing of the revised Programme of Action (1992), in 1993–94, the central government launched two new schemes: (i) Area Intensive Programme for Educationally Backward Minorities, a scheme that gives intensive attention to educational development in areas identified as having large concentration of educationally backward religious minorities, and (ii) Financial Assistance for Modernisation of Madrasa Education, a scheme that encourages the traditional Muslim educational institutions like the *madrasa* and *maktab* to introduce science, mathematics, social studies, Hindi, and English in their curriculum.

In the ultimate analysis, however, the impetus for the educational progress of the Muslims has to come from within the community itself, just as it has come about in the case of the Christians and other religious minorities. M.R.A. Baig (1974), a reputed Muslim intellectual, has traced the roots of the community's stagnation to the general orthodoxy imposed upon it by the intermingling of religion and socio-economic issues. Thus, it cannot be denied that the immense responsibility of carving out a progressive worldview to draw the Muslims into the mainstream of national life and ensure their progress within it lies with the leadership of the community itself. The quintessential element of this progressive worldview has to be modern education.

Multicultural Education: Problems and Prospects

As noted earlier, India is a multicultural country *par excellence*; its diversities are socio-historically rooted and politically entrenched. In such a country, nation-building is a problematic exercise: it involves fostering national unity, on the one hand, and addressing cultural specificities of the country's multifarious communities, on the other. For the political managers, whatever their ideological orientation, the task of balancing between the majoritarian strain for uniformity and the multiculturality of the populace is daunting indeed. The problems and prospects of multicultural education in India have to be understood in the background of this socio-political challenge.

In the preceding three sections, we have examined the relation between multiculturalism and education from the vantage point of egalitarianism or the equality of opportunities. The issue was discussed keeping in view the constitutional guarantees as they relate to the principles of federalism (or centre-state relationship) and the rights of the linguistic and religious minorities. Important as it obviously is, the problem of equality of educational opportunities does not exhaust multiculturalism's concern with education. In what follows let us analyse two salient issues of multicultural education in India, namely, symbolic representation of different communities and cultures, and religious instruction in schools.

There is no gainsaying that, in inter-community dynamics, especially in the context of cultural differences and majority-minority relations, apart from the considerations of material possessions and availability of opportunities, the socio-psychological phenomenon of identity of the community and its symbolic representation becomes important. Often, the claims and counterclaim for symbolic representation are more important than material concerns. Thus, not surprisingly, the first issue concerning multicultural education consists of the symbolic representation of different communities in the curriculum and textbooks. This is particularly so in subjects such as history, social sciences or social studies, and the languages.

During the colonial period, the curricula and the textbooks used were filtered through the western, particularly the British, lens. They were indifferent to or prejudiced against the native cultures, philosophy, events, and heroes of India. The textbooks were mostly written by British authors or by Indian authors who would toe the British line. These textbooks were imported into India or published by branch agencies that had their head offices in Great Britain. For some time after Independence too, the implanted curricula and imported textbooks remained in currency in Indian education. However, gradually, becoming conscious of their biases and prejudices, these curricula and textbooks were replaced to present a 'correct' picture from an Indian nationalist point of view.

As the euphoria of Independence and nationalism (vis-à-vis the British colonialism) began waning and sub-nationalism and cultural differences raised their heads, representations and interpretations in curricula and textbooks became contentious. A reference to the contentions about the curricula and textbooks prepared by NCERT, under the influence of the central government committed to the ideology of 'cultural nationalism', was made earlier. However, such contentions are not restricted to the NCERT textbooks. School curricula and textbooks have been equally contentious within each state, highlighting the essential multiculturality of the population across the country.

The contentions in curricula and textbooks concern the cultural space allocated to specific communities or cultural groupings. They concern the representation of the 'heroes' or champions of the community, region, or locality and their role or contribution to the national, regional, or local life. They may also concern the representation of key events – the freedom struggle, reform movements, cultural contributions – in which the community had a role. Since the symbolic meaning that these 'heroes' and events carry for different communities or cultural groupings is not necessarily shared by others, the interpretation of their representations in textbooks often becomes controversial and lead to agitations and even violence. In India, thus, addressing multiculturalism in curriculum development and preparation of textbooks is challenging.

The second point of contestation has centred on religious instruction in schools. In the case of schools run by minority religious communities, the Constitutional provisions guarantee their right to impart religious instruction. While the Muslim *madrasas* have religious instruction as their primary objective, given their excessive religious orientation and often the use of Urdu as the medium of instruction, schools run by the Muslims seldom have children belonging to other religious communities. The educational institutions run by the Christians, whatever be the denomination (the Roman Catholic or Jesuit, Protestant Missionaries, or others), are broad based in their student intake, as these institutions are more open, and often western too, in their orientation. In these institutions, while religious instruction is invariably provided for Christian students (or at least those belonging to the particular denomination), non-Christian students are offered a veiled and less objectionable form of religious instruction, euphemistically called 'moral education'.

However, the situation in government schools and non-minority grant-in-aid private schools (that is, schools receiving financial assistance from the government) is problematic. These schools have to think of a religion-neutral moral/value education, which is difficult; or smuggle in Hindu religious instruction, if it is not objected to; or eschew religious instruction altogether, in case of confrontation, real or anticipated. But sometimes, in these schools, the practice of commencing the day's work with prayers or recitation of national songs, or even the national anthem, has been objected to on religious grounds and provoked controversy. Similarly, most government and grant-in-aid private schools display the photographs or idols of Hindu gods or goddesses in their premises, especially that of Saraswati, the goddess of learning. This too, has sometimes become a matter of controversy. There are also cases of teachers and students belonging to minority communities demanding a prayer-break during school/college hours and a place for prayers within the school/college premises.

It must be noted that contestations over the cultural content of education have increased in number and intensity during the last thirty-five years. These contestations have not remained democratic in spirit and confined to public discourse in the media or the legislature or petitions in the courts. They have resulted in political mobilisation and protests, often becoming violent. That such contestations are now more than ever before is explained by the fact that, with the spread of educational facilities, the composition of teachers and students has been becoming ever more heterogeneous. The entrance of the first generation of students and teachers from the communities and cultural groupings which had no exposure to education earlier, and their becoming culturally assertive and engaging in identity politics are significant developments in the Indian educational scene. Furthermore, there is now greater heterogeneity between the teachers and the taught and greater scope for the interplay of multifarious belief and value systems. It is in this context that we have to understand the controversy over the central government's prescriptions for 'strengthening culture and values in education' and directions for teaching fundamental duties as part of the school/college curriculum (see A. Roy 2003).

Before concluding this section, we should allude to a different strain of educational thought and development in India. *À la* Ivan Illich and Paulo Freire, it has been argued by some scholars that school, as it exists as a model for learning in Indian society, is inappropriate to the diversity of its cultures and structures at the local level: '... ideologically it is the notion of schooling that stands as a barrier to the development of learning and that it is to the liberation of learning that we should give due attention as we also ponder on more general social liberation' (Shotton 1998: 62). Drawing from the traditional Indian teaching-learning systems (for example, the *Guru-Shishya Parampara*) and the educational philosophy of Sri Aurobindo, Mahatma Gandhi, Jiddu Krishnamurti, and Rabindranath Tagore, there have emerged alternative educational initiatives in Indian tradition.[13] Significant as these alternative politico-educational projects are, given their circumscribed approach and extremely limited coverage (excepting the literacy campaigns/programmes, perhaps), one tends to be sceptical about their being a realistic solution to the educational challenge confronting contemporary India.

Epilogue: Towards a Grammar of Multicultural Education

By surviving as a single political entity for more than five and half decades, India has belied the prophets of pessimism.[14] More important, but for the brief dark interregnum of the Emergency era in the mid-1970s, her track record as a functioning democracy, with the largest electorate in the world, has been enviable. Democratic politics, no doubt, has a tendency to politicise all aspects of life, including region, language, and religion. Accordingly, nation-building in India has necessarily implied the need to address the question of reconciling effectively majoritarianism and multiculturalism.

Since diversity of cultures is an existential reality of India, multiculturalism appears to be her ineluctable ideological option. This, however, does not gainsay the importance of national unity. The relation between unity and diversity is complementary, rather than antagonistic – 'Unity in diversity', as the clichè encapsulates succinctly. One cannot be exaggerated without jeopardising the other. Paradoxical as it may sound, however, it appears on closer scrutiny that diverse cultures need an underlying unity, for the singularity of each culture is meaningful only in the context of general unity. However, what diversity can benefit from unity neither is automatic nor can it be taken-for-granted. It calls for a constant vigil against encroachment of one's cultural rights and a willingness to make sacrifices for coexistence. This is more easily said than done.

Education has a significant role in multiculturalism as in nation-building: after all, before entering the adult world, it is within educational institutions that children and adolescents first encounter and negotiate the reality of cultural diversity. It is often asked, whether such diversity is a bane or boon for the education of children. The consequences of diversity could be beneficial: it may contribute to 'creative problem solving, growth in cognitive and moral reasoning, increased perspective-taking ability, improved relationships, and general sophistication in interacting and working with peers from a variety of cultural and ethnic backgrounds'. The consequences could be harmful, too: it may result in 'closed-minded rejection of new information; increased egocentrism; and negative relationships characterised by hostility, rejection, divisiveness, scapegoating, bullying, stereotyping, and prejudice'. As such, cultural diversity in education may increase or lower academic achievement and productivity depending upon other exigent circumstances (see Johnson and Johnson 2002: 1–2).

The Indian experience informs us that assertions, contentions, and demands of multiculturalism will continue; just as the strain for unity and uniformity will remain pressed with vigour. Those concerned with the formulation of educational policies and programmes, as also those in charge of the implementation of these policies and programmes, have to be extra-sensitive to the demands of multiculturalism in education and the problems of multicultural education. It is important to bear in mind that there is no readymade or straitjacket formula for multicultural education. The grammar of multicultural education has been and will continue to evolve over a period, making adjustments and readjustments, constantly addressing and accommodating the new demands and gradually forging and stabilising the national framework.

Notes

1. Significantly, *The Fontana Dictionary of Modern Thought* (edited by Bullock and Stallybrass) published in 1977 carried no entry on 'multiculturalism', but *The New Fontana Dictionary of Modern Thought* (edited by Bullock and Trombley) published in 1999 has a prominent entry on this item by Andrew J. Miller (see Bullock and Trombley 1999: 550). Laconically, we may define a multicultural society as a society composed of people who belong to different cultures. However, it is important to recognise their cultural differences 'as springing from a universally shared attachment of importance to culture and to an implicit acknowledgement of the equality of all cultures' (Watson 2002: 2).

2. In the Lok Sabha (the Lower House of India's Parliament) elections held in 1984, BJP won only two seats. In the Lok Sabha elections held in 2014, BJP contested 428 of 543 seats and won 282 with a vote share of 31 per cent; the Indian National Congress contested 464 seats and won only 44 with a vote share of 19.31 per cent (Election Commission of India 2014). Thus, increasing its tally steadily over the successive elections, BJP has now emerged as the single largest political party in the country. That BJP has been able to garner 'votes that have been let loose from the shredded net of Congress' (Ludden 1996: 18) is explained, at least partly, by its ability to sell the ideology of 'cultural nationalism'. This is a political phenomenon that can hardly be brushed aside.
3. In writing this chapter, I have drawn on my earlier work on multiculturalism and nation-building (Jayaram 2000a), the language question in higher education (Jayaram 1993), and the educational backwardness of Indian Muslims (see Chapter 11).
4. In view of India's quasi-federalism and her project to build a centralised nation-state going awry, some political scientists justifiably argue that there is an imminent need 'to rethink our federal polity and plural society in order to design a *federal India* which can successfully combine "federalism" and "pluralism" in the institutional framework of "*self-rule with shared rule*"' (Khan 1997: v; emphasis in original).
5. *Kendriya Vidyalayas* (Central Schools, established since 1963) are mainly intended to cater to children of the employees of the Central Government agencies, public sector undertakings, and armed forces – employees who are periodically transferred across the country. But they are open to local residents subject to the availability of vacancies. There are 877 such schools (some outside the country, too) catering to 7,50,000 students. They are managed by Kendriya Vidyalaya Sangathan, an autonomous body set up by the Central Government's Ministry of Education in December 1965.
6. *Navodaya Vidyalayas* (Model Schools, launched in 1985–86) are intended to provide 'good quality modern education' to talented children from the rural areas. Admission to these residential schools commences at VI Standard and is based on an entrance test conducted by the National Council of Educational Research and Training (NCERT). There are 389 such schools, at least one in each district (administrative zone) of every state.
7. 'Saffronisation' is a euphemism for the majoritarian exclusivist 'Hindu nationalism'. It is often used as a sobriquet to dub the

ideological praxis of BJP and its allied quasi-political organisations like the Rashtriya Swayamsevak Sangh (RSS).

8. In educational parlance, 'first language' is a new expression put together through a sort of back-formation from the familiar concept of a second language. Its vogue may be traced to the Gokak Committee Report in Karnataka state, which, in seeking to stress the primacy of Kannada in the language curricula in the schools, found it necessary to avoid any mixing up of the two concepts of 'mother tongue' and 'regional language'.
9. Ludden has argued that 'the ideas that define Hinduism as a religion ... deeply discourage the formation of a collective Hindu religious identity among believers and practitioners. Hindu identity is multiple, by definition ...' (1996: 7). Nevertheless, it should be recognised that Hindu identity can be and has been selectively articulated at various levels, depending upon the context and the other identities in question.
10. Besides Fundamental Rights enshrined for all citizens irrespective of religion, caste or creed, Articles 29 and 30 of the Constitution of India specifically guarantee the rights of minorities to conserve their 'distinct language, script and culture' and 'to establish and administer educational institutions of their choice'.
11. Naidu cites historian B.B. Misra's coinage of the term 'minority effect' to refer to that fact that 'in the pre-Independence Indian states wherever the minority community had the least concentration, they were more urban, more educated and more vigorous as a community as compared to the states where they were numerically in the majority' (1980: 33).
12. Kumar (2002) has drawn attention to the selective narrations, contrary imaginations, and contrasting interpretations of the freedom struggle in the school texts currently used in India and Pakistan. The deadweight of unrelenting hostility implicit in the Indian school texts is not without implications for the Muslim minority there.
13. Shotton (1998: Ch 3) has surveyed the alternative educational initiatives in India by classifying them into three general types:
    (i) Learner-centred Literacy Projects: Jan Vigyan Manch, Bihar; Dungarpur Total Literacy Campaign (TLC), Rajasthan; Ernakulam Total Literacy Programme, Kerala; TLC, Tamil Nadu; and TLC, Haryana.

(ii) Rural-based Development Education Schemes: Charvaha Vidyalaya, Turki, Bihar; PROPEL, Maharashtra; Shiksha Karmi Project, Rajasthan; and Lok Jumbish Project, Rajasthan.

(iii) Experimental Schools: Mirambika, Sri Aurobindo Ashram, New Delhi; Bangalore Education Centre (The Valley School), Mumbai Centre, Rajghat Education Centre, Varanasi; Rishi Valley Education Centre, near Madanapalle in Andhra Pradesh; and The School KFI, Chennai run by the Krishnamurti Foundation India; Neel Bagh School, Andhra Pradesh; Deepalaya Education Society, New Delhi; and Bhubaneswar School, Orissa.

14. One may recall here that Selig S. Harrison's analysis of 'the most dangerous decades' of post-Independence India begins with Suniti Kumar Chatterji's ominous warning that she 'stands the risk of being split into a number of totalitarian small nationalities' (1960: 3).

17

Educational Muddle and Degeneration of Democracy

Political philosophers and educationists have from time immemorial debated on the relation between education and democracy.[1] In his famous treatise *Democracy and Education*, first published in 1916, the noted American educationist and philosopher, John Dewey (1916: 108–10) suggested that the character of the educational system has a definite bearing on the polity of a democratic country. Since then liberal political philosophy has come to view education as a *sine qua non* of democracy. Today, every politician mouths this idea as a cliché.

However, there is more to this political doctrine linking education to democracy than as a mere exercise in rhetoric. Analysing the comparative data on the educational level of a nation's population and its chances for democracy, Seymour Martin Lipset observed that 'The educational enrolment per thousand total population at three different levels – primary, post-primary, and higher educational – is ... consistently related to the degree of democracy' (1983: 38–39). He also found that

> the evidence on the contribution of education to democracy is even more direct and strong on the level of individual behaviour *within* countries than it is in cross-national correlations .... The higher one's education, the more likely one is to believe in democratic values and support democratic practices. All the

relevant studies indicate that education is more significant than either income or occupation (ibid.: 39–40).

This is so because 'Education presumably broadens man's outlook, enables him to understand the need for norms of tolerance, restrains him from adhering to extremist doctrines, and increases his capacity to make rational electoral choices' (ibid.: 39). Lipset, therefore, concluded that 'If we cannot say that a "high" level of education is a *sufficient* condition for democracy, the available evidence suggests that it comes close to being a *necessary* one' (ibid.: 40; emphasis in original).

Sound as this thesis on education and democracy may apparently seem to be, it is not difficult to pick holes in it. It is not my purpose here to controvert Lipset's thesis by adducing fresh comparative data. Such an exercise, for reasons which would become clear later, would be futile in an effort to understand either the educational crisis or the political mess in an individual country, as, for instance, in India. Furthermore, to attempt such an understanding it would be necessary to state the unstated assumptions of the liberal education-democracy thesis.

This thesis conceives of people as atomised units behaving, by and large, in a rational manner. It assumes people to be homogeneous and living in an open, though stratified, society. It conceives of education as formal schooling (in the western 'secular' sense) which is equally open to all. It assumes, *à la* Tom Paine, that democracy is the best form of government and it alone is the legitimate form of government under all conditions. It also assumes that the leaders who are elected by the people are the enlightened ones who endeavour to work for the common weal not only without self-interest, but even at the cost of their own self. It further presumes that the election of the leaders is a fair and free mechanism, in which the people make a rational choice. Education attained by the people is supposed to influence their choice of the leaders and to induce them to engage themselves in a discourse on their policy.

Although this thesis does not necessarily posit a *status quo*ist concept of society, it nevertheless emphasises change as a peaceful process of transition involving readjustments within or tinkering of the social system. It excludes change *of* the system. After all, if people are dissatisfied with those who are in charge of the government, they can be changed at the next elections. While conflict is not ruled out – in fact, in some forms and under certain conditions, it is even regarded as functional – all violence is dubbed as uncivilised behaviour. Here again, education is expected to play a positive role in enabling the people to resolve a conflict situation through peaceful dialogue.

In the light of all this, it is easy to understand how the liberal political philosophy was led by its internal logic to declare 'the end of ideology'.[2] Both education and government are viewed as 'value neutral' and, if there is any value-commitment at all, it is to democracy as an *abstract absolute*. Education and democracy, in brief, are treated as given entities. No wonder then, textbooks on liberal political philosophy, and even political science, generally eschew any discussion on the socio-economic and cultural context of the operation of democracy, save for some illustrative purpose.

Does this facile thesis of liberal political philosophy, reiterated often by academicians and politicians alike, hold good with reference to the social dynamics of a polity like India? Is it substantiated by, let alone explain, the experience of India over the last six decades? What the education-democracy linkage is as witnessed in India? I have attempted a tentative examination of these questions in this essay, which is not conceived as an exegesis either on democracy or on education *per se*. Hence, on both these aspects my analysis would be inadequate in coverage and superficial in treatment. Rather, my objective here is to delineate the education-democracy linkage as it evolved in the pre-Independence era and as it is functioning today.

The Colonial Legacy

In India, the institutions of 'modern' education and parliamentary democracy are both British colonial legacies.[3] The earliest attempt to impart English education in India can be traced to the missionary activities following the establishment of the East India Company and the measures adopted by Warren Hastings as early as 1773. The protracted controversy that had been generated by these initial efforts was finally resolved by William Bentinck, barely a month after Thomas Babington Macaulay had penned his (in)famous Minute (on 2 February 1835). This policy was reaffirmed by Charles Wood's Despatch of 1854 and, with minor modifications, continued throughout the British rule.

Historians of education have now adequately laid bare the fact that the 'spreading (of) English education was not an act of disinterested magnanimity' (A. Basu 1978: 57). On the contrary, it was the outcome of a complex combination of motives, and not the least of which was the political motive of consolidating and maintaining the dominance of the British in the country. Charles Trevelyan (1838: 189–90), a distinguished civil servant of the British Raj, clearly perceived the political pay off of English education. The English-educated Indians, he hoped, would cease to consider their rulers as foreigners; on the contrary, he expected them to become 'intelligent and zealous co-operators' (ibid.: 190).

This does not mean that the British embarked on a programme of mass English education in India. What they were interested in was only the creation of a small class of English-educated Indians, who may act, in Macaulay's words, as 'interpreters between us and the millions whom we govern – a class of persons Indian in blood and colour, but English in tastes, in opinions, in morals and intellect' (in Sharp 1965: 116). This class was expected to filter down to the masses the knowledge and values it had acquired and internalised. This, it was hoped, would eventually stabilise the Raj.

The system of education that the British introduced in India was modelled after the system prevalent in their Mother country. From the time of its inception it was urban-based, top-heavy, and elitist. The masses gradually got estranged from the polity because of the emphasis on English in the administrative, judicial, and commercial institutions established by the British. Since they were vitally affected by these new institutions and were not able to understand the modalities of their operation, they were forced to depend upon those who were English-educated and who consequently came to be bestowed with unprecedented prestige and power.

Although in the shorter run English education did contribute to the political stability of the Raj, in the longer run it proved to be the undoing of the British stranglehold on the country. The educated class, which had been exposed to the values of 'liberty, equality, and fraternity' espoused in Europe and elsewhere in the West after the French Revolution, became more and more vocal in its criticism of the Raj. The Sedition Committee, which investigated the revolutionary conspiracies in India, reported in 1918 that most of the conspirators were educated young men. As it turned out, almost all the leaders in the forefront of the nationalist movement belonged to the English-educated elite (see McCully 1940; Seal 1982).

Although the English-educated elite turned from 'zealous co-operators' to 'freedom fighters', they could not rise equal to the historic task of liberating the nation. The nationalist movement, led predominantly by the English-educated bourgeoisie, was not a radical revolution premised upon mass involvement and directed towards changing the fundamental institutions and cultural values of society (see A.R. Desai 1966). Nowhere is this more perspicuous than in the gradual adoption of the western – mostly British – institutions of administration, justice, and commerce, and the hammering out of the republican constitution by the Constituent Assembly after Independence (see Austin 1972). It is to this mere change of complexion of the elite from 'white' to 'brown' that we owe the rather smooth transfer of power from the colonial masters to the indigenous English-educated bourgeoisie, which was accomplished without any major breakdown or transformation of the English-implanted institutions, including education and parliamentary democracy.

In brief, the backdrop for a discussion on education-democracy linkage in India is provided by the implantation and development of an elitist system of education superimposed on existing inequalities, a gradual socialisation into a parliamentary form of government and the adoption of a republican constitution by the English-educated bourgeoisie with strong underpinnings of liberal political philosophy. That India has been able to survive as a democracy – irrespective of the modalities of its operation – for over six decades, notwithstanding the innumerable fissiparous tendencies, belying all doubts (see, for example, S.S. Harrison 1960) is something remarkable by itself. However, the glaringly unequal distribution of the fruits of planned development reinforcing the already existing inequalities, and the persistence of poverty, illiteracy, and exploitation of large sections of the population reveal that the system is no panacea for all our socio-economic ills.

Illiteracy: Failure on the Education Front

What would perhaps appear to be the most glaring and at the same time the quite significant point of irreconcilability of India's experience with Lipset's thesis is the survival and functioning of her democracy in spite of the rampant illiteracy and indigence of the masses. One may recall here that Prime Minister Rajiv Gandhi in his Jodidi Lecture delivered at the Harvard University on 18 October 1987 (Ministry of External Affairs 1987) expressed the rather naive opinion that India's experience has proved that illiteracy, after all, is not a stumbling block for the functioning of democracy. This paradox raises certain important questions about the nature of the democracy which prevails in the country as well as the nature of the educational development that has taken place after Independence.

The most unpardonable failure of our educational system is evidenced by the pathetic literacy rates. While the percentage of literates had increased at a snail's pace from 16.67 in 1951 to 36.23 in 1981, the number of illiterates has shot up from approximately 300 million to 437 million in the same period, and is expected to cross the 500 million mark by CE 2000.[4] Of the 125 countries listed by the World Bank, only twenty-six had literacy rates worse than ours. And, the Bank estimates that India would have the largest concentration (54.8% in 15–19 age-group) of illiterate population in the world by that year.

As Paul Harrison says, 'illiteracy is a personal tragedy, and a powerful force in preserving inequalities and oppressions' (1981: 305). Besides being a disqualification standing in the way of better-paid employment, it is a source of cultural deprivation. It weighs heaviest on those groups – women, scheduled castes and tribes, the poor, and those in rural areas – which are already disadvantaged in other ways. What has Independence and democracy brought to these hapless sections of our countrymen, and what meaning has democracy for them?

It is in this context that universalisation of elementary education, which has unfortunately not been the primary concern for the political elite all these years, notwithstanding the specific directive in this regard in the Constitution, assumes greatest significance. In fact, the deadline set for the realisation of the Constitutional directive regarding universalisation of elementary education has already been extended thrice, and the so-called 'new' education policy does not even set a deadline for this as a priority! It is true that most children now have a primary school within one kilometre of their homes. But the facilities available in most of these schools and the quality of instruction imparted there are, as confessed by the 'new' education policy statement, anything but satisfactory:

> Forty per cent (of these schools) have no *pucca* buildings, 39.72 per cent have no black boards, and 59.50 per cent have no drinking water. Thirty-five per cent (of these) schools have a single teacher to teach three or four different classes (see Ministry of Education 1985: 35).

What is more disconcerting, out of 100 children enrolled in Class I only twenty-three reach Class VIII.

In marked contrast to this scenario, excessive emphasis has been laid on higher education. While the expansion at this level has been more rapid, the percentage of the relevant age-group in institutions of higher education constitutes is still insignificant. With the rapid expansion of higher education the associated problems have multiplied and the resulting crisis has accentuated over the years.[5] The legion problems include the irrelevance of the present system of higher education to the needs of the society, the decline in the quality of education, the mismatch between education and employment and the consequent unemployment or misemployment of the educated persons, the devaluation of degrees and escalation of qualifications for jobs, and the alienation of the educated persons.[6] But more important from our point of view here is that while the system of education has insignificantly contributed to the levelling of inequalities, it has significantly contributed to the stabilisation and perpetuation of ascribed status or status retention (see Jayaram 1987a). Alas, the much talked about 'new' education policy has only turned out to be a programme *par excellence* of elitist education (see Chapter 19).

It must be pointed out here that the 'formal' equality of opportunities, which is emphasised following its enshrinement in the Constitution, is essentially a conservative notion, and 'as a recipe for social engineering it merely makes for mobility within the *status quo*' (Entwistle 1978: 9). If formal equality is fallacious in conception, it is unjust in practice. In fact, the moral assumptions about equality are ingeniously reconciled with the functionalist economic, sociological, and psychological arguments for inequality in the ideology of meritocracy (see Jayaram 1987b: 101–05). Worse still, the resulting thinking individualises failure and shifts the blame for people's predicaments from society to individuals.

The Electoral Game and Manipulation of Consent

The survival of democracy, even if it be in a truncated form, amidst rampant illiteracy and chronic poverty, necessitates an analysis of the manipulation of the consent of the people and the engineering of its legitimation by the regime. The most effective instrument for such a manipulation in a democracy is the game of elections. Election is considered as the bedrock of democracy as it gives to the people the freedom to choose their own rulers, and thereby recognises the sovereignty of the people. The political party which has mastered the rules of the game of elections and knows how to use them fully to its advantage can play it successfully. The advantageous position in which a ruling party is placed vis-à-vis other parties can hardly be exaggerated.

Without going into the details of the electoral dynamics, it is enough to note that at the national level a party has been able to rule for decades without even getting 50 per cent of the total votes cast in the elections. In other words, 'the democratic swindle', as Karl Marx appropriately dubbed it (see Draper 1978: 306–07), amounts to the vast masses of the people being used through the periodical ritual of elections to legitimise the rule of a party which is controlled by the ruling class.[7]

The absence of any sincere and dedicated opposition party to match the strength, skills and resources of the Congress party and the government led by it has no doubt enabled it to remain in power at the national level, but for the brief Janata interregnum, and provide a stable government. But its position as far as the states are concerned has seen a sea change. It is significant to note that it is precisely in the backward states of the Hindi heartland with rates of literacy below the national average that the Congress has been able to retain its stranglehold. The elected representatives from these states together constitute a majority in the Lok Sabha.[8]

In those states outside the Hindi heartland, where the rates of literacy are above the national average, parties other than the Congress have had a chance to come to power.[9] In fact, Kerala, the state which has been politically most volatile in the country, has the highest literacy rate. In other states, where in spite of the rate of literacy being lower than the national average non-Congress parties have been able to come to power – for example, as in Andhra Pradesh and Assam – it has been mainly due to the ability of the indigenous educated elites to successfully raise the banner of revolt against the affront to the state's self-esteem and the unimaginative handling of the state's affairs by the Congress at the centre.

A curious paradox of the Indian political scenario has been that while the leaders have been, by and large, educated, the educated people themselves are observed to be politically apathetic. The Constitution of India does not prescribe any educational qualifications for the membership of either Parliament or the State Assembly. Despite this, the educational levels of the members of the Lok Sabha have not only remained relatively high but also seem to be going up in every successive Lok Sabha. The majority of the Lok Sabha members have been graduates and holders of higher academic qualifications, and the Eighth Lok Sabha had, in fact, the distinction of having the highest percentage of members (71.1) belonging to the category of 'graduates and above' (Lok Sabha Secretariat 1986: 5–8). The situation in the various State Assemblies may not be very different.

On the other hand, studies on voting behaviour seem to reveal that the illiterate and below matriculate electorate are more enthusiastic in casting their votes than their college-educated counterparts. In a case study of the Fourth General Elections in Rajasthan, S.P. Varma et al., found that 'literacy is not a precondition for political mobilisation and participation' (1973: 24). Similar findings have been reported by other studies (see, for example, Sirsikar 1973: 276–81; Ganguly and Ganguly 1975: 50–52).

As Varma et al. observe,

> What appears to motivate the electorate more to become a voter is its sense of political efficacy. People who have faith in the efficacy of the political system in general and the ballot box in particular and who as such have a stake in both of them feel motivated to vote (1973: 366).

The average educated citizen, though more exposed to the socio-economic realities and who, therefore, can even be expected to be politically more conscious and be aware of the political processes, tends to be more alienated from the political system and the electoral process. The educated electorate constitute a comparatively large percentage of non-voters.

Nevertheless, it can hardly be denied that if the educated persons decide to vote at all it will be to protest against the ruling party and its perceived omissions and commissions. This was witnessed in a characteristic fashion in the 1977 General Elections when the Congress party was voted out of power not only in the Centre but in many states too. Available evidence confirms that the main support of the Congress comes from 'the illiterate and the half-literate voters', whereas the non-Congress parties receive 'support from the better educated strata of the society' (Sirsikar 1973: 276–77). N.G.S. Kini's analysis of the voting behaviour in the General Elections of 1967 in Nagpur revealed that 'a vote for Congress varies inversely with the educational level and for non-Congress directly with the educational level of the voter. Congress thrives on the vote of illiterates while the non-Congress vote is more enlightened' (1974: 256).

The inference is obvious then that both the apathy of the educated non-voter and the illiteracy of the enthusiastic voter constitute the strength of the bourgeoisie ruling party, be it Congress or Janata or some other. No wonder then, the ruling party at the Centre and in most states as well as the parties in the opposition have manifested a studied apathy to the spread of literacy or, more appropriately, a vested interest in the perpetuation of rampant illiteracy and ignorance.

It is obvious that in a democratic political game where the electorate has to choose between parties which are basically bourgeois in character, a change in the party in power cannot bring about any significant change for the masses. Should the 'revolutionary', 'anti-bourgeois' parties then participate in the electoral game and parliamentary politics? Moin Shakir has quite convincingly argued that it is only through participation in elections that such parties can 'educate and enlighten the masses' (1986: 125). He regards the 'left' governments as 'transitional instruments' of the working class from which miracles cannot be expected. But what is important, he emphasises, is that 'the left can show an alternative to the people' who would otherwise 'obey the existing system, with a sense of inevitability' (ibid.: 125–26).

Populism, Protest, and Suppression

But how is the meek consent of the illiterate majority manipulated by the ruling class for the perpetuation of its own power and interests. After Independence, and especially since the mid-1960s, we have been witnessing what is best called the politics of populism and sloganeering: *'garibi hatao'*, old and new '20-Point Programmes', loan *melas*, subsidised sale of rice, free supply of textbooks and *mangalasutras*, mid-day meal scheme, and so on. In addition to squandering the valuable scarce resources on unimaginative ephemeral schemes, this weird brand of 'leftist-centrist' politics has resulted in rousing the people's unrealistic expectations and aspirations, besides breeding a sense of dependence in them. Their ambitious dreams are further whipped up by the culture of consumerism to which they are exposed by the media and the demonstration effect of the way our leaders, the elite and the *nouveau riche* lead their lives.

Considering the inexorable constraints of resources, the nature and rate of feasible economic growth and the structural limitations, these aspirations are chimerical and Utopian. Since people do not or, rather, cannot realise this and as the government is neither interested in nor capable of educating them in this regard, the latter can counter the resulting unrest and attempt to maintain itself in power only through the politics of expediency. It often even tries to divert the attention of the people from the real issues. But such an exercise in political hoodwinking is, of course, not always successful.

The periodic sporadic outbursts of protest and struggle, often taking an extremist turn, should be viewed as symptomatic of the subterranean contradictions of the above situation. The successive governments have facilely treated such protests and struggles as essentially a problem of law and order, and have stubbornly refused to grapple with the underlying contradictions. As a consequence, we notice a growing authoritarianism on the part of the government, on the one hand, and political alienation among the people, on the other. This has the danger of destroying the democratic edifice itself in the long run.[10]

What is worse and not surprising is that instead of identifying themselves with the state and the government, sections of the people have come to view the latter as their exploiter and to orient themselves towards them in a belligerent manner. Such an attitude comes to be mutually rationalised considering that the police and the law-enforcement machinery have been politicised, the frequency of police firing and the deployment of the army to tackle civilian disorder has increased, and the number of obnoxious laws curbing dissent and democratic rights is increasing (see A.R. Desai 1986).

The fact that state aggrandisement and alienation of the people have resulted in a people-government relationship worse than the one prevalent in the pre-Independence period is tied up with a unique form of political identification which has emerged. It is observed that the country is identified with the government, the government with the ruling party, and the ruling party with its leader. This trend was characteristically illustrated by a statement such as 'Indira is India', expressed by a Congress party politician in the 1980s. With reference to the Congress (I) at the Centre, this is understandably explained by reference to the historic role of the Indian National Congress in the freedom movement and the hold of a particular family which was deeply involved in the movement over the party. But one does see such a phenomenon even in states run by political parties which have only a recent history.

Whatever may be the roots of this phenomenon, one consequence of it is certain. That is, any criticism, however genuine it may be, of the leader of the party or the party itself, comes to be viewed as an attack on the government and the country. As a result, we have a situation where 'if you are not with me, you must be against me', and patriotism, whatever it may mean, has become the monopoly of the ruling party and its leader(s).

The dynamics of the foregoing situation has thrown up a new genre of leadership, which being socialised in the new wave politics is, by and large, totally oblivious to any higher political values and commitments and is content to pursue narrow selfish or sectional interests. It is well known that among our 'leaders' today we have tax evaders, smugglers, hijackers, *goondas*, and even proclaimed absconders! Political intimidation, group skirmishes, and murders are part of a syndrome which is best described by the sobriquet 'the criminalisation' or 'the lumpenisation' of politics.

A direct deleterious consequence of the general drift and the politics of expediency is the gradual erosion of the existing institutions. Rule of law has almost disappeared from our jurisprudence;

people's faith in the judiciary is under strain; the universities have so much deteriorated that much of what goes on in the name of education there is only to be experienced to be believed (see Chapter 12); intra-party democracy has become extinct; and corruption, nepotism, and inefficiency have come to be institutionalised as something inevitable. The fact that we are now resigned to live with these aberrations is a tragedy too deep for words.

That ordinary citizens have reconciled themselves, however reluctantly, to his present predicament about which they feel helpless is easy to understand. But what is not so easy to understand and still more difficult to excuse is the apathy of the intellectuals, and the gradual disappearance of what Arun Shourie calls 'the national discourse' (1988). There are, no doubt, a few journalists who have taken up cudgels against autocracy, corruption, nepotism, exploitation, and the violation of human rights. But, by and large, our social scientists have cut a very sorry figure in this regard. It is, of course, true that hardly six per cent of the population knows English and only a small section of even this has the time and the inclination to read about the present state of our society and polity; therefore, the overall impact of what is written in English is far less than what is expected. Can this be an apology for apathy by a section of the population which can understand and owes a duty to make others understand too?

Conclusion: Education for Liberation

The need for a radical socio-economic transformation or a 'total revolution' has been repeatedly voiced. To speak of such a transformation or revolution is not to embark on its course. An important prerequisite for it is the recognition that it can come about only through a process of education whose aim is what Paulo Freire calls 'conscientisation': it refers 'to learning to perceive social, political, and economic contradictions, and to take action against the oppressive elements of reality' (1972b: 15). This implies that, using education as a catalyst of social regeneration, a people can be awakened to their suppressed and deprived conditions and armed with the means of changing these conditions. A small section of the people getting higher education and becoming individually mobile does not help spread conscientisation. Rather, it would act as a wet blanket on conscientisation, keeping social awareness in swaddling-bands.

The spread of literacy and oracy through lower levels of education can play an important role in bringing about social transformation. But it is precisely at this level that the present system of schooling has failed. At the snail's pace at which the rate of literacy is growing it would take many many more decades to reach a significant level. How long will it take for the oppressed sections in rural areas to reach the general level of literacy is anybody's guess. Leave alone the physical limits, the present system of education premised upon mobility ideology and welfare state philosophy cannot be expected to undertake the historic task of social transformation. In fact, it seems to be an effective instrument for the reproduction of the social division of labour and the maintenance of the *status quo*.

In a highly insightful paper on the failure of American education, Stephanie Coontz concluded, 'When people know that what they think will actually make a difference, what they think about is likely to expand considerably' (1974: 42). There is an urgent need to rekindle a national discourse on what should the future society be like and how do we go about realising it (see Shourie 1988). At the same time, parties and organisations which are genuinely interested in bringing about a radical socio-economic transformation should primarily devote themselves to the rapid spread of literacy and oracy among the masses and set in motion a process of conscientisation, instead of being excessively preoccupied with electoral politics which only legitimises the existing system and its operators all the more. After all, 'a journey of a thousand miles must begin with a single step' (Lao-tzu).

Notes

1. The concept of democracy is a hard nut which I do not propose to crack here.
2. Among the chief representatives of the 'end-of-ideology' thesis are Daniel Bell, Seymour Martin Lipset, and Clarke Kerr. The empirical generalisations in which this thesis is embedded are summarised by Giddens (1973: 283). For a critical assessment of this ideology, see Moskvichov (1974).

3. In outlining the colonial legacy in education, I have borrowed heavily from Chapter 4. For a succinct account of the colonial legacy of our democratic polity, see Morris-Jones (1971: 16–48), and Hanson and Douglas (1972: 11–31).
4. According to Census of India, in 2001, that is, five decades after planned programme of development, the rate of literacy had increased to only 64.84 per cent (75.26% for males; 53.67% for females). That is, 35 per cent of the population was still illiterate. Only four states and four union territories had a literacy rate over 80 per cent, with Kerala (90.86%) ranking first. Incidentally, Bihar ranked the lowest (47%) (Ministry of Information and Broadcasting 2010: 10, 11–13).
5. For more recent discussion on the crisis confronting higher education in India, see Jayaram (2006, 2014 and Chapter 12).
6. The 'new' education policy document bemoaned that the preponderant majority (of the students) come out of the institutions of higher education, perhaps with a little more of book learning and of course a degree, but with very little capacity for self-study, poor language and communication skills, a highly limited worldview and hardly any sense of social or national responsibility (Ministry of Education 1985: 8–9).
7. Analysing the class nature of the state in India is a complex and difficult task, and a straitjacket mechanical application of the Marxian concepts is futile (see Shakir 1986: 31–62). However, the concentration of economic power in the hands of the industrial bourgeoisie in the urban areas and the class of rich peasants and landlords in the rural areas, and its bearing on the 'state managers' (cutting across party lines) can hardly be gainsaid. It is to refer to this political combine that the terse label 'ruling class' is used here.
8. This political scenario in the country has changed to some extent, first with the rule of the Bharatiya Janata Party-led National Democratic Alliance during 1999–2004 and its thumping victory in the Lok Sabha elections in 2014. Will this regime change bring about changes in plight of the people at large is a moot question.
9. It must be noted that ideologically, organisationally, and functionally these parties are not necessarily different from the Congress.
10. A.R. Desai (1986) provides an excellent documentation on and analysis of the various aspects of the repressive state in India.

18

Peace and Conflict vis-à-vis Education

Ironic as it may sound, even a cursory reflection seems to suggest a correlation between educational development and the propensity for discord. The country which dropped the first ever atom bomb on Hiroshima on 6 August 1945 killing 78,000, badly injuring 70,000 and exposing most of the remainder of the population to some long-term radiation damage, and destroying two-thirds of that city is a highly educated one. The countries which are spending enormous amounts on the development and deployment of increasingly destructive weapons, and which are extending the area of international rivalry into space through 'star wars' programme are well known for their educational development.

Such a correlation seems to hold good intra-nationally also. For instance, the country which set about to exterminate Jews, the country which is characterised by the highest number of race riots, and the county which has perhaps the highest rate of crimes against individuals, and the countries which allow if not patronise 'schools' for training terrorists and the country which is most intolerant of individual dissension are all highly educated. Sociological evidence seems to indicate that, in our own country, more than the illiterate masses, it is the educated elite which plays an important role in aggravating the communal situation (see

Engineer 1984). We hear of violence and destruction of public property indulged in more by university and college students than by other categories of the population.

The inference that one is tempted to draw from the foregoing observations is that education by itself would not ensure peace. However, unfortunate such an inference may seem, it nevertheless raises a host of issues – conceptual, empirical, and prognostic. In this chapter, I have attempted to deal with some of these issues.

Connotation of Peace and Conflict

The word peace is generally used with reference to international relations or what P. Wehr and M. Washburn euphemistically call the 'world order system' (1976). In fact, the primary dictionary meaning of the word peace is 'freedom form, cessation of, war; ratification or treaty of peace between powers previously at war'. This is obviously a circumscribed usage of the term peace. On the other hand, one comes across the word peace being used in a much broader sense and even loosely, to refer to absence of strife of all sorts, and even to 'quiet, tranquillity; mental calm'. Such a usage tends to be bereft of any analytical meaning. In either case, it is to be noted that the concept of peace is defined in negative terms.

Between the peace assured by the absence of war between nations and the peace obtaining in the absence of haggling between a shopkeeper and a customer in a market place there are a variety of situations which could be designated as peace. Sociologically speaking, the notion of peace, or more appropriately, its absence manifesting in the form of social conflict (see Jayaram and Saberwal 2012), becomes significant when it is shown to be linked to certain specific social structural arrangements and conditions. This necessarily theoretical point of view implies that the problem of peace or absence of it can be scientifically discussed neither in pristine abstraction and isolation of other social realities nor by reference to specific orientation of populations and of historical *deus ex machina* (see Dahrendorf 1969b: 214–15).

This line of thought emphasises the point that, as used in both academic and popular parlances, 'peace', like 'justice', 'equality', etc. is a metaphysical notion, an abstract value, and a desired ideal. It is, in the terminology of Raoul Naroll's 'socionomics', a 'core value' (1983: 47–48). In reality, what we experience is its binary opposite, namely, conflict, strife, and contention. It is, therefore, much easier to recognise and study conflict or lack of peace. As Johan Galtung says, 'social science has uncovered more knowledge about war (and other conflicts) than about peace', and 'peace thinking has had a tendency to become Utopian and to be oriented toward the future' (1968: 487). Thus, the general tendency to crave for and talk about peace, which is something which we lack, is easy to understand. It is also not surprising that there are such expressions as 'firmed peace' and 'conflict-readiness as a deterrent'. Considering all this, it would seem more appropriate to speak of dealing with or resolving real conflicts than beating about the ideal peace bush.

That peace is a desired ideal or a 'core value' does not mean that it is a virtue by itself. Quite the contrary. When Lord Willingdon claimed that he had brought back peace to the Raj after quelling the Civil Disobedience Movement during the early 1930s, Mahatma Gandhi dubbed it as 'a peace of the graveyard'. It is significant that one of the meanings of the word peace is 'silence'. A situation in which people passively acquiesce in the existing 'order' may be characterised as being one of 'peace', however unjust and exploitative that order may be. The celebrated Brazilian educationalist Paulo Freire succinctly and appropriately described the peace obtaining in such an order as a manifestation of 'the culture of silence' (1972b: 12). The educational system, as he has exposed, is a key instrument for the maintenance and fostering of this culture.

The history of societies round the world is replete with illustrations of the impenitent use of violence in the ruthless suppression of civil liberties in the name of maintaining peace, an euphemism for perpetuating the *status quo* in the interests of the dominant sections. Journalists, political analysts, and academicians have started using such expressions as 'state terrorism', 'encounter killings', and so on. Thus, it is imperative to ask the question in whose interest is peace sought, by whom, and why?

Conversely, it could be argued that conflict is not something intrinsically and inevitably bad. 'It is the bad side', as Karl Marx said, 'that produces the movement which makes history, by providing a struggle' (1975: 113). This should not be misunderstood as a plea for focussing on the functional aspects of social conflict, of the sort made *à la* sociologists of the functionalist ilk.

For instance, Lewis A. Coser, following Georg Simmel, is concerned with 'those consequences of social conflict which make for an increase rather than a decrease in the adaptation or adjustment of particular social relationships or groups' (1956: 8) Such a functionalised view of conflict blurs the distinction between structurally rooted conflicts and superficial ones and veils 'the actual conflicts of interest within a group, organisation, or society' and 'the relationships of domination that characterise them' (Zeitlin 1973: 107).

Thus, when pacifists oppose war *per se,* they think of war in the abstract, without reflecting on the real aims of the nations at war and the classes in whose interest it is fought. It is necessary to distinguish between imperialistic wars, which are unequivocally unjust, and wars of liberation, which are both inevitable and just. Similarly, when other methods fail to resolve basic contradictions and thereby to eradicate exploitation and oppression by the dominant sections and establish a just society, a revolution by the oppressed will become a historical necessity.

'Development', Vladimir I. Lenin said, 'is the "struggle" of opposites' (n.d.: 360). This is expressed by the essence of the dialectical law of the unity and conflict of opposites: 'the process of development from the lower to the higher takes place not as a harmonious unfolding of phenomena, but as a disclosure of the contradictions inherent in things and phenomena, as a "struggle" of opposite tendencies which operate on the basis of these contradictions' (Stalin 1976: 841). Thus, before a value judgement is made on a conflict, however violent and destructive it may be, one should understand its nature, sources, and the expected outcome.

Conflict: Experience and Explanation

Conceptual issues apart, international and intra-societal conflicts are essentially social experiences, though unpleasant and lamentable, and a source of education, though mainly in the negative sense. Indeed, academic concern with conflict dates back to Kautilya, Polybius, Cicero, and Dante (see Martindale 1961: 127–49). Apart from courses on 'peace studies' offered in some universities, there are international institutions like the Consortium on Peace Research, Education and Development, and Institute of World Order specialising in 'peace research'. There has also been a steady flow of papers and books and a never ending series of seminars and symposia on peace. But, practically, have human beings learnt anything from six thousand years of organised violence? Unfortunately, nothing praiseworthy. If anything, they have perfected the art of conflict and escalated its scope and scale.

One is led to ask why this is so. In his fascinating book, *The Anatomy of Human Destructiveness,* the famous psycho-analyst Erich Fromm (1973) has provided an extensive critique of the various theories about human being's propensity for aggression, conflict, and destruction. One theory which has had a very wide currency, in spite of being insufficiently substantiated, is instinctivism, associated with such great names as Charles Darwin, William James, William McDougall, Sigmund Freud, and Konard Lorenz.

Instinctivism views conflict as a part of the 'nature' of human beings, which is characteristically expressed in the Hobbesian notion of *Homo Ferox,* man-the-quarrelsome. But, instead of explaining the phenomenon in question, instinctivism explains it away and puts it outside the purview of sociological explanation. Also, it makes peace chimerical, and leaves us without hope.

However, it is necessary to emphasise that the structurally significant conflicts arise out of conditions contrived by human beings. And to the extent that the structural contradictions can be resolved, there is yet hope. One can share Bertrand Russell's optimism that 'man can look forward to a future immeasurably longer than his past, inspired by a new breadth of vision, a continuing hope perpetually fed by a continuing achievement' (1961: 127). In the realisation of this hope of peace, as much as in the analysis of the significant conflicts leading to it, education could play an important role. In what follows, I shall deal with intra-societal conflict as it is manifest in relation to our educational system, in general, and with reference to our youth, in particular.

Context of Conflict

Ours is a transitional polity with a chequered past and an uncertain future, where the subjective consciousness of the objective realities of life is pitifully feeble and is obfuscated by a variety of ideologies, religious and political. Though freed formally from colonial bondage the elite is yet to overcome the colonial hangover. The process of planned social change, which is wedded to liberal ideology, has not been able to accomplish a radical break with the past. There are far too many programmes which are implemented with far too little efficacy. As a consequence, while some notable achievements have taken place, the basic problems are yet far from being solved.

In a society where political freedom is not premised upon economic freedom, the problem of legitimacy is as complex as it is crucial. One aspect of this problem is the tendency among the ruling groups to hold on to power at all costs. As a part of their strategy to gain political power, or hold on to it having gained it once, in addition to invoking the grand promises enshrined in the Constitution, all political parties, not excluding the ones with left-leanings, have over the years whipped up people's ambitions. To me, the crux of the matter seems to lie here.

Basically, two types of chasms can be identified with reference to ambitions. Firstly, there is a gap between the ever-soaring ambitions of the people and the consistently decreasing prospects of realising them. Secondly, there is the disjunction between the ambitions of the people, on the one hand, and their quality or worthiness and their willingness to put in the requisite efforts or make the necessary sacrifices in realising the ambitions, on the other.

In the normal circumstances, soaring ambitions do not constitute a problem. Nay, they may even be an important catalyst of development (see McClelland 1961). But, under conditions of perpetual scarcity of resources and opportunities, the chasms associated with ambitions can have untoward consequences.

The constitutional commitment to the principle of distributive justice makes the problem worse confounded. We have witnessed the pernicious results of the politicisation of the strategy of protective discrimination for the amelioration of the status of the traditionally indigent sections of the society. There has been a growing opposition to indefinite protective discrimination from those who do not benefit from it, and this has even taken a violent turn as was witnessed in the anti-reservation agitations in Gujarat and elsewhere. Exploitation of the volatile situation by the vested interests worsens it and makes the problem even more intractable. The fact that the union government had once advised all state governments to keep the reservation issue in abeyance is not only a proof of the sensitive nature of the issue, but also an indication of the government's inability to effectively grapple with it without making compromises by yielding to sectional interests.

A cue from this has been taken by other dominant sections of society, and the innumerable committees and commissions charged with the investigation of the problem of backwardness have been dismayed by the large number of petitions and deputations proclaiming backwardness in order to be listed for benefits. Knowing full well the implications of the pressure potential of these groups, the government has extended the cover of the policy to several non-scheduled castes and communities with the result that the *raison d'être* of the policy of protective discrimination is itself lost.

From the government's perspective, the policy of protective discrimination is an effective instrument of social control of groups which could otherwise prove to be potentially disruptive. The ablest among the indigent sections are weaned away and absorbed by the ruling groups, and combined with the individualisation of failure an illusion for the entire class of the oppressed is created. Their attention is diverted from the full extent of the problem and its roots in the overall socio-economic framework.

Unrest on the Campus

Nowhere is the conflict associated with our system of education more pronounced than on the campus itself (see Chapter 15). Campus unrest and agitation, which were once exclusively associated with students, are now normal and regular phenomena with reference to their teachers also. Intrusion by the police into a university or college campus has become a frequent occurrence and is no longer news. Police outposts and police stations have, in fact, become a part of the campus in quite a few universities. The situation on our campus is, no doubt, a reflection of what is happening in the society at large and is, therefore, least unexpected.

Most of the incidents of student unrest and agitations are basically misdirected and are destructive, however symptomatic they may be. They, by and large, fit into Edward Shils characterisation as a manifestation of 'juvenile delinquency' (1968b:

74–92). The manifestations are severe and recurrent as some impunity is always assured. But, in the absence of political patronage and support, they tend to be unstable and short-lived. The more serious development on our campuses is, however, the growing *goonda*ism and the political mobilisation of what could be called the 'schooled lumpens'.

To be sure, student unrest is not always necessarily a manifestation of juvenile delinquency and, given certain conditions, can change into an articulated constructive movement (Jayaram 1981b). The student movements of 1974 in Gujarat and Bihar, which were ruthlessly crushed during the Emergency, are a case in point. But the main problem in mobilising students and providing the necessary direction to their movement is the fact that they are a transitory element in the system and that orientation to restructuring the society is not a goal held out to them by the educational system.

While teachers are a relatively more permanent element of the system, the organisation of teachers seems to have been more on trade union lines and economism. But unlike trade unions, teachers' unions evoke neither feelings of solidarity nor of professional pride, despite the often high calibre of leadership (see Chapter 14). Considering the state which the academic profession is now in, it is too much to expect any intellectual direction from it.

Media and Violence

Education, defined broadly to mean the process of learning, is not confined to what takes place within the four walls of the classroom. The mass media of communication, as sources of informal education, have a significant influence on the people. C. Wright Mills has observed that 'between consciousness and existence stand communications, which influence such consciousness as men have of their existence .... The mass communication system ... reflects society, but selectively; it reinforces certain features by generalizing them...' (1951: 332, 334).

In a country where the growth of rate of literacy has been shockingly slow, and where a tradition of reading is not institutionalised as a cultural value, the press, no doubt, does not play a crucial role. Nevertheless, there is a noticeable tendency on the part of the press to sensationalise crime and conflict. A glance at our newspapers and magazines confirms this. A visit to a book stall will show the number of bestsellers displayed reflecting this, even with reference to the books meant for children.

For a majority, however, this communication is available through such media as the cinema, radio, television, and now the Internet. Of these, the cinema is perhaps the most powerful, closely followed by its cousin television, as 'the attention absorbed by the images on the screen's rectangle dominates the darkened public' (ibid.: 336). The intense impact of cinema on the conscious and subconscious minds of the audience can hardly be exaggerated.

Conflict and violence of various sorts are an integral part of our cinema. The 'formula films' have a quota of fight-sequences, with a variety of techniques and gadgets used, and murders and acts of violence on women attempted or committed. The audience keeps a count of each one of these elements and evaluates a film on that basis. The films are advertised as 'action-packed entertainers', 'deadly thrillers', and so on, and the heroes of such films become real-life heroes. According to a recent report on the trends in film- and video-viewing in the West, watching violence, cruelty, torture, and killing is the latest craze.

Not a little of this is due to the commercialisation of films, in particular, and other media, in general. Incidentally, the film which is reported to have grossed the highest ever collection at the Hindi box-office happens to be a movie which is known for depicting senseless conflict and violence in their crudest forms. It is noteworthy that advertisements of such innocuous commodities of everyday consumption like vests, ghee, and even baby food have to use fighting screen heroes.

It is only to be expected that what is seen on the screen is enacted in real life by some. In fact, not a few criminals have claimed inspiration for the crimes committed by them from similar episodes watched by them on the screen. Insensitiveness, or at least indifference, engendered amongst our youth by habitual viewing of violence on the screen is indeed disconcerting. In brief, the mass media have been sufficiently responsible for perpetrating and perpetuating senseless violence and aimless conflict.

Education and Social Change

For too much seems to be expected of education as a peaceful solvent of all social ills and a prime mover of social change. But 'education seldom rises above the socio-economic and socio-political situation in which it is embedded' (Kamat 1985: v), and it can hardly be expected to make amends for social deficiencies. This also means that the crisis confronting the educational system cannot be separated from the crisis characterising other facets of life in our society. Thus, educational restructuring can come about only as a part of a radical transformation of society.

An important prerequisite for such a transformation of society is the recognition that it can come about only through a process of education whose aim is what Freire calls 'conscientisation': it refers 'to learning to perceive social, political, and economic contradictions, and to take actions against the oppressive elements of reality' (1972b: 15). The spread of literacy or oracy through lower levels of education can certainly facilitate conscientisation. But it is precisely at this level that the present system of schooling has failed.

Lasting peace for all will remain a distant dream as long as the fundamental problems remain unaddressed and society remains untransformed. If sincere attempts are not made to resolve such problems from within the democratic framework, then large-scale conflict and violence are bound to occur. Should one aim at containing intermittent conflict and establish instant peace by sweeping under the carpet the basic problems or should one strive to come to grips with such problems and aim at lasting peace? The answer to this question depends on who is seeking peace and in whose interest?

19

'New' Educational Policy, 1985

A Critique

Challenge of Education: A Policy Perspective, the 119-page document prepared by the Union Ministry of Education (since reorganised as the Ministry of Human Resources Development) and presented to Parliament in August 1985, is a somewhat unorthodox exercise in policy formulation. Unlike in the past when a committee or commission was appointed to survey the situation and counsel the government, this time the government itself has come out with this document which is intended to act as a catalyst and elicit the views and opinions of all those dealing with or interested in the complex task of 'restructuring the system of education' confronted by a crisis. However, behind this new approach is a design to pass on the buck by a government which being weighed down by vested interests and populist policies is in no hurry to take the hard decisions which are long overdue. It has nevertheless to be conceded that the document is perhaps the most remarkably candid and forthright one to have come from the government, admitting the failures on several fronts and acknowledging the innumerable mistakes.

The apparent honesty of approach of the document cannot hide the fact that it is basically an updated record of the all too familiar statistics on our educational achievements and blunders, and a restatement of many of the old educational ideas, whose roots can easily be traced to the umpteen unimplemented or inadequately or improperly implemented reports of various committees and commissions. A closer scrutiny of the document reveals that some of the problems have been toned down and that on others, as for instance on 'capitation fee', there is a studied reluctance on the part of the government to commit itself. The statement of 'goal-orientation' is grandiose and couched in vague epithets. One hopes that in the dust that is raised by the document the directions will not be lost.

The fundamental failing of the document is the unbridled faith that it reposes in education as the prime mover of socio-economic change. Operating with a now debunked 'investment in human capital' thesis, sedulously propagated by Theodore Schultz and his associates wedded to growth-brand developmental economics, it views, education as 'the most effective means for equalizing opportunities and reducing disparities between human beings' (p. 40)[1] and the only means to 'imbue people with the knowledge, the sense of purpose and the confidence essential for building a dynamic, vibrant and cohesive nation capable of providing its people with the wherewithal for creating better, fuller and more purposeful life' (p. 1).

The available evidence, however, seems to suggest that education seldom rises above the socio-economic and socio-political situation in which it is embedded. Those who have drafted the document are themselves well aware that 'an education system does not operate in a vacuum' (p. 7). That is, the crisis confronting the educational system cannot be separated from the crisis characterising the other facets of life in our society. Piecemeal efforts to stem the tide will only be mere palliatives and the desired radical restructuring can come about only as a part of the general restructuring of society. Keeping this in mind, let us now turn to the perspectives of the document.

It is not disputed that the educational system which is being subjected to severe indictment 'has produced scholars, engineers, technologists, doctors and management personnel of a quality comparable with the very best products of the best universities in the world'. But they form only a small minority, while

> the preponderant majority come out of the institutions of higher education, perhaps with a little more of book learning and of course a degree, but with very little capacity for self-study, poor language and communication skills, a highly limited world-view and hardly any sense of social or national responsibility (pp. 8–9).

The most glaring and unpardonable failure of our educational system is evidenced in the pathetic literacy rates. While the percentage of literates has increased from 16.67 in 1951 to 36.23 in 1981, the number of illiterates has shot up from approximately 300 million to 437 million in the same period, and is expected to cross 500 million by CE 2000.[2] The situation on the literacy front is more distressing with reference to women, scheduled castes and tribes and those in rural areas. Of the 125 countries listed by the World Bank, only twenty-six had literacy rates worse than ours. And the Bank estimates that India would have the largest concentration (54.8% in 15–19 age-group) of illiterate population in the world by the year 2000. This must indeed be the most bitter pill for those who are looking forward to enter the 21st century with trumpets blaring.

It is in this context that universalisation of elementary education, which has unfortunately not been the primary concern for the ruling class all these years, notwithstanding the specific directive in this regard in the Constitution, assumes the greatest significance. No doubt, most children now have a primary school within one kilometre of their homes. But the facilities available in most of these schools and the quality of instruction imparted there are anything but satisfactory: Forty per cent (of these schools) have no *pucca* buildings, 39.72 per cent have no blackboards, and 59.50 per cent have no drinking water. Thirty-five per cent (of these) schools have a single teacher to teach three or four different classes (p. 35). What is more disconcerting, out of 100 children enrolled in Class I only twenty-three reach Class VIII. To put it with brutal frankness, the root cause of this distressing situation is poverty, which is largely the warp and woof of our socio-economic fabric.

There are inter-state variations in the achievement of targets for universalisation of elementary education. This, the document argues, is because of the fact that under the present arrangement, the 'availability of educational facilities has been dependent, not upon the commitment of the nation as a whole, but upon the vicissitudes of the resources allocated by states' (p. 65). The remedy for this does not certainly lie in levelling down the achievements in other states through the centre's intervention. In fact, all the six states (Bihar, Rajasthan, Uttar Pradesh, Madhya Pradesh, Orissa, and Assam) whose achievement is poor have been ruled for most of the time by the same political party, namely, the Congress, which is ruling at the centre (in 1985). It should not have been difficult for the centre to take these states to task at the political level.

The document proposes that 'with the help of *Anganwadis* under the Integrated Child Development Scheme programme, pre-primary education would be provided for three years and thereafter in continuation and conjunction, at the same location, primary education would be organised' (p. 92). This is expected to lead to better participation in education at later stages and also to the increased participation of girls in education. This could be given a fair trial, as studies have shown positive results. But, along with this, the document also proposes the introduction of non-formal education from the Class VII stage to meet the educational needs of the drop-outs. What will be the shape and content of this non-formal education is not clear. Going by the experience of the way schemes have been implemented so far, one cannot be optimistic of the effectiveness of non-formal education at this level in rural areas.

More crucial in eradicating illiteracy is adult education. 'UNESCO studies have revealed that an adult literacy level of 70 per cent is the critical threshold for universalisation of elementary education' (pp. 42–43). The Adult Education Programme has been implemented till now with neither seriousness nor sincerity. Opportunities for linking it with other programmes of development have remained unutilised.

In this context, we can recall with profit the experience of the former Soviet Russia and the People's Republic of China. In both these countries, the revolutionary parties which came to power had the spread of literacy and education as both a party and a national goal. The party cadres did substantial work in eradicating illiteracy and spreading education. But, in our country, the ruling party at the centre and those in the states, as well as the parties in opposition, all of which depend mostly on the votes of illiterate masses, have shown absolutely no interest in eradicating illiteracy, let alone spreading education, among the masses.

In spite of the phenomenal expansion of secondary education (from 4,000 schools in 1947 to 52,279 in 1982–83) only 22 per cent of the students in the age-group corresponding to classes IX and X are in school. The '10+2+3' pattern has not been implemented in quite a few states, and in others, where it has been implemented, it has been a mere arithmetical exercise. With some notable exceptions, the facilities available in most secondary schools are hardly commensurate with or conducive to any meaningful teaching.

Instead of proposing measures for stemming the rot in secondary education, the document emphasises the need for setting up 'pace-setting Model Schools' in the central sector. These schools to be set up, one in each district, are expected 'to demonstrate what good instruction and a good curriculum can do to raise the competence of boys and girls for entering the world of work or institutions of higher education' (p. 45). The country's experience with trendsetters has been that they become the exclusive preserves for grooming the elite and the nurseries for status retention. Instead of fostering equality, the model school concept will add yet another tier to the already stratified schools system and reinforce inequalities and inegalitarian tendencies.

The document hints at Constitutional changes for establishing a uniform 'core curriculum' throughout the country. This is intended 'to strengthen unity within diversity and also to facilitate mobility from one part of the country to another' (p. 4). Whether this idea can ever take root in a country ridden with linguistic chauvinism and exclusiveness is a moot question. Furthermore, the concept of core curriculum is closely related to the more controversial issue of the value component in learning. Fears have already been expressed about whose values will be included, as education is also an ideological and emotional process (see Chapter 9).

Another well-known concept reiterated by the document is that of vocationalisation of education. It places particular emphasis on vocationalisation as part of the '10+2' stage of secondary education and also before this stage and outside the system. In addition to industry, it is sought to be aligned with agriculture, the service sector, and various programmes of rural development providing opportunities for self-employment.

As of now, vocationalisation has not made much headway. The enrolment in vocational courses at the secondary stage is estimated to be only about nine per cent of the total. This, according to the document, is partly due to 'the cultural prejudices towards skill-oriented education' (p. 76). The Standing

Committee of the Central Advisory Board of Education has identified lack of clear knowledge on the subject, inadequate data on employment opportunities and manpower needs at the 'middle' level, paucity of trained instructors, lack of interest on the part of private entrepreneurship in the area, and the high cost involved as the major hurdles in the vocationalisation of education. It is also necessary to note that there are not sufficient employment opportunities for vocational certificate and diploma holders and the incidence of unemployment among them is already quite high. Unless more jobs are created and we know what types of jobs will be available, the expansion of vocational education may not only be wasteful but also lead students into a blind alley.

The document lays the utmost emphasis on higher education, as it 'can provide ideas and men to give shape to the future and also sustain all the other levels of education' (p. 6), and is, therefore, 'the single most important indicator of ... country's future' (p. 47). While the expansion at the tertiary level has been most rapid, the percentage of the relevant age-group enrolled in institutions of higher education constitutes is still insignificant. Much of what goes on in the name of higher education is totally irrelevant and, therefore, a waste of precious resources. The high public subsidisation coupled with growing unemployment among the educated has resulted in devaluation of degrees and escalation of qualification for jobs without any necessary relation to more effective job performance or sophistication demanded by the economy.

A key policy measure with reference to higher education hinted at in the document is the delinking of degrees from jobs. This idea has been toyed with off and on for nearly five decades now, but it has remained a cliché. It is *inter alia* expected along with a National Merit Examination Scheme to reduce the scramble for university seats, raise the standards of higher education, match jobs and skills, cut down 'educated unemployment', and avoid wastage of scarce resources. However, delinking degrees from jobs may not be a panacea by itself, and may even prove to be counter-productive (see Chapter 5).

It is naive to imagine that with 'delinking' the pressure for university seats would automatically be reduced. On the contrary, indications are that it may increase. In the case of recruitment to jobs based on competitive examinations requiring advanced academic knowledge, irrespective of whether the degree or certificate acts as an eligibility criterion, prospective competitors will tend to go to college or university or such other institutions to enhance their chances of passing the examinations. If the competitive examinations now in vogue are any indication, they are at best a mirror image of university examinations.

As noted earlier, enrolment in institutions of higher education as a percentage of the population in the relevant age-group is very low. But more important, according to estimates of the 32nd round of the National Sample Survey (1977–78), only 2.07 per cent of the total labour force in the country has a qualification of 'graduation and above'. Of about seven million added to the labour force annually, only about half a million are 'higher educated'. That is, only one out of fourteen persons added to the labour force is a graduate. Why accentuate the malady by wrongly diagnosing it?

The superficial link between education (qualification-earning) and jobs, as also the problem of unemployment among the educated and degree devaluation are the outcome of the conventional growth-oriented socio-economic strategy embarked upon in the country. This strategy hinges on the urban-based capital-intensive modern sector and engenders consumption culture and raises the cost of living. The vision of a golden future held out by this strategy is chimerical considering the limitations of resources of various kinds, and is one which we will never be able to catch up with. And, even if we can mobilise the requisite resources, should we continue to tread the same path, knowing full well its limitations as experienced by the advanced capitalist societies?

There are two other policy measures in relation to higher education which are worth noting. The document calls for 'diversification of courses' 'with a view to establishing greater relevance to personal development, socio-economic problems and the world of work' (p. 95). It further proposes that 'a moratorium should be placed on further expansion of the traditional pattern of colleges and universities' (p. 110).

More important, the document proposes selective admission to higher education based on 'scholastic interest and aptitude' (p. 96). This is particularly relevant at the postgraduate level, where admission should be confined to those 'who have a good academic record' (ibid.). To consider higher education as a birth right of every citizen is a costly luxury which this poor country can ill afford at present. But selectivity raises questions of the basis and method of selection, which if not intelligently, sympathetically, and effectively handled could have disastrous consequences as far as our avowed objective of removing prevailing social inequalities is concerned and defeat the programme of protective discrimination. Be that as it may, selectivity could neither be practicable nor desirable until and unless alternative avenues of employment and training are made available to those who are denied higher education.

Instead of improving the facilities in the existing institutions and toning up their functioning, the document contemplates the modernisation of the existing ones and the establishment of new 'centres of excellence' 'to take care of our critical requirements of enlightened, sophisticated and creative manpower' (p. 11). Before we embark on such costly misadventures, solely for the purpose of keeping up with international Joneses, we should realise who has been benefitting so far from such centres of excellence. The growing incidence of the brain drain from the country can hardly be exaggerated. According to the American Consul at Madras, in 1984, all the chemical engineering graduates from the Indian Institute of Technology Madras, went to the United States of America for employment or study. One of the causes of this is that we are not in a position to utilise the talent produced at a huge cost and this makes its relevance itself questionable. For instance, '45 per cent of PhDs and 69 per cent of Masters in engineering are engaged in activities unconnected with research and development' (p. 107). There is an urgent need to redefine the role of institutions of higher learning, including the existing 'centres of excellence' which have only excelled in draining the country of its native talent, before we embark upon a 'more the merrier' programme.

Perhaps the most far-reaching of the measures contemplated by the document has to do with decentralisation of educational planning, administration, and monitoring. For the first time we are hearing of multi-level planning as 'a crucial process for formulating programmes, maintaining reliable data systems and evaluating the functional efficiency of the system on an objective basis' (p. 116). There are two aspects to this: one is treating the district or the block as the basic unit and the other is involving, 'not nominally but effectively', the local communities in the management of schools (p. 85). To what extent and in what manner the decision-making powers are going to be delegated is to be seen.

The document hints that, in a polity like ours, education cannot be the sole responsibility of the state, and there is enormous scope to increase the involvement of voluntary agencies. Considering that no such plea has been put forward with reference to programmes benefitting the rich, one would be justified in viewing this as an abdication of responsibility by the state, especially in regard to the Constitutional commitment to universalisation of elementary education. (Incidentally, the document, unlike the Constitution, does not even set a deadline for universalisation of elementary education!). Some state governments have expressed reservations regarding the role of voluntary agencies. While it is necessary to associate as many individuals and agencies as possible in realising our educational aims, we should bear in mind the imperative need to define clearly the specific role of voluntary agencies vis-à-vis education.

In this context, it is significant to note that private donations and endowments for education have declined considerably. They formed 11.6 per cent of the total expenditure on education in 1950–51 and only about 3 per cent in 1980–81. The document suggests 'encouraging private entrepreneurs to contribute to educational development, particularly in respect of vocational and professional streams, by giving suitable rebates in taxes' (p. 89).

Although one should not fail to place on record the invaluable service rendered by some of the private institutions for the cause of education in the country, one cannot at the same time be oblivious to the fact that many of these institutions are functioning as 'teaching shops' run on purely commercial lines or to serve sectional or communal interests. More disturbing is the practice of charging sizeable amounts as 'capitation fee', especially in professional courses and by the English medium schools. Strangely enough, while the document mentions this pernicious practice in one paragraph (4.8 on p. 98), it is totally non-committal on this important issue.

Teachers constitute the most important element of the educational system, and over 70 per cent of the educational expenditure is incurred by way of salaries paid to them. Expectations about their commitment and efficiency are, therefore, high. Unfortunately, however, teaching has become 'the last choice in the job market' and attracts, by and large, only the dregs and leftovers. The mental equipment with which people enter the teaching profession is sadly deficient and the decline in their commitment to the profession is even more deplorable (see Jayaram 2003).

The document is vague as to what action should be taken to rectify this situation. (Nevertheless, some heart-searching and self-criticism on the part of teachers would not be asking for too much). The document repeatedly emphasises the need for a code of conduct for teachers. The idea that every occupational or professional group should have a code of conduct is apposite. But the task of preparing such a code for teachers should be entrusted only to them, and in any case, the government is not morally competent to perform this task lacking as it does a code of conduct of its own. In a society where no facet of life is free from the canker of corrosion of the moral fibre, starting with the government and its handmaid the bureaucracy, it is unfair to single out teachers for special treatment.

The most unsatisfactory element of our educational system is examination, which has become 'the tail that wags the educational dog' (A. Singh 1984). The criticism that we do not have an educational system but only an examination system is serious enough. But worse still is the fact that the system has become a fertile ground for nepotism, cheating, corruption, and violence. The document reiterates the need to modify the present system of annual examination and introduce continuous assessment. This is nothing new and has failed along with other aspects of examination reform for want of sincerity, vigour, and sustained action in implementation.

The most glaring omission in the document is perhaps the language question. It makes a passing admission of the central government's failure to 'ensure the faithful implementation of the three-language formula', but underlines the need 'to ensure that language does not become a barrier to mobility in India of tomorrow' (p. 81). It is precisely this feared development which is happening and is already there and is likely to gather strength in future. The document raises the question of tenability of the 'so-called English medium schools', but is again non-committal. A time has come to sort out the language tangle in general and in particular the place of English, which can be given up only with catastrophic consequences in education. Let not short-sighted emotion override far-sighted reason on such a crucial issue of national importance.

Although the document is non-committal on many crucial issues, it seems to be hell bent on de-politicisation of the academia. Let us admit that politics (not politicking) is a natural and an essential part of human existence, and there is no reason why a healthy democracy should fight shy of it. Are not our universities in several other aspects politicised? Teachers are not robots and their organisations cannot but take on a political colouring, though this may have some negative consequences. Notwithstanding any possible attendant risk, the time has come to associate the academia in all aspects of policy formulation, implementation, and evaluation.

A reference should be made here to the document's proposal to strengthen the University Grants Commission (UGC) 'to save the universities and colleges from insularity and politicisation which inevitably follows from inbreeding and parochialism' (p. 99). Given the stranglehold of the central government on UGC, and under changing centre-state relations, this may not be in the interest of state universities, especially in those states which are ruled by parties other than the one ruling at the centre.

Such a fear also acquires emphasis by the tendency of the central government for aggrandisement manifest in the document. One may view this as the centre's obsession with the 'Concurrent List' syndrome. But the danger signals in it are loud enough not to be ignored. This has grave implications for both the autonomy and accountability of all those engaged in higher education.

Paucity of resources is a familiar refrain that we have been hearing for quite some decades now. But, considering the way public money is being squandered on costly government *tamashas,* image-making schemes, and on populist policies, one wonders whether it is the paucity of resources or lack of a sense of priorities which is the crux of the problem. A government given to squandering will never overcome financial constraints.

It is true that education still constitutes the second highest sector of budgeted expenditure, after defence. However, excepting the Third Five-Year Plan, the share of education has been declining from one Plan to another: from 7.2 per cent in the First Plan to 2.6 per cent in the Sixth. The share of primary education has declined from 43 per cent in 1950–51 to 27 per cent in 1976–77. Any government worth its salt should set right the skewed priorities. Garnering resources and checking leakages apart, the highest priorities must be accorded to school and adult education, and the high subsidisation of higher education must be slashed.

We educate now to reap the benefit twenty years hence. Any measure to change the educational system should, therefore, be in tune with the vision of a society that we would like to create. This vision must essentially be a politico-ethical one, and not just a demographic or technical one. Among other things this vision has to take into account such issues as appropriate technology, developmental priorities and strategies, national income and wage policy, and a definition of a minimum standard of life. We now have an opportunity to debate on 'the desirable society' and work out strategies for realising it. If we let this opportunity pass, we may well be faced with a similar situation in future discussing another document prepared by another set of bureaucrats.

Notes

1. All references in this Chapter are to Ministry of Education (1985).
2. For more recent data on the literacy front, see Chapter 17, En 4 in this book.

References

Abercrombie, N., S. Hill, and B.S. Turner. 2000. *The Penguin Dictionary of Sociology* (4th edition). London: Penguin Books.

Acharya, Arabinda and S.K. Mohanty. 2010. 'Youth Unemployment in India: A Situational Analysis', *Journal of Educational Planning and Administration,* 24 (2): 115–33.

Adam, W. 1941. *Reports on the State of Education in Bengal, 1835 and 1838* (ed. A.N. Basu). Calcutta: University of Calcutta.

Agarwal, B.L. 1985. 'Nexus between Jobs and Degrees', in J.V. Raghavan (ed.): *Higher Education in the Eighties* (52–76). New Delhi: Lancer International.

Ahir, D.C. 1990. *The Legacy of Dr Ambedkar.* Delhi: B.R. Publishing Corporation.

Ahmad, I. 1978. *Caste and Social Stratification among Muslims in India.* New Delhi: Manohar.

——. 1981. 'Muslim Educational Backwardness: An Inferential Analysis', *Economic and Political Weekly,* 16 (36): 1457–65.

Aikara, J. 1994. *Sociology of Education (Research in Sociology and Social Anthropology: Third Survey, Monograph 2).* New Delhi: Indian Council of Social Science Research.

——. 2004. *Education: Sociological Perspectives.* Jaipur: Rawat Publications.

Alam, A. 2013. 'Controlling Minds, Disciplining Bodies: Life Inside a Madrasa', in G.B. Nambissan and S.S. Rao (eds.): *Sociology of Education in India: Changing Contours and Emerging Concerns* (224–44). New Delhi: Oxford University Press.

Altbach, P.G. 1968a. *Student Politics in Bombay*. Bombay: Asia Publishing House.

——. 1968b. 'Student Politics and Higher Education in India', in P.G. Altbach (ed.): *Turmoil and Transition* (17–73). Bombay: Lalvani.

——. 1971. 'The Transformation of the Indian Student Movement', in A. DeConde (ed.): *Student Activism* (204–20). New York: Charles Scribner's Sons.

——. 1974. 'Bibliography on Indian Higher Education', in A. Singh and P.G. Altbach (eds.): *The Higher Learning in India* (421–46). Delhi: Vikas Publishing House.

——. 1975. *Publishing in India*. Delhi: Oxford University Press.

——. 1998. 'Gigantic Peripheries: India and China in the World Knowledge System', in P.G. Altbach (ed.): *Comparative Higher Education* (189–206). Hong Kong: Comparative Education Research Center, University of Hong Kong.

Altbach, P.G. and T. Umakoshi (eds.). 2004. *Asian Universities: Historical Perspectives and Contemporary Challenges*. Baltimore, Maryland: Johns Hopkins University Press.

Althusser, L. 1971. 'Ideology and Ideological State Apparatuses', in L. Althusser: *Lenin and Philosophy and Other Essays* (tr. B. Brewster) (121–73). London: New Left Books.

Ambedkar, B.R. 1925. *The Evolution of Provincial Finance in British India*. London: P.S. King and Sons.

——. 1927. *The Problem of the Rupee*. London: P.S. King and Co.

——. 1943. *Mr Gandhi and the Emancipation of the Untouchables*. Jullundur: Bheem Patrika Publications.

——. 1946. *Who were the Shudras? How They Came to be the Fourth Varna in the Indo-Aryan Society?* Bombay: Thacker and Co.

——. 1957. *The Buddha and His Dhamma*. Bombay: People's Education Society.

Anderson, B. 1983. *Imagined Communities: Reflections on the Origin and Spread of Nationalism*. London: Verso.

Anderson, C.A. and P.J. Foster. 1964. 'Discrimination and Inequality in Education', *Sociology of Education*, 38 (1): 1–18.

Anderson, W. and A. Pant. 1970. 'Student Politics at Allahabad University', *Economic and Political Weekly*, 5 (23): 910–16 and 5 (24): 941–48.

Andreski, S. 1974. *Prospects of a Revolution in the USA*. New York: Harper and Row.

Andrews, R. 1987. *The Routledge Dictionary of Quotations*. London: Routledge and Kegan Paul.

Ashby, E. and M. Anderson. 1966. *Universities: British, Indian, and African*. London: Weidenfield and Nicholson.

Association of Indian Universities, New Delhi. 1985. *Universities Handbook, 1985–86*. New Delhi: Association of Indian Universities.

Aurora, G.S. 1970. 'Teachers as a Professional Group and Their Organizations', in S.P. Ruhela (ed.): *Sociology of the Teaching Profession in India* (12–21). New Delhi: NCERT.

Austin, G. 1972. *The Indian Constitution*. Bombay: Oxford University Press.

Baig, M.R.A. 1974. *The Muslim Dilemma in India*. Delhi: Vikas Publishing House.

Baig, T.A. 1976. *India's Woman Power*. New Delhi: S. Chand.

Baldridge, J. 2002. 'Reconciling Linguistic Diversity: The History and the Future of Language Policy in India', *Language in India*, 2 (3 May), http://www.languageinindia.com/may2002/baldridgelanguagepolicy.html (accessed on 6 September 2014).

Banks, O. 1976. *The Sociology of Education* (3rd edition). London: B.T. Batsford.

Barnett, M.R. 1976. *The Politics of Cultural Nationalism in South India*. Princeton, NJ: Princeton University Press.

Barrow, R. 1978. *Radical Education*. London: Martin Robertson.

Basant, R. and A. Shariff (eds.). 2009. *Handbook of Muslims in India: Empirical and Policy Perspectives*. New Delhi: Oxford University Press.

Basu, A. 1978. 'Policy and Conflict in India: The Reality and Perception of Education', in P.G. Altbach and G.P. Kelly (eds.): *Education and Colonialism* (53–68). New York: Longman.

——. 2002. 'Indian Higher Education: Colonialism and Beyond', in P.G. Altbach and V. Selvaratnam (eds.): *From Dependence to Autonomy: The Development of Asian Universities* (167–86). Chestnut Hill, Mass.: Center for International Higher Education, Boston College.

Basu, A.N. (ed.). 1952. *Indian Education in Parliamentary Papers, Part I (1832)*. Bombay: Asia Publishing House.

Bauer, C. 1956. 'The Pattern of Urban and Economic Development: Social Implications', *The Annals of the American Academy of Politics and Social Science*, 305: 60–67.

Bernstein, B. 1961. 'Social Class and Linguistic Development: A Theory of Social Learning', in A.H. Halsey, J. Floud, and C.A. Anderson (eds.): *Education, Economy, and Society* (288–314). New York: The Free Press.

——. 1971. 'On the Classification and Framing of Educational Knowledge', in M.F.D. Young (ed.): *Knowledge and Control: New Directions for the Sociology of Education* (47–69). London: Collier Macmillan.

——. 1973. 'Education Cannot Compensate for Society', in J. Raynor and J. Harden (eds.): *Equality and City Schools* (79–84). London: Routledge and Kegan Paul in association with Open University Press.

——. 1974a. 'A Critique of the Concept of "Compensatory Education"', in D. Wedderburn (ed.): *Poverty, Inequality and Class Structure* (109–22). London: Cambridge University Press.

——. 1974b. 'Sociology and the Sociology of Education: A Brief Account', in J. Rex (ed.): *Approaches to Sociology* (145–59). London: Routledge and Kegan Paul.

Berreman, G.D. 1981. *The Politics of Truth.* New Delhi: South Asian Publishers.

Béteille, A. 1981. 'The Problem', *Seminar,* 268: 10–13.

——. 2000. 'Universities as Institutions', in A. Béteille: *Antinomies of Society: Essays on Ideologies and Institutions* (153–71). New Delhi: Oxford University Press.

Bhagat-Ganguly, V. 2014. 'Revisiting the Nav Nirman Andolan of Gujarat', *Sociological Bulletin,* 63 (1): 95–112.

Blackledge, D.A. and B.D. Hunt. 1985. *Sociological Interpretations of Education.* Beckenham: Croom Helm.

Blaug, M. (ed.). 1972. *Economics of Education (Vol. 1).* Harmondsworth, Middlesex: The English Language Book Society and Penguin Books.

Blaug, M., R. Layard, and M. Woodhall. 1969. *The Causes of Graduate Unemployment in India.* London: Allen Lane.

Borkotoky, K. and S. Unisa. 2014. 'Educational Deprivation of Children in India: Insights from Recent National Level Household Survey', *Journal of Educational Planning and Administration,* 28 (1): 39–53.

Boudon, R. 1974. *Education, Opportunity and Social Inequality.* New York: John Wiley and Sons.

Bourdieu, P. 1973. 'Cultural Reproduction and Social Reproduction', in R. Brown (ed.): *Knowledge, Education and Cultural Change* (71–112). London: Tavistock.

——. 1974. 'The School as a Conservative Force: Scholastic and Cultural Inequalities' (tr. J.C. Whitehouse), in J. Eggleston (ed.): *Contemporary Research in the Sociology of Education* (32–46). London: Methuen.

Bowles, S. 1977. 'Unequal Education and the Reproduction of the Social Division Labour', in J. Karabel and A.H. Halsey (eds.): *Power and Ideology in Education* (137–53). New York: Oxford University Press.

Bowles, S., H. Gintis, and P. Meyer. 1975–76. 'Education, IQ, and the Legitimation of the Social Division of Labour', *Berkeley Journal of Sociology*, 20: 233–64.

Brass, P. 1975. *Language, Religion and Politics in North India.* Delhi: Vikas Publishing House.

Brim, O.G. 1958. *Sociology and the Field of Education.* New York: Russell Sage Foundation.

Brookover, W.B. 1955. *A Sociology of Education.* New York: American Book Company.

Brookover, W.B. and D.A. Gottlieb. 1964. *A Sociology of Education* (2nd edition). New York: American Book Co.

——. 1970. 'Toward a Definition', in D.F. Swift (ed.): *Basic Readings in the Sociology of Education* (5–9). London: Routledge and Kegan Paul.

Brown, F.J. 1961. *Educational Sociology* (2nd Modern Asia edition). Tokyo: Charles E. Tuttle Company.

Brown, R. (ed.). 1973. *Knowledge, Education, and Cultural Change.* London: Tavistock.

Buckman, P. (ed.). 1975. *Education without Schools* (Indian edition). Calcutta: Rupa.

Bullock, A. and O. Stallybrass (eds.). 1977. *The Fontana Dictionary of Modern Thought.* London: Fontana Books.

Bullock, A. and S. Trombley (eds.). 1999. *The New Fontana Dictionary of Modern Thought.* London: Harper Collins.

Calhoun, C.J. and F.A.J. Ianni (eds.). 1976. *The Anthropological Study of Education.* The Hague: Mouton.

Cannon, C. 1970. 'The Influence of Religion on Educational Policy, 1902–1944', in P.W. Musgrave (ed.): *Sociology, History and Education* (162–79). London: Methuen.

Carnoy, M. 1974. *Education as Cultural Imperialism.* New York: Longman.

Carnoy, M. and H.M. Levin (ed.). 1976. *The Limits of Educational Reform.* New York: David McKay.

Census of India. 2001a. Language. http://www.censusindia.gov.in/Census_Data_2001/Census_Data_Online/Language/Statement5.aspx (accessed on 30 August 2014).

Census of India. 2001b. Religion. http://www.censusindia.gov.in/Census_Data_2001/India_at_glance/religion.aspx (accessed on 30 August 2014).

Chakravarty, R. 1980. *Communists in the Indian Women's Movement, 1940–1950*. New Delhi: People's Publishing House.

Chanana, K. 2001. *Interrogating Women's Education: Bounded Visions, Expanding Horizons*. Jaipur: Rawat Publications.

——. 2013. 'Sociology of Education and Sociology in India: Disciplinary Boundaries and Institutional Spaces', in G.B. Nambissan and S.S. Rao (eds.): *Sociology of Education in India: Changing Contours and Emerging Concerns* (46–64). New Delhi: Oxford University Press.

Chatterjee, P. (in collaboration with N. Banerjee, A.K. Baruah, S. Deshpande, P.R. de Souza, K. Hachhethu, B.K. Jahangir, M.S.S. Pandian, N. Wikramasinghe, S.A. Zaidi, and I. Abraham). 2002. *Social Science Research Capacity in South Asia: A Report (SSRC Working Paper Series – Vol. 6)*. New York: Social Science Research Council.

Chaturvedi, M.G. and B.V. Mahale. 1976. *Position of Languages in School Curriculum in India*. New Delhi: NCERT.

Chaturvedi, M.G. and S. Singh. 1981. *Third All-India Educational Survey: Languages and Media of Instruction in Indian Schools*. New Delhi: NCERT.

Chen, Xiangming. 2003. 'The Academic Profession in China', in P.G. Altbach (ed.): *The Decline of the Guru: The Academic Profession in Developing and Middle-Income Countries* (107–34). New York: Palgrave.

Chitnis, S. 1974a. 'Sociology of Education: A Trend Report', in Indian Council of Social Science Research: *A Survey of Research in Sociology and Social Anthropology (Vol. II)* (166–232). Bombay: Popular Prakashan.

——. 1974b. 'Teachers in Higher Education', in A. Singh and P.G. Altbach (eds.): *The Higher Learning in India Delhi* (237–48). Delhi: Vikas Publishing House.

——. 1977. 'Education and Equality', in A. Kloskowska and G. Martinotti (eds.): *Education in a Changing Society* (73–106). London: Sage Publications.

——. 1981. A *Long Way to Go…* . New Delhi: Allied Publishers.

——. 1985. 'Sociology of Education', in Indian Council of Social Science Research, *Survey of Research in Sociology and Social Anthropology, 1969–1979 (Vol. II)* (209–51). New Delhi: Satvahan.

——. 2013. 'Sociology of Education in India: A Personal Account', in G.B. Nambissan and S.S. Rao (eds.): *Sociology of Education in India: Changing Contours and Emerging Concerns* (27–45). New Delhi: Oxford University Press.

Clarke, F. 1940. *Education and Social Change*. London: Sheldon Press.

Commissioner for Scheduled Castes and Scheduled Tribes. 1980. *Twenty-sixth Report, 1978–79* (2 parts). Delhi: Controller of Publications, Government of India.

Coombs, P. 1964. *The Fourth Dimension of Foreign Policy.* New York: Harper and Row.

Coontz, S. 1974. 'The Failure of American Education', *International Socialist Review,* 35 (7): 6–11 and 30–42.

Corwin, R.G. 1965. *A Sociology of Education.* New York: Appleton-Century-Crofts.

Coser, L.A. 1956. *The Functions of Social Conflict.* New York: The Free Press.

Cosin, B.R., I.R. Dale, G.M. Esland, and D.F. Swift. 1971. *School and Society.* London: Routledge and Kegan Paul in association with the Open University Press.

Crossland, A. 1962. *The Conservative Enemy.* London: Jonathan Cape.

Dadhich, N. 2004. 'Indian Science Experiment', *Economic and Political Weekly,* 39 (21): 2181–84.

Dahrendorf, R. 1969a. 'On the Origin of Inequality among Men', in A. Béteille (ed.): *Social Inequality* (16–44). Harmondsworth, Middlesex: Penguin Books.

——. 1969b. 'Toward a Theory of Social Conflict' (tr. A. Rapaport), in W. L. Wallace (ed.): *Sociological Theory* (213–26). London: Heinemann.

Dasgupta, S. 1974. *The Great Gherao of 1969.* New Delhi: Orient Longman.

Dattagupta, S. 2005. 'The State of Physics', *Seminar,* 547: 19–22.

Davies, I. 1971. 'The Management of Knowledge: A Critique of the Use of Typologies in the Sociology of Education', in M.F.D. Young (ed.): *Knowledge and Control: New Directions for the Sociology of Education* (267–88). London: Collier Macmillan.

Davis, K. and W.E. Moore. 1945. 'Some Principles of Stratification', *American Sociological Review,* 10 (2): 242–49.

De Bary, W.T., S. Hay, R. Weiler, and A. Yarrow. 1963. *Sources of Indian Tradition.* Delhi: Motilal Banarsidas.

Demaine, J. 1981. *Contemporary Theories in the Sociology of Education.* London: Macmillan.

Desai, A.R. 1966. *Social Background of Indian Nationalism* (4th edition). Bombay: Popular Prakashan.

——. 1967. 'Social Change and Educational Policy', in M.S. Gore, I.P. Desai, and S. Chitnis (eds.): *Papers in the Sociology of Education in India* (91–126). New Delhi: National Council of Educational Research and Training.

——. (ed.). 1986. *Violation of Democratic Rights in India (Vol. I)*. Bombay: Popular Prakashan.

Desai, B.G. 1967. *The Emerging Youth*. Bombay: Popular Prakashan.

Desai, I.P. 1953. *High School Students in Poona*. Poona: Deccan College.

——. 1981. 'Anti-Reservation Agitation and Structure of Gujarat Society', *Economic and Political Weekly*, 16 (18): 819–23.

De Souza, A. 1974. *Indian Public Schools*. New Delhi: Sterling Publishers.

Dewey, J. 1899. *The School and Society: Being Three Lectures*. Chicago, IL: The University of Chicago Press.

——. 1916. *Democracy and Education: An Introduction to the Philosophy of Education*. New York: Macmillan.

Dhar, T.N., A.S. Ilchman, and W.F. Ilchman. 1976. *Education and Employment in India*. Calcutta: Minerva Associates.

Dharmpal. 1983. *The Beautiful Tree*. New Delhi: Biblialmpex.

Dholakia, J. 1977. *Unemployment and Employment Policy in India*. New Delhi: Sterling Publishers.

Di Bona, J.E. 1972. *Change and Conflict in the Indian University*. Bombay: Lalvani.

——. 1974. 'Gurus and Graduates: The Realization of Higher Education in the Punjab', in J.E. Di Bona (ed.): *The Context of Education in Indian Development* (155–88). North Carolina: Duke University Press.

——. 1983. *One Teacher, One School*. New Delhi: Biblia Impex.

Dore, R. 1976. *The Diploma Disease*. London: George Allen and Unwin.

Douglas, J.W.B. 1964. *The Home and the School: A Study of Ability and Attainment in the Primary Schools*. London: MacGibbon and Kee.

Draper, H. 1978. *Karl Marx's Theory of Revolution (Vol. I)*. New York: Atherton Press.

Dubashi, J. 1983. 'Unemployment: Jobs for the Jobless', *India Today*, 8 (18): 82–83.

Dube, S.C. 1992. *Indian Society*. New Delhi: National Book Trust, India.

Durkheim, E. 1956/1922. *Education and Sociology* (tr. with an Introduction by S.D. Fox). New York: The Free Press.

——. 1961/1925. *Moral Education*. New York: The Free Press.

——. 1977/1938. *The Evolution of Educational Thought: Lectures on the Formation and Development of Secondary Education in France* (tr. Peter Collins). London: Routledge and Kegan Paul.

Dushkin, L. 1972. 'Scheduled Caste Politics', in J.M. Mahar (ed.): *The Untouchables in Contemporary India* (165–226). Tucson, Arizona: The University of Arizona Press.

Dutt, S. 1970. 'Toward a True Profession of Teaching', in S.P. Ruhela (ed.): *Sociology of the Teaching Profession in India* (3–11). New Delhi: NCERT.

Edwardes, M. 1967. *British India, 1772–1947.* London: Sidgwick and Jackson.

Eggleston, J. 1978. 'Stability or Change?: On Education and Society', *Encounter*, 51 (6): 64–70.

Eisenstadt, S.N. 1963. 'Archetypal Patterns of Youth', in E.H. Erikson (ed.): *Youth: Change and Challenge*. New York: Basic Books.

Election Commission of India. 2014. 'Partywise Performance and List of Party Participated', http://eci.nic.in/eci_main1/GE2014/ge.html (accessed on 30 August 2014).

Emmerij, L. and D. Ghai. 1976. 'Employment Problems in Developing Countries: Lessons from the World Employment Programme', in A. Cairncross and M. Puri (eds.): *Employment, Income and Development Strategy* (56–70). London: Macmillan.

Engineer, A.A. (ed.). 1984. *Communal Riots in Post-Independence India.* Hyderabad: Sangam Books.

Entwistle, H. 1978. *Class, Culture and Education.* London: Methuen.

Fairchild, H.P. (ed.). 1970. *Dictionary of Sociology and Related Sciences.* Totowa, NJ: Littlefield, Adams and Co.

Fletcher, R. 1972. *The Making of Sociology* (Vol. 1). London: Thomas Nelson and Sons.

Floud, J.E. and A.H. Halsey. 1958. 'The Sociology of Education', *Current Sociology*, 7: 165–93.

Floud, J.E., A.H. Halsey, and F.M. Martin. 1957. *Social Class and Educational Opportunity.* London: Heinemann.

Foster, P.J. 1971. 'Access to Schooling', in D. Adams (ed.): *Education in National Development* (13–33). London: Routledge and Kegan Paul.

Frank, A.G. 1981. 'The Development of Underdevelopment', in M. Smith, R. Little, and M. Shackleton (eds.): *Perspectives on World Politics* (291–300). London: Croom Helm in association with the Open University.

Franklin, E.W. 1970. 'Professional Organization of Teachers in India', in S.P. Ruhela (ed.): *Sociology of the Teaching Profession in India* (22–28). New Delhi: NCERT.

Freire, P. 1972a. *Cultural Action for Freedom.* Harmondsworth, Middlesex: Penguin Books.

——. 1972b. *Pedagogy of the Oppressed.* Harmondsworth, Middlesex: Penguin Books.

Frith, S. and P. Corrigan. 1977. 'The Politics of Education', in M. Young and G. Whitty (eds.): *Society, State and Schooling* (253–68). Lewes, Sussex: The Falmer Press.

Fromm, E. 1973. *The Anatomy of Human Destructiveness.* New York: Fawcett Crest by arrangement with Holt, Rinehart and Winston.

Furnivall, J.S. 1944. *Netherlands India: A Study of Plural Economy.* Cambridge: Cambridge University Press.

——. 1948. *Colonial Policy and Practice: A Comparative Study of Burma and Netherlands India.* Cambridge: Cambridge University Press.

Galtung, J. 1968. 'Peace', in D.L. Sills (ed.): *International Encyclopedia of Social Sciences (Vol. XI)* (487–96). New York: The Macmillan Co. and The Free Press.

Ganguly, B. and M. Ganguly. 1975. *Voting Behaviour in a Developing Society: West Bengal.* New Delhi: Sterling Publishers.

Gardanov, V.K. 1976. 'Fosterage', in C.J. Calhoun and F.A.J. Ianni (eds.): *The Anthropological Study of Education* (29–40). The Hague: Mouton.

Giddens, A. 1973. *The Class Structure of the Advanced Societies.* London: Hutchinson.

Gintis, H. 1972. 'Towards a Political Economy of Education: A Radical Critique of Ivan Illich's *Deschooling Society*', *Harvard Educational Review,* 42 (1): 70–96.

Glaser, B.G. and A.L. Strauss. 1967. *The Discovery of Grounded Theory.* London: Weidenfeld and Nicolson.

Glaser, W. 1978. *The Brain Drain.* Oxford: Pergamon Press.

Glass, D. (ed.). 1954. *Social Mobility in Britain.* London: Routledge and Kegan Paul.

Goldschmidt, W. 1971. *Exploring the Ways of Mankind* (2nd edition). New York: Holt, Rinehart and Winston.

Goldthorpe, J.H. 1973. 'Social Inequality and Social Integration in Modern Britain', in J. Raynor and J. Harden (eds.): *Equality and City Schools* (4–27). London: Routledge and Kegan Paul in association with the Open University.

Goodman, P. 1971. *Compulsory Miseducation.* Harmondsworth, Middlesex: Penguin Books.

Goody, J. (ed.). 1968. *Literacy in Traditional Societies.* Cambridge: Cambridge University Press.

Goody, J. and I. Watt. 1968. 'The Consequences of Literacy', in J. Goody (ed.): *Literacy in Traditional Societies* (27–68). Cambridge: Cambridge University Press.

Gorbutt, D. 1972. 'The "New" Sociology of Education', *Education for Teaching*. 89 (1): 3–11.

Gore, M.S. 1993. *The Social Context of an Ideology*. New Delhi: Sage Publications.

Gore, M.S. and S. Chitnis. 1967. 'Sociology and Educational Research', in M.S. Gore, I.P. Desai, and S. Chitnis (eds.): *Papers in the Sociology of Education in India* (335–56). New Delhi: NCERT.

Gore, M.S. and I.P. Desai. 1967. 'The Scope of a Sociology of Education', in M.S. Gore, I.P. Desai, and S. Chitnis (eds.): *Papers in the Sociology of Education in India* (1–32). New Delhi: NCERT.

Gore, M.S., I.P. Desai, and S. Chitnis (eds.). 1967. *Papers in the Sociology of Education in India*. New Delhi: NCERT.

——. 1970. *Field Studies in the Sociology of Education*. New Delhi: NCERT.

Government of Karnataka. 1975. *Report of the Karnataka Backward Classes Commission* (4 Vol.). Bangalore: Government Press.

——. 1980. *Universities in Karnataka: Report of the Review Commission*. Bangalore.

Government of Maharashtra. 1982. *Dr Babasaheb Ambedkar Writings and Speeches (Vol. 2)*. Bombay: Government of Maharashtra.

——. 1991. *Dr Babasaheb Ambedkar Writings and Speeches (Vol. 9)*. Bombay: Government of Maharashtra.

Govinda, R. 2003. 'Dynamics of Decentralised Management in Primary Education: Policy and Practice in Rajasthan and Madhya Pradesh', in R. Govinda and R. Diwan (eds.): *Community Participation and Empowerment in Primary Education* (203–35). New Delhi: Sage Publications.

Govinda, R. and R. Diwan. 2003. 'Introduction: Emerging Issues and Practices', in R. Govinda and R. Diwan (eds.): *Community Participation and Empowerment in Primary Education* (11–30). New Delhi: Sage Publications.

Gross, N. 1965. 'The Sociology of Education', in R.K. Merton, L. Broom, and L.S. Cottrell (eds.): *Sociology Today* (Vol. 1: 128–52). New York: Harper and Row.

Grugeon, E. 1993. 'Gender Implications of Children's Playground Culture', in P. Woods and M. Hammersley (eds.): *Gender and Ethnicity in Schools: Ethnographic Accounts* (11–33). London: Routledge in association with The Open University.

Guha, A. 1980. 'Little Nationalism Turned Chauvinist: Assam's Anti-Foreigner Upsurge, 1979–80', *Economic and Political Weekly*, 15 (41–43): 1699–1720.

Halsey, A.H. 1973. 'Political Ends and Educational Means', in L. Raynor and J. Harden (eds.): *Equality and City Schools* (85–98). London: Routledge and Kegan Paul in association with Open University Press.

——. 1997. 'Preface', in A.H. Halsey, H. Lauder, P. Brown, and A.S. Wells (eds.): *Education: Culture, Economy, and Society* (v–vi). Oxford: Oxford University Press.

Halsey, A.H., J.E. Floud, and C.A. Anderson (eds.). 1961. *Education, Economy, and Society*. New York: The Free Press.

Halsey, A.H., H. Lauder, P. Brown, and A.S. Wells (eds.). 1997. *Education: Culture, Economy, and Society*. Oxford: Oxford University Press.

Hammersley, M. and P. Atkinson. 1983. *Ethnography: Principles in Practice*. London: Tavistock.

Hansen, D.A. 1967. 'The Uncomfortable Relation of Sociology and Education', in D.A. Hansen and J.E. Gerstl (eds.): *On Education: Sociological Perspectives* (3–35). New York: John Wiley.

Hanson, A.H. and J. Douglas. 1972. *India's Democracy*. Delhi: Vikas Publishing House.

Haq, E. 1981. *Education and Political Culture in India*. New Delhi: Sterling Publishers.

Hardy, P. 1972. *The Muslims of British India*. Cambridge: Cambridge University Press.

Harrison, P. 1981. *Inside the Third World* (2nd edition). Harmondsworth, Middlesex: Penguin Books.

Harrison, S.S. 1960. *India: The Most Dangerous Decades*. Madras: Oxford University Press.

Hartog, P. 1939. *Some Aspects of Indian Education: Past and Present* (being three Joseph Payne Lectures for 1935–36 delivered in the Institute of Education, University of London). London: Oxford University Press.

Hasan, M. 1979. *Nationalism and Communal Politics in India, 1916–1928*. New Delhi: Manohar.

Herndon, J. 1968. *The Way it Spozed to Be*. New York: Simon and Schuster.

Hobsbawm, E.J. 1975. 'Equality in the Past', in J. Vaizey (ed.): *Whatever Happened to Equality* (31–40). London: British Broadcasting Corporation.

Holmes, B. (ed.). 1985. *Equality and Freedom in Education*. London: George Allen and Unwin.

Hunter, W.W. 1872. *The Indian Mussalmans* (2nd edition). London: Trubner and Co.

Hussain, S.A. 1965. *The Destiny of Indian Muslims.* Bombay: Asia Publishing House.

Illich, I.D. 1973. *Deschooling Society.* Harmonsworth, Middlesex: Penguin Books.

Inkeles, A. 1965. *What is Sociology? An Introduction to the Discipline and Profession.* New Delhi: Prentice Hall of India.

Issacs, H. 1965. *India's Ex-Untouchables.* New York: John Day and Co.

Jackson, J.A. 1970. 'Professions and Professionalization: Editorial Introduction', in J.A. Jackson (ed.): *Professions and Professionalization* (3–15). Cambridge: Cambridge University Press.

Jayaram, N. 1976. *Education and Social Structure,* Ph.D. Thesis in Sociology. Bangalore: Bangalore University.

——. 1977. 'Social Implications of Medical Education in India', *Journal of Higher Education,* 3 (2): 207–20.

——. 1978. 'Higher Education as Status Stabilizer: Students in Bangalore', in S. Saberwal (ed.): *Process and Institutions in Urban India* (169–91). Delhi: Vikas Publishing House.

——. 1981a. 'Fresh Look at Harijan Question', *Mainstream,* 19 (38): 10–14.

——. 1981b. 'Sadhus No Longer: Recent Trends in Indian Student Activism', in P.G. Altbach (ed.), *Student Politics: Perspectives for the Eighties* (214–33). Metuchen, NJ: The Scarecrow Press.

——. 1985a. 'Education: Jobs and Degrees', *The Herald Review,* 1 (25): 32–5 and 37.

——. 1985b. 'Brain Drain: A Non-Refundable Deposit', *The Herald Review,* 1 (39): 41–42.

——. 1987a. *Higher Education and Status Retention.* New Delhi: Mittal Publications.

——. 1987b. *Introductory Sociology* (An adaptation of the original by Tony Bilton et al.). Madras: Macmillan India.

——. 1990. 'Ethnicity and Education: A Socio-Historical Perspective on the Educational Backwardness of Indian Muslims', *Sociological Bulletin,* 39 (1–2): 115–29 (Republished as Chapter 11 in this book).

——. 1992. 'India', in B.S. Cooper (ed.): *Labour Relations in Education: An International Perspective* (157–69). Westport, Conn.: Greenwood Press.

——. 1993. 'The Language Question in Higher Education: Trends and Issues', in S. Chitnis and P.G. Altbach (eds.): *Higher Education Reform in India: Experience and Perspectives* (84–114). New Delhi: Sage Publications.

——. 2000a. 'Multiculturalism and Nation-Building: A South Indian Perspective', *Journal of Social and Economic Development*, 3 (2): 274–90.

——. 2000b. 'Sociology of Youth in India', in M.S. Gore (ed.): *Third Survey of Research in Sociology and Social Anthropology (Vol. I)* (221–95). New Delhi: Indian Council of Social Science Research and Manak Publications.

——. 2003. 'The Fall of the Guru: The Decline of the Academic Profession in India', in P.G. Altbach (ed.): *The Decline of the Guru: The Academic Profession in Developing and Middle-Income Countries* (199–230). New York: Palgrave Macmillan.

——. 2004a/1992. 'Emancipation through Proselytism? Some Reflections on the Marginal Status of the Depressed Castes', in R. Robinson (ed.): *Sociology of Religion in India* (256–72). New Delhi: Sage Publications India (originally published in *Sociological Bulletin*, 41 (1 and 2), 1992: 67–80).

——. 2004b. 'Higher Education in India: Massification and Change', in P.G. Altbach and T. Umakoshi (eds.): *Asian Universities: Historical Perspectives and Contemporary Challenges* (85–112). Baltimore, Maryland: The Johns Hopkins University Press.

——. 2006. 'India', in J.J.F. Forest and P.G. Altbach (eds.): *International Handbook of Higher Education (Part Two: Regions and Countries)* (747–67). Dordrecht, The Netherlands: Springer.

——. 2007. 'Beyond Retailing Knowledge: Prospect of Research-Oriented Universities in India', in P.G. Altbach and J. Balán (eds.): *World Class Worldwide: Transforming Research Universities in Asia and Latin America* (70–94). Baltimore: The Johns Hopkins University Press.

——. 2009. 'Higher Education in India: The Challenge of Change', in D. Palfreyman and T. Tapper (eds.): *Structuring Mass Higher Education: The Role of Elite Institutions* (95–112). New York: Routledge.

——. 2010. 'Disparities in Access to Higher Education in India: Persistent Issues and the Changing Context', in F. Lazin, M. Evans, and N. Jayaram (eds.): *Higher Education and Equality of Opportunities* (161–81). Lanham, Maryland: Lexington Books.

——. 2012. 'Academic Salaries and Career Advancement: Tuning the Professoriate for a Knowledge Economy in India', in P.G. Altbach, L. Reisberg, M. Yudkevich, G. Androushchak, and I.F. Pacheco (eds.): *Paying the Professoriate: A Global Comparison of Compensation and Contracts* (155–65). New York/London: Routledge.

——. 2013. 'India: Streamlining the Academic Profession for a Knowledge Economy', in P.G. Altbach, G. Androushchak, Y.

Kuzminov, M. Yudkevich, and L. Reisberg (eds.): *The Global Future of Higher Education and the Academic Profession* (93–125). Basingstoke, Hampshire and New York: Palgrave Macmillan.

——. 2014. 'Whither Innovations in Higher Education in India', in A. Maldonado–Maldonado and R.M. Bassett (eds.): *The Forefront of International Higher Education: A Festschrift in Honor of Philip G. Altbach* (195–205). Dordrecht: Springer.

Jayaram, N. and G. Sivaramakrishnan. 1976. 'Recruitment to Teaching in Higher Education', *Vidya Bharathi*, 2 (1): 69–72.

Jayaram, N. and S. Saberwal (eds.). 2011/1996. *Social Conflict* (Oxford in India Readings in Sociology and Social Anthropology) (2nd revised edition). New Delhi: Oxford University Press.

Jensen, G.E. 1967. *Educational Sociology*. Englewood Cliffs, NJ: Prentice-Hall.

Jodhka, S.S. 2001. 'Introduction', in S.S. Jodhka (ed.): *Community and Identities: Contemporary Discourses on Culture and Politics in India* (13–31). New Delhi: Sage Publications in association with The Book Review Literary Trust, New Delhi.

Johnson, D.W. and R.T. Johnson. 2002. *Multicultural Education and Human Relations: Valuing Diversity*. Boston, MASS: Allyn and Bacon.

Jones, D.E. and R.W. Jones. 1977. 'The Scholars' Rebellion: Educational Institutions and Agitational Politics in Gujarat', *Journal of Asian Studies*, 36 (3): 457–76.

Joseph, K. and J. Sumption. 1979. *Equality*. London: John Murray.

Joshi, B.R. 1982. *Democracy in Search of Equality: Untouchable Politics and Indian Social Change*. Delhi: Hindustan Publishing Corporation.

Joshi, K. 1983. *Report of the Working Group to Review Teachers' Training Programme (in the Light of the Need for Value-Orientation)*. New Delhi: Ministry of Education and Culture.

Kabra, K.N. 1976. *Political Economy of Brain Drain*. New Delhi: Arnold-Heinemann.

Kadam, K.N. 1991. *Dr Babasaheb Ambedkar and the Significance of His Movement: A Chronology*. Bombay: Popular Prakashan.

Kamat, A.R. 1972. 'The Educational Situation', *Economic and Political Weekly*, 7 (26): 1229–37.

——. 1980. 'Ethno-Linguistic Issues in the Indian Federal Context', *Economic and Political Weekly*, 15 (24–25), 1053–66.

——. 1985. *Education and Social Change in India*. Bombay: Somaiya.

Kantha, V.K. and D. Narain. 2003. 'Dynamics of Community Mobilisation in a Fragmented and Turbulent State', in R. Govinda and R.

Diwan (eds.): *Community Participation and Empowerment in Primary Education* (122–50). New Delhi: Sage Publications.

Kapur, P. 1974. *The Changing Status of the Working Women in India.* Delhi: Vikas Publishing House.

Karabel, J. and A.H. Halsey. 1977a. 'Educational Research: A Review and an Interpretation', in J. Karabel and A.H. Halsey (eds.): *Power and Ideology in Education* (1–85). New York: Oxford University Press.

——. (ed.), 1977b. *Power and Ideology in Education.* New York: Oxford University Press.

Kareem, P.A. 1988. *Education and Socio-economic Development.* New Delhi: Ashish.

Karlekar, M. 1975. 'Higher Education and the Scheduled Castes', *Journal of Higher Education,* 1 (2): 179–87.

Kaur, K. 2003. *Higher Education in India (1781–2003).* New Delhi: University Grants Commission.

Kaur, R. 2001. 'The Eclipse or the Renaissance of "Community"? The Career of the Concept', in S.S. Jodhka (ed.): *Community and Identities: Contemporary Discourses on Culture and Politics in India* (80–94). New Delhi: Sage Publications in association with The Book Review Literary Trust, New Delhi.

Keddie, N. 1971. 'Classroom Knowledge', in M.F.D. Young (ed.): *Knowledge and Control: New Directions in the Sociology of Education* (133–60). London: Collier Macmillan.

Keer, D. 2009/1954. *Dr Ambedkar: Life and Mission* (4th edition). Bombay: Popular Prakashan.

——. 1982. *Dr Ambedkar: A Memorial Album.* Bombay: Popular Prakashan.

Khan, R. (ed.). 1997. *Rethinking Indian Federalism.* Shimla: Inter-University Centre for Humanities and Social Sciences, Indian Institute of Advanced Study.

Kini, N.G.S. 1974. *The City Voter in India.* New Delhi: Abhinav.

Kirpal, V. 1978. 'Higher Education for the Scheduled Castes and Scheduled Tribes', *Economic and Political Weekly,* 13 (4–5): 165, 167–69.

Kozol, J. 1967. *Death at an Early Age.* Boston: Houghton Mifflin.

Krishna, G. 1982. 'Indian Muslims in the Nation-Formation Process', in G. Krishna (ed.): *Contributions to South Asian Studies (Vol. 2)* (110–45). Delhi Oxford University Press.

Krishna, S. 1991. *India's Living Languages: The Critical Issues.* New Delhi: Allied Publishers.

Kumar, K. 1989. *Social Character of Learning.* New Delhi: Sage Publications.

——. 1991. *Political Agenda of Education: A Study of Colonialist and Nationalist Ideas.* New Delhi: Sage Publications.

——. 2002. *Prejudice and Pride: School Histories of the Freedom Struggle in India and Pakistan.* New Delhi: Penguin Books.

Ladd Jr, E.C. and S.M. Lipset. 1975. *The Divided Academy.* New York: McGraw-Hill.

Laponce, J.A. 1960. *The Protection of Minorities.* Berkeley, CA: University of California Press.

Leitner, G.W. 1973. *History of Indigenous Education in the Punjab since Annexation, and in 1882, 1883.* Patiala: Languages Department (reprint edition).

Lenin, V.I. n.d. *Collected Works (Vol. 38).* Moscow: Progress Publishers.

Levitas, M. 1974. *Marxist Perspectives in the Sociology of Education.* London: Routledge and Kegan Paul.

Levy Jr, M.J. 1966. *Modernization and the Structure of Societies.* Princeton, NJ: Princeton University Press.

Liebow, E. 1972. 'The Human Costs of Unemployment', in A.M. Okun (ed.): *The Battle against Unemployment* (1–11). New York: W.W. Norton.

Lipset, S.M. 1967. 'White Collar Workers and Professionals: Their Attitudes and Behaviour towards Unions', in W.A. Faunce (ed.): *Readings in Industrial Sociology* (525–48). New York: Appleton-Century-Crofts.

——. 1983. *Political Man: The Social Bases of Politics* (expanded and updated edition). London: Heinemann Educational Books.

Lipset, S.M. and H.L. Zetterberg. 1966. 'A Theory of Social Mobility', in R. Bendix and S.M. Lipset (eds.): *Class, Status and Power* (2nd edition) (561–73). New York: The Free Press.

Little, A. and J. Westergaard. 1964. 'The Trend of Class Differentials in Educational Opportunity in England and Wales', *British Journal of Sociology,* 15 (4): 301–15.

Lokhande, G.S. 1977. *Bhimrao Ramji Ambedkar: A Study in Social Democracy.* New Delhi: Sterling Publishers.

Lok Sabha Secretariat. 1986. *Members of Lok Sabha: A Study in Socio-Economic Background.* New Delhi: Lok Sabha Secretariat.

Ludden, D. 1996. 'Introduction: Ayodhya – A Window on the World', in D. Ludden (ed.): *Making India Hindu: Religion, Community and the Politics of Democracy in India* (1–23). New Delhi: Oxford University Press.

Lukes, S. 1975. *Emile Durkheim*. Harmondsworth, Middlesex: Penguin Books.

Lynch, O. 1972. 'Dr Ambedkar: Myth and Charisma', in J.M. Mahar (ed.): *The Untouchables in Contemporary India* (91–112). Tucson, Arizona: The University of Arizona Press.

MacIver, R.M. and C.H. Page. 1962/1950. *Society: An Introductory Analysis*. London: Macmillan.

Madan, T.N. 1983. *Culture and Development*. New Delhi: Oxford University Press.

Madan, T.N. and B.G. Halbar. 1972. 'Caste and Community in the Private and Public Education of Mysore State', in S.H. Rudolph and L.I. Rudolph (eds.): *Education and Politics in India* (121–47). Delhi: Oxford University Press.

Majumdar, D.N. and T.N. Madan. 1956. *An Introduction to Social Anthropology*. Bombay: Asia Publishing House.

Mannheim, K. 1940. *Man and Society in an Age of Reconstruction*. London: Kegan Paul, Trench, Trubner and Co.

——. 1952. *Essays on the Sociology of Culture*. London: Routledge and Kegan Paul.

Mannheim, K. and W.A.C. Stewart. 1962. *An Introduction to the Sociology of Education*. London: Routledge and Kegan Paul.

Marshall, T.H. 1971. 'Social Selection in the Welfare State', in E. Hopper (ed.): *Readings in the Theory of Educational Systems* (38–55). London: Hutchinson.

Martindale, D. 1961. *The Nature and Types of Sociological Theory*. London: Routledge and Kegan Paul.

Marx, K. and F. Engels. 1970. *Selected Works (Vol. III)*. Moscow: Progress Publishers.

——. 1975. *The Poverty of Philosophy*. Moscow: Progress Publishers.

——. 1976. *Manifesto of the Communist Party* in *Collected Works (Vol. VI)* (477–519). Moscow: Progress Publishers.

Matthews, M.R. 1980. *The Marxist Theory of Schooling*. Sussex: The Harvester Press.

Mayhew, A. 1926. *The Education of India*. London: Faber and Gwyer.

Mazumdar, V. 1975. 'Higher Education of Women in India', *Journal of Higher Education*, 1 (2): 155–65.

McClelland, D.C. 1961. *The Achieving Society*. Princeton, NJ: D. Van Nostrand.

McCully, B.T. 1940. *English Education and the Origins of Indian Nationalism*. New York: Columbia University Press.

Mead, M. 1930. *Growing Up in New Guinea.* New York: W. Morrow and Co.

——. 1936. *Coming of Age in Samoa.* New York: Blue Ribbon Books.

Mendelsohn, O. and M. Vicziany. 1990. 'The Untouchables Today', in J. Masselos (ed.): *India: Creating a Modern Nation* (254–86). New Delhi: Sterling Publishers.

Merton, R.K. 1968. *Social Theory and Social Structure* (enlarged edition). New York: The Free Press.

Mills, C.W. 1951. *White Collar.* New York: Oxford University Press.

Min, Weifang. 2004. 'Chinese Higher Education: The Legacy of the Past and the Context of the Future', in P.G. Altbach and T. Umakoshi (eds.): *Asian Universities: Historical Perspectives and Contemporary Challenges* (53–83). Baltimore, Maryland: The Johns Hopkins University Press.

Ministry of Education, Government of India. 1971. *Education and National Development (Report of the Education Commission, 1964–66)* (reprint edition). New Delhi: NCERT.

——. 1985. *Challenge of Education: A Policy Perspective.* New Delhi: Ministry of Education, Government of India.

Ministry of External Affairs, Government of India. 1987. *Foreign Affairs Records,* 33 (10): 340–46.

Ministry of Human Resource Development (MHRD), Government of India. 1986. *Programme of Action: National Policy on Education.* New Delhi: The Controller of Publications.

——. 1991. *Towards an Enlightened and Humane Society: Report of the Committee for Review of National Policy on Education 1986.* New Delhi: The Controller of Publications.

——. 1992. *National Policy on Education – 1986: Program of Action – 1992.* New Delhi: Publications Division, Government of India.

——. 2007. *Selected Educational Statistics – 2004–05.* New Delhi: Statistics Division, Department of Higher Education, MHRD, Government of India.

——. 2008. 'Higher Education in India', www.education.nic.in/stats 0405.asp (accessed on 24 April 2008).

Ministry of Information and Broadcasting (MIB), Government of India. 1987. *India 1986: A Reference Annual.* New Delhi: Publications Division, MIB, Government of India.

——. 2010. *India 2010: A Reference Annual* (54th edition). New Delhi: Publications Division, MIB, Government of India.

Misra, B.B. 1961. *The Indian Middle Classes: Their Growth in Modern Times.* London: Oxford University Press.

Mohan, N.S., M.D.G.D. Dutt, and Piush Antony. 2003. 'Community Participation in Primary Education: The Karnataka Experience', in R. Govinda and R. Diwan (eds.): *Community Participation and Empowerment in Primary Education* (151–81). New Delhi: Sage Publications.

Morris-Jones, W.H. 1971. *The Government and Politics of India.* London: Hutchinson.

Moskvichov, L.N. 1974. *The End of Ideology Theory.* Moscow: Progress Publishers.

Mujeeb, M. 1967. *The Indian Muslims.* London: George Allen and Unwin.

Murdock, G.P. 1934. *Our Primitive Contemporaries.* New York: Macmillan.

Myrdal, G. 1968. *Asian Drama* (Vol. III). Harmondsworth, Midllesex: Penguin Books.

Naidu, R. 1980. *The Communal Edge to Plural Societies: India and Malaysia.* Delhi: Vikas Publishing House.

Naik, J.P. 1965. *Educational Planning in India.* Bombay: Allied.

——. 1982. *The Education Commission and After.* New Delhi: Allied Publishers.

Nambissan, G.B. 2014. 'Sociology of School Education in India: A Review of Research, 2000–10', in Y. Singh (ed.): *Indian Sociology (ICSSR Research Surveys and Explorations, Vol. 2: Development and Change)* (66–101). New Delhi: Oxford University Press.

Nambissan, G.B. and S.S. Rao. 2013a. 'Introduction: Sociology of Education in India: Trajectory, Location, and Concerns', in G.B. Nambissan and S.S. Rao (eds.): *Sociology of Education in India: Changing Contours and Emerging Concerns* (1–23). New Delhi: Oxford University Press.

——. (eds.). 2013b. *Sociology of Education in India: Changing Contours and Emerging Concerns.* New Delhi: Oxford University Press.

Narlikar, J.V. 2003. 'How to Recapture the Thrill for Basic Sciences in Higher Education' (UGC Golden Jubilee Lecture Series). New Delhi: University Grants Commission.

Naroll, R. 1983. *The Moral Order: An Introduction to the Human Situation.* Beverly Hills, CA: Sage Publications.

National Assessment and Accreditation Council (NAAC). 2010. *NAAC News,* 10 (2).

National Commission on Teachers. 1985. *Report of the National Commission on Teachers – II, 1983–85.* Delhi: Controller of Publications.

National Knowledge Commission (NKC). 2007. *Report to the Nation – 2006.* New Delhi: NKC, Government of India.

National Sample Survey Organisation (NSSO). 2006. *Employment and Unemployment Situation in India* (NSSO 61st Round, July 2004–June 2005). New Delhi: NSSO, Ministry of Statistics and Programme Implementation, Government of India.

Noronha, A. 2003. 'The Community in Charge: Shades of Experience from Madhya Pradesh', in R. Govinda and R. Diwan (eds.): *Community Participation and Empowerment in Primary Education* (99–121). New Delhi: Sage Publications.

Oommen, T.K. 1974. 'Student Politics in India: The Case of Delhi University', *Asian Survey*, 14 (9): 777–94.

Parhar, M. 2002. 'Enrolment Projection in Higher Education', *University News*, 40 (27): 1–4.

Parkin, F. 1972. *Class Inequality and Political Order*. Frogmore, St Albans: Granada.

——. 1974. 'Strategies of Social Closure in Class Formation', in F. Parkin (ed.): *The Social Analysis of Class Structure* (1–18). London: Tavistock.

Parmaji, S. 1979. *Education and Jobs*. Delhi: Leeladevi.

Parulekar, R.V. 1951. *A Source Book of History of Education in Bombay Province, Part I (Survey of Indigenous Education, 1820–30)*. Bombay: Asia Publishing House.

Pathak, A. 2009. *Recalling the Forgotten: Education and Moral Quest*. Delhi: Aakar Books.

——. 2013/2002. *Social Implications of Schooling: Knowledge, Pedagogy and Consciousness*. Delhi: Aakar Books.

Pattanayak, D.P. 1981. *Multilingualism and Mother Tongue Education*. Delhi: Oxford University Press.

Pattnaik, S.K. 1982. *Student Politics and Voting Behaviour*. New Delhi: Concept Publishing Company.

Patwardhan, S. 1973. *Change among India's Harijans*. New Delhi: Orient Longman.

Payne, E.G. 1928. *Principles of Educational Sociology: An Outline*. New York: New York University Press.

Pearsall, J. (ed.). 1999. *The Concise Oxford Dictionary* (10th edition). New Delhi: Oxford University Press.

Peer, M. 1988. *Muslim Education in India: Problems and Prospects*. Mangalore: Karnataka Muslim Pragathi Parishat.

Phadnis, U. 1990. *Ethnicity and Nation-Building in South Asia*. New Delhi: Sage Publications.

Philips, C.H. 1962. *The Evolution of India and Pakistan, 1858–1947* (Select Documents). London.

Planning Commission. 1981. *Sixth Five Year Plan, 1980–85*. New Delhi: Government of India.

Premi, M.K. 2008. 'The Power of People', *One India One People*, 12 (3): 8–9.

Preston, P.W. 1982. *Theories of Development*. London: Routledge and Kegan Paul.

Public Accounts Committee (V Lok Sabha). 1975. *Report No. 167: Foreign Participation or Collaboration in Research Projects in India*. New Delhi: Lok Sabha Secretariat.

Puttaswamaiah, K. 1977. *Unemployment in India*. New Delhi: Oxford and IBH.

Rajagopalan, C. 1978. *Social Mobility among the Scheduled Castes*. Bangalore: Department of Sociology, Bangalore University.

Ramachandran, V. 2003. 'Community Participation and Empowerment in Primary Education: Discussion of Experiences from Rajasthan', in R. Govinda and R. Diwan (eds.): *Community Participation and Empowerment in Primary Education* (54–74). New Delhi: Sage Publications.

Rangan, P.S. 2014. 'An Unequal Childhood', *Outlook*, 54 (35): 20–26.

Rao, S.S. 2013. 'Structural Exclusion in Everyday Institutional Life: Labelling of Stigmatized Groups in an IIT', in G.B. Nambissan and S.S. Rao (eds.): *Sociology of Education in India: Changing Contours and Emerging Concerns* (199–223). New Delhi: Oxford University Press.

Rao, V.K.R.V. 1961. *University Education and Employment*. Bombay: Asia Publishing House.

Ray, A.B. 1977. *Students and Politics in India*. New Delhi: Manohar Book Service.

Raza, M., Y.P. Aggarwal and M. Hasan. 1985. 'Higher Education in India: An Assessment', in J.V. Raghavan (ed.): *Higher Education in the Eighties* (95–173). New Delhi: Lancer International.

Reddy, A.K.N. 1974. 'The Brain Drain', in A. Singh and P.G. Altbach (eds.): *The Higher Learning in India* (373–94). Delhi: Vikas Publishing House.

Reid, I. 1978. *Sociological Perspectives on School and Education*. London: Open Books.

Reimer, E. 1971. *School is Dead*. Harmondsworth, Middlesex: Penguin Books.

Roberts, B. 1973. 'Education, Urbanization, and Social Change', in R. Brown (ed.): *Knowledge, Education and Cultural Change* (141–62). London: Tavistock.

Robinson, F. 1975. *Separatism among Indian Muslims: The Politics of the United Provinces' Muslims, 1860–1923*. Cambridge: Cambridge University Press.

Robinson, J. 1937. *Essays in the Theory of Employment*. London: Macmillan.

Rodrigues, V. 1989. 'Religion as an Ideological Apparatus: The Role of the Catholic Church in Dakshina Kannada', in M. Shakir (ed.): *Religion, State and Politics in India* (249–70). Delhi: Ajanta Publications.

——. (ed.). 2002. *The Essential Writings of B.R. Ambedkar*. New Delhi: Oxford University Press.

Ross, A.D. 1969. *Student Unrest in India*. Montreal: McGill-Queen's University Press.

Roy, A. 2003. 'Making Good Citizens: Teaching Fundamental Duties in Schools', *Economic and Political Weekly*, 38 (25): 2470–73.

Roy, K. 2002. 'National Textbooks for the Future?', *Economic and Political Weekly*, 37 (51): 5083–85.

Rudolph, S.H., L.I. Rudolph, and K. Ahmad. 1971. 'Student Politics and National Politics in India', *Economic and Political Weekly*, 6 (30–32): 1655–68.

Russell, B. 1961. *Has Man a Future?* Harmondsworth, Middlesex: Penguin Books.

Saberwal, S. 1978. 'Focus and Milieu', in S. Saberwal (ed.): *Process and Institutions in Urban India* (241–46). Delhi: Vikas Publishing House.

——. 2006. 'On the Making of Muslims in India Historically', *Sociological Bulletin*, 55 (2): 237–66.

——. 2008. *Spirals of Contention: Why India was Partitioned in 1947*. New Delhi: Routledge.

SAHMAT. 2002. *Saffronised and Substandard: A Critique of the New NCERT Textbooks*. New Delhi: SAHMAT.

Saran, A.K. 1971. 'Higher Education and Social Change in Independent India', in S.C. Malik (ed.): *Management and Organization of Indian Universities* (241–46). Simla: Indian Institute of Advanced Study.

Sarangapani, P.M. 2003. *Constructing School Knowledge: An Ethnography of Learning in an Indian Village*. New Delhi: Sage Publications.

Sarup, M. 1978. *Marxism and Education*. London: Routledge and Kegan Paul.

Saxena, N.C. 1989. 'Public Employment and Educational Backwardness among the Muslims in India', in M. Shakir (ed.): *Religion, State and Politics in India* (155–99). Delhi: Ajanta Publications.

Saxena, S. 2003. 'Community Participation and Literacy: Beyond Semantics', in R. Govinda and R. Diwan (eds.): *Community Participation and Empowerment in Primary Education* (75–98). New Delhi: Sage Publications.

Schaefer, R.T. 1979. *Racial and Ethnic Groups*. Boston: Little Brown and Co.

Schermerhorn, R.A. 1978. *Ethnic Plurality in India*. Tucson, Ariz.: University of Arizona Press.

Schultz, T.W. 1963. *The Economic Value of Education*. New York: Columbia University Press.

Seal, A. 1968. *Emergence of Indian Nationalism: Competition and Collaboration in the Late Nineteenth Century*. Cambridge: Cambridge University Press.

Sen, A.K. 1971. 'The Crisis in Indian Education', in S.C. Malik (ed.): *Management and Organisation of Indian Universities* (248–78). Simla: Indian Institute of Advanced Study.

——. 1975. *Employment, Technology and Development*. Delhi: Oxford University Press.

Seshadri, C. 1976. 'Equality of Educational Opportunity: Some Issues in Indian Education', *Comparative Education*, 12 (3): 219–30.

Shah, B.V. and S.D. Joshi. 1979. 'Sociology of Education: A Trend Report', in M.B. Buch (ed.): *A Survey of Research in Education* (70–122). Baroda: SERD.

Shah, G. 1977. 'Revolution, Reform or Protest? A Study of the Bihar Movement', *Economic and Political Weekly*, 12 (15): 505–14, 12 (16): 642–55, and 12 (17): 695–702.

Shah, G., H. Mander, S. Thorat, S. Deshpande, and A. Baviskar. 2006. *Untouchability in Rural India*. New Delhi: Sage Publications.

Shah, R.C. 1968. 'Student Politics and Student Leadership in an Indian University', in P.G. Altbach (ed.): *Turmoil and Transition* (190–201). Bombay: Lalvani.

Shah, V.P. and T. Patel. 1977. *Who Goes to College?* Ahmedabad: Rachana Prakashan.

Shakir, M. 1986. *State and Politics in Contemporary India*. Delhi: Ajanta.

Shariff, A. 2007. 'Problem of Numbers: Skills Shortage Could Scupper High Growth Rates', *The Times of India* (Lucknow), 22 November 2007: 12.

Shariff, A. and P.K. Ghosh. 2000. 'Indian Education Scene and the Public Gap', *Economci and Political Weekly*, 35 (16): 1396–1406.

Sharma, G.S. 1973. *Educational and Cultural Rights of the Minorities*. New Delhi: Indian Council of Social Science Research.

Sharma, K.D. 1978. *Education of a National Minority: A Case Study of Muslim Community in Delhi.* New Delhi: Kalamkar.

Sharp, H. 1965. *Selections from Educational Record, Part I, 1781–1839* (reprint edition). New Delhi: Published for the National Archives of India by the Manager of Publications, Government of India.

Sheth, P.N. 1977. *Nav Nirman and Political Change in India.* Bombay: Vora.

Shils, E. 1961. *The Intellectual between Tradition and Modernity.* The Hague: Mouton.

——. 1968a. 'Students, Politics, and Universities in India', as Introduction to P.G. Altbach (ed.): *Turmoil and Transition* (1–13). Bombay: Lalvani.

——. 1968b. 'Indian Students: Rather Sadhus than Philistines', in P.G. Altbach (ed.): *Turmoil and Transition* (74–92). Bombay: Lalvani.

——. 'The Academic Profession in India', *Minerva,* 7 (3): 345–72.

Shipman, M.D. 1968. *The Sociology of the School.* London: Longman.

Shotton, J.R. 1998. *Learning and Freedom: Policy, Pedagogy and Paradigms in Indian Education and Schooling.* New Delhi: Sage Publications.

Shourie, A. 1988. 'Converting Clamour into Discourse' and 'Restoring Discourse', *Indian Express* (Bangalore), 19 and 26 June.

Simon, B. 1960. *Studies in the History of Education (Vol. 1).* London: Lawrence and Wishart.

Singh, A. 1984. *Commonsense about Examinations.* New Delhi: Oxford University Press.

——. 2004. *Fifty Years of Higher Education in India: The Role of the University Grants Commission.* New Delhi: Sage Publications.

Singh, A.K. 2006. 'Degree Devaluation in Higher Education: Unemployment and Unemployability among Graduates in India', *Journal of Educational Planning and Administration,* 20 (4): 411–28.

Singh, K.S. 1992. *People of India: An Introduction.* Calcutta: Anthropological Survey of India.

——. 1993. *People of India: An Anthropological Atlas (Ecology and Cultural Traits; Languages and Linguistic Traits; Demographic and Biological Traits).* New Delhi: Oxford University Press.

Singh, M.K. 2006. 'Higher Education: A Disqualification?', *Sunday Times of India* (Mumbai), 1 January 2006: 8.

Singh, N. 1983. *Education and Under Siege.* New Delhi: Concept Publishing Company.

Singh, Y. 2000. *Culture Change in India: Identity and Globalization.* Jaipur: Rawat Publications.

Singhal, S. 1977. *Academic Leadership and Student Unrest*. New Delhi: Newman Group of Publishers.

Sirsikar, V.M. 1973. *Sovereigns without Crowns*. Bombay: Popular Prakashan.

Smith, M.G. 1965. *The Plural Society in the British West Indies*. Berkeley, CA: University of California Press.

Smith, P.M. 1959. 'Educational Sociology', in J.S. Roucek (ed.): *Contemporary Sociology* (383–405). London: Peter Owen.

Smith, W.R. 1917. *Introduction to Educational Sociology*. Boston: Houghton Mifflin Co.

Srinivasan, N. 1981. *Identity Crisis of Muslims: Profiles of Lucknow Youth*. New Delhi: Concept Publishing Company.

Srivastava, K. 2014. 'Very Few Dalit Elites Help Their Community: Study', *DNA* (Mumbai), 15 August: 4.

Stalcup, R.J. 1968. *Sociology and Education*. Columbus, Ohio: C.E. Merrill.

Stalin, J.V. 1976. *Problems of Leninism*. Peking: Foreign Languages Press.

Stella, A. and A. Gnanam. 2003. *Foundations of External Quality Assurance in Indian Higher Education*. New Delhi: Concept Publishing Company.

Stewart, W.A.C. 1962. 'Introduction' to K. Mannheim and W.A.C. Stewart: *An Introduction to the Sociology of Education* (vii–xvii). London: Routledge and Kegan Paul.

Tawney, R.H. 1964. *Equality*. London: George Allen and Unwin.

Taylor, W. 1966. 'The Sociology of Education', in J.W. Tibbie (ed.): *The Study of Education* (179–213). London: Routledge and Kegan Paul.

Thapan, M. 2006/1991. *Life at School: An Ethnographic Study* (2nd edition). New Delhi: Oxford University Press.

——. (ed.). 2014. *Ethnographies of Schooling in Contemporary India*. New Delhi: Sage Publications.

Tharakan, P.K.M. 2003. 'Community Participation in School Education: Experiments in the State of Kerala', in R. Govinda and R. Diwan (eds.): *Community Participation and Empowerment in Primary Education* (31–53). New Delhi: Sage Publications.

The Task Force on Higher Education and Society. 2000. *Higher Education in Developing Countries: Peril and Promise*. Washington, DC: The World Bank.

The Times of India. 2009. 'Vacant: Ideas to Create Jobs', *The Times of India* (Mumbai), 19 March 2009: 2.

Thirtha, N.V. and M. Mukhopadhyay. 1974. 'Sociology of Education: A Trend Report', in M.B. Buch (ed.): *A Survey of Research in Education*

(83–134). Baroda: Centre for Advanced Study in Education, M.S. University of Baroda.

Thomas, P.M. and D. Tiwari. 2005. 'Two-Room University!', *The Week*, 23 (13): 36–37.

Thorat, S. 2009. *Dalits in India: Search for a Common Destiny*. New Delhi: Sage Publications.

Tickoo, C. 1980. *Indian Universities*. Madras: Orient Longman.

Tilak, J.B.G. 1996. 'Higher Education under Structural Adjustment', *Journal of Indian School of Political Economy*, 8: 266–93.

——. 2002. 'Privatization of Higher Education in India', *International Higher Education*, 29 (1), 11–13.

——. 2004. 'Absence of Policy and Perspective in Higher Education', *Economic and Political Weekly*, 39 (21), 2159–64.

Tilak, J.B. (ed.). 2007. *Women's Education and Development*. New Delhi: Gyan Publishing House.

Times News Network. 2008a. 'Employment Scenario Bleak, Says Report', *The Times of India* (Mumbai), 13 December 2008: 14.

——. 2008b. 'More Job Cuts, Closure of Industrial Units Likely', *The Times of India* (Mumbai), 13 December 2008: 25.

Tönnies, F. 1957. *Community and Society (Gemeinschaft und Gesellschaft)* (tr. and ed. by C.P. Loomis). New York: Harper and Row Publishers.

Trevelyan, C.E. 1838. *On the Education of the People of India*. London: Longman, Orme, Green, and Longmans.

Tropp, A. 1967. 'The English Case', in D.A. Hansen and J.E. Gerstl (eds.): *On Education: Sociological Perspectives* (284–91). New York: John Wiley.

Tumin, M.M. 1969. *Social Stratification* (Indian edition). New Delhi: Prentice-Hall of India.

United Nations Population Division. 2004. *World Population Prospects: A 2004 Revision Population Database*. New York: United Nations Organisation.

——. 2006. *World Population Prospects: The 2006 Revision, Volume II – Sex and Age Distribution of the World Population*. New York: United Nations Organisation.

——. 2007. *World Population Ageing – 2007*. New York: United Nations Organisation.

University Education Commission (1948–49). 1985. 'Extracts', in J.V. Raghavan (ed.): *Higher Education in the Eighties* (Appendix I: 240–47). New Delhi: Lancer International.

University Grants Commission (UGC). 2002–03. *Annual Report 2002–2003*. New Delhi: UGC.

Upadhya, C. 2001. 'The Concept of Community in Indian Social Sciences: An Anthropological Perspective', in S.S. Jodhka (ed.): *Community and Identities: Contemporary Discourses on Culture and Politics in India* (32–58). New Delhi: Sage Publications in association with The Book Review Literary Trust, New Delhi.

Vaizey, J. 1968. 'Some Dynamic Aspects of Inequality', in L. Sussman (ed.): *Special Objectives in Educational Planning*. Paris: Organisation for Economic Co-operation and Development.

——. 1972. *The Political Economy of Education*. London: Gerald Duckworth.

van Gennep, Arnold. 1960. *The Rites of Passage* (tr. M.B. Vizedom and G.L. Caffee). London: Routledge and Kegan Paul.

Varma, S.P. et al. 1973. *Voting Behaviour in a Changing Society*. Delhi: National.

Verghese, N.V. 1996. 'Decentralisation of Educational Planning and District Primary Education Programme' (Occasional Paper No. 22). New Delhi: National Institute of Educational Planning and Administration.

Verma, H.S. 1974. 'Intelligence Work through Collaborative Research in India', *Social Scientist*, 2 (9): 59–66.

Vijayakumar, B. 2003. 'Regeneration of Quality Research in Higher Education: Ways Ahead', *University News*, 41 (41): 3–7.

Vishwa Yuvak Kendra. 1973. *The Dynamics of Student Agitations*. Bombay: Somaiya.

Vollmer, H.M. and D.L. Mills (eds.). 1966. *Professionalization*. Englewood-Cliffs, NJ: Prentice-Hall.

Wankhede, G.G. 2001. 'Educational Inequalities among Scheduled Castes in Maharashtra', *Economic and Political Weekly*, 36 (18): 1553–58.

Ward, L.F. 1883. *Dynamics Sociology: Or Applied Social Science*. New York: D. Appleton and Co.

Watkins, M.H. 1965. 'The West African Bush School', in G. Spindler (ed.): *Education and Culture* (426–43). New York: Harper, Row and Winston.

Watson, C.W. 2002. *Multiculturalism*. New Delhi: Viva Books.

Watson, K. 1983a. 'Introduction: Youth, Education and Employment: The Challenge of the 1980s', in K. Watson (ed.): *Youth, Education and Employment*. London: Croom Helm.

——. (ed.). 1983b. *Youth, Education and Employment*. London: Croom Helm.

Weber, M. 1965. 'Ethnic Groups', in T. Parsons et al. (eds.): *Theories of Society: Foundations of Modern Sociological Theory* (305–09). New York: The Free Press.

Wehr, P. and M. Washburn. 1976. *Peace and World Order Systems*. Beverly Hills, CA: Sage Publications.

Weiner, M. 1963. *The Politics of Scarcity*. Bombay: Asia Publishing House.

Weiner, M. and M.F. Katzenstein (with K.V.N. Rao). 1981. *India's Preferential Policies: Migrants, the Middle Classes and Ethnic Equality*. Chicago: University of Chicago Press.

Westergaard, J. and H. Resler. 1975. *Class in a Capitalist Society*. London: Heinemann.

Wheeler, R.S. 1970. *The Politics of Pakistan: A Constitutional Quest*. Ithaca: Cornell University Press.

Williams, R. 1976. *Keywords: A Vocabulary of Culture and Society*. Glasgow: Fontana/Croom Helm (William Collins).

Williamson, B. 1974. 'Continuities and Discontinuities in the Sociology of Education', in M. Flude and J. Ahier (eds.): *Educability, Schools and Ideology* (3–14). London: Croom Helm.

Wilson, J. 1966. *Equality*. London: Hutchinson.

Wirth, L. 1965. 'The Problem of Minority Groups', in T. Parsons et al. (eds.): *Theories of Society: Foundations of Modern Sociological Theory* (309–15). New York: The Free Press.

Young, M. 1961. *The Rise of the Meritocracy, 1870–2033: An Essay on Education and Equality*. Harmondsworth, Middlesex: Penguin Books.

Young, M.F.D. 1971a. 'Introduction', in M.F.D. Young (ed.): *Knowledge and Control: New Directions for the Sociology of Education* (1–46). London: Collier Macmillan.

Young, M.F.D. (ed.). 1971b. *Knowledge and Control: New Directions for the Sociology of Education*. London: Collier Macmillan.

Zeitlin, I.M. 1973. *Rethinking Sociology*. New York: Appleton-Century-Crofts.

Zelliot, E. 1972. 'Gandhi and Ambedkar: A Study in Leadership', in J.M. Mahar (ed.): *The Untouchables in Contemporary India* (69–95). Tucson, Arizona: The University of Arizona Press.

Znaniecki, F. 1970. 'The Scientific Function of Sociology of Education', in D.F. Swift (ed.): *Basic Readings in the Sociology of Education* (10–24). London: Routledge and Kegan Paul.

Index